"The author clearly demonstrates academic mastery of relevant material and offers a fresh look at a broad range of the literature on a timely and important subject matter. I congratulate the author on a rich and differentiated treatment of the topic".

Professor Marc Oliver Bettzüge, Director,
Institute of Energy Economics, University of Cologne, Germany

"The book is a reliable analysis on energy security from the exporters' perspective. Even though there has been many works on energy security devoted to the importing nations' viewpoint, this book is important as it delivers the exporting nations' angle. In this well-structured, content-rich book author makes an attempt to analyse all key aspects connected to the topic each time supporting the analysis with extensive and numerous references".

Professor Jan Jakub Michałek, Department of Macroeconomics and International Trade Theory, Faculty of Economic Sciences,
University of Warsaw, Poland

Economics of Energy Security

There has been a burgeoning interest in energy security in recent years due to the transformation of the energy landscape through deepening market deregulation, rising environmental challenges, growing energy hunger, and significant political changes. Depicting energy security as an evolving concept that absorbs economic and political conditions, this book adopts an economic approach to energy security in the international gas market. Uniquely, this book explores the theoretical assumptions and practical consequences attached to both demand and supply-side security in global energy markets. It investigates why energy exporters are so protective of independence in energy exports. This book also looks at the critically important issue of environmental aspects of energy security, particularly around climate change. It also analyses the potential for a cartel in the international gas market, similarly to the oil industry. This book will be of much interest to readers in energy economics, energy security, energy policy, IR/security studies, and relevant policy-makers.

Honorata Nyga-Łukaszewska, PhD, is an assistant professor in the SGH Warsaw School of Economics, Poland.

Routledge Explorations in Environmental Economics
Edited by Nick Hanley,
University of Stirling, UK

Pricing Carbon Emissions
Economic Reality and Utopia
Aviel Verbruggen

Economics and Engineering of Unpredictable Events
Modelling, Planning and Policies
Edited by Caterina De Lucia, Dino Borri, Atif Kubursi and Abdul Khakee

Environmental Finance and Green Banking
Contemporary and Emerging Issues
Edited by Sergey Sosnovskikh and Samsul Alam

Economic Growth and Environmental Quality in a Post-Pandemic World
New Directions in the Econometrics of the Environmental Kuznets Curve
Edited by Muhammad Shahbaz, Daniel Balsalobre Lorente and Rajesh Sharma

Low Carbon Transition in Emerging Economies
Climate Policy, Carbon Pricing and the Effect on Employment
Erkin Erdoğan

Economics of Energy Security
Perspectives of Natural Gas Exporters
Honorata Nyga-Łukaszewska

For more information about this series, please visit: www.routledge.com/Routledge-Explorations-in-Environmental-Economics/book-series/REEE

Economics of Energy Security

Perspectives of Natural Gas Exporters

Honorata Nyga-Łukaszewska

Routledge
Taylor & Francis Group
LONDON AND NEW YORK

First published 2024
by Routledge
4 Park Square, Milton Park, Abingdon, Oxon OX14 4RN

and by Routledge
605 Third Avenue, New York, NY 10158

Routledge is an imprint of the Taylor & Francis Group, an informa business

British Library Cataloguing-in-Publication Data
A catalogue record for this book is available from the British Library

Library of Congress Cataloging-in-Publication Data
Names: Nyga-Łukaszewska, Honorata, author.
Title: Economics of energy security : perspectives of natural gas exporters / Honorata Nyga-Łukaszewska.
Description: Abingdon, Oxon ; New York, NY : Routledge, 2024. | Series: Routledge explorations in environmental economics | Includes bibliographical references and index. |
Identifiers: LCCN 2023034199 | ISBN 9780367510602 (hardback) | ISBN 9780367510619 (paperback) | ISBN 9781003052241 (ebook)
Subjects: LCSH: Energy security—Economic aspects. | Gas industry—Security measures. | Gas industry—Economic aspects.
Classification: LCC HD9502.A2 N94 2023 | DDC 333.79—dc23/eng/20230822
LC record available at https://lccn.loc.gov/2023034199

ISBN: 978-0-367-51060-2 (hbk)
ISBN: 978-0-367-51061-9 (pbk)
ISBN: 978-1-003-05224-1 (ebk)

DOI: 10.4324/9781003052241

Typeset in Times New Roman
by codeMantra

To Stanley and Sophia

Contents

About the Author

Honorata Nyga-Łukaszewska, PhD, is an assistant professor in the SGH Warsaw School of Economics, Poland. She is active in teaching assignments and scientific research devoted to international economics and energy markets. She is the author of various publications within these areas. She is a member of international and national scientific associations specialising in the analysis of energy markets. She is graduate of the International Energy Agency training programme devoted to international energy markets and energy security.

Acknowledgements

This book is an effect of the author's studies on the economics of the energy security phenomenon and its characteristics in different countries carried out in SGH Warsaw School of Economics, Poland. The author would like to thank all employees of the Collegium of World Economy, and its dean – Professor Mariusz Próchniak, in particular – for invaluable support which contributed to the creation of this book.

The author would like to extend particular gratitude to Professor Adam Budnikowski, whose scientific and organizational support directed research efforts on this book. Received suggestions and advice refined the book's idea and approach and finally structured it. However, the last version of the presented manuscript is also an effect of valuable comments provided in the process of detailed scientific review by two distinguished scholars (in alphabetical order): Professor Marc Oliver Bettzüge – chair of the Energy Economics Department at the University of Cologne, Germany, and Professor Jan Jakub Michałek – from the Department of Macroeconomics and Theory of Foreign Trade, Faculty of Economic Sciences, University of Warsaw, Poland.

I owe special thanks to my publisher at Routledge for providing me the space for this book and for patience and forbearance that was of great value in the manuscript's preparations.

Most of all I would like to thank my family for continuous support and encouragement without which none of this would happen.

Introduction

Natural resources are an indispensable element of our lives. The diversity of natural resources, from biological, environmental through non-energy to energy resources, affects their different perception in economic terms. Economics, as a science discipline, since the times of classical economics, has focused on the analysis of the importance of natural resources for the economy. Natural resources for Thomas Malthus, David Ricardo, and John Stuart Mill were a factor of production indispensable to economic development. The main analysis focused at that time on land as a factor of production determining the ability of economies to develop. In neoclassical economics, whose origins date back to the second half of the 19th century, the question of resource scarcity changed considerations from absolute to relative dimension, and in the methodological sense shifted to the area of marginal productivity analysis as did William Stanley Jevons and Carl Menger (Perman et al., 2003). The contribution of both researchers referred to the concept of natural resource scarcity and related price increase or possibility of resources' substitution. The Hotelling (1931) principle[1] created in this trend later became the basis for the analysis of prices and the optimal level of exploitation of non-renewable natural resources, including energy resources.

Although the Hotelling (1931) work referred to, among other things, energy resources, they gained an established place in the economy only around the 1970s with the publication of reports of the Club of Rome. The vision of the catastrophic development of mankind with an exponential growth in the population, environmental pollution, consumption, extraction of natural resources, and simultaneous increase in technology progress, was to become a reality 100 years after the publication of the first report (Meadows, Randers, and Bahrens, 1973). The limits to growth described in this way have become the object of criticism related primarily to the assumptions adopted in the econometric modelling or too far-reaching simplification of the reality. One of the most prominent critics was Robert Solow – the Nobel Prize winner in economics, who claimed that report had not accounted for innovation capacity or pace of technological progress (Solow, 1973, 1974; Clement, 2002). Although the second report of the Club of Rome was slightly more optimistic and presented a statement that most of the elements included in the modelling of human economic development are under human control, it did not rebound in the economic and political discussion as widely as the first report (Mesarović et al., 1977).

DOI: 10.4324/9781003052241-1

The last[2] of the most famous reports of the Club of Rome is the third one, prepared under the direction of Jan Tinbergen – the laureate of the Noble Prize in economics. This report, sometimes called "Tinbergen report"(Tinbergen, 1978), focused mainly on the causes of unequal economic development in poorly developed and highly developed countries, proposing changes to the international monetary system or the organization of international trade. This report also highlighted the issue of rationalizing of the use of natural resources, in particular energy.

Discussion on energy resources within the Club of Rome reports imprinted on the energy landscape of the 20th and 21st centuries. Contemporary energy picture has been additionally conditioned by regulatory and geopolitical changes that have been reinforced by natural gas market developments. Although the analysis of the geopolitical aspects is beyond the scope of this book, it is impossible not to, at least, mention them while outlining the contemporary conditions for the development of energy markets. Regulatory developments are represented by the global climate protection agreements that started with Kyoto Protocol and since then have permanently introduced greenhouse gas emissions' reductions into energy production and consumption patterns. Geopolitical changes relate to the emergence of new energy powers on the world map, such as the most recent examples of the USA or Russia. The former has just become an important hydrocarbon market player in the aftermath of the shale gas discovery, while the latter's role has risen with the global shift towards gas – as the cleanest fossil fuel. Moreover, in the recent years, there have been unprecedented supply shocks in the natural gas market (e.g., 2008/2009), resulting in increased supply security concerns within the European Union (EU) group, which at the beginning of the new century has admitted a large group of countries heavily dependent on imports of Russian hydrocarbons. Gas supply disruption threats have been additionally strengthened by the risk of market cartelization which emerged with the creation of the Gas-Exporting Countries Forum (GECF) in 2001.

Shaped in this way the energy landscape of the 21st century puts in the foreground, among other things, issues related to energy security. This is not a new phenomenon as its origins date back to the 1970s. The first three reports of the Club of Rome described above also referred to energy crises, which evoked energy security concerns across the globe. Due to changes on international energy markets, crude oil exports were suspended, and for the first time in modern history, the world became aware of its reliance on imported energy resources. The International Energy Agency (IEA), created in the aftermath of the oil crises, was established to prevent a similar problem in the future. The IEA's system of stocks of crude oil and petroleum products in the OECD (Organization for Economic Cooperation and Development) member countries, as well as the implementation of the monitoring and reporting mechanism on the stocks, built the foundations for the energy security of the OECD energy-importing countries. Nevertheless, the issue of energy security has also evolved with the passage of time and changes in energy markets. That refers to the perception of the phenomenon, fuel lying at the centre of the analysis, as well as the groups of countries that have become the subject of research.

Currently, the energy security analysis focuses mainly on the natural gas market. This is due to the fact that the mechanisms ensuring energy security, implemented by the IEA, function efficiently in the crude oil market. However, the crude oil market, due to its global nature and the relatively well-researched structure of supply, demand and prices, offers fewer potential research *nichés*. On the other hand, the natural gas market, regional in its nature, with a clearly divided supply according to the supply chain elements, relatively unclear conditions for determining price formulas, and with still infant cartel-like structures, constitutes an interesting research field from the point of view of energy security. It is worth noting that the natural gas market, due to the supply disruptions, is considered mainly from the perspective of importing countries in energy security analyses. But in the 21st century, more and more often, appeared the perspective of energy security of energy exporters.[3] As indicated by Bollino and Galkin (2021), Dike (2013), Karatayev and Hall (2020), Romanova (2013), Novikau (2022), there is a significant **research gap** regarding energy security of energy exporters, and as noted by Nowrouzi et al. (2019) or Ye et al. (2021), in particular, in the natural gas market. Additionally, as highlighted by Antoniadis (2017) and Karatayev and Hall (2020), there is a need for a broader geographical analysis of energy-exporting countries which extends beyond than so far studies of developing or in-transition economies.

The proposed book fits into the above-described research gap by answering a following **research question**: how does energy demand security look like in the natural gas market in the 21st century and is it a determinant of the comparative advantage of high-income net natural gas-exporting nations. The novelty of this approach lies in theoretical and empirical aspects. In the theoretical dimension, this book is innovative in three ways. Firstly, it focuses on the analysis of the energy demand security in the natural gas market on the grounds of international economics while majority of existing research efforts in energy demand security analysis employs either political or general economic perspective. This research narrows down the analysis to international economics by using the Ricardian and Heckscher-Ohlin frameworks with the latest extensions to investigate the perspective of energy demand security. Secondly, this book presents a scoping literature review to identify the nature and extent of research evidence on the analysed phenomenon. While using different literature-mapping strategies have already been introduced in energy supply security research (e.g., Esfahani et al., 2021), energy demand security studies have so far followed solely descriptive and narrative literature reviews. This way a scoping literature review precedes deeper critical literature synthesis and analysis. Thirdly, this study builds on existing energy supply security achievements, integrating them with energy demand security, and further extending into a comprehensive theoretical framework of the analysed phenomenon. In the empirical layer, the novelty of the described in the book approach includes two aspects. Firstly, the study offers a comprehensive, but also, critical overview of existing empirical methods assessing quantitatively energy demand security, which builds upon the development of energy supply security estimates. Secondly, this research employs Amoroso et al.'s (2011) framework to estimate energy demand security within empirical approach to Ricardian and Heckscher-Ohlin hypotheses.

Apart from theoretical and methodological novelties included in this book, below-described research focuses on the demand security phenomenon in the group of developed countries, which are net natural gas exporters. This way, the analysis diverges from existing research efforts, which usually focus on individual countries or their clusters from the group of the biggest energy or oil and gas exporters (considered together), being either developing countries or economies in transition. So far studies have included the energy demand security perspective of following nations: Russia (Boussena and Locatelli, 2013; Romanova, 2013; Bollino and Galkin, 2021), Iran (Nowrouzi et al., 2019), or their groups regarded as geographic clusters: the Caspian region such as, Azerbaijan, Kazakhstan, Turkmenistan, and Uzbekistan (Karatayev and Hall, 2020) or organizational clusters, such as Organization of the Petroleum Exporting Countries (OPEC) (Dike, 2013). Studies resembling the most the geographical scope of the below research include Bollino and Galkin (2021) and Nyga-Łukaszewska and Napiórkowski (2022). The former describes energy demand security in the case of Australia and Canada next to Iran, Nigeria, Russia, but also OPEC and GECF (Gas-Exporting Countries Forum). The latter study presents the phenomenon on the example of developed, OECD economies including Canada, the Netherlands, Norway, and the USA.

Therefore, **the aim of this book** is to describe and analyse energy demand security phenomenon with its determinants in the 21st century and to test its comparative advantage relevance for high-income, net natural gas exporters. This goal can be broken down into theoretical and empirical subgoals. Within the former, the author aims to systemize and organize energy demand security research within a broader energy security and international economics fields, while within the latter, the author intends to describe the natural gas market in the 21st century with energy demand security determinants and analyse the phenomenon's influence over comparative advantage of high-income, OECD net gas exporters.

The choice of the countries' sample results on the one hand from the research gap (identified in the literature review), and these economies' rising importance in the natural gas trade, on the other hand. OECD members had increased their share of (only) liquified natural gas (LNG) exports from less than 10% in 2000 to 40% in 2021 (BP, 2022).[4] This growth has been even strengthened in 2022 by recent geopolitical events in Ukraine when Russian gas supplies to the European Union countries were substituted by American LNG deliveries. This trend is expected to continue in the future or may be even reinforced as European Union member countries, globally one of the biggest gas importers,[5] announced in 2022 withdrawal from Russian fossil fuel imports for a deeper cooperation in LNG imports with the USA, Canada, and Norway (European Commission, 2022). Thus, investigating the potential influence of energy demand security on the economies of Canada, the Netherlands, Norway, and the USA may open new and promising research field offering the possibility for future scientific dialogue.

Period of analysis ranges between 1997 and 2019 and results from, on the one hand, data availability constraints and, on the other, willingness to capture the phenomenon in possibly the broadest time dimension. This way, analysis starts at the verge of centuries and ends before COVID-19 pandemic. Even though international databases offered longer time series at the time of the final book preparations, including data from 2020 and in some cases 2021, these data points were excluded from the analysis. Rationale for such an approach includes the fact that the pandemic stormed through economies and energy markets leaving substantial traces in the macroeconomic and energy data. Thus, including the latest available data points in this research might have distorted the research results. Description of the pandemic effects on oil and gas markets and price dimension of energy security of energy-importing and energy-exporting nations can be found, for instance, in Nyga-Łukaszewska and Aruga (2020).

The research **tests the hypothesis** according to which, on the one hand, energy demand security research has gained on the importance in the 21st century and, on the other, that energy demand security has determined comparative advantage of high-income net gas-exporting countries. The above assumption is checked with the use of various scientific methods. Firstly, research employs critical literature review enriched by elements of the scoping review with an aim to investigate and organize the current state of the research on energy demand security. Secondly, the study uses the descriptive analysis of the secondary data to provide an overview of the contemporary developments in the natural gas market and position of different natural gas exporters. Thirdly, the research employs the econometric modelling to understand the relationship between energy demand security and the comparative advantage idea.

The structure of this three-chaptered book corresponds with the research goals and hypothesis. The first part includes a theoretical introduction to the energy security framework. This chapter opens with an analysis of the depletable resources exploitation basics, which are crucial to understand specifics of fossil fuel resource base and their economic characteristics. Yet, as this part serves solely as an introduction to further analysis of energy markets, and natural gas in particular, its scope is limited. It refers only to selected aspects of depletable resources' economics. This way the author admits that even though the research uses only chosen concepts referring to depletable and energy resources in a broader dimension, this part relates to natural resource economics, which might be of use in a similar analysis, but taking the research goal into consideration, they are limited to fossil fuel characteristics. This introduction is needed in the latter part of Chapter 1, in which the author introduces the energy security concept. The idea is said to be one of the most vaguely defined scientific concepts. Only between 2000 and 2014, there had been more than 80 papers delivering 100 different energy security definitions (Ang, Choong, and Ng, 2015). Such vigorous scientific debate on the understanding of energy security created "semantic chaos"[6] in energy security studies. Thus, part of Chapter 1 delivers possible explanations behind the varied understandings of energy security along with evolution of the phenomenon since the 1970s. The main body of this chapter constitutes literature review in the form of scoping and partially systematic approach. The goal of the review is to identify possible research gaps in the energy security (mainly demand) studies. Detected *niché* on relatively rare economic research in the demand security analysis became the focal point of considerations developed in Chapter 2.

Chapter 2 opens with an introductory analysis of energy demand security which centres around supply security concept and methods used to assess it. Including supply security perspective, in this part of this book, results from the fact that demand security originates from supply security idea. The author holds the view that understanding demand security, without looking at its conceptual origins, might have been called a flawed perspective. That is why this chapter provides synthesis of selected supply security concepts and later uses them as a basis for further comparison with energy demand security.[7] These concepts are later analysed with reference to conceptual frameworks used in supply security studies in order to present the perspective of this book's author on demand security. Theoretical considerations precede analysis on that empirical assessment of the demand security. Presented methods are divided into a few groups. They range from simple through complex and aggregated measures to portfolio theory approach. In each of these categories, this book offers a catalogue of indicators used to assess energy demand security. Discussion on these indexes is summarized with a reflection on their developments in the light of supply security research methods. The last part of Chapter 2 embeds the energy demand security analysis in selected neoclassical approaches of international economics. The analysis opens with a description of the trade theories division criteria and then moves to the description of relevance of these approaches to the analysis of energy demand security. Considerations include, on the one hand, the factor endowment theory and its extensions, and, on the other hand, Leontief's paradox and neo-factor theories. This part builds upon the Heckscher-Ohlin approach and its extensions including exhaustible natural resources (Long, 1974; Kemp and Suzuki, 1975; Kemp and Long, 1979, 1982; Ono, 1982; Osei and Lapan, 1995) along with Leontief's paradox natural resource-related explanations provided in Vanek's (1959, 1963), Leamer's (1984) or Baldwin's (2008), and Trefler's (1993, 1995) studies. Additionally, the research includes energy-centred neoclassical theoretical framework using the Dutch disease theorem with the latest developments (Opp, Sonnenschein, and Tombazos, 2009) including the role of institutions (Mehlum, Moene, and Torvik, 2006; Robinson and Torvik, 2013).

Theoretical analysis in Chapter 2 is followed by an empirical research delivered in the third part of this book. This last part describes the energy security phenomenon in the global gas market along with its determinants. The global gas market is depicted in terms of global natural gas supply, demand, and prices. Apart from that, the description includes world trade in natural gas and organization of the world gas market with a special, but synthesized, focus on the Gas-Exporting Countries Forum (GECF).[8] Division of determinants of energy security in the international natural gas market reflects Bohi and Toman's (1996) approach including volume and price aspects. The former group of determinants refers to resource and infrastructure base, non-price terms of energy contracts and energy policy. The latter pertains to price terms of contracts, energy subsidies, and sovereign wealth funds. This chapter closes the description of the econometric modelling approach used to test hypothesis on the demand security influence over comparative advantage of high-income net gas-exporting countries. This part ends with the book's summary.

This book's last part concludes on theoretical and empirical research results with reference to the research question, goals, and tested hypothesis. Apart from that, this section includes concluding remarks following each of the book's chapters accompanied by the author's own reflections on the demand security developments in the future. Inherent segments of this part are also research constraints' description on the one hand, and next research steps recommendations on the other.

Materials used to prepare the book include topic-relevant books, monographs, scientific articles, or reports published by leading research institutions or recognized scientists in the field of energy economics or international economics. Empirical data used in this book was derived, on the one hand, from international databases of World Bank, World Trade Organization, International Energy Agency, Organization for Economic Cooperation and Development, and World Energy Council and, on the other, was obtained from regional energy-specialized bodies such as Energy Information Administration or Sovereign Wealth Found Institute.

For the sake of language coherence and clarity, this book uses phrases "energy security", "energy supply security", and "energy demand security" in different conceptual settings. The first notion is used to describe issues relevant from the point of view of supply and demand security. The second concept, sometimes interchangeably called "supply security" for short or "energy security of importers/importing nations", refers only to energy-importing nations. On the contrary, the third idea, sometimes interchangeably called "demand security" for short or "energy security of exporters/exporting nations", pertains only to exporting nations. Other phrases, which are used interchangeably in this book are the following: "natural gas" and "gas", "crude oil" and "oil", and "natural resources" and "raw materials" or "commodities".

Additionally, in a number of places, this book uses abbreviations. That includes: bcm – which stands for billion cubic metres, mBtu – accounting for million British thermal units, mt – meaning million tons, and Mtoe – standing for million tons of oil equivalent.

Notes

1 According to this concept, the prices of non-renewable resources should increase at the rate determined by the increase in the interest rate (Hotelling, 1931).
2 Later several other reports were published under the auspices of the Club of Rome, but none of them gained the same fame as the first three reports.
3 It is worth noting that the perspective of the countries that transit energy belongs to the same research stream as the energy security of importers.
4 This rise is even more impressive in absolute figures, in 2000 exports of OECD members in total LNG exports amounted to 12 bcm, while in 2021, it was 206.7 bcm (BP, 2022).
5 European Union member countries accounted for ca. 40% of gas pipeline imports in 2021, what made them the incomparably biggest gas importer in the world, while in the LNG imports Europe (with the United Kingdom, UK) accounted for ca. 20% of global LNG imports with foreign gas purchases similar to Japan and China. BP statistics in LNG imports refer to Europe, rest of Europe, Turkey, and the UK, while in pipeline imports to the EU. Thus, here they are presented in the original source manner (BP, 2022).

6 As called by Nyga-Łukaszewska (2018).
7 A detailed conceptual approach on supply security, which is beyond the scope of this book, can be found, for instance, in the analysis of supply security measures in: Bożyk and Nyga-Łukaszewska (2013). Description of different energy demand security definitions with their detailed considerations is provided in the second part of this chapter.
8 More detailed explanation on the GECF as an imperfect market competition type of organization and its possibility of influencing world gas market can be found in Nyga-Łukaszewska (2009).

References

Amoroso, N., Chiquiar, D., and Ramos-Francia, M. (2011) 'Technology and endowments as determinants of comparative advantage: evidence from Mexico', *The North American Journal of Economics and Finance*, 22(2), pp. 164–196. doi:10.1016/j.najef.2011.01.004.

Ang, B.W., Choong, W.L., and Ng, T.S. (2015) 'Energy security: definitions, dimensions and indexes', *Renewable and Sustainable Energy Reviews*, 42(February), pp. 1077–1093.

Antoniadis, I. (2017) 'Exploring the linkage between oil and gas sector and competitiveness: a panel data analysis for the countries of the Black Sea region', *Scientific Bulletin – Economic Sciences*, 16, pp. 34–44. Available at: http://economic.upit.ro/repec/pdf/2017_1_4.pdf (Accessed: 21 December 2021).

Baldwin, R. (2008) *The development and testing of Hecksher-Ohlin trade models*. Cambridge: Massachusetts Institute of Technology, pp. 89–90.

Bohi, D.R. and Toman, M.A. (1996) *The economics of energy security*. 1st edn. Boston, MA: Kluwer Academic Publishers.

Bollino, C.A. and Galkin, P. (2021) 'Energy security and portfolio diversification: conventional and novel perspectives', *Energies*, 14(14), p. 4257. doi:10.3390/en14144257.

Boussena, S. and Locatelli, C. (2013) 'Energy institutional and organisational changes in EU and Russia: revisiting gas relations', *Energy Policy*, 55, pp. 180–189. doi:10.1016/j.enpol.2012.11.052.

Bożyk, P. and Nyga-Łukaszewska, H. (2013) 'Pojęcie i miary bezpieczeństwa energetycznego', in Bożyk, P. (ed.), *Bezpieczeństwo energetyczne Polski w ujęciu autonomicznym i z zintegrowanym z Unią Europejską*. Warszawa: Akademia Finansów i Biznesu Vistula, pp. 9–26.

BP (2022), *BP Statistical Review of World Energy 2022*. Available at: https://www.bp.com/en/global/corporate/energy-economics/statistical-review-of-world-energy/downloads.html (Accessed: 4 April 2023).

Clement, D. (1 September 2002). 'Interview with Robert Solow'. Federal Reserve Bank of Minneapolis. Available at: https://www.minneapolisfed.org/article/2002/interview-with-robert-solow (Retrieved: 29 November 2017).

Dike, J.C. (2013) 'Measuring the security of energy exports demand in OPEC economies', *Energy Policy*, 60, pp. 594–600. doi:10.1016/j.enpol.2013.05.086.

Esfahani, A.N. et al. (2021) 'The knowledge map of energy security', *Energy Reports*, 7, pp. 3570–3589. doi:10.1016/j.egyr.2021.06.001.

European Commission (2022) *REPowerEU: A Plan to Rapidly Reduce Dependence on Russian Fossil Fuels and Fast Forward the Green Transition*. Available at: https://ec.europa.eu/commission/presscorner/detail/en/ip_22_3131 (Accessed: 27 March 2023).

Hotelling, H. (1931) 'The economics of exhaustible resources', *Journal of Political Economy*, 39(2), pp. 137–175. doi:10.1086/254195.

Karatayev, M. and Hall, S. (2020) 'Establishing and comparing energy security trends in resource-rich exporting nations (Russia and the Caspian Sea region)', *Resources Policy*, 68(October), p. 101746 doi:10.1016/j.resourpol.2020.101746.

Kemp, M. and Long, N. (1979) 'International trade with an exhaustible resource: a theorem of Rybczynski type', *International Economic Review*, 20(3), pp. 671–677.

Kemp, M. and Long, N. (1982) 'Rybczynski's theorem in a context of exhaustible resources: the case of time-contingent prices', *International Economic Review*, 23(3), pp. 699–710. doi:10.2307/2526384.

Kemp, M. and Suzuki, H. (1975) 'International trade with a wasting but possibly replenishable resource', *International Economic Review*, 16(3), pp. 712–732.

Leamer, E. E. (1984). *Sources of comparative advantage: Theory and evidence*. Cambridge, MA: MIT Press.

Long, N. (1974) 'International borrowing for resource extraction', *International Economic Review*, 15(1), pp. 168–183.

Meadows, D.L., Randers, J., and Bahrens, W.W. (1973) *Granice wzrostu*. Warszawa: Państwowe Wydawnictwo Ekonomiczne.

Mehlum, H., Moene, K., and Torvik, R. (2006) 'Institutions and the resource curse', *The Economic Journal*, 116(508), pp. 1–20. doi:10.1111/j.1468-0297.2006.01045.x.

Mesarović, M.D. et al. (1977) *Drugi Raport dla Klubu Rzymskiego*. Warszawa: Państwowe Wydawnictwo Ekonomiczne.

Novikau, A. (2022) 'Rethinking demand security: between national interests and energy exports', *Energy Research & Social Science*, 87, p. 102494. doi:10.1016/j.erss.2022.102494.

Nowrouzi, A. et al. (2019) 'Optimizing Iran's natural gas export portfolio by presenting a conceptual framework for non-systematic risk based on portfolio theory', *Energy Strategy Reviews*, 26, p. 100403. doi:10.1016/j.esr.2019.100403.

Nyga-Łukaszewska, H. (2009) 'Czy porozumienie głównych producentów gazu ma szanse stać się nowym OPEC w światowym handlu gazem ziemnym?' *International Journal of Management and Economics*, 26, pp. 127–148.

Nyga-Łukaszewska, H. (2018) 'Bezpieczeństwo energetyczne: u źródeł chaosu semantycznego', in Gryz, J., Podraza, A., and Ruszel, M. (eds.), *Bezpieczeństwo energetyczne: koncepcje, wyzwania, interesy*. Warszawa: Wydawnictwo Naukowe PWN, pp. 69–79.

Nyga-Łukaszewska, H. and Aruga, K. (2020) 'Energy prices and COVID-immunity: the case of crude oil and natural gas prices in the US and Japan', *Energies*, 13(23), p. 6300. doi:10.3390/en13236300.

Nyga-Łukaszewska, H. and Napiórkowski, T.M. (2022) 'Does energy demand security affect international competitiveness? Case of selected energy-exporting OECD countries', *Energies*, 15(6), p. 1991. doi:10.3390/en15061991.

Ono, H. (1982) 'Note on "international trade with an exhaustible resource: a theorem of Rybczynski type"', *International Economic Review*, 23(1), pp. 165–170. doi:10.2307/2526470.

Opp, M.M., Sonnenschein, H.F., and Tombazos, C.G. (2009) 'Rybczynski's theorem in the Heckscher–Ohlin world – anything goes', *Journal of International Economics*, 79(1), pp. 137–142. doi:10.1016/j.jinteco.2009.05.005.

Osei, E. and Lapan, E. (1995) *The generalized H-O model with different natural resource intensities*. Economic Staff Paper Series, 253. Ames: Iowa State University. Available at: http://lib.dr.iastate.edu/econ_las_staffpapers/253 (Accessed: 3 March 2020).

Perman, R. et al. (2003) *Natural resource and environmental economics*. 3rd edn. Essex: Pearson Education Limited.

Robinson, J. and Torvik, R. (2013) 'Institutional comparative statics', in Acemoglu, D., Arellano, M., and Dekel, E. (eds.), *Advances in economics and econometrics*. Tenth World Congress, Volume II: Applied Economics. Cambridge: Cambridge University Press, pp. 97–134.
Romanova, T. (2013) 'Energy demand: security for suppliers?' in Dyer, H. and Trombetta, J. (eds.), *International handbook of energy security*. Cheltenham: Edward Elgar, pp. 239–249.
Solow, R.M. (1973) 'Is the end of the world at hand?' *Challenge*, 16(1), pp. 39–50.
Solow, R.M. (1974) 'Intergenerational equity and exhaustible resources', *The Review of Economic Studies*, 41, pp. 29–45. doi:10.2307/2296370.
Tinbergen, J. (1978) *O Nowy Ład Międzynarodowy*. Warszawa: Państwowe Wydawnictwo Ekonomiczne.
Trefler, D. (1993) 'International factor price differences: Leontief was right!' *Journal of Political Economy*, 101(6), pp. 961–987.
Trefler, D. (1995) 'The case of the missing trade and other mysteries', *The American Economic Review*, 85(5), pp. 1029–1046.
Vanek, J. (1959) 'The natural resource content of foreign trade, 1870–1955, and the relative abundance of natural resources in the United States', *The Review of Economics and Statistics*, 41(2), pp. 146–153.
Vanek, J. (1963) *The natural resource content of foreign trade, 1870–1955*. Cambridge: Cambridge University Press.
Ye, R. et al. (2021) 'Natural gas security evaluation from a supply vs. demand perspective: a quantitative application of four As', *Energy Policy*, 156, p. 112425. doi:10.1016/j.enpol.2021.112425.

1 Energy security

Introduction to theoretical framework

1.1 Depletable/Natural resource exploitation

Natural resources can be classified based on their physical properties and the timescale of relevant adjustment processes. Sweeney (2006) suggests that under the criterion of physical characteristics, natural resources can be broken down into biological, non-energy mineral, energy, and environmental resources. Examples of biological resources include fish, flowers, wild animals, and most agricultural products. Non-energy minerals include resources such as gold, platinum, iron ore, salt, and soil. Energy resources encompass wood, solar radiation, natural gas, crude oil, etc. Environmental resources would include air, the ozone layer, forests, and water. Sweeney (2006) adds that based on the timescale of the relevant adjustment processes, natural resources can be divided into the expendable, renewable, and depletable categories (Table 1.1). Depletable resources are those with a slow adjustment speed, while renewables adjust more rapidly, and expendables exhibit a fast adjustment process. Depletable resources are provided by nature only once, and once used up, they cannot be renewed. Prototypical examples are crude oil and natural gas deposits but also endangered species, the ozone layer, gold, and salt minerals. Renewable resources do not deplete and can be renewed naturally within a certain timescale. These include fish, livestock, wood, geothermal energy and also animal populations. Expendable resources are replaceable and changes within their stock in one period have no or little effects in subsequent periods. This includes agricultural production, salt, solar radiation, hydropower, and also noise pollution and non-persistent air pollution.

Depletable resources meet four distinctive criteria. Firstly, the resource stock decreases over time whenever it is being used. This can be described by equation 1.

$$S_t = S_{t-1} - h(E_t) \tag{1}$$

S_t – resource stock at the end of time period t,

E_t – quantity of the resource extracted in period t (in physical quantities: tins, barrels),

$h(E_t)$ – extraction rate under the assumption of linear stock dynamics (stock is reduced by one unit for every unit of the resource extracted) $h(E_t) = E_t$.

DOI: 10.4324/9781003052241-2

Table 1.1 Examples of natural resources

Availability	*Physical properties*			
	Biological	*Non-energy minerals*	*Energy*	*Environmental*
Expendable	Agricultural resources: corn, grains, etc.	Salt[a]	Solar radiation, hydropower, ethanol	Noise pollution, air pollution, water pollution
Renewable	Forest products, fish, livestock, wild animals, wood, whales, flowers, insects		Wood, hydropower, geothermal	Ground water, air, animal populations, forests
Depletable	Endangered species	Minerals: gold, iron ore, bauxite, salt, etc.	Crude oil, natural gas, coal, uranium, etc.	Ozone layer, water in some aquifers, virgin wilderness

Source: Compiled by the author based on Sweeney (2006).

[a] Most non-energy minerals are depletable. Sweeney gives an example of salt as being both an expendable and depletable resource, explaining that salt evaporated from the San Francisco Bay can be viewed as an expendable resource since the separation of an area of seawater for salt extraction has virtually no impact on the availability of seawater in the Bay.

Secondly, stock never increases over time, as described in equation 2.

$$h\left(E_t\right) \geq 0 \quad \text{and} \quad E_t > 0 \rightarrow h\left(E_t\right) > 0 \tag{2}$$

Thirdly, the rate of stock decrease is a monotonically increasing function of the rate of resource use, as described in equation 3.

$$E_t' > E_t \rightarrow h\left(E_t'\right) > h\left(E_t\right) \tag{3}$$

Fourthly, resource use is not possible without its positive stock, as being described in equation 4.

$$S_t \geq 0 \tag{4}$$

One may claim that stocks of non-renewable resources are not fixed at all times. This is partially true as mineral deposits – in solid, liquid, and gaseous forms – are biologically accumulated over time. However, their rate of formation is slow enough in a timescale relevant to humans that it is reasonable to label them as non-renewables (Perman et al., 2003). That is why, in a physical sense, it may seem inappropriate to refer to non-renewable resources as a fixed resource base. However, with time, the resource base – the resource stock physically available for extraction – may change as technology develops. The resource potential is the estimate of the upper limit of the extractable resource given current or expected technologies. For economists, it is important to look at resources not only from the point of view of their physical potential but also with regard to the feasibility of their extraction under specific circumstances. This means that not only technically feasible resources will be of interest but also potential supplies adjusted by market prices, costs of extraction, and expected profitability (Perman et al., 2003). This approach is common in energy business practice. However, in economic modelling, fixed resource stock (or resource base) is often used as a simplifying assumption (Perman et al., 2003). It should be noted, at this point, that business practice has proved that the resources that were estimated as potential years ago have since been tapped with new technology development. One of such examples is the exploration of the unconventional hydrocarbons across the world in the 21st century.

There are numerous international standards for the classification of mineral deposits. They serve as a benchmark for national geological reporting systems (Saługa, Uberman, and Mazurek, 2018). Resource producers have adjusted their systems to international standards. These benchmarks include

- Combined Reserves International Reporting Standards Committee (CRIRSCO),
- United Nations Framework Classification (UNFC), and
- Petroleum Resources Management System (PRMS).

CRIRSCO has its roots in the mid-1990s and is used to describe specifically solid mineral stocks: solid fuels – coal, gold, industrial, and precious metal ores. It does not refer to hydrocarbons (Saługa, Uberman, and Mazurek, 2018). According to CRIRSCO, resources can be divided into (Figure 1.1)

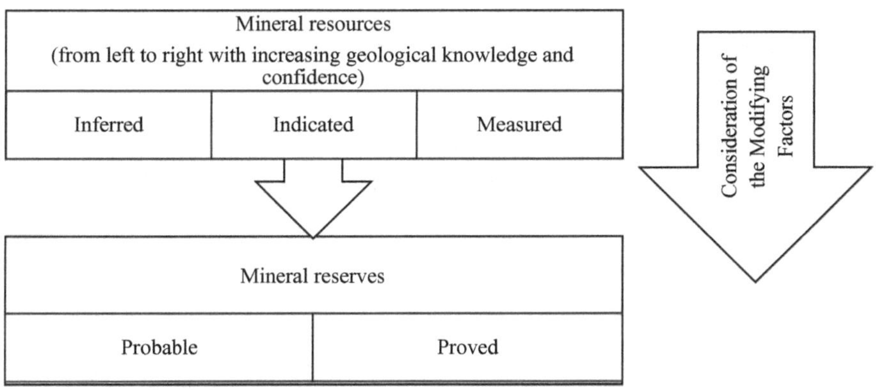

Figure 1.1 General relationship between Exploration Results, Mineral Resources and Mineral Reserves according to CRIRSCO.

Source: Compiled by the author based on PERC (2021).

reserves – which in the case of some countries might be equivalent to exploitable or operational resources; reserves broadly fall into two subcategories: proven and probable reserves,

resources – current balance resources; occurring in the subcategories: measured, indicated, and inferred.

Modifying factors are considerations used to convert resources to reserves include, but are not limited to, mining, processing, metallurgical, infrastructure, economic, market, legal, environmental, social, and governmental factors.

Inferred mineral resources are those resources whose quantity, grade, and quality have been estimated on the basis of limited geological evidence and sampling. Indicated resources are described in terms of quantity, grade or quality, densities, shape, and physical characteristics with enough confidence to allow the application of modifying factors to support mine planning and evaluation of the economic viability of the deposit. Measured resources are those with quantity, grade or quality, densities, shape, and physical characteristics assessed with sufficient confidence to enable the application of modifying factors to support detailed mine planning and final evaluation of the economic viability of the deposit.

Reserves are part of indicated resources that is viable for production under economic, financial, and environmental conditions. Feasibility of production is assessed with modifying factors. Probable reserves are economically mineable indicated resources with sufficient quality to serve as the basis for a decision on the development of the deposit. Proved reserves have a higher level of confidence than probable reserves and constitute an economically mineable part of a measured resource (PERC, 2021).

Like CRIRSCO, the United Nations Framework Classification of Resources and Reserves (UNFC) was developed in the 1990s and refers mainly to stocks of solid resources. The UNFC is a principles-based system in which resources are classified on the basis of three fundamental criteria: environmental-socio-economic viability, technical feasibility, and degree of confidence in the estimate. Combinations of these criteria create a three-dimensional system (United Nations, 2020). In all these criteria, there are sets of subcategories. Environmental and socio-economic viability relies on market prices and relevant legal, regulatory, social, environmental, and contractual conditions that affect resource extraction projects. Technical feasibility includes the maturity of technology, studies, and commitments necessary to implement the project. Degree of confidence designates the reliability of the estimate of the quantities of products that can be obtained from the resource extraction. This way, resource production can be divided into several project classes in a three-dimensional reality (captured to some extent in Figure 1.2). These include viable projects, potentially viable projects, non-viable projects, prospective projects, and projects with remaining products not developed from prospective projects.

Viable projects are those with confirmed environmental-socio-economic viability and technical feasibility. Viable projects are divided into three groups: "on-production", "approved for development", and "justified for development". "On-production" activities are those involving an actual production and sale of products. While the implementation of such projects may not be complete, the on-production project is assumed to have all necessary approvals and contracts in

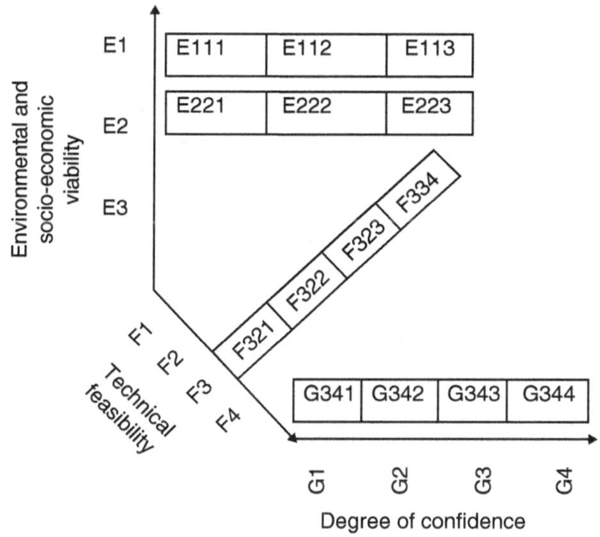

E111, E112, E113 – viable projects

E221, E222, E223 – potentially viable projects

F321, F322, F323 – non-viable projects

F334 – prospective projects

G341, G342, G343, G344 – remaining products not developed

Figure 1.2 UNFC Categories and Subcategories of resources.

Source: Compiled by the author based on United Nations (2020).

place, and capital funds committed. As with on-production projects, those falling within the "approved for development" class also require all approvals/contracts to be in place, with capital funds committed. However, the additional difference between these two types of projects concerns the availability of project facilities. In the case of "approved for development" activities, some machinery might be still under construction or due to start immediately. Project failure might only arise from an unforeseeable change in circumstances. The last group of viable projects includes those "justified for development". They are projects whose technical feasibility and environmental-socio-economic viability have already been confirmed, for which all necessary approvals/contracts for project development and operation are expected to be obtained in the foreseeable future (United Nations, 2020).

Potentially viable projects are the ones for which environmental-socio-economic viability and/or technical feasibility have yet to be confirmed. They are divided into two groups: "development pending" and "development on hold" activities. Development pending activities require the acquisition of additional data (e.g., appraisal drilling) or the completion of project feasibility studies to determine the optimum development scenario. These projects may demonstrate non-technical contingencies expected to be resolved positively within a reasonable time frame. That is why development pending activities are forecasted to have a high probability of achieving viability, in contrast with development on hold projects. Development on hold activities are assumed to face significant contingencies such as environmental or social issues that are objective and cannot be addressed by project developers. Thus, the outcome of the project is under significant uncertainty (United Nations, 2020).

Like potentially viable projects, non-viable projects are characterized by the lack of confirmed environmental-socio-economic viability and/or technical feasibility. They can be divided into two groups: "development unclarified" and "development not viable" activities. The former category covers projects that are in the early stages of technical and environmental-socio-economic evaluation or which will require the acquisition of additional data. That may include, for instance, a recent new discovery of resource deposits. The latter category is used to describe technically feasible projects but with no possibility to remove contingencies affecting project viability. These projects might be considered for future development in case of a major change in technology or environmental-socio-economic conditions (United Nations, 2020).

The "prospective projects" class features insufficient information on the source to assess the project's environmental-socio-economic viability and technical feasibility, while remaining products not developed from projects cover a category of resource quantities that might be produced in the future due to the development of new technology (where no technically feasible projects have been previously identified) (United Nations, 2020).

The Petroleum Resources Management System (PRMS) is a system developed for consistent and reliable definition, classification, and estimation of hydrocarbon resources in 2007 and updated in 2018. This classification, like the UNFC, is considered on a project basis. Resources include all quantities of petroleum naturally occurring within the Earth's crust, both discovered and undiscovered (whether recoverable or unrecoverable), plus those quantities already produced. Resources are classified based on their chance of commerciality and estimates of recoverable and marketable quantities associated with each project reflected under the uncertainty criterion (so-called discovery status) (Figure 1.3). Commerciality

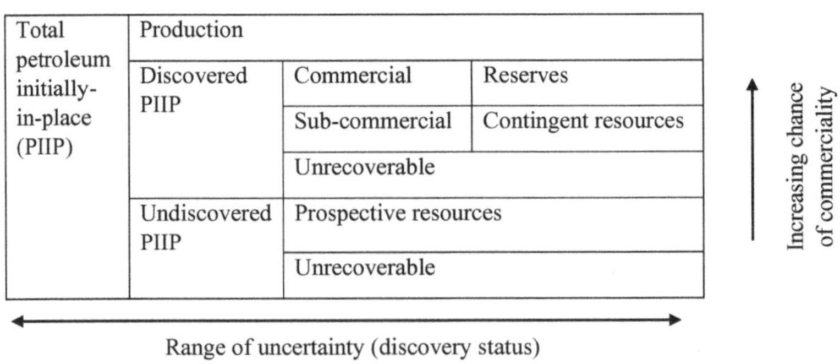

Figure 1.3 PRMS resources classification framework.

Source: Compiled by the author based on SPE (2018).

is determined by the existence of evidence of a technically mature, feasible development plan; financial support to implement the project; assessment of positive economic and investment criteria (cash flow assessment for the investment decision); existence of demand for forecasted sales quantities and similar confidence that all produced streams (e.g., CO_2, water) can be managed appropriately (stored, re-injected, or properly disposed of); suitable necessary production and transportation facilities; legal, contractual, environmental, regulatory, and government approvals. All that has to be achieved in a reasonable time frame. Discovery status is described through petroleum accumulation in one or more exploratory wells that have been established through testing, sampling, and/or logging the existence of a significant quantity of potentially recoverable hydrocarbons (SPE, 2018).

Total petroleum initially-in-place (PIIP) includes all estimated quantities of petroleum that exist in naturally occurring accumulations, discovered and undiscovered, before production. Total petroleum initially-in-place (PIIP) can be broken down into discovered and undiscovered stocks. Discovered PIIP refers to the quantity of petroleum that is estimated, as of a given date, to be contained in known accumulations before production. Discovered PIIP may be subdivided into commercial, sub-commercial, and the portion remaining in the reservoir as unrecoverable, while undiscovered PIIP is the quantity of petroleum estimated, as of a given date, yet to be discovered in known deposits. Unrecoverable discovered petroleum in-place resources are evaluated, as of a given date, as those that cannot be recovered by commercial and sub-commercial projects. Reserves are those quantities of petroleum anticipated to be commercially recoverable. Reserves have to meet the following criteria: be discovered, recoverable, commercial, and remaining (as of the evaluation effective date) based on the development project(s) applied. Contingent resources are those quantities potentially recoverable from known accumulations but not currently considered to be commercial due to one or more contingencies. Contingent resources may include projects for which there are currently no viable markets, or where commercial recovery is dependent on technology under development, or where evaluation of the accumulation is insufficient to clearly assess commerciality. Prospective resources are those quantities of petroleum estimated to be potentially recoverable from undiscovered accumulations. Prospective resources have a chance of geologic discovery and a chance of development. Unrecoverable resources in undiscovered PIIP may never be recovered because of physical/chemical constraints associated with the stocks. Production is the cumulative quantities of petroleum that have been recovered at a given date. Production can be reported in terms of the sales product specifications, but for project evaluation purposes raw production (sales plus non-sales) quantities are taken into account (SPE, 2018).

According to a simple resource depletion model proposed by Perman et al. (2003), in an economy producing a single good (Q) using a non-renewable resource (R) and manufactured capital (K) as inputs, the production function is written as in equation 5.

$$Q = Q(K, R) \tag{5}$$

Q – good produced in the economy,
R – non-renewable resource input,
K – manufactured capital input.

It is assumed that a non-renewable resource is essential for production of the good Q if without the resource (R), the output is zero. This relationship is described in equation 6.

$$Q = Q(K, R = 0) = 0 \text{ for any } K > 0 \tag{6}$$

The use of manufactured capital and the resource for the production is conditioned by their elasticity of substitution (σ), which is a proportionate change in the ratio of capital to the depletable resource in response to a proportionate change in the ratio of the marginal products of capital and that resource, with the output (Q) remaining constant, as described in equation 7.

$$\sigma = \frac{\dfrac{d(K,R)}{\dfrac{K}{R}}}{\dfrac{d\left(\dfrac{Q_k}{Q_R}\right)}{\dfrac{Q_k}{Q_R}}} \quad Q = \text{constant} \tag{7}$$

where:

$$Q_R = \frac{\sigma Q}{\sigma R} \text{ – marginal product of the resource,} \tag{8}$$

$$Q_K = \frac{\sigma Q}{\sigma K} \text{ – marginal product of manufactured capital.} \tag{9}$$

The elasticity of substitution lies between zero (0) and infinity (∞). If $\sigma = 0$, it means that there are no substitution effects between the depletable resource and manufactured capital, while when $\sigma = \infty$ there is a perfect substitution between those two inputs. Usually, $0 < \sigma < \infty$, if σ value is high, resource scarcity will not be of importance for the production of Q, as the economy can easily replace the resource if σ value is low, resource scarcity, with limited substitutability, will have severe effects for the production of Q. Graphically, elasticities of substitution are depicted with isoquants as in Figure 1.4. The depletion of the resource both in the case of low and high substitutability pushes up the relative price of the resource.

Estimation of substitution elasticities between energy and capital (in general) was motivated by the first oil price shock of 1973 (Zweifel, Praktiknjo, and Erdmann, 2016). Policy-makers were interested whether and how easy it was to

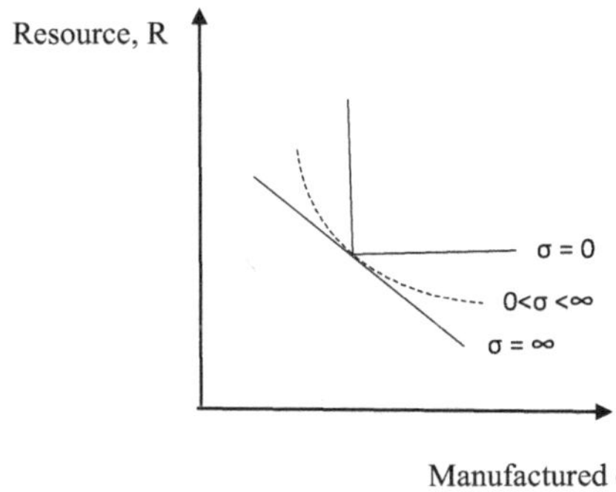

Figure 1.4 Production function isoquants with different elasticities of substitution.

Source: Compiled by the author based on Perman et al. (2003).

substitute energy for capital. However, econometric studies carried out after the oil shocks and even more recently have brought contradictory results claiming that there is either substitutability or complementarity between energy and capital. As Zweifel, Praktiknjo, and Erdmann (2016) suggest, the exact relationship between energy and capital (in general) cannot be clearly determined to this day. Possible explanations behind this ambiguity include limited validity of aggregated data, problems with distinguishing between long and short term[1] or challenges connected with isolating the effects of technological change. Apart from that, it is worth noting that the substitution effect is not considered only between energy and capital but also between different energy resources. In practice, there are different energy resources that can be substituted for one another depending on the purpose of use. Additionally, energy deposits differ in quality. With time, once high-grade resources are depleted, production turns to lower-grade minerals, usually with higher extraction costs.

Dasgupta (2006) described nine different mechanisms for resource substitution arguing at the same time that they are often overlapping and simultaneously occurring. The first mechanism includes an innovation which allows a given resource to be used for a given purpose. The author highlights that this kind of innovation enables a resource "to become". One of the examples of this mechanism is the development of the techniques using coal in the refining of pig-iron. The second type of resource substitution refers to the development of new materials. Dasgupta gives an example of synthetic fibres being a substitute for natural materials such as cotton, wool, etc. Technological developments increasing the efficiency of resource production processes are named as a third mechanism behind resource substitution. An example of that is the use of large-scale earthmoving equipment facilitating economically viable strip-mining of low-grade mineral deposits. The fourth mechanism comprises of scientific and technological discoveries decreasing the costs of exploration activities, e.g., seismology and aerial photography. Technological developments are also crucial in increasing the efficiency of resource use, and as such they are presented by Dasgupta as the fifth mechanism. The author gives an example of reduced amount of coal needed to produce electricity. In the period from

1900 to the 1960s, the quantity of that resource required to produce a kilowatt-hour of electricity fell from seven pounds to less than one pound. The sixth mechanism of resource substitution is the development of techniques allowing the exploitation of low-grade but abundant deposits. Dasgupta gives an example of the use of froth-flotation, which allowed low-grade sulphide ores to be concentrated in an economical manner. Continuous development of recycling techniques is the seventh mechanism of possible resource substitution. Recycling lowers resource costs in a natural way and indirectly increases the stock available for future production. As an example, one may refer to aluminium production in the world. Nowadays, due to improved recycling techniques, most of the aluminium used in the world markets is recycled. The eighth mechanism, as Dasgupta stresses, is more prosaic and not much connected with technological development. It involves the substitution of depleting high-grade resources by low-grade deposits. This results in higher resource extraction and refining costs. Examples of that mechanism include the worldwide production of fossil fuels. The last mechanism is the possibility of substitution of fixed, manufactured capital for depleting resources. As Dasgupta points out, such possibilities are limited. Referring to Dasgupta and Heal (1979), it is worth noting that beyond a point fixed capital in production is complementary to energy resources. The elasticity of substitution is less than one. The ninth mechanism has already been under investigation by economists such as Solow (1974). As can be seen, mechanisms one to seven are triggered by technological discoveries while the eighth and the ninth rely on the existing knowledge. A detailed economic analysis of the eighth mechanism is available in Hotelling's theory of exhaustible resources (Hotelling, 1931).

Depletable energy resources are still the most common sources of energy in the world. Even though their share in total final energy consumption[2] as reported by the International Energy Agency (IEA) decreased from 75% in 1973 to 67% in 2018, they maintain a relatively strong position in global energy use (IEA, 2020). Uneven geographical distribution of proven resources deposits across the world and relatively limited resource substitution in the short and medium term forces energy-scarce countries to buy fuels abroad. Such trade relationship evokes challenges including physical supply disruption and price volatility. Both of these constitute prime concerns in the energy security research.

1.2 Energy security evolution

Energy security is one of the most vaguely defined scientific concepts. Most studies dealing with this issue begin with the statement that energy security is a concept which is either complex (Knox-Hayes et al., 2013) or elusive (Kruyt et al., 2009, p. 609; Loeschel, Moslener, and Ruebellke, 2010) or it is a notion difficult to be defined (Wright, 2005; Kruyt et al., 2009).

Researchers analysing the way of understanding energy security have not reached a consensus so far (Kisel et al., 2016; Garcia-Gusano, Iribarren, and Garrain, 2017; Holley and Lecavalier, 2017). For this reason, there is no single

Table 1.2 Energy security descriptions

Description	*Author*
"difficult"	Wright (2005)
"elusive"	Kruyt et al. (2009)
"exact definition is hard to give as it has different meanings to different people at different moments of time"	
"no common interpretation"	Checchi, Behrens, and Egenhofer (2009)
"blurred"	Loeschel, Moslener, and Ruebellke (2010)
"ubiquitous"	Chester (2010)
	Sovacool and Mukherjee (2011)
	Erdal (2015)
"term is not clearly defined"	Winzer (2012)
"complex nature of energy security"	Knox-Hayes et al. (2013)
"complex concept"	Sumskis (2015)
"definition is another widely disputed matter in the literature"	Kisel et al. (2016)
"difficulty in interpreting its definition"	Li, Shi, and Yao (2016)
"actual definition of energy security has not yet reached consensus"	Garcia-Gusano, Iribarren, and Garrain (2017)
"complex phenomenon"	Jones, Kaklamanou, and Lazuras (2017)
"remains poorly defined"	Glynn, Chiodi, and Gallachoir (2017)
"there is little consensus"	Holley and Lecavalier (2017)

Source: Compiled by the author.

interpretation of this phenomenon (Checchi, Behrens, and Egenhofer, 2009). A detailed list of terms used in relation to energy security is presented in Table 1.2.

The lack of a common definition is surprising, especially considering the fact that the analysed phenomenon is not a new concept. The first references to energy security date back to the beginning of the 20th century. The interest in this issue has increased in the wake of the 1970s oil crises. In the years 1973–1974 (the first oil crisis) and 1979–1982 (the second oil crisis), the supply of crude oil on world markets was reduced and its prices increased. Both of these events triggered negative supply shocks[3] in the global oil markets and sparked a lively discussion on the energy security of fuel-importing countries. In the following years, the interest in energy security shifted towards both a different fuel and a different geographical region. As a result of political changes in Europe in the late 1980s and early 1990s, the existing political and economic ties were loosened and the nature of cooperation between Central and Eastern European countries changed. The culmination of interest in the issues of energy security falls after the accession of this group of countries to the European Union and is associated with the suspension of natural gas supplies by Russia to the EU countries in the winter of 2008/2009.

Despite the relatively long history of research on energy security, there is no single common definition of energy security. There are at least several reasons for this. Here they will be discussed only synthetically. These include the evolution of the phenomenon over time, the level of economic development, the interdisciplinary nature of research on energy security, research horizon, geographical scope of the analysis, and research approach: aggregated versus disaggregated.[4]

One of the basic reasons why there is no one universally accepted definition of energy security is its continuous evolution over time (Figure 1.5).

The perception of energy security has been constantly changing since the 1970s. Initially, it was associated with supply shocks in the crude oil market. Hence, the first works on this subject dealt with the issue of estimating the impact of changes in oil prices on GDP. It can be concluded that in the 1970s and 1980s, energy security was studied mainly from the point of view of energy supply and effects of disrupted supplies to importing nations.

There was a change in the last decade of the 20th century. With the progressive liberalization of energy markets, both primary[5] and secondary,[6] access to energy/energy services has become more important than energy supply itself. This concerned, in the microeconomic sense, the position of the consumer/recipient in the energy market and, in the macroeconomic sense, continuing the consumption of Russian energy in Central and Eastern Europe.[7] Therefore, it can be concluded that in the 1990s, the analysis of energy security focused mainly on the demand side and position of energy suppliers.

In the new century, the way energy security is understood has changed again. This is due to factors influencing both the supply and demand side of energy. The former

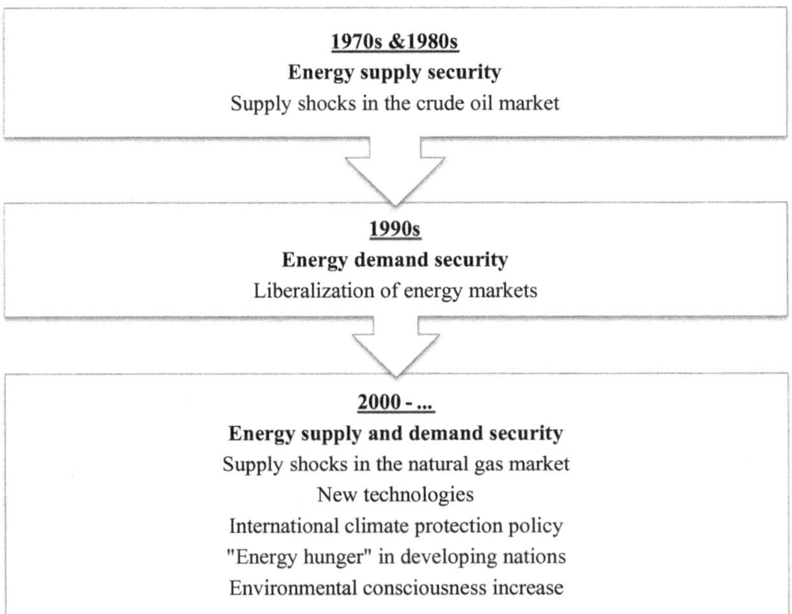

Figure 1.5 Energy security evolution.

Source: Compiled by the author.

includes supply shocks on the natural gas market resulting from the reduction in the exports of Russian gas through Ukraine in 2009.[8] The group of demand-side factors which shaped the understanding of energy security in the 21st century includes, first of all, the constantly tightening global standards of fuel consumption and the growing pressure for a more rational use of fossil energy sources. In addition, with the increase in raw material prices and the development of new technologies, renewable/alternative energy sources (e.g., photovoltaic panels/methane production from landfills) have gained importance. More and more often, aspects related to the social acceptance of energy have come to the fore in the discussion on the way of understanding energy security (Jones, Kaklamanou, and Lazuras, 2017; Wang and Zhou, 2017). Additionally, in the group of developing countries, the growing demand for energy, dictated by the fast pace of economic development, has become an important element. Hence, it can be concluded that in the 21st century the way of understanding energy security included the issues of supply and demand for energy.

Summing up the stages of the evolution of the way of understanding energy security, it can be noted that the 1970s and 1980s were a period when the analysis of this phenomenon was dominated by the issue of access to energy resources. Treating energy as a production factor, one can define the research that emerged in that period as a resource trend in the energy security studies. In the 1990s, the researchers' attention was drawn to market mechanisms serving to ensure the security of energy supply. Therefore, this line of research can be described as the market dimension of energy security. On the other hand, the first decades of the new century, dominated by the issues of sustainable energy management, can be described as the environmental and social dimension of energy security (Figure 1.6).

The described stages of the evolution of energy security reflect the gradual maturing of the way of understanding this phenomenon. However, it should be noted that energy security is not evolving at the same pace worldwide. The development of the way of perceiving the phenomenon is a result of the maturity of the economy, which is determined, among others, by the effectiveness of market mechanisms and highly developed ecological awareness of society. The evolution of the way of understanding energy security from the factor (resource) dimension to the market dimension and then to the environmental and social dimension, is conditioned by a sufficiently high level of socio-economic development.

Frei's pyramid of energy needs (Frei, 2004) can be used to explain the evolution of the way of understanding energy security. Frei (2004) based his idea on Maslow's

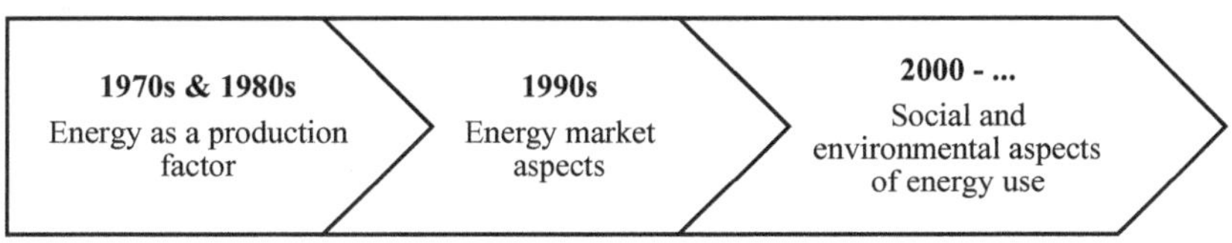

Figure 1.6 Evolution of the concept of energy security since the 1970s.

Source: Compiled by the author.

hierarchy of needs, a common concept in managerial sciences. He applied Maslow's approach to energy markets. Referring to the pyramid, it can be noticed that only in societies where access to energy (energy resources) is provided, it is possible to liberalize the energy market and then take into account public acceptance (or lack thereof) as one of the elements determining the country's energy policy. Frei (2004) claimed, citing Maslow, that once the lower-order needs were satisfied, countries concerned themselves with higher-order needs. However, when basic needs were not met, higher-order needs did not exist. Thus, when access to energy, resource-efficiency needs are met, environmental and social aspects of energy use are placed high on the countries' policy agendas. Germany is an example of a country that might be treated as the most advanced on Frei's energy needs pyramid. A balanced energy mix and a deregulated energy market make it possible for this country to decide to withdraw from nuclear energy due to the lack of social acceptance for this source of energy.

This is where another factor responsible for the lack of a uniform definition of energy security becomes apparent – that is, the diversified level of economic development. For developing countries, access to energy remains the key issue, whereas for developed countries it is social acceptance for a specific energy security profile. The examples of Nigeria and Germany can be used to illustrate these differences (Table 1.3). Comparing these two countries, clear differences can be seen in economic development (GDP), access to energy (the level of electrification and energy consumption), and the attitude of society to environmental protection (index representing environmental protection activities). The high level of economic development in Germany is accompanied by a full electrification rate, high energy consumption, and a high (tenth) position in the ranking taking into account activities for environmental protection. In contrast, Nigeria, with its weak economic development, a low electrification rate, and relatively low energy consumption, is ranked among the lowest positions (151st) for environmental protection activities.

Table 1.3 Selected indicators comparing Nigeria and Germany in the years 2014, 2019, and 2020

Indicator	*Nigeria*	*Germany*
GDP (current prices, USD bn) 2019	573	3,888
Access to electricity (% of population)[a]2019	55	100
Electric power consumption (kWh per capita) 2014	145	7,035
Energy use (kg of oil equivalent per capita) 2014	764	3,818
Environmental Performance Index – rank in 2020 (out of 180 countries)	151	10

Source: Compiled by the author based on World Bank (2022) and Yale (2022).

[a] The most recent data in the World Bank database for electric power consumption (kWh per capita) and energy use (kg of oil equivalent per capita) was available for 2014

1.3 Energy supply and demand security evolution – Theoretical approach

1.3.1 Method description

Scoping literature review is an "approach to finding the most notable studies in the field, minimal attempts to evaluate them for quality, [and] a rudimentary attempt at synthesis" (Booth, Sutton, and Papaioannou, 2016). A scoping review identifies the nature and extent of research evidence (including ongoing research). This type of review is a mapping effort within a predefined scope and sample. Scoping reviews identify the existence of significant work in progress to inform future reviews and reveal research gaps. Weaknesses of scoping reviews connected with search and appraisal according to the SALSA framework (Search, Appraisal, Synthesis and Analysis) (Booth, Sutton, and Papaioannou, 2016) have been overcome in this study by employing, wherever possible, systematic-literature review elements. This way, the searched documents have not been accepted on their face value but, especially in the last stages of the research, were appraised against their abstracts or, if needed, full text versions. To avoid susceptibility to bias, the study has adopted a drop-out rather than contamination strategy (Petticrew and Roberts, 2006). The appraisal strategy has employed a hierarchy of evidence, while synthesis and analysis followed the narrative approach.

The systematic review employed in this study is a type of advanced literature review. It is widely used in different scientific disciplines. The most detailed methodological approach to systematic reviews has been developed in medical and biological sciences. Social sciences also use it as "another research method, and in many respects they are very similar to a survey – though in this case they involve a survey of the literature, not of people" (Petticrew and Roberts, 2006). Systematic reviews have grown in importance since they provide an effective way of handling substantial quantities of information. They have been increasingly used by policymakers, as this method integrates research with decision-making. The systematic review offers a retrospective research. When comparing different data-producing techniques, a systematic review can neither be called a primary research technique nor a secondary one, as it does not produce primary data in a way that, for instance, surveys do, but it can (especially when employed for theory testing) generate valuable research pools (Petticrew and Roberts, 2006). Petticrew and Roberts (2006) describe several situations in which a systematic review might be of use. They argue that it is especially effective when it is generally known that there is a wide range of research on a subject but key questions remain unanswered. They also claim that systematic review should precede any primary research effort, arguing that it should be part of good scientific practice or even a condition for grant application. Systematic reviews can, but do not have to, include a meta-analysis – a quantitative approach to the researched literature (Littell, Corcoran, and Pillai, 2008).

Following the logic of systematic literature reviews, the research is organized into the following stages. First, the research question has been described. Secondly, a detailed report on the literature search has been established. The third step included a multistage database search, selection of relevant documents, which were analysed according to the inclusion and exclusion criteria stated in the next phase and comparison of the results in the form of meta-analysis (Orłowska, Mazur, and Łaguna, 2017). Accordingly, materials taken into consideration in this research met the following criteria: (1) were published between January 2000 and (late) November 2020, (2) appeared in one of the most popular scientific databases – Web of Science Core Collection or Scopus, and (3) fall into the category of economics or management discipline of social sciences. In order to avoid language bias (Littell, Corcoran, and Pillai, 2008), the study did not limit the research to English only. However, as shown later, the majority of records described energy security in that language. In order to find the best possible scientific description of energy security, the two largest scientific databases have been searched: Web of Science Core Collection (WoS) and Scopus. Web of Science launched in 1997 and renamed Web of Science Core Collection in 2014 offered 79 m records with more than 21,419 journals at the end of October 2020. WoS covers a wide range of science areas ranging from life sciences, biomedical sciences through engineering to social sciences, arts and humanities (Web of Science, 2020). Scopus, established in 2004 and often called a "newcomer" (Zhu and Liu, 2020), offered nearly 80 m different records with more than 25,100 titles dominated by 23,452 journals as of January 2020. Scopus covers a wide range of areas in the fields of science, technology, medicine, social science, and arts and humanities (Scopus, 2020). The world's third leading scientific database is PubMed, which covers more than 30 m records but, being limited to medical and biological sciences, it is not included in this research.

The database search took place in November 2020. Access to resources was obtained with a licence held by the SGH Warsaw School of Economics. The search was focused on such terms as "energy security", "energy supply security", and "energy demand security". In each of these cases, search-limiting criteria included in the first stage (i.e., the period 2000–2020) and in the second stage (i.e., the subject area) were employed. As the study was designed within the framework of economics, subject areas were delineated as economics, business, and management for WoS, and economics, econometrics and finance, business and accounting, and management for Scopus. The latter database offered a more detailed discipline breakdown. Both WoS and Scopus provided the year of record publication, authors, type of document, organization (in WoS) and/or affiliation (in Scopus), funding sources, language, and either research area (in WoS) or subject area (in Scopus).

1.3.2 Research results

The first stage of the scoping review showed that between 2000 and 2020, there was a growing trend in the energy security research within both databases (Figure 1.7). There was a drop in publication records in both databases in 2020, but it can be attributed to the fact that the study gathered data in November, when full-year data for 2020 did not yet exist. Scopus responded with more (51,614) records than WoS (29,462). The majority of records in both databases (around 30%) were

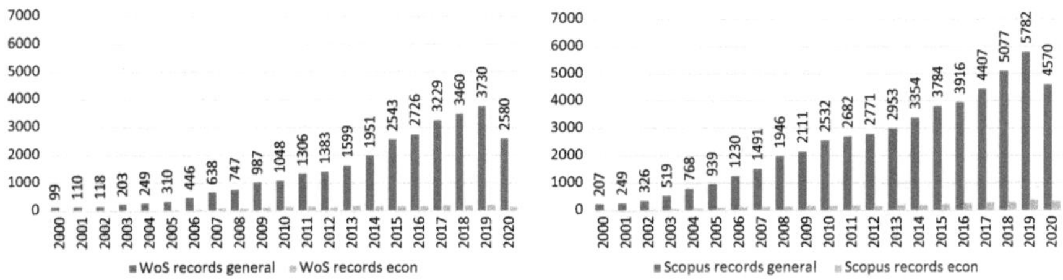

Figure 1.7 Comparison of "energy security" search in the Scopus and WoS general databases and limited to the economics field between 2000 and 2020.

Source: Compiled by the author based on the Scopus and WoS databases.

reported in the period 2017–2019. A longer examined period (2000–2020) showed a growing trend in energy security research within the economics area. *Scopus econ* offers more than 3,000 records in economics, econometrics and finance, business and accounting, and management, whereas *WoS econ* includes 2,000 items in the economics, business, and management fields.

Articles hold a dominant position in both the Scopus and WoS general databases (54% and 45%, respectively) (Figure 1.8). Another popular way of reporting energy security research results in both Scopus and WoS is through proceedings papers or conference papers (25% and 38%, respectively). Book chapters were used more often in WoS (6%) than in Scopus (3%), whereas reviews are of the same importance in both cases (5% each). Similar document types with a share in the databases of around and less than 1% have not been presented in Figure 1.8. In Scopus, this includes books, retracted publications, news items, meeting abstracts, letters, data papers, and corrections; and in WoS, books, notes, business articles, short surveys, editorials, letters, errata, retracted publications, abstract reports, and data papers.

A similar document breakdown is observed in *Scopus econ* and *WoS econ* (Figure 1.9), covering 3,300 and 2,028 research items, respectively. Articles seem to be the most popular form of research reporting in the area of economics, especially with *WoS econ* (72%). Conference and proceedings papers have comparable shares, at 13% (*Scopus econ*) and 15% (*WoS econ*). Book chapters are more popular in *Scopus econ* (13%) than in *WoS econ* (7%). Similar document types with a share in the databases of around and less than 1% have not been presented in Figure 1.9. In *Scopus econ*, this includes short surveys, conference reviews, editorials, retracted publications, and letters; in *WoS econ*, reviews, books, early access publications, and corrections.

Looking at the institutions that publish energy security research in general, the Scopus and WoS databases show that the top three affiliations come from China (Table 1.4). Interestingly, the top two in both databases are the same: the Chinese Academy of Sciences and Tsinghua University, which is a major research university in Beijing. Asian research institutions enjoy a dominant position, constituting the top nine affiliations in Scopus and seven of the top ten

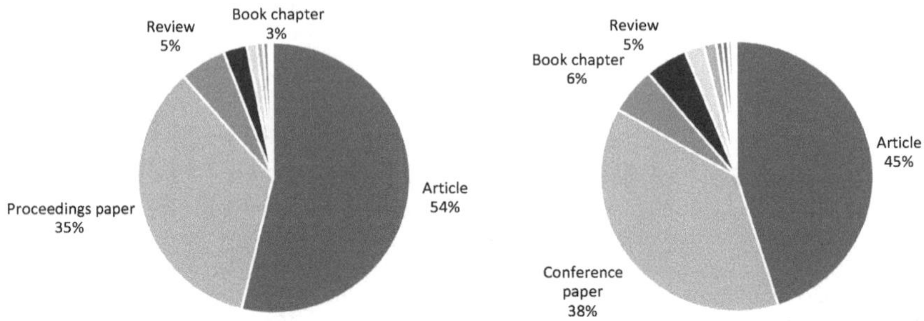

Figure 1.8 Comparison of "energy security" search in the Scopus (left) and WoS (right) general databases according to document type.

Source: Compiled by the author based on the Scopus and WoS databases.

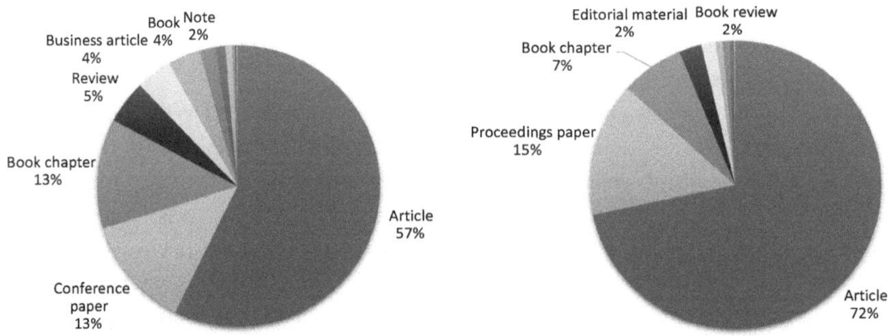

Figure 1.9 Comparison of "energy security" search in the Scopus econ (left) and WoS econ (right) databases according to document type.

Source: Compiled by the author based on the Scopus and WoS databases.

in WoS. Due to the size difference between both databases, the actual record count for institutions is higher in Scopus. In both databases, high positions are also held by the Massachusetts Institute of Technology (MIT), ranked 13th in Scopus and 12th in WoS, the Georgia Institute of Technology – 15th and 12th, respectively, Southeast University – 18th and 17th, and Nanyang Technological University, 17th and 18th, respectively. No Central European research institutions are recorded in this comparison.

Scopus, unlike WoS, also offers a possibility to identify the territory or region represented by a researcher. During the 2000–2020 period, the largest proportions of research items came from two countries, the USA and China, which accounted for 16% and 14%, respectively, of "energy security" records in the Scopus general database. Among the top ten regions representing "energy security" research, European countries account for 13%, with the UK, Germany, Italy, and France as contributors. Interestingly, among the group of the Central European countries, Poland leads with a 0.8% share, followed by Romania (0.5%), Czechia (0.39%), Hungary (0.25%), and Lithuania (0.25%).

Table 1.4 Comparison of "energy security" search in the Scopus (left) and WoS (right) general databases according to affiliation or organization (top ten records)

Affiliation	*Scopus general records*	*Organization*	*WoS general records*
Chinese Academy of Sciences	610	Chinese Academy of Sciences	474
Tsinghua University	559	Tsinghua University	292
Ministry of Education, China	519	North China Electric Power University	213
North China Electric Power University	328	National University of Singapore	181
Shanghai Jiao Tong University	235	Islamic Azad University	168
Zhejiang University	225	Zhejiang University	159
National University of Singapore	218	University California Berkeley	152
Beijing University of Posts and Telecommunications	216	Purdue University	147
Xi'an Jiaotong University	216	Xi'an Jiaotong University	143
Institute of Electrical and Electronics Engineers	213	Shanghai Jiao Tong University	141

Source: Compiled by the author based on the Scopus and WoS databases.

Scopus econ and *WoS econ* reveal a greater geographical diversity in energy security research within the economics field (Table 1.5). The Chinese Academy of Sciences leads in both databases along with the University of Cambridge, with the University of Cambridge leading in *Scopus econ* and the Chinese Academy of Sciences in *WoS econ*. In contrast to general databases search results, in the field of economics there are, in addition to North American and Asian contributors, also European (Eurasian) institutions. In the case of *Scopus econ*, these are the Bucharest University of Economic Studies and three Russian representatives: the Russian Academy of Sciences, Plekhanov Russian University of Economics, and the Financial University under the Government of the Russian Federation. In *WoS econ*, there are (apart from the Bucharest University of Economic Studies) the University of Sussex, the International Institute for Applied Systems Analysis, and also the Central European University. The Bucharest University of Economic Studies enjoys a relatively strong position, being ranked third in *WoS econ* just after the University of Cambridge (with a difference of only one record item). Geographical and institutional diversity is also visible in the rest of *Scopus econ* and *WoS econ* records. In *Scopus econ*, there are the German Institute of Economic Research, Imperial College London, the University of Manchester, ETH Zürich, Aarhus University, the University of Sussex and Technische Universität Dresden. In *WoS econ*, there are the University of Oxford, Aarhus University, Lund University, Vilnius University, the Cracow University of Economics, the Economic University of Bratislava, and

Table 1.5 Comparison of "energy security" search in the Scopus econ (left) and WoS econ (right) databases according to affiliation or organization (top ten records)

Affiliation	*Scopus econ records*	*Organization*	*WoS econ records*
University of Cambridge	38	Chinese Academy of Sciences	31
Chinese Academy of Sciences	25	University of Cambridge	27
Russian Academy of Sciences	24	Bucharest University of Economic Studies	26
The Australian National University	22	University of California, Berkeley	22
Plekhanov Russian University of Economics	22	National University of Singapore	21
Bucharest University of Economic Studies	22	University of Sussex	21
National University of Singapore	21	International Institute for Applied Systems Analysis	19
Cambridge Judge Business School	17	Tsinghua University	18
Tsinghua University	16	Stanford University	17
Financial University under the Government of the Russian Federation	16	Central European University	15

Source: Compiled by the author based on the Scopus and WoS databases.

KU Leven. Central European research units investigating energy security from the economic point of view are better represented in the *WoS econ* database.

A *Scopus econ* country breakdown shows that between 2000 and 2020, the largest proportions of research items came from three countries: the USA, China, and the UK, which accounted for 14%, 8%, and 8%, respectively, of "energy security" records in the database. Among the top ten regions for "energy security" research, European countries account for 18%. Apart from the UK, this includes Germany (5%), Italy (3%), and France (2%). Central European countries with the highest records are represented by Romania (1%), Poland (1%), Lithuania (1%), Czechia (0.6%), Hungary (0.5%), and Slovakia (0.4%).

Looking at the subject (Scopus) or research (WoS) area within energy security studies, similarities can be observed in both databases. The leading positions are held by engineering (23% and 22%, respectively), computer science (18%–13%), energy/energy fuels (14%–12%), and environmental science (7% each). In Scopus, the subjects "Business, management and accounting" (2,292 research items) and "Economics, econometrics and finance" (1,662 research items) each have a 2% share in total Scopus energy security records. In WoS, "Business economics" (2,028 research items) account for nearly 7% of records.

The most prolific author between 2000 and 2020 in both databases, regardless of their general or economic character, was Benjamin Sovacool. He authored or co-authored 95 research items in the general Scopus database, 91 in WoS, 14 in *Scopus econ*, and 25 in *WoS econ*. Similarly, Andreas Goldthau produced 18 research items in the general Scopus database, six in *Scopus econ*, eight in *WoS econ*, even though was not included in the WoS general database. Manuela Tvaronavičienė's publications had eight and five records in *Scopus econ* and *WoS econ*, respectively. Benjamin Sovacool – a leading researcher in both databases, repeatedly published under the most popular *WoS econ* title, *Energy Policy*, in which nearly 40% of all research items were published in the 2000–2020 period. The leading journal in *Scopus econ* – *the Journal of Cleaner Production* – was less popular among researchers than *Energy Policy* and published 12% of database records in the same period. An overwhelming majority of research published in scientific databases, regardless of their general or economic character, is written in English (97%).

1.3.2.1 Energy supply security

The next stage of the scoping review search added the "energy supply security" as a criterion for inclusion. The narrowing down of the analysis yielded 9,975 research items in Scopus, 5,335 in WoS, 1,093 in *Scopus econ*, and 707 in *WoS econ*. Analysis shows that between 2000 and 2020, there was a growth trend in energy security research within both databases (Figure 1.10). However, WoS, compared to Scopus, offers a significantly lower number of energy supply security records. The period 2017–2019 brought a significant number of new energy security research record items. Interestingly, even though 2020 has not been fully captured in the research, unlike energy security within the economic field, the number of research items with economic focus (in *Scopus econ*) on energy supply security was only slightly lower (two items) than in the previous year. That dynamic might be a sign of a more detailed analysis and understanding. In 2000, there were seven research items on energy supply security in *Scopus econ* and a closer look at them shows that they mainly referred to oil markets, economics of natural resource availability and exploration. None of them applied scientific methodology to security of supply in the natural gas market. The only documents describing topics within this field were information in

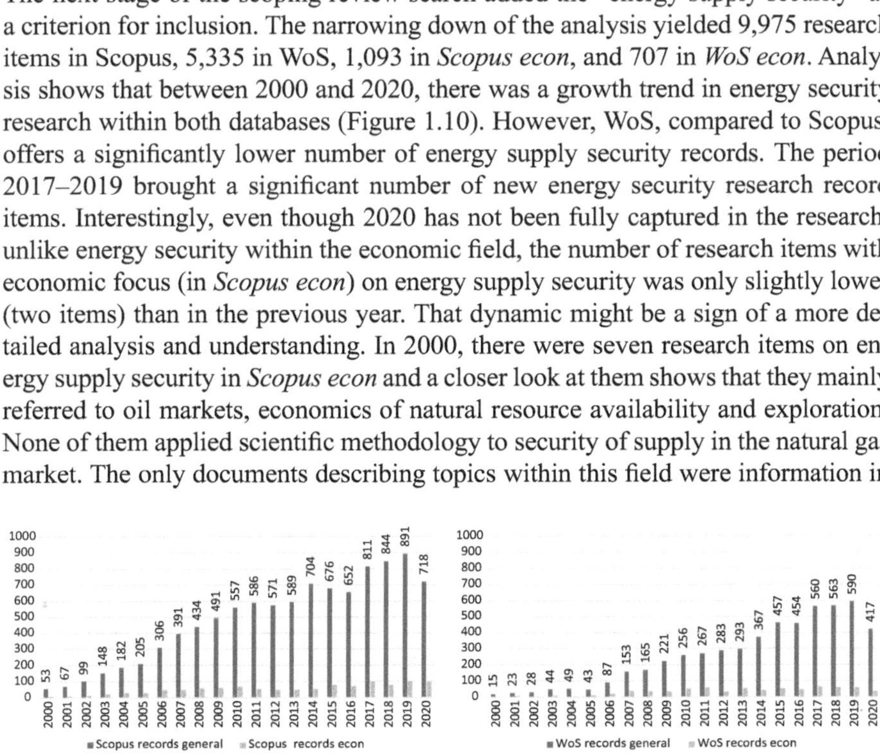

Figure 1.10 Comparison of "energy supply security" search in the Scopus and WoS general databases and limited to the economics field between 2000 and 2020.

Source: Compiled by the author based on the Scopus and WoS databases.

Petroleum Economist about discussions during the World Gas Conference 2000 in Nice, France, and a report in *Petroleum Review* based on discussions with energy experts and organizations throughout the EU following the European Commission's analysis of issues associated with the EU's reliance on natural gas imports.

The dominance of articles as a primary method of "energy supply security" reporting is even stronger than in case of "energy security". Articles in the Scopus and WoS general databases represent 52% and 60%, respectively (Figure 1.11). Another popular way of reporting energy security research results is through proceedings in Scopus (27%) and WoS (29%). Unlike energy security research, book chapters are more often used in Scopus (7%) than in WoS (3%), whereas reviews are of the same importance in both cases (8% each). Figure 1.11 presents a complete characterization of WoS document types. For Scopus, research items with a database share of around or less than a 2% have not been presented in the figure. In Scopus, this includes book notes, conference reviews, short surveys, editorials, letters, abstract reports, errata, and retracted publications.

A similar document breakdown, resembling even more our "energy security" search in *Scopus econ* and *WoS econ*, is presented in Figure 1.12. The analysis included 1,093 and 707 research items, respectively. Articles are the most popular form of research reporting in the area of economics, especially with *WoS econ* (81%). Conference and proceedings papers have comparable shares, at 10% (*Scopus econ*) and 13% (*WoS econ*). Again, book chapters are more popular in *Scopus econ* (10%) than in *WoS econ* (3%). It seems that moving to a more detailed analysis level (from the general idea of "energy security" to "energy supply security") increases the overall article share. Similar document types with a share in the databases of around or less than 2% have not been presented in Figure 1.8. In *Scopus econ*, this includes conference reviews, short surveys, editorials, and letters; and in *WoS econ*, reviews, editorial materials, early access materials, book reviews, and corrections.

Looking at institutions that publish energy supply security research in the general Scopus and WoS databases reveals that the Chinese Academy of Science again leads, with the notable presence of Tsinghua University (Table 1.6). Asian

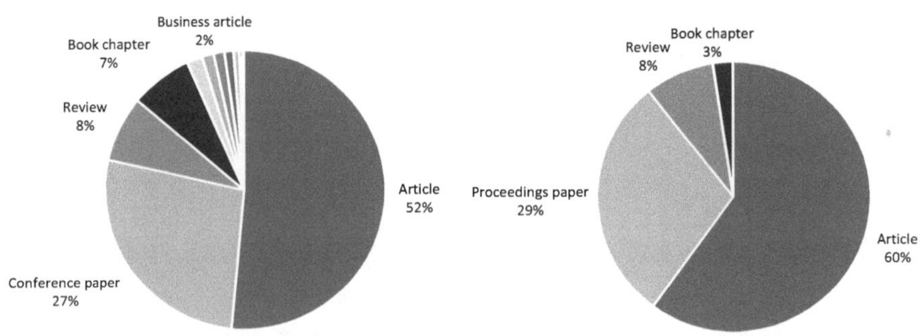

Figure 1.11 Comparison of "energy supply security" search in Scopus (left) and WoS (right) general databases according to document type.

Source: Compiled by the author based on the Scopus and WoS databases.

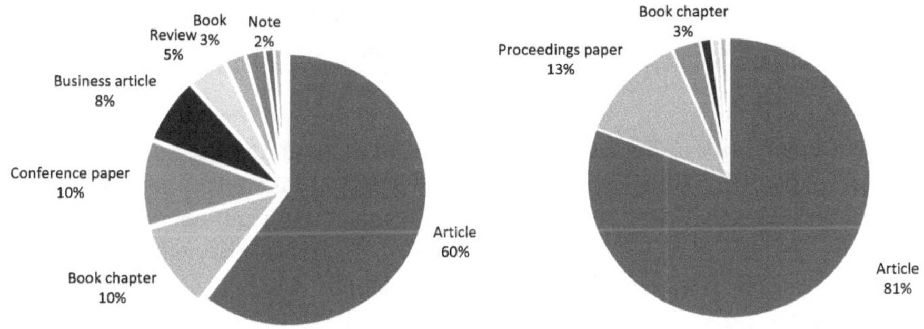

Figure 1.12 Comparison of "energy supply security" search in the Scopus econ (left) and WoS econ (right) databases according to document type.

Source: Compiled by the author based on the Scopus and WoS databases.

Table 1.6 Comparison of "energy supply security" search in Scopus (left) and WoS (right) general databases according to affiliation or organization (top ten records)

Affiliation, Scopus general	*Scopus general records*	*Organizations, WoS general*	*WoS general records*
Chinese Academy of Sciences	128	Chinese Academy of Sciences	86
Imperial College London	83	North China Electric Power University	55
Tsinghua University	81	Tsinghua University	41
European Commission Joint Research Centre	78	European Commission	38
North China Electric Power University	71	International Institute for Applied Systems Analysis, Luxemburg	38
University of Cambridge	61	University of Manchester	36
Ministry of Education, China	58	University of Cambridge	35
International Institute for Applied Systems Analysis, Luxemburg	56	Delft University of Technology	34
University of Manchester	48	Islamic Azad University	33
ETH Zürich	48	Kyoto University	30

Source: Compiled by the author based on Scopus and WoS databases.

research institutions' dominance in "energy supply security" is not as strong as in the case of "energy security". Among the top ten Scopus "energy supply security" positions, four affiliations are Asian, against nine in "energy security" (see Table 1.5), whereas in the top ten WoS affiliations, only three represent Asia as opposed to seven in "energy security". Asian dominance is undermined in both cases by strong representation of European institutions, such as the European Commission Joint Research Centre, the University of Cambridge, the International Institute for Applied Systems Analysis, the University of Manchester, and ETH Zürich (in Scopus); and, apart from those, the University of Manchester and Delft University of Technology (in WoS). In both databases, a similarly high position is also held by Beijing Normal University, ranked 15th in Scopus and 12th in WoS, the National University of Singapore – 16th in Scopus and 13th in WOS, the University of California, Berkeley – 20th in Scopus and 16th in WoS, and Rheinisch-Westfälische Technische Hochschule Aachen – 22nd in Scopus and 18th in WoS.

According to Scopus, the largest proportions of "energy supply security" research between 2000 and 2020 again came from two countries, the USA and China, which accounted, respectively, for 12% and 9%, respectively, of "energy supply security" records in the Scopus general database. Among the top ten regions representing "energy security" research, European countries account for 13%, with the UK, Germany, and Italy predominating. Interestingly, the group of the Central European countries is again led by Poland with a 1% share, followed by Romania (0.6%), Hungary (0.5%), and Lithuania (0.4%).

In *Scopus econ* and *WoS econ*, Asian dominance is even weaker (Table 1.7). Both databases are led by the University of Cambridge, followed by the German

Table 1.7 Comparison of "energy supply security" search in the Scopus econ (left) and WoS econ (right) databases according to affiliation or organization (top ten records)

Affiliation Scopus econ	*Scopus econ records*	*Organization*	*WoS econ records*
University of Cambridge	21	University of Cambridge	17
German Institute for Economic Research	13	Chinese Academy of Sciences	16
Chinese Academy of Sciences	10	University of London	15
Beijing Normal University	10	International Institute for Applied Systems Analysis	13
Cambridge Judge Business School	10	University of California	13
Australian National University	9	Centre National De La Recherche Scientifique	11
Imperial College London	9	European Commission Joint Research Centre	11
Technische Universität Dresden	9	University of Oxford	11
The Royal Institute of Technology KTH	8	Stanford University	8
RWE AG	8	University of California, Berkeley	8

Source: Compiled by the author based on the Scopus and WoS databases.

Institute for Economic Research (in *Scopus econ*) and the Chinese Academy of Sciences (in *WoS econ*). In contrast to "energy security" search results in the general databases, in the field of economics, "energy supply security" research is dominated by European organizations. In *Scopus econ*, there are, apart from the institutions already mentioned, Cambridge Judge Business School, Imperial College London, Technische Universität Dresden, KTH Royal Institute of Technology, and RWE AG. In *WoS econ*, there are, apart from the University of Cambridge, the University of London, the International Institute for Applied Systems Analysis, Centre National De La Recherche Scientifique, the European Commission Joint Research Centre, and the University of Oxford.

Both in *Scopus econ* and *WoS econ* records, there is a marked presence of German institutions. Apart from the ones already mentioned, in *Scopus econ*, these are the Karlsruhe Institute of Technology, the Fraunhofer Institute for Systems and Innovation Research ISI, Deutsches Zentrum für Luft-Und Raumfahrt, the Technical University of Berlin, the University of Cologne, Universität Leipzig, Universität Duisburg-Essen, Universität Stuttgart, Rheinisch-Westfälische Technische Hochschule Aachen, Helmholtz Zentrum für Umweltforschung, Potsdam Institut für Klimafolgenforschung, Freie Universität Berlin, Ruhr-Universität Bochum, and Technische Universität Kaiserslautern; in *WoS econ*, there is additionally the Helmholtz Association. Central European research units investigating energy supply security from the economic point of view are equally represented in the *WoS econ* and *Scopus econ* databases. The former includes the Central European University and the University of Economics, Bratislava. The latter lists the Bucharest University of Economic Studies and the Lithuanian Energy Institute.

In *Scopus econ*, a country breakdown shows that during 2000–2020, the largest proportions of research items came from two countries, the UK and the USA, each with a share of 10% in "energy supply security" records in the database. Among the top ten regions representing this research type, European countries account for 29%. Apart from the UK, this includes Germany (8%), Italy (5%), and France (3%). Central European countries with the highest records are represented by Poland (more than 1%), followed by Lithuania (0.9%), Romania (0.7%), and Hungary (0.6%).

Looking at the subject (Scopus) or research (WoS) area within energy supply security studies, similarities can be observed in both databases. The leading positions by topic are energy (Scopus)/energy fuels (WoS) (24% and 40%, respectively), engineering (18% and 34%, respectively), and environmental science (13% and 21%, respectively). In Scopus, the subjects "Business, management and accounting" (733 research items) and "Economics, econometrics and finance" (521 research items) have a 4% and 3% share, respectively, in the total of Scopus energy supply security records. In WoS, "Business economics" (712 research items) account for more than 13% of records.

The author who published the most works between 2000 and 2020 in both databases, regardless of their general or economic character, is again Benjamin Sovacool. He has authored or co-authored 34 research items in the general Scopus database, 28 in WoS, and seven in *WoS econ*. In *Scopus econ*, Derek Brower is the leader, who published eight articles in *Petroleum Economist* during that same period. Similar record counts are found in *Scopus econ* for Jean-Michel Glachant (six) and Franziska Holz (five). The most popular *WoS econ* title between 2000 and 2020 was *Energy Policy*, where nearly 50% of energy supply security research in the economics field was published. *Scopus econ*'s leading title *Journal of Cleaner Production* was less popular among researchers than *Energy Policy*, publishing 13% of database records in the same period. The majority of research published in scientific databases, regardless of their general or economic character, is written in English (97%). In the field of energy supply security, as well as energy security, *Scopus econ* and *WoS econ* offer a greater variety of works in languages such as Chinese, Slovak, or Polish.

1.3.2.2 Energy demand security

The next stage of the scoping review search added "energy demand security" as a criterion for inclusion. The narrowing down of the analysis yielded 7,499 research items in Scopus, 4,926 in WoS, 637 in *Scopus econ*, and 1,310 in *WoS econ*. Analysis shows that between 2000 and 2020 there was a growth trend in energy security research within both databases (Figure 1.13). However, WoS, compared to Scopus, offers a significantly lower number of energy demand security records. Interestingly, even though 2020 has not been fully captured in the research, the number of research items with economic focus (in *Scopus econ*) on energy demand security was even higher (four items) than in the previous year. Comparing *Scopus econ* and *WoS econ* energy demand security records, it can be seen that both databases are on the rise, but within the same time period, *Scopus econ* records grew from 6 to 69, while *WoS econ* rose from 0 to 23.

The dominance of articles as a primary method of "energy demand security" research reporting is similar to the case of "energy security". Articles in the Scopus and WoS general databases represent 48% and 58%, respectively (Figure 1.14). Another popular way of reporting energy security research results is through proceedings in Scopus (33%) and WoS (29%). Unlike energy security research, and as with energy supply security, book chapters are more often used in Scopus (7%) than in WoS (2%), whereas reviews are of similar importance in both cases (Scopus-7%, WoS-9%). Figure 1.14 presents a characterization of WoS and Scopus document types with excluded research items representing around or less than 1% of the database entries. In Scopus, this includes books, business articles, conference reviews, short surveys, editorials, letters, abstract reports, errata, and retracted publications. In WoS, editorial materials and early access materials.

A similar document breakdown, resembling even more our "energy supply security" search in *Scopus econ* and *WoS econ*, is presented in Figure 1.15. Articles are the most popular form of research reporting in the area of economics, especially with *WoS econ* (87%). Conference and proceedings papers enjoy the same shares of 12% in both databases. Again, book chapters are more popular in *Scopus econ* (12%) than in *WoS econ* (2%). It seems that moving to a more detailed analysis level

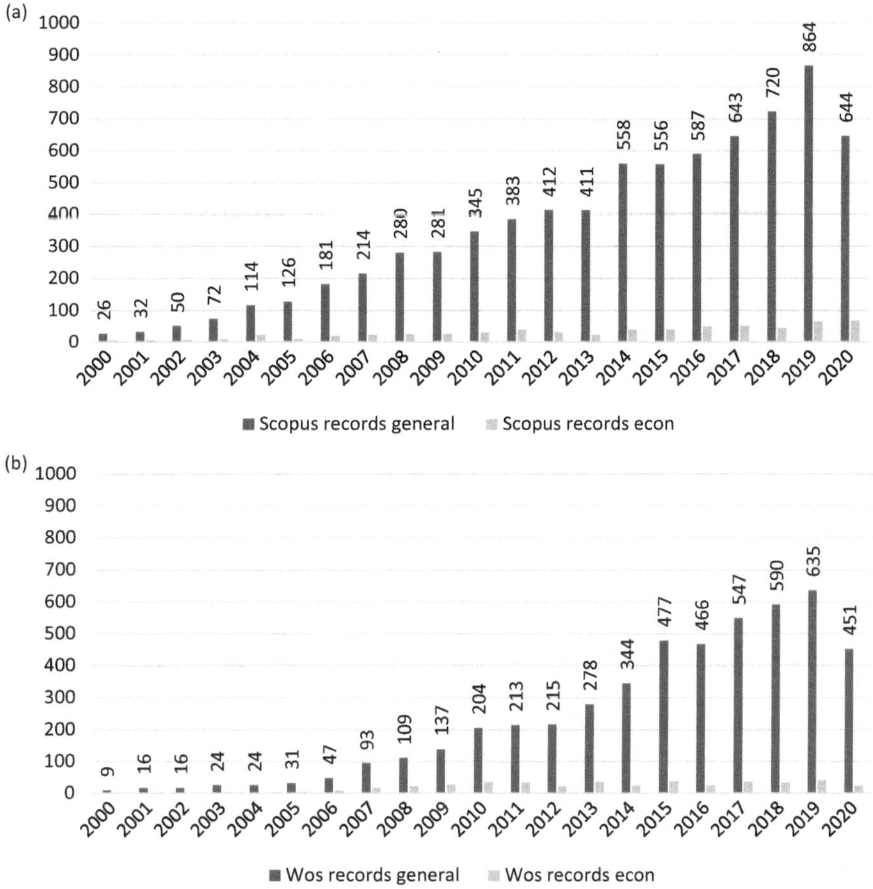

Figure 1.13 Comparison of "energy demand security" search in the Scopus and WoS general databases and limited to the economics field between 2000 and 2020.

Source: Compiled by the author based on the Scopus and WoS databases.

(from the general idea of "energy security" to "energy supply security" and "energy demand security") increases the overall article share. Document types with a share in the databases of around or less than 1% have not been presented in Figure 1.15. In *Scopus econ*, this includes notes, conference reviews, short surveys, and editorials; and in *WoS econ*, reviews, editorial materials, and early access materials.

Looking at institutions that publish energy demand security research in the general Scopus and WoS databases reveals that the Chinese Academy of Sciences leads again, with the notable presence of Tsinghua University (Table 1.8). Asian research institutions' dominance in "energy demand security" is as strong as in case of "energy security". In the top ten Scopus "energy demand security" positions, seven affiliations are Asian against nine in "energy security" (see Table 1.4), whereas in the top ten WoS affiliations, only four represent Asia as opposed to

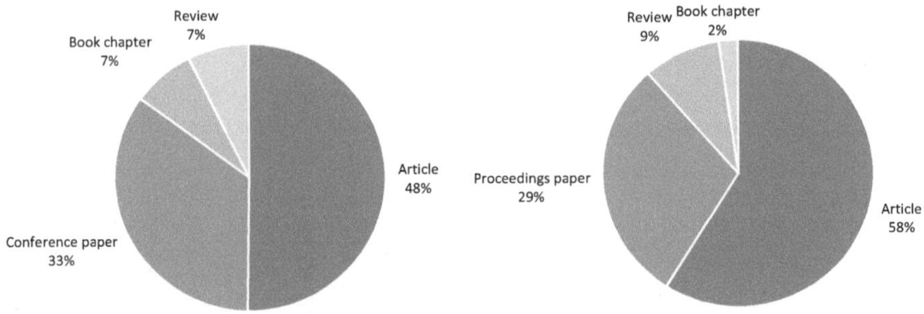

Figure 1.14 Comparison of "energy demand security" search in the Scopus (left) and WoS (right) general databases according to document type.

Source: Compiled by the author based on the Scopus and WoS databases.

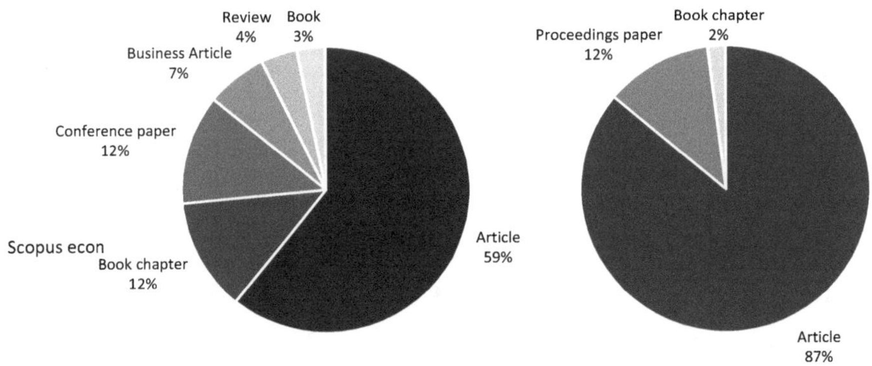

Figure 1.15 Comparison of "energy demand security" search in the Scopus econ (left) and WoS econ (right) databases according to document type.

Source: Compiled by the author based on the Scopus and WoS databases.

In *Scopus econ*, a country breakdown shows that during 2000–2020, the largest proportions of research items came from two countries, the UK and the USA, with respective shares of 11% and 7% in "energy demand security" records in the database. Other leading countries are India, Germany, and China – each with a share of 6%. In *WoS econ*, the USA leads again (20%), followed by China (13%), the UK (12%), and Germany (9%). Central European universities are underrepresented in economic research on energy demand security in both the Scopus and WoS databases, with one notable exception of Poland ranked 16th in the *WoS econ* database (2% share).

Looking at the subject (Scopus) or research (WoS) area within energy demand security studies, similarities can be observed in both databases. In Scopus, the subject "Business, management and accounting" accounts for 410 research items and "Economics, econometrics and finance" includes 326 records. In the WoS database, 42% of records fall into the category of business economics. The most popular

Table 1.8 Comparison of "energy demand security" search in the Scopus (left) and WoS (right) general databases according to affiliation or organization (top ten records)

Affiliation, Scopus general	*Records in Scopus general*	*Organizations, WoS general*	*Records in WoS general*
Chinese Academy of Sciences	73	Chinese Academy of Sciences	102
Tsinghua University	73	US Department of Energy	100
Imperial College London	64	Indian Institute of Technology System IIT	78
North China Electric Power University	64	University of California	66
Ministry of Education, China	60	North China Electric Power University	52
ETH Zürich	40	Helmholtz Association	49
State Grid Corporation of China	39	Imperial College London	49
Shanghai Jiao Tong University	38	Tsinghua University	49
University of Waterloo	37	Islamic Azad University	48
China Electric Power Research Institute	37	University of London	46
Aalborg University	37		

Source: Compiled by the author based on the Scopus and WoS databases.

seven in "energy security". Asian dominance is accompanied by representation of the North American or European research institutes. In the case of Scopus, these are the Canadian University of Waterloo, Imperial College of London, and Aalborg University; in WoS, the US Department of Energy and the University of California compete in the top ten with German Helmholtz Association and Britain's Imperial College London and the University of London.[9]

In *Scopus econ* and *WoS econ*, Asian dominance is weaker than in the general databases (Table 1.9). Even though in *WoS econ* the Chinese Academy of Sciences takes the lead, it enjoys a similar position as the University of Cambridge, which is also ranked top of the *Scopus econ* database. European dominance is especially strong in *Scopus econ*. The top three ranks in *Scopus econ* are held, in addition to the above-mentioned University of Cambridge, by Imperial College London and Cambridge Judge Business School. The institutions enjoying high positions in both rankings are the German Institute for Economic Research, Tsinghua University, and the National University of Singapore.

Table 1.9 Comparison of "energy demand security" search in the Scopus econ (left) and WoS econ (right) databases according to affiliation or organization (top ten records)

Affiliation Scopus econ	*Records in Scopus econ*	*Organization WoS econ*	*Records in WoS econ*
University of Cambridge	13	Chinese Academy of Sciences	11
Imperial College London	7	University of Cambridge	11
Cambridge Judge Business School	7	Stanford University	7
German Institute for Economic Research	6	Tsinghua University	7
Purdue University	6	University of California	7
The Australian National University	5	University of Oxford	7
National University of Singapore	5	Asian Institute of Technology	6
Parthenope University of Naples	5	National University of Singapore	6
Tsinghua University	5	Aristotle University of Thessaloniki	5
Aalto University	5	German Institute for Economic Research	5

Source: Compiled by the author based on the Scopus and WoS databases.

titles for publishing energy demand security research in *WoS econ* in 2000–2020 were *Energy Policy* (50% of papers published), *Energy Economics* (8%), *Food Policy* (1%), *Ecological Economics* (1%), *Energy Journal* (1%), and *Technological Forecasting and Social Change* (1%). In contrast to *WoS econ*, in *Scopus econ* there was no clear leading title. The most popular ones included the *Journal of Cleaner Production* (14% of papers published), *Petroleum Economist* (8%), *Petroleum Review* (7%), and *Energy Economics* (7%). It is visible that *Energy Economics* is published in both databases; thus, its importance is greater than what would appear from analysis of a single database. In *Scopus econ*, the authors publishing the most between 2000 and 2020 on energy demand security were Derek Brower (publishing mostly in *Petroleum Economist*) and Tooraj Jamasb,[10] while the most prolific contributor to *WoS econ* was Larry Hughes.[11]

1.3.2.3 Comparison of energy supply and demand security research

Comparing Scopus and WoS databases based on search for "energy demand security" (left) and "energy supply security" (Figure 1.16) reveals that the Scopus database offers a greater variety of records in both topics. During the period of 2000–2020, each year the Scopus database significantly exceeded the number of

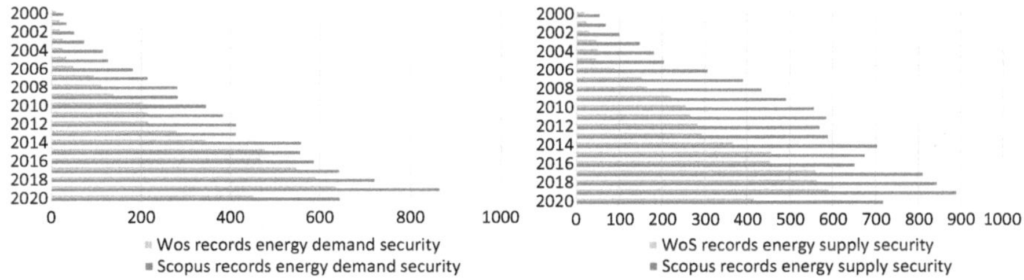

Figure 1.16 Comparison of "energy demand security" (left) and "energy supply security" (right) search in the Scopus and WoS databases.

Source: Compiled by the author based on the Scopus and WoS databases.

documents published within the search areas. This difference between the databases was even more visible in the case of energy supply security research. Due to its historical importance, this topic was more often an area of scientific investigation than energy demand security. Interestingly, in the years 2019 and 2020, Scopus offered a comparable number of documents on energy supply and demand security, which might be a sign of increasing importance of the energy demand security research.

Analysing the economic part of the Scopus and WoS databases reveals a similar trend though not that strong (Figure 1.17). Again, during period 2000–2020, Scopus (here, *Scopus econ*) was publishing more than WoS (here, *WoS econ*) on energy supply and demand security topics. However, that superiority was not stable within the analysed time horizon. There were years in which *WoS econ* clearly published more records than *Scopus econ*. That was the case in the years 2009–2010 in energy demand security research and 2013 in energy supply security. Similarly to the general WoS and Scopus databases, also in their economic parts, the number of papers published on energy supply security was greater than on energy demand security. This proves that energy supply security research still prevails in energy security studies in different research fields.

Looking at the general Scopus and WoS databases against their economic dimension (Figure 1.18), it is visible that there are some differences in energy supply and demand security research. General databases offer a wider spectrum of papers in terms of their quantity. Between 2000 and 2020, Scopus and WoS entries outnumbered *Scopus econ* and *WoS econ* around eight times. In the economic part of the databases, research on energy supply and demand security, even though it appeared in 2000, resulted in only six and eight papers, respectively, on energy supply and demand security. In 2020, the respective figures increased to 92 and 133. At the same time, in the Scopus and WoS general databases, the total number of records for energy demand security amounted to 1,095 and for energy supply security to 1,135. Such a huge difference in records between the general and economic parts of the databases may suggest that both energy supply and demand security are rarely investigated topics from the economic point of view.

Since affiliations have been compared earlier in this chapter, at this point there will be no detailed analysis covering the origins of energy supply and demand

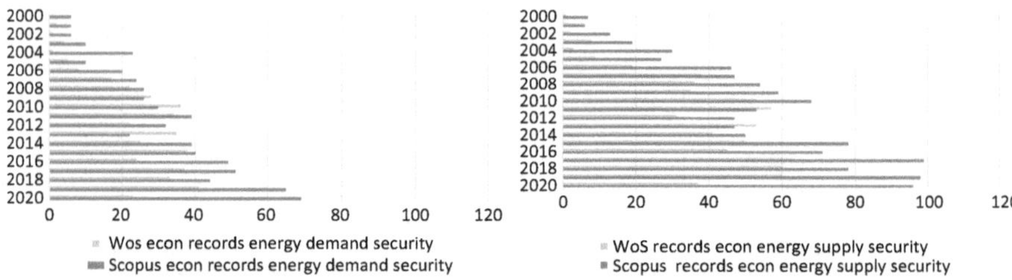

Figure 1.17 Comparison of "energy demand security" (left) and "energy supply security" (right) search in the Scopus econ and WoS econ databases.

Source: Compiled by the author based on the Scopus and WoS databases.

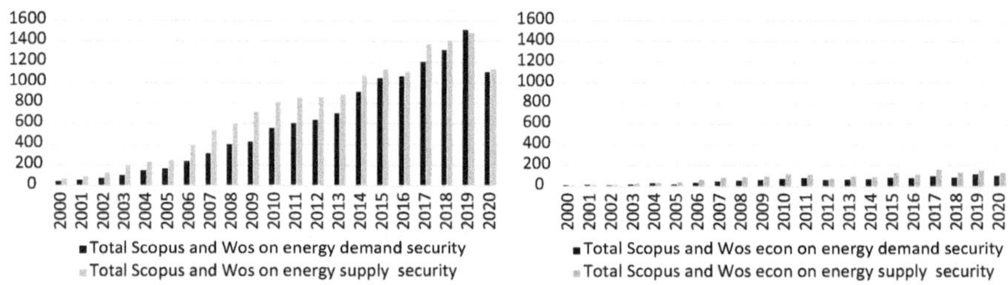

Figure 1.18 Comparison of "energy demand security" and "energy supply security" search in the general databases (left) and in the Scopus econ and WoS econ (right) databases.

Source: Compiled by the author based on the Scopus and WoS databases.

security research. One thing worth noting is the fact that in the general databases, a majority of research institutions originates from Asia (mainly China), while in economics – Asian leaders give way to European and American universities.

The above literature review shows that energy supply and demand security studies are on the rise in the 21st century in the two most popular scientific databases. Interestingly, both of the areas are underrepresented in the field of economics (and/or business/management science). This constitutes a possible research gap in a merit and technical layer.

However, that *niché* has already been investigated by researchers from various science disciplines. What emerges as a new phenomenon, underrepresented in energy security studies, is demand security showing the perspective of energy exporters. Economists (or business/management scientists) tend to be silent on this issue. Thus, what is expected to be one of the most promising research gaps (in a merit sense) in energy security studies in future is demand security analysed from the economic point of view.

Additionally, in a technical sense, majority of the research in energy demand security published in the form of journal articles, thus book emerges as a new way of presenting research results in this area. Moreover, in energy demand security research, unlike in energy supply security, the point of view of European, or even Central/Eastern European research centres is missing. Thus, this book's angle on energy demand security constitutes different geographical perspective in a scientific debate on energy demand security.

This, new in merit and technical sense, perspective is reflected in the next chapters. Energy demand security as dealt with in this book addresses the above-described research gap narrowing down the analysis to demand security from the perspective of international economics as trade in energy resources is of a predominantly transboundary character.

Notes

1 Capital and energy resources might be complementary in the short term but are substitutional in the long term (Zweifel, Praktiknjo, and Erdmann, 2016).
2 Including crude oil, natural gas, coal, biofuels and waste, and electricity.
3 Supply shock is a macroeconomic phenomenon, the explanation of which is based on the AS-AD (Aggregated Supply – Aggregated Demand) model. A supply shock is a phenomenon that changes the aggregate supply of goods on the market, in this case energy resources.
4 Attempts to explain the reasons why it is so difficult to define energy security can be found in Wright (2005) and Radovanovic, Filipovic, and Pavlovic (2017). For more on this topic, see Nyga-Łukaszewska (2018).
5 For instance, natural gas.
6 For instance, electricity.
7 Along with geopolitical changes in Europe, the fear of a change in the direction of supplies of hydrocarbons imported by the post-Soviet countries was real.
8 This corresponds with the classic understanding of energy security – referring to supply shocks.
9 A country breakdown similar to that in the "energy security" and "energy supply security" analysis was not available for "energy demand security".
10 Other authors active in *Scopus econ* were Buzhyn, O.A.; Copeland, A.; Djamarani, M.; Haine, I.; Haney, A.B.; Holz, F.
11 Other authors active in *WoS econ* were Karatza, E.; Shrestha, R.M.; Balta-Ozkan, N.; Britvic, J.; Buzhyn, O.A.; Huntington, H.G.; Jewell, J.; Markandya, A.; Sadorsky, P.; Shi, X.P.

References

Booth, A., Sutton, A., and Papaioannou, D. (2016) *Systematic approaches to a successful literature review*. 2nd edn. London: SAGE Publications. Available at: https://www.researchgate.net/profile/Andrew_Booth/publication/235930866_Systematic_Approaches_to_a_Successful_Literature_Review/links/5da06c7f45851553ff8705fa/Systematic-Approaches-to-a-Successful-Literature-Review.pdf (Accessed: 28 November 2020).

Checchi, A., Behrens, A., and Egenhofer, C. (2009) *Long-term energy security risks for Europe: a sector-specific approach*. CEPS Working Paper No. 309. Brussels: Centre for European Policy Studies.

Chester, L. (2010) 'Conceptualising energy security and making explicit its polysemic nature', *Energy Policy*, 38(2), pp. 887–895. doi:10.1016/j.enpol.2009.10.039.

Dasgupta, P. (2006) 'Natural resources in an age of substitutability', in Kneese, A.V. and Sweeney, J.L. (eds.), *Handbook of natural resource and energy economics*. 4th edn. Amsterdam: Elsevier, pp. 1111–1130.

Dasgupta, P.S. and Heal, G.M. (1979) *Economic theory and exhaustible resources*. 1st edn. Cambridge: Cambridge University Press (Cambridge Economic Handbooks), pp. 193–226. doi:10.1017/CBO9780511628375.

Erdal, L. (2015) 'Determinants of energy supply security: an econometric analysis for Turkey', *Ege Akademik Bakis*, 15(2), pp. 153–163. doi:10.21121/eab.2015217981.

Frei, C.W. (2004) 'The Kyoto Protocol – a victim of supply security? or: if Maslow were in energy politics', *Energy Policy*, 32(11), pp. 1253–1256. doi:10.1016/j.enpol.2003.12.012.

Garcia-Gusano, D., Iribarren, D., and Garrain, D. (2017) 'Prospective analysis of energy security: a practical lice-cycle approach focused on renewable power generation and oriented towards policy-makers', *Applied Energy*, 190, pp. 891–901. doi:10.1016/j.apenergy.2017.01.011.

Glynn, J., Chiodi, A., and Gallachoir, B.O. (2017) 'Energy security assessment methods: quantifying the security co-benefits of decarbonising the Irish Energy System', *Energy Strategy Reviews*, 15, pp. 72–88. doi:10.1016/j.esr.2016.11.005.

Holley, C. and Lecavalier, E. (2017) 'Energy governance, energy security and environmental sustainability: a case study from Hong Kong', *Energy Policy*, 108, pp. 379–389. doi:10.1016/j.enpol.2017.06.010.

Hotelling, H. (1931) 'The economics of exhaustible resources', *Journal of Political Economy*, 39(2), pp. 137–175. doi:10.1086/254195.

IEA (2020) *Key World Energy Statistics 2020. Total Final Consumption*. Available at: https://www.iea.org/reports/key-world-energy-statistics-2020/final-consumption (Accessed: 31 February 2022).

Jones, C.R., Kaklamanou, D., and Lazuras, L. (2017) 'Public perceptions of energy security in Greece and Turkey: exploring the relevance of pro-environmental and procultural orientations', *Energy Research & Social Science*, 28, pp. 17–28. doi:10.1016/j.erss.2017.04.002.

Kisel, E. et al. (2016) 'Concept of energy security matrix', *Energy Policy*, 95, pp. 1–9. doi:10.1016/j.enpol.2016.04.034.

Knox-Hayes, J. et al. (2013) 'Understanding attitudes toward energy security: results of a cross-national survey', *Global Environmental Change*, 23(3), pp. 609–622. doi:10.1016/j.gloenvcha.2013.02.003.

Kruyt, B. et al. (2009) 'Indicators for energy security', *Energy Policy*, 37(6), pp. 2166–2181. doi:10.1016/j.enpol.2009.02.006.

Li, Y., Shi, X., and Yao, L. (2016) 'Evaluating energy security of resource-poor economies: a modified principle component analysis approach', *Energy Economics*, 58, pp. 211–221. doi:10.1016/j.eneco.2016.07.001.

Littell, J.H., Corcoran, J., and Pillai, V. (2008) *Systematic reviews and meta-analysis*. Oxford: Oxford University Press.

Loeschel, A., Moslener, U., and Ruebellke, D.T.G. (2010) 'Indicators of energy security in industrialised countries', *Energy Policy*, 38(4), pp. 1665–1671. doi:10.1016/j.enpol.2009.03.061.

Nyga-Łukaszewska, H. (2018) 'Bezpieczeństwo energetyczne: u źródeł chaosu semantycznego', in Gryz, J., Podraza, A., and Ruszel, M. (eds.), *Bezpieczeństwo energetyczne. Koncepcje-wyzwania-interesy*. 1st edn. Warszawa: Wydawnictwo Naukowe PWN, pp. 69–80.

Orłowska, A., Mazur, Z., and Łaguna, M. (2017) 'Systematyczny przegląd literatury: na czym polega i czym różni się od innych przeglądów?' *Ogrody Nauk i Sztuk*, 7(7), pp. 350–363. doi:10.15503/onis2017.350.363.

PERC (2021) *PERC Reporting Standard 2021. Pan-European Standard for the Public Reporting of Exploration Results, Mineral Resources and Mineral Reserves*. Available at: https://percstandard.org/perc-standard/ (Accessed: 22 March 2022).

Perman, R. et al. (2003) *Natural resource and environmental economics*. 3rd edn. Essex: Pearson Education Limited, pp. 473 504.

Petticrew, M. and Roberts, H. (2006) *Systematic reviews in the social sciences. A practical guide*. Oxford: Blackwell Publishing.

Radovanovic, M., Filipovic, S., and Pavlovic, D. (2017) 'Energy security measurement – a sustainable approach', *Renewable and Sustainable Energy Reviews*, 68, pp. 1020–1032. doi:10.1016/j.rser.2016.02.010.i

Saługa, P., Uberman, P., and Mazurek, S. (2018) 'Cele harmonizacji klasyfikacji zasobów złóż kopalin stałych', *Przegląd Geologiczny*, 66(6), pp. 353–360.

Scopus (2020) 'Scopus Content Coverage Guide'. Elsevier. Available at: https://www.elsevier.com/?a=69451 (Accessed: 28 November 2020).

Solow, R.M. (1974) 'The economics of resources or the resources of economics', *The American Economic Review*, 64(2), pp. 1–14. http://www.jstor.org/stable/1816009.

Sovacool, B.K. and Mukherjee, I. (2011) 'Conceptualizing and measuring energy security: a synthesized approach', *Energy*, 36, pp. 5343–5355. doi:10.1016/j.energy.2011.06.043.

SPE (Society of Petroleum Engineers) (2018) *Petroleum Resources Management System*. Available at: https://netherlandsewell.com/wp-content/uploads/2018/12/SPE_Petroleum_Resources_Management_System_2018.pdf (Accessed: 10 January 2021).

Sumskis, V. (2015) 'Economic implications of energy security in the short run', *Ekonomika*, 94(3), pp. 119–138. doi:10.15388/Ekon.2015.3.8791.

Sweeney, J. (2006) 'Economic theory of depletable resources: an introduction', in Kneese, A. and Sweeney, J. (eds.), *Handbook of natural resource and energy economics*. 3rd edn. Oxford: Elsevier, pp. 759–850.

United Nations (2020) 'United Nations Framework Classification for Resources. Update 2019', *ECE Energy Series*, 61, pp. 1–28.

Wang, Q. and Zhou, K. (2017) 'A framework for evaluating global national energy security', *Applied Energy*, 188, pp. 19–31. doi:10.1016/j.apenergy.2016.11.116.

Web of Science (2020) *Clarivate Web of Science*. Available at: https://clarivate.libguides.com/webofscienceplatform/coverage (Accessed: 28 November 2020).

Winzer, C. (2012) 'Conceptualizing energy security', *Energy Policy*, 46, pp. 36–48. doi:10.1016/j.enpol.2012.02.067.

World Bank (2022) *Indicators*. Available at: https://data.worldbank.org/indicator (Accessed: 28 November 2022).

Wright, P. (2005) 'Liberalisation and the security of gas supply in the UK', *Energy Policy*, 33(17), pp. 2272–2290. doi:10.1016/j.enpol.2004.04.022.

Yale (2022) *Environmental Performance Index*. Available at: https://epi.yale.edu/ (Accessed: 28 February 2021).

Zhu, J. and Liu, W. (2020) 'A tale of two databases: the use of Web of Science and Scopus in academic papers', *Scientometrics*, 123(1), pp. 321–335. doi:10.1007/s11192-020-03387-8.

Zweifel, P., Praktiknjo, A.J., and Erdmann, G. (2016) *Energy economics. Theory and applications*. 1st edn. Berlin: Springer.

2 Energy security theoretical approach

2.1 Energy supply security concept and methods of assessing energy supply security

The multitude of works on the analysis of the way of understanding energy security makes the literature studies a great research challenge. Studies in political science and engineering have been omitted as they are beyond the scope of this book. Only those studies that are of an interdisciplinary or economic nature are taken into consideration in the analysis below.

Recognizing the book's goal, various definitions of energy supply security will be presented in a synthetic way. However, it should also be noted that this is an extensive research area. The ways of understanding energy security can be classified according to various criteria, including the subject and time of analysis, etc. A broader discussion on this topic is presented, among others, by Ang, Choong, and Ng (2015), Winzer (2012), and Nyga-Łukaszewska (2013).

The energy security definitions presented below can be divided into several groups. The first one takes into account the issue of energy origin, the second one is based on the estimation of the costs of interruptions in energy supplies, the third one covers a set of various criteria (including geological and geopolitical ones), and the fourth one concerns threats related to energy security.

2.1.1 Supply security concept

The definitions developed on the basis of the criterion of the origin of energy make it possible to distinguish energy supply security in the national (internal) and international (external) dimensions. References to this way of understanding the phenomenon can be found in the works of, *inter alia*, Checchi, Behrens, and Eggenhofer (2009) and Czerpak (2006).[1]

The internal dimension concerns the functioning of the national energy systems (here, energy infrastructure) in the context of the liberalization of energy markets. The process of deregulation of the energy sector is perceived as a threat to the continuity of energy supplies in a country. As part of this approach, the issue of the impact of the national energy system on the natural environment is also considered. In turn, the external dimension reflects, as emphasized by the International Energy

DOI: 10.4324/9781003052241-3

Agency (IEA, 2004), a traditional approach to energy supply security and refers to energy imports.

The external dimension, mainly related to energy imports, is visible in studies devoted to the structure of imported energy (Vivoda, 2009; Cohen, Joutz, and Loungani, 2011; Austvik, 2016). These are works which estimate the concentration of foreign suppliers in the volume of energy imported to a country. For this purpose, various indicators of concentration or dispersion of international trade are used. The key concept here is the diversification of imported energy supplies. More on this topic can be found in Bożyk and Nyga-Łukaszewska (2013).

The structure of energy imports and the related concentration of foreign suppliers establish another dimension in which energy supply security can be defined. This approach is in line with the concept of economic dependence, widely known in economics. This idea emerged in the 1960s in the Latin America region and already then sparked a discussion in the scientific community, mainly among representatives of developing countries. The authors of the first works describing this phenomenon were, *inter alia*, Frank (1970), Dos Santos (1970), Cardoso and Faletto (1979), and Caporaso (1978). What the approaches represented by these researchers have in common is the focus on the relations of Latin America with developed countries and the perception of economic dependence is an asymmetric trade relationship. Among the factors determining trade relations between Latin American countries and developed countries, the authors mention the international division of labour and differences in the endowment with production factors.

The concept of economic dependence refers to the ideas of Hans Singer and Raul Preibisch, commonly known as the Preibisch-Singer thesis. According to it, in long-term relations between developing and developed countries, the terms of trade of developing countries gradually deteriorate due to the established structure of export of cheaper commodities and import of more expensive industrial goods. Among the contemporary works devoted to the problem of economic dependence from the point of view of international economics, Wysokińska's output (Wysokińska, 1995) is a notable example. She notes that the literature most often describes economic interdependence rather than economic dependence. The criterion differentiating both phenomena is the symmetry of trade relations between economic partners. According to this assumption, economic dependence is described by the asymmetry of trade relations, which is indicated by both Wysokińska (1995) and by Gwiazda (1985) and Bożyk (2008). Depending on the analysis criteria adopted, economic dependence can be categorized, e.g., as one-sided or multilateral, and as merchandise/capital/technology-based (Figure 2.1).

Iskra (2004) and Bożyk (2008) define one-sided dependence as dependence of one entity on another, and multilateral dependence as dependence on a larger number of entities. Trade dependence is the trading of merchandise, technological dependence is related to technology trading, and capital dependence is related to international capital flows. Gwiazda (1985) additionally indicates that specific varieties can be distinguished as part of trade dependence. The basis for their selection is the types of goods traded. Thus, Gwiazda indicates energy, resource, food, and financial dependence.

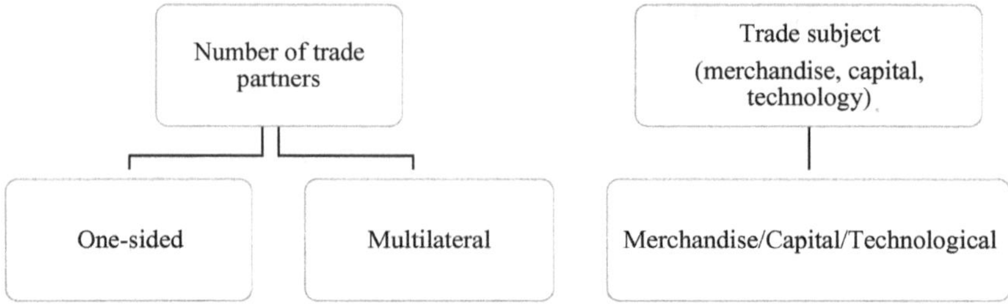

Figure 2.1 Selected economic dependence types.

Source: Compiled by the author based on Bożyk (2008).

Energy dependence relates to dependence on imported fuels. The way to reduce it, which Gwiazda (1985) believes can be achieved only in the long run, is through the rationalization of energy consumption and the substitution of imported fuels. It seems that energy dependence is a special case of general resource dependence, which relates to dependence on imports of commodities, including precious metals and minerals. Due to the fact that fuels (in particular primary energy) are also commodities, energy dependence in this case is a type of resource/commodity dependence. For its part, food dependence is related to technological progress, which, thanks to increased production efficiency, enables developed countries to export food. On the other hand, financial dependence involves the indebtedness of developing countries with developed countries. According to Gwiazda, energy and resource dependence refers to developed countries' reliance on developing ones, whereas food and financial dependence is the other way round.

When analysing energy security in the context of energy import, an analogy can be observed with the idea of energy dependence, in which (in general) developing countries act as suppliers of imported energy, and developed countries become its recipients. Due to the different structure of suppliers of imported energy, one can speak of one-sided or multilateral economic dependence. In this sense, energy supply security is a special case of economic dependence on trade related to energy resources.

Energy import is the starting point for yet another way of defining energy supply security, which focuses on the costs of energy supply disruptions. It has already been mentioned by a number of authors (e.g., Bohi and Toman, 1996b; Huntington, 2004; Davis et al., 2005; Greene and Leiby, 2006; Arnold and Hunt, 2009; Chester, 2010; Loeschel, Moslener, and Ruebellke, 2010; Winzer, 2012). In this perspective, energy supply security relates to the lack of energy availability and its impact on GDP. This phenomenon is seen in terms of external costs of fuel import. Empirical research within this area assesses how changes in the prices of energy, mainly crude oil, affect the welfare of societies (Constantini and Gracceva, 2004; Sumskis and Giedraitis, 2015). One of the academic centres involved in the development of this research is the Stanford University in California (the USA), where this type of research is carried out and where some of the most prestigious studies on this

Table 2.1 Crude oil price increase effects

Independent variable	*Dependent variable*	*Changes in the dependent variable (%)*	*Research sample*
Crude oil price increase (+50%)	GDP	From −0.1 to −0.8	Eurozone[a]
Doubling the existing crude oil prices	GDP	−3.7	The USA (1960–1998), Eurozone[a]
Maintained crude oil price increase at the level of 20%	GDP growth rate	−0.25 (in the first four years)	World[a]
	Trade balance (deficit, USD bn)	−USD 7.8 bn	Eurozone[a]
Crude oil price increase (+50%) in the first year and decrease to the base level (starting point level) in the third year	Inflation	+0.2	Industrialized countries[a]

Source: Compiled by the author based on Arnold and Hunt (2009).

[a] According to research ranging from 2000 to 2004.

subject come from (Beccue and Huntington, 2005). Table 2.1 illustrates the effects of rising oil prices and their effects on GDP in various countries.

Bohi and Toman (1996b) present a detailed classification of the external costs[2] of energy security related to energy imports, distinguishing external costs related to the volume of imports, the price of the imported energy, and military expenditures. Military expenses are understood as expenditures for maintaining a military presence in regions rich in energy resources (Figure 2.2). The first category of the above-listed external costs is medium to long term, and the second is short term. The authors do not describe military expenditure in terms of time, even though it seems that they should be classified as short term.[3]

Externalities referring to the volume of imported energy can be broken down into (Bohi and Toman, 1996b):

- direct externalities, which involve the use of market power[4] by exporters or importers to influence the quantity of fuel sold or bought, as appropriate; an example of the use of market power by exporters is the operation of OPEC (Organization of Petroleum Exporting Countries) on international oil markets; importers, on the other hand, can only exploit their market power in a monopsony situation;
- indirect externalities, which relate to increased inflation, negative impact on the trade/payment balance, and employment in domestic industries producing energy.

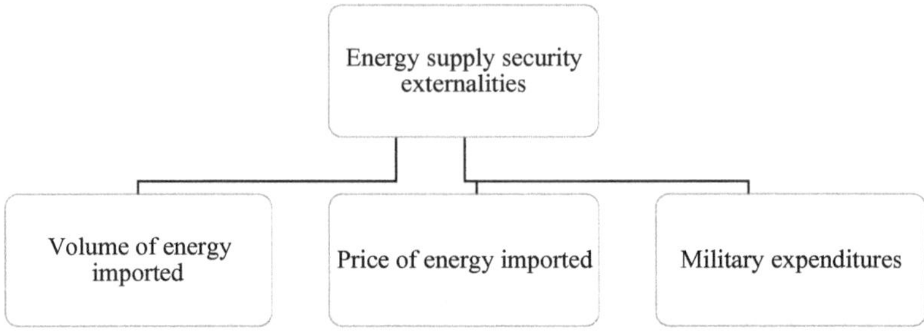

Figure 2.2 Energy supply security externalities.

Source: Compiled by the author based on Bohi and Toman (1996b).

Among the external costs of energy supply security related to the price of imported fuel, one can distinguish the following: lack of hedging against fluctuations in resource prices (mainly within the private sector), decrease in employment, and decrease in production. These effects may apply to both broadly understood energy markets and markets not directly related to it.

It is argued that military expenditure is often an additional social cost of energy import (mainly crude oil),[5] assuming that spending for military purposes is a necessary condition for gaining access to energy resources in areas of armed conflicts. However, as noted by Bohi and Toman (1996b), the costs of military presence are to a greater extent a political rather than economic goal and, therefore, due to the material scope of the work, they are not given much attention here.

Most of the work devoted to research on the external costs of energy supply security is based on quantitative analysis (Leiby et al., 1997; Barsky and Kilian, 2004), although in some of them, the authors use qualitative research, e.g., in the form of interviews with experts (Beccue and Huntington, 2005). The common feature of the above-mentioned studies is the determination of the impact of the increase in crude oil prices on GDP (including its growth rate), inflation, and the balance of trade.

The third group of definitions are those referring to the concept popular in the scientific community, proposed in 2007 by the Asia Pacific Research Centre ("4 As" approach). In this approach, energy security is analysed in terms of:

- geological availability of energy resources (*availability*),
- geopolitical and geoeconomic accessibility of energy resources (*accessibility*),
- acceptability of the use of particular energy resources (*acceptability*),
- affordability of the respective energy resources (*affordability*) (APERC, 2007).

Geological availability is associated with the presence of specific deposits of energy resources. It also concerns access to renewable energy sources for which geological issues (apart from geothermal) do not play a significant role. Geopolitical and geoeconomic accessibility is associated with various types of barriers to access to energy, such as cartelization of energy markets as well as infrastructural, legal, and financial limitations. Geopolitics and geoeconomics apply to all types of primary energy – both non-renewable and renewable. The third dimension of energy supply security is related to the acceptability of the use of specific energy sources in the country's energy mix from the point of view of environmental policy. This aspect reflects the international standards for reducing greenhouse gas emissions. The fourth dimension concerns affordability and shows the price of energy and the price elasticity of demand – in a microeconomic sense. In a broader – macroeconomic – approach, it refers to the needs of investing in the energy sector. Due to the multitude of analysed aspects, the way of understanding energy supply security proposed by APERC can be described as multidimensional.

The concept of the "4 As" approach has been adopted in research on energy security. It was the starting point for creating extensive definitions along with a proposal for a quantitative assessment of the phenomenon (Kruyt et al., 2009; Brown et al., 2014; Kocaslan, 2014). One of the broadest energy security concepts based on this idea was proposed by Sovacool and Mukherjee (2011), who presented more than 250 different energy supply security measures.

According to the opinion of author in this book, the popularity of the "4 As" approach results from its semantic capacity and ease of application. Each of the indicated dimensions is formulated so generally that it can be freely supplemented and expanded. On the other hand, the lack of a formalized methodological analysis means that this concept can be used by researchers representing various fields of science. Nevertheless, the "4 As" approach did not escape criticism in 2014. Cherp and Jewell (2014) rightly noticed that it lacks a description for whom energy supply security should be guaranteed and what threats this phenomenon involves.

A similar understanding of supply security as proposed by APERC can be seen in the works of such authors as Staśko and Kaliski (2006), Gracceva and Zeniewski (2014), Johansson (2013), Mansson, Johansson, and Nilsson (2014), Mitchell (2002), and Checchi, Behrens, and Eggenhofer (2009). However, escaping the above criticism, they highlight various methods of energy supply security analysis, including its subject, object (type of threat) within the spatial (geographical) and temporal dimensions. The subject of supply security may be a country, its region, or a company that uses imported energy. In this sense, energy supply security has its macro- and microeconomic dimensions. The subject of threats to energy security may include, for example, depletion of energy resources and the related supply constraints, restriction of access to deposits for foreign investors, as well as extreme weather conditions or technical infrastructure malfunctioning (for more, see Nyga-Łukaszewska, 2013). In the spatial dimension, Staśko and Kaliski distinguish local, regional, and global supply security. Additionally, all of the above aspects may be analysed in the short, medium, and long term. However, the typology of their determination is conventional. Mitchell describes the short-term perspective in energy security studies as spanning a period of 12–18 months, medium term – 3–5 years, and long term – 10–15 years. Other researchers do not provide time limits when analysing energy supply security. However, it can be assumed that Mitchell's typology converges with the economic distinction between the short term, the medium term, and the long term, according to which production factors have no chance to adapt to changes taking place in the market in the short term. This becomes possible only in the long run.

Referring this analysis to the natural gas market, Cabalu (2010) additionally combines the time horizon of supply security with its threats, arguing that the short-term dimension of this phenomenon is associated with interruptions in fuel supplies and the long-term dimension with inadequate adjustment of the level of investment in production/transmission infrastructure and transport of energy, with the level of energy demand, as well as an undiversified structure of imports. Ciborski (2006) adds that one of the long-term threats is the already-mentioned issue of depletion of energy deposits. A similar distinction between short- and long-term energy security is also provided by the IEA (2018), followed by Kocaslan (2014).

The fourth group of definitions covers the analysis of energy security in the context of related threats. It includes works of such authors as Eggenhofer (2004) or Checchi, Behrens, and Eggenhofer (2009). It is worth noting here that the analysis of energy security in the context of its threats is a cross-sectional approach. This is due to the fact that studies in this field simultaneously address the issues of the research time horizon (short, medium, or long term) (Mitchell, 2002) or the origin of energy (domestic or imported) (Stern, 2002; Luciani, 2004). More on energy supply security threats can be found in Nyga-Łukaszewska (2013).

On the basis of the existing literature, several types of dangers can be distinguished in a cross-sectional way (Figure 2.3). The first category consists of short-term (12–18 months) threats of an external nature. They include fluctuations in the prices of commodities in the world markets or failures of the cross-border transmission infrastructure. These are risks of an economic and technical nature, respectively. From the perspective of the domestic market, the malfunctioning of the national transmission infrastructure is also mentioned in the category of short-term dangers.

The second category includes medium-term threats. In the domestic market, they may relate to the liberalization process, which shifts the responsibility for

Dimension External/Internal	Short term 12–18 months	Medium term 3–5 years	Long term 10–15 years
	Malfunctioning of the domestic transmission infrastructure	Liberalization of the domestic energy market	Underinvestment in infrastructure for energy import
	Malfunctioning of the cross-border transmission infrastructure Price volatility in the global markets	Formation of a cartel in the market of energy producers	Depletion of energy resources Underinvestment in cross-border infrastructure for energy import

Figure 2.3 Selected short-, medium-, and long-term threats to energy supply security in the external and internal dimensions.

Source: Compiled by the author based on Checchi, Behrens, and Eggenhofer (2009), Mitchell (2002), Stern (2002), Luciani (2004), and Czerpak (2006).

ensuring supply security from the state to private entities (Eggenhofer and Lege, 2001). On the other hand, in foreign markets, the formation of an international cartel of raw material producers may be a medium-term threat.

The third group of threats includes long-term dangers (10–15 years), such as lack of investment in infrastructure for the transmission of energy, may refer to both in domestic and foreign markets. Internally, this applies in particular to the infrastructure used for energy imports (Czerpak, 2006), and externally to global energy transport.

An additional trend in research on energy security of importing countries is the perspective of transit countries. Its omission, at this point, would be unjustified, but the author of this book admits that this perspective is beyond the scope of this study. It should be borne in mind that this is a relatively new theoretical approach that has not yet been thoroughly analysed. There is no separate energy security concept for transit countries in the literature. There are works in which the energy security of this group of countries is considered in terms of the security of energy supply (Yafimava, 2011; Energy Charter Secretariat, 2015; Pirani and Yafimava, 2016). Such treatment of energy transit is justified by the need to analyse the entire energy supply chain – from its production through transport to the final consumer. Energy transit is, thus, an element of fuel transport, and, therefore, it is inextricably linked with the security of energy supply. An additional argument in favour of treating energy transit as an element of supply security is the fact that threats to energy security are similar both with regard to the importer and the transit country. In both cases, we are dealing with the provision of supplies at an acceptable price.

To sum up the current considerations on the way of conceptualizing energy supply security, it can be noted that they are linked by the issue of supplies (import volume) and the price of imported energy. The IEA itself defines supply security as a continuous supply of energy at an affordable price (IEA, 2018). Given the prestige of this OECD energy-oriented agenda, many scientists are embracing this research perspective, including Ćwiek-Karpowicz (2016), Jones, Kaklamanou, and Lazuras (2017), Labandeira and Manzano (2012), Wang and Zhou (2017), and Erahman et al. (2016).

2.1.2 Supply security assessment methods

Due to the lack of an unambiguous perception of energy supply security, there are many methods of quantifying the phenomenon. According to research by Sovacool and Mukherjee (2011), by 2011, about 320 simple and 52 complex indicators were used as a part of energy supply security assessment. No single measure has so far been unilaterally accepted by the scientific community (Kocaslan, 2020). Instead of that, there is a variety of assessment methods which due to the book's goal will only be synthetically presented at this point. However, it should be noted that their analysis deserves much broader attention. To some extent, this task was performed by Bożyk and Nyga-Łukaszewska (2013), but due to language bias (available in Polish only) and publishing date, it cannot nowadays serve as an insightful review of energy supply security assessment methods. Interesting contribution supplementing the above approach might be the work of Azzuni and Breyer (2020), who present trends in energy security assessment between 2011 and 2021. These developments include next to quantitative nature of studies, desire to create composite indicators, periodical refinement/update of indicators also building indicators serving international competitiveness goals and introducing energy security measurement into economic security dimension (like in case of Ukraine). Similar, but newer than Azzuni and Breyer (2020), source of information on energy supply security measurement might be Krikštolaitis et al. (2022). The authors provide a brief literature review on indicators assessing energy supply security while building composite supply security measure for Germany, France, Italy, and Spain between 2006 and 2018.

Following this book's goal, energy supply security assessment methods are described only synthetically from the point of view of their methodological evolution indicating contemporary research trends within analysed area. That is why, in each category of measures, only selected, representative methods are presented. The rationale behind their choice includes their advancement level and representation potential for the analysed group of measures. That is why in some cases indicators/formulas are provided and in others description of the method is given. When analysing these measures, one can notice their evolution resulting from changes in the way of understanding supply security. The methods of assessing this phenomenon can be divided into several groups.

The first group of methods for the quantitative assessment of energy supply security are measures that allow the concentration of fuel imports to be estimated. These measures refer to a wider category of imports' diversification, which is popular in energy supply security measurement studies (Vivoda, 2009; Cohen, Joutz, and Loungani, 2011). This group includes measures based on the Herfindahl-Hirschman Index (HHI) on the one hand, and on the Stirling index on the other. Both methods describe the structure of imports: the first in terms of concentration in trade, the second in terms of dispersion in trade. Measures based on the HHI are used, among others, by Blyth and Lefevre (2004), Gupta (2007), Le Coq and Paltseva (2008). On the other hand, indicators based on the trade dispersion index are used by Jansen, van Arkel, and Boots (2004), Neumann (2004), and Neumann and Hirschhausen (2006). The use of the HHI in energy supply security research is justified by the fact that along with its use, the importance of the largest suppliers increases (Le Coq and Paltseva, 2008). For this reason, the HHI is well suited to assess the situation of countries with the dominant role of a single supplier of energy resources, such as Poland and in such capacity was used, for instance, by Nyga-Łukaszewska (2013).

Energy supply security measures based on trade concentration or dispersion indicators, apart from the above-mentioned indices, contain elements specific to the energy market. These include primary energy supply in a given country and resource depletion rates in the exporter and importer country. In addition, a factor that is commonly included in many ways is the political stability of energy suppliers. To present the discussed methods of estimating supply security, two of them are presented below: one that takes into account the concentration index, and the other one, trade dispersion measures.

One of the most advanced measures using the HHI is the REES (Risky External Energy Supply) indicator developed by Le Coq and Paltseva (2008). The HHI is visible in the REES index as the sum of the squares of the quotient of the net imports (from a specific country) and the total consumption of an energy resource. This construction of the REES index is a response to the energy supply security index proposed by Blyth and Lefevre (2004), and in particular to the way of including the so-called net export potential (for more, see Le Coq and Paltseva, 2008; Bożyk and Nyga-Łukaszewska, 2013).

The REES index includes also share of resource in total energy consumption of country and so-called fungibility of fuel imports, political stability of energy supplier and distance between countries. Fungibility describes the possibility of substituting means of transport for fuel. Higher values correspond to less substitutable fuels and thus energy types. The value of 1 means that the flow of energy is fungible and it includes all global commodity markets. A value of 2 indicates a less fungible flow of energy, e.g., energy types transported via pipeline. For instance, coal, oil, and LNG markets are highly fungible and, thus, their fungibility equals 1, whereas for the pipeline gas market fungibility equals 2. But if a respective supplier delivers gas to an importing country by pipeline and LNG tankers, then fungibility is a weighted average between 1 and 2. Weights refer to share of LNG imports and pipeline imports in total exports.

Political stability of the energy supplier is calculated with the use of political stability index delivered by the PRS Group. The higher the values of the calculated index, the lower the political stability of the supplier. The distance between the supplier and consumer of energy resource is determined within range from 1 to 3. It reaches 1, if the distance between the exporter's and importer's capitals $< 1{,}500$ km; 2, if the distance between the exporter's and importer's capitals $< 4{,}000$ km; and 3, when $\geq 4{,}000$ km. The greater the distance between national capitals, the greater the risk of energy supply disruption.

On the other hand, trade diversity is measured, for instance, by index that is compiled by Jansen, van Arkel, and Boots (2004). This measure, similarly to REES, takes into consideration role of the fuel for country's (here in the form of share of a given energy resource in the primary energy balance) and its imports (here in the form of share of net energy imports in the primary energy balance for fuel and share of energy resource imports from a given country in total imports of energy) captured in a different manner. Instead of trade concentration measure, authors use the trade dispersion index, here the Shannon index. The index is adjusted by geopolitical stability of the exporting region, which relies on geopolitical stability index provided by United Nations Human Development Indicator (HDI). Additionally, in contrast to the REES index, Jansen, van Arkel, and Boots (2004) include in the most advanced form of their index a set of measures characterizing energy resources from the geological point of view. In this way, index takes into consideration depletion rates of the imported energy resource in importing and exporting country along with exporter's Resources to Production ratio of a respective energy resource. These measures are corrected by a parameter characterizing the speed of depletion of resources. The greater it is, the faster the resources are depleted. The authors propose the value of 2 for that parameter to be considered. Arbitrary way of adopting the value of parameter suggested by authors and using Human Development Index as a determinant of the supplier's political stability seem to be main methodological concerns behind Jansen, van Arkel, and Boots (2004) measure.

The second group of methods of quantifying energy supply security comprises measures estimating the costs of energy supply disruptions (Leiby et al., 1997; Barsky and Kilian, 2004; Constantini and Gracceva, 2004; Beccue and Huntington, 2005; Davis et al., 2005). Some of them are not even directly defined as energy supply security measures. Instead, they are called *disruption costs* (Leiby et al., 1997; Constantini and Gracceva, 2004; Beccue and Huntington, 2005). As mentioned earlier, this line of considerations focuses on the effects of supply shocks in the economy.

One of such indices was presented by Hedenus, Azar, and Johansson (2010). The authors analyse the supply disruption cost in the crude oil market for 25 EU countries.[6] This cost is composed of three elements: wealth transfer, macroeconomic adjustment mechanisms, and loss of consumer surplus.[7] The first of these includes the wealth transfer achieved by exporters when oil prices in the world markets remain above its production costs. This transfer is assessed using crude oil price and its net import volume before and after the supply shock. The import volume depends, on the one hand, on the demand for crude oil and its short-term price elasticity, and on the other on the price elasticity of domestic crude oil supply and the level of its production. The second element of supply disruption costs includes macroeconomic adjustment mechanisms induced by the energy price increase. They are represented in terms of changes in GDP, which move in the opposite direction to changes in oil prices. If oil prices rise, GDP falls, and *vice versa*. The costs of macroeconomic adjustment mechanisms are assessed with the reference to GDP values without supply shock and GDP elasticity with reference to energy prices (here crude oil). The third element in estimating supply disruption costs is the loss of consumer surplus due to the rise in oil prices. Consumer loss is considered to be a cost incurred as part of macroeconomic adjustment mechanisms. All of these three elements are discounted by the probability of supply shock and volume of energy supply decrease (here, oil) resulting from supply shock and additionally multiplied by number of supply shocks. Although Hedenus, Azar, and Johansson (2010) chose the crude oil market for their analysis, the presented methodology can also be applied to the natural gas market.[8]

Due to the multidimensional influence of the supply shocks to economies combined with scientific desire to capture the phenomenon in a comprehensive manner, construction of such measures is relatively complex. Examples of simple disruption costs quantification include, for instance, the work of Davis et al. (2005), whose approach depicts the GDP change resulting from changes in the terms of trade for imported energy products. This method, called simple net import model, takes additionally into consideration net imports of energy in relation to the GDP and price elasticity of energy demand. An example of its use apart from Davis et al. (2005) – for Ukraine, is also Nyga-Łukaszewska (2018a) – for Poland.

Nowadays, most attention is paid to complex measures of energy supply security, taking into account the multidimensionality of the phenomenon. Such indicators constitute the third group of measures estimating supply security. More can be found in Cabalu (2010); Kocaslan (2014); Mansson, Johansson, and Nilsson (2014); Boehringer and Bortolamedi (2015); Kisel et al. (2016); and Garcia-Gusano, Iribarren, and Garrain (2017). What these works have in common is the analysis of energy supply security from the point of view of the structure of the country's energy balance, domestic fuel resources, reliability of transmission infrastructure, and dependence of the importer's economy on foreign energy resources. A similar multidimensional perspective on energy supply security is represented by Erahman et al. (2016); Li, Shi, and Yao (2016); Radovanovic, Filipovic, and Pavlovic (2017); Wang and Zhou (2017); Zeng, Streimikiene, and Balezentis (2017); and Abdullah et al. (2020). These works, additionally, share a similar research methodology. In all the above-mentioned studies, complex indicators of energy security are constructed on the basis of the principal component analysis (PCA). The use of the PCA method avoids assigning arbitrary weights to individual components in complex measures (Erahman et al., 2016).

An example of a complex energy supply security measure built with the use of PCA is the Energy Security Indicator (ESI) presented in 2017 by Wang and Zhou (2017). The text and Table 2.2 title use original wording of the authors, but it is worth mentioning that index is a supply security measure. It includes three categories (Table 2.2). The first is energy supply and delivery. It includes variables describing domestic energy resources, dependence on (net) energy imports, domestic production of energy resources, diversification of the country's energy mix, diversification of electricity generation, as well as electricity transmission losses and the time (calculated in days) necessary to obtain a connection to the power grid. The second category (so-called equity and environmental sustainability dimension) consists of variables showing, on the one hand, access to energy, and on the other hand, the impact of the energy sector on the natural environment. For this purpose, such aspects as the level of final energy consumption per capita, average annual gasoline prices, access to the electricity grid and the use of fuels other than coal in electricity production, energy consumption of the economy, and CO_2 emissions are taken into account. The third category is determined by the political and social stability of the country that imports energy resources, which is presented using the criteria for economic development established by the World Bank. This group of indicators includes regulatory quality and the rule of law in the country, corruption control, and GDP per capita as a determinant of the strength of the economy. Variables from all ESI index categories are subject to statistical normalization. They are then weighted and aggregated into a composite ESI index. Index provides a new evaluation technique based on the integrated application of subjective and objective weight allocation methods—SOWA (Subjective & Objective Weight Allocation) and places different weighs on each of the three dimensions. Energy supply and delivery and equity and environmental sustainability dimensions are equally weighed 0.40, while political and social stability enters the index with weigh 0.20 (Wang and Zhou, 2017). Various weights given to index components make it very

Table 2.2 Components of the *Energy Security Indicator* (ESI)

	Category	*Dimension*	*Variable*
Energy security indicator	Energy supply and delivery	Supply	Total domestic energy production/total domestic energy consumption (–)[a]
			Share of net energy imports in total energy consumption (%)
			Domestic natural gas reserves (tcf)
			Domestic coal reserves (m t)
			Domestic crude oil reserves (bbl)
			Energy mix diversity (–)
			Electricity generation diversity (–)
		Delivery	Time needed to get access to electricity grid (days)
			Losses in electricity transmission/net electricity produced (–)
	Sustainable character of energy use	Energy access	Final energy consumption *per capita* (kgoe[b] *per capita*)
			Share of population having access to electricity (%)
			Share of population having access to non-solid fuels (%)[c]
			Average annual gasoline prices (USD in PPP)[d]
		Environmental protection	Share of renewables in total primary energy supply (%)
			Share of electricity produced from renewable sources in total electricity production (%)
			CO_2 emissions/primary energy consumption (t/toe)[e]
			Energy intensity (mtoe/1,000 USD GDP in 2005 constant prices)
	Political and social stability		Geopolitical stability and lack of terror acts (–)
			Regulatory quality (–)
			Effectiveness of public authorities (–)
			Rule of law (–)
			Corruption control (–)
			GDP *per capita* (USD in current prices)

Source: Compiled by the author based on Wang and Zhou (2017).

[a] Dimensionless quantity.
[b] kgoe = kg of oil equivalent.
[c] Hydrocarbons and renewable energy sources.
[d] USD including purchasing power parity (PPP).
[e] Original term: *carbon factor*.

subjective. Such approach does not escape criticism. Stavytskyy et al. (2021) argue that in the long run only equal weighting seems to be a reasonable solution as economic and political conditions change drastically and thus one year they can be of greater importance for index construction but in the other period may seem to matter less. In general discussion on the logic and techniques of weighting of the components in composite indexes is a lively scientific debate visible or instance in Azzuni and Breyer (2020), Badea et al. (2011), or Stavytskyy et al. (2021). Wang and Zhou's (2017) index is created for 162 countries which are categorized on a scale from excellent through good, limited or weak to poor. In this way, ESI offers a possibility of international comparisons just like other ranking-like measures described later in this chapter.

The ESI index allows a comprehensive assessment of the energy supply security phenomenon. It takes into account more aspects than the previously discussed measures based on trade concentration/dispersion indices or similar complex energy security indicators based on the general (Computable General Equilibrium – CGE) (Boehringer and Bortolamedi, 2015) or partial equilibrium model (Gracceva and Zeniewski, 2014).

When examining the complex methods of energy supply security assessment, it can be noticed that the dominant way of understanding this phenomenon is the approach proposed by APERC – the "4 As". The approach to supply security in the four aspects described above was presented by Kruyt et al. (2009), Sovacool and Mukherjee (2011), Erdal (2015), Sumskis and Giedraitis (2015), and others. Interestingly, Erdal and Sumskis and Giedraitis are among the few in this research field to use time series regression analysis, while the majority of energy supply security empirical studies focuses on analysing the phenomenon in a precise moment in time.

Apart from developing original measures for energy supply security, researchers leaned towards applying existing empirical methods from various disciplines. One of such empirical efforts involved the use of the portfolio theory, deeply rooted in finance, to assess the structure and risk of energy import. This includes research by Mansson, Johansson, and Nilsson (2014) and Bigerna, Bollino, and Galkin (2020).

Another interesting trend in supply security assessment refers to the use of qualitative methods such as questionnaires or case studies. The use of questionnaire surveys is visible, *inter alia*, in Knox-Hayes et al. (2013); Ćwiek-Karpowicz (2016); Biresselioglu et al. (2017b); Jones, Kaklamanou, and Lazuras (2017); and Biresselioglu et al. (2017a). The main goal behind these empirical efforts was to understand either individual (Knox-Hayes et al., 2013; Ćwiek-Karpowicz, 2016; Jones, Kaklamanou, and Lazuras, 2017) or group (corporate) (Biresselioglu et al., 2017a, 2017b) respondents' perception on energy supply security. On the other hand, supply security research with the use of case studies was performed, *inter alia*, by Cherp and Jewell (2013).

Equally important research stream includes efforts to build international rankings allowing to compare energy security across the world. That involves next to individual engagement in creating worldwide rankings comparing energy supply security performance, significant contribution of international organizations/

bodies. The former includes works of Azzuni and Breyer (2020) or Stavytskyy et al. (2021). The latter refers to the most popular classifications sponsored by the IEA, the World Energy Council (WEC), and the Global Energy Institute.

Even though all of the above-mentioned efforts offer unified comparison of all countries, only Azzuni and Breyer (2020) eliminate subjectivity in energy supply security index calculations. The authors provide 15 parameters for energy security covered within 78 different indicators for 229 countries. Indicators range from country area, population, health expenditures, or democracy index to net energy imports, energy use per capita, energy use per area (km^2), income loss due to power outage. In a transparent way, Azzuni and Breyer (2020) build composite index ranging from 0 to 100, which is later used to create ranking. The higher the index values, the better position in the ranking. Another ranking is prepared by Stavytskyy et al. (2021) based on 29 indicators for 45 countries between 2000 and 2020. Indicators refer to the access, consumption, and depletion of natural resources, efficiency of their use, possibility of introducing new energy sources or pollution from mining activities. The proposed index offers the possibility to compare the energy security index with 1 (value for the European average). If a country has an energy security index greater than 1, it means that its energy security is currently better than the European average, and if it is lower than 1, it means that it is worse than the European average.

In 2011, the IEA created a model for assessing short-term energy security, called MOSES (Model of Short-Term Energy Security) for short. The model includes 35 simple indicators relating to various types of energy (primary and secondary), dependence on fuel import, storage capacity, diversification of fuel import, and political stability of suppliers. Taking this into account and relating the analysis to various types of primary energy (coal, oil, natural gas, nuclear energy), the IEA creates a complex index. The index on a scale from "low" to "high" allows the level of threats to a country's energy security and its ability to counteracting these dangers to be determined. In this manner, MOSES estimates energy supply security for 28 IEA member states (Jewell, 2011).

The models of the World Energy Council and the Global Energy Institute have a greater geographic scope than MOSES. While the WEC has developed an index called the Energy Trilemma Index (ETI), which takes into account data from 125 countries around the world, the Energy Security Risk Index (ESRI) prepared by the Global Energy Institute covers 75 countries with the highest energy consumption in the world.

The ETI consists of three sub-indices. These are energy security (original wording), access to energy, and sustainable energy management. Each of them has an equal 30% share in the ETI index. The remaining 10% accounts for a country's characteristics in terms of GDP, FDI inflow, political, and regulatory stability. Each sub-index consists of several variables. Energy security is measured by indicators describing the diversification of the primary energy balance and the structure of electricity generation, the relation of energy consumption to GDP, dependence in fuel import, energy storage, and the quality of human capital in the energy sector. Each of the variables has an equal 5% share in the sub-index concerning energy security (WEC, 2017).

On the other hand, the ESRI takes into account eight categories of variables with different weight attached to them. It consists of indicators in categories such as resources, production, consumption, prices, and import of energy resources (coal, crude oil, natural gas), and energy expenditure, energy intensity in the transport industry, and CO_2 emissions. The ESRI value is influenced the most by energy expenditures (weighting 20%), import structure (weighting 17%), energy prices (weighting 15%), and resources and energy consumption (14% each) (GEI, 2018). ESRI, like ETI, presents the results in the form of rankings, which makes it possible to compare countries on a global scale but also provide a framework for deeper analysis of a single country, like for instance – USA (as in Nyga-Łukaszewska, 2018b). However, the ESRI did not escape scientific criticism. Podbregar et al. (2020), using stepwise regression, principal component analysis, and Promax oblique rotation, came to the conclusion that the index relies to a high extent on crude oil price and global coal reserves ratios, as they explain 90% of the variance of the index. They add that if 100% of the variance of the index is to be explained, the global coal reserves variable loses its significance, which is an important indication that this variable is contained in other variables. The authors suggest that the variables used in the ESRI are of a general type and often contained in each other, which is methodologically unacceptable.

The latest (and relatively rarely represented in the research) trends in empirical assessment of energy supply security involve the use of artificial intelligence, combination of linear programming, and energy modelling, introducing the probabilistic approach and decision-making methodologies. The first of these research methods was used by Šimić et al. (2021), who implemented the so-called fuzzy logic analysis to support energy policy and the supply security decision-making process in particular. While a mix of IKARUS linear programming and the GAS-OPT optimization model was implemented by Gillessen et al. (2019) to derive both scenario-based future gas demands and load flow problems for the German economy, the first-of-a-kind probabilistic study on energy supply security was presented by Augustis et al. (2015) to assess the ex-ante perspective to supply security as opposed to prevailing ex-post analyses in energy security studies. Theory of the decision-making methodologies in supply security assessment is used, for instance, in Badea et al. (2011) and Ren and Sovacool (2014). The former uses aggregation rule derived from the group decision theory to build the composite indicator, which allows to define a threshold for a critical situation of a country and thus could be a starting point for risk-prone or risk-averse energy supply security decisions. The latter uses DEMATEL (Fuzzy Decision-making Trial and Evaluation Laboratory) to conclude that availability and affordability dimensions of the Chinese energy supply security matter the most in energy security strategies.

Looking at the evolution of energy supply security measurement studies, one may observe its gradual change (Figure 2.4). The beginnings of the research were marked by supply disruption analysis and its consequences for GDP. Later, the attention shifted towards the import dependence phenomenon and possibilities of trade diversification. It does not mean that both of the above-described research trends have been missing in the current empirical debate. They are still present, but

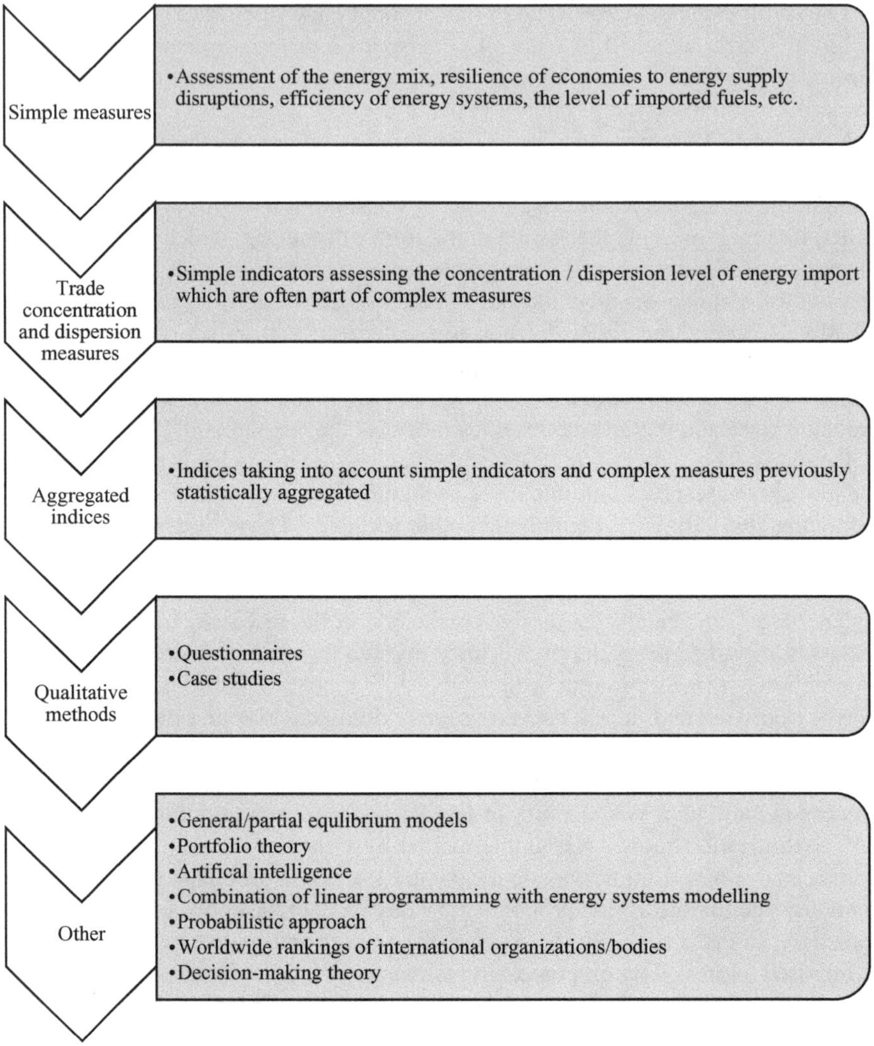

Figure 2.4 Evolution of supply security measures.

Source: Compiled by the author.

the second decade of the 21st century saw more efforts aimed at constructing complex or aggregated measures often using statistical or econometric methods of data aggregation. In parallel with these analyses, there have been several other research trends in assessment of energy supply security. First, computable equilibrium modelling (general or partial), the portfolio theory approach and the application of qualitative research methods in energy security analysis. It is worth noting the trend visible especially in the recent years when researchers have shifted towards the use of artificial intelligence methods, combination of energy modelling with energy systems optimization techniques, or probabilistic approaches. This proves that energy supply security has undergone thorough evolution and can be treated as an exemplary case for demand security empirical studies.

2.2 Energy demand security concept

2.2.1 Research gap

Discussion on energy security in general is dominated by the perspective of energy importers, often called supply security. The point of view of energy exporters tends to be missing from the energy security debate. This results mainly from the historical developments of energy markets. Oil crises of the 20th century triggered the debate on supply security. Later, as the new fuel – natural gas – had become popular in international energy markets, attention shifted in the 21st century towards gas supply disruptions. Still, regardless of the time and analysed fuel, scientists focused mainly on energy supply security. Its importance in the energy markets was strengthened by the establishment of the International Energy Agency (IEA). The IEA's main responsibility is to safeguard energy supply security. Even though there is no clear distinction for whom that security has to be guaranteed, the Agency's activity proves that importing nations are at the centre of the IEA's focus. The Agency's nearly half a century's experience in energy market surveillance proves that supply security has for many years dominated the energy security debate. Interestingly, there is no international and generally accepted organization safeguarding exporters' interests. Even though the Organization for Petroleum Exporting Countries (OPEC) and the Gas Exporting Countries Forum (GECF) are in place, they do not have the status of an international organization and act more as "cartel-like bodies".[9] That is why, while the IEA offers clear a definition of supply security, there is no such internationally recognized explanation for energy demand security, as suggested by Bollino and Galkin (2021). Interests of energy exporters are not treated uniquely in the international arena. Apart from general rules applying to energy trade, as any other traded goods (Shih, 2009),[10] the regulations of the World Trade Organization provide no other measures that can be applied specifically to exporters. A derivation of the WTO rules is also included in the International Energy Charter, which is a political initiative aimed at promoting cooperation between signatory states. As of 2022, countries such as Qatar, Russia, or Saudi Arabia were not among treaty signatories, unlike Norway, the United Arab Emirates, or the United States. An organization that represents the interests of energy exporters, to some extent, is the International Energy Forum, promoting itself as an energy dialogue platform. The diverse membership of that organization includes Norway, Russia, Qatar, United Arab Emirates, or Venezuela and also traditional energy importers such as Germany, Hungary, or Japan.

Novikau (2022) rightly claims that "energy, like any traded commodity, inevitably has two sides – supply and demand". That is why these "two sides" also have to be included in the scientific debates concerning different energy resources. That is why, it seems that the assumption adopted by Nowrouzi et al. (2019) of supply security being focused solely on the crude oil market does not escape criticism.

Indeed, when the discussion on energy supply security originally emerged, the majority of works referred to crude oil markets, but in the 21st century not only scientific but also political attention has moved towards natural gas. Some scientific examples are offered by Wright (2005), Cabalu (2010), Austvik (2016), or Gillessen et al. (2019). This does not mean that oil market research is missing nowadays from the supply security debate, as it is represented, for instance, by Brown and Huntington (2013, 2015) or Beccue et al. (2018). In the case of demand security, as Ye et al. (2021) suggest, the research gap mainly refers to the natural gas market. One possible explanation for that may be the historical development of energy security research. Starting from the crude oil market and supply disruptions, researchers focused on the effects of the volatility of crude oil prices on both importers and exporters. But later, their attention shifted towards supply disruptions and situation of natural gas importers. It seems that with development of institutional measures safeguarding supply security for importing nations, research naturally moves towards the group of natural gas exporters underrepresented in scientific investigations. Table 2.3 presents selected and detailed descriptions of the research gap on energy demand security.

2.2.2 Definitions

Energy demand security is an inherent part of the energy security research. Bollino and Galkin (2021) suggest that including exporters' view would make energy security a more comprehensive phenomenon. Demand security is treated in the same manner by Romanova (2013), who believes that energy supply and demand security are interconnected. Boussena and Locatelli (2013) even claim that energy supply versus demand security emerges as the "new duel" in the 21st century.

In order to conceptualize demand security better, it is worth referring to some general assumptions on energy security. According to these, in analysing energy security, it is important to answer a few questions. They can be summarized as follows: "Energy security for whom?", "In what time horizon?", "What kind of fuel is in question?" (Konoplyanik, 2005). Firstly, it should be reflected what kind of subject of energy security the analysis refers to. Is it a country, region, company, or individual citizen? If the analysis pertains to a country, it is relevant to define the nation's role in the international division of labour, specifically to answer the question whether the country is an energy-exporting or -importing nation, and, apart from that, additionally whether the country is a developed or developing nation. In this book, distinction between developed and developing nations follows international economics' perspective and country's role in the international division of labour described, for instance, in Carbaugh (2012). If the analysis concerns a region, then its boundaries and participating nations/minorities have to be delineated. When energy security research pertains to a company, probably its ownership structure and assets endowment might be in question, while in case of an individual citizen – their vulnerability to either energy price volatility or to sudden supply disruption might be of relevance. Secondly, the energy security analysis should clearly define the time frame. Risks and challenges are time-sensitive. Sudden blackouts require ad-hoc short-term intervention within hours, days, or

Table 2.3 Selected descriptions of the research gap on energy demand security

Author	*Description*
Bollino and Galkin (2021)	(…) *energy security has been primarily viewed from the consumer's (or importer's) perspective. The predominant body of literature on the subject has been produced in the energy-importing economies and tends to employ language that reflects this bias. Formal definitions of energy security and relevant policy documents often refer to the security of 'supply' rather than the more neutral 'energy,' and describe prices using words such as 'affordable' rather than 'fair,' 'reasonable,' or 'stable,' which would also reflect the energy producer's/exporter's interests.* *The inclusion of exporters' viewpoints also allows a more comprehensive methodological approach to energy security research.* *(...) Unlike their demand and import-focused counterparts, the international organizations for energy exporters do not present a clear definition of energy security in their key policy documents.*
Dike (2013)	*In the energy economics literature, very little contributions exist in this area of study as regards energy exports demand security risks. However, there are numerous contributions in the literature on the external energy supply security risks.*
Karatayev and Hall (2020)	*While the concept of energy security has received less attention in resource-rich countries with high exports, global geopolitical, environmental, and energy transition trends, mean energy security is gaining political importance for resource-rich energy-exporting countries.*
Nowrouzi et al. (2019)	*Studies conducted on energy security and risk have focused thus far on countries depending on energy import, especially crude oil.*
Romanova (2013)	*The vast majority of papers on energy security look at it from the consumer's point of view, making security of supply the key preoccupation. (...) Preoccupations of suppliers are not new; they emerged in the 1980s and have grown in scope ever since.*
Novikau (2022)	*In recent decades, energy security literature has included an increasing number of voices with a critical view of the supply-centred conceptualization of energy security. The critique is based on the logic that energy, like any traded commodity, inevitably has two sides – supply and demand. Since energy balance can shift in either direction, energy security concerns should be equally related to both supply and demand. Yet, in contrast to energy supply, energy demand has been less investigated in the energy security literature.*
Ulatowski (2016)	*Most publications focus on the importer's perspective (supply security).* (Translation from Polish)
Ye et al. (2021)	*According to the literature review, most scholars focus their studies from the perspective of energy-importing countries. There are few with emphasis on natural gas security from a demand perspective, needless to mention a supply vs. demand perspective.*

Source: Compiled by the author.

weeks. But capital-intensive infrastructural investments need long-term planning for years ahead. The last question that has to be addressed is about the energy resource and in particular the possibilities for its substitution. In this chapter, security of energy-exporting nations is analysed, both for developed and developing ones, from the theoretical point of view; thus, any short- and long-term challenges will be included. In order to better understand the phenomenon, the hydrocarbon market will be put into considerations.

The origins of demand security date back to the 1980s. As Romanova (2013) claims, that was the time when OPEC members made their first requests for demand security as a result of reduced energy consumption in the European countries (after the oil crises of the 1970s). In the 1980s, demand security boiled down to price stability and quantity of exported resources. It was limited at that time to oil, as that was a globally traded commodity. In the 1990s, exporting nations' concerns became more sophisticated. Romanova suggests that oil producers were more preoccupied with stable cash flows and their influence on investments in oil extraction, transportation, and processing. The 1990s were also marked by rising environmental pressure and liberalization of energy markets in oil-importing nations. Environmental arguments undermined the position of fossil fuels and encouraged European nations to develop climate-neutral energy carriers/technologies, such as renewables. Liberalization, on the other hand, aroused producers' concerns about the unbundling principle, which partially took away producers' control over pipelines.[11] The turn of the new millennium changed the rhetoric of oil-producing nations regarding demand security. Exporters were still focused on price stability and guaranteed export volumes but highlighted more often that export revenues were crucial for supporting economic growth and social progress in producing nations. As of now, such argument might be perceived as a type of moral blackmail justifying high oil prices. Nevertheless, for countries with budgets heavily relying on oil export revenues, a sudden change in that respect might truly result in economic turmoil and humanitarian disaster. The new millennium also brought natural gas into the limelight of the energy security analysis with concerns for producers similar to those related to oil unbundling. Table 2.4 presents selected definitions in an alphabetical order by author's name on energy demand security, which are described below. Detailed discussion of definitions is carried out within "from the general to specific" logic. It means that analysis starts with explanation of the broadest concepts and ends with the most substantial ones.

The most comprehensive description of energy demand security is offered by Romanova (2013) and Bollino and Galkin (2021). Romanova points out that demand security is underpinned by economic and political aspects. The former includes price stability, stability of oil and gas consumption in importing nations, taxes in importing nations, stability of regulation, and competition in export markets, whereas the latter refers to stable revenues for national budgets, development of a new legal regime taking exporters' interests into account, objection to any form of politicization of energy relations (Figure 2.5).

In further analysis, price stability will be one of the most recurring aspects. In this dimension, stability does not refer to the idea, well known from the supply security studies, namely that of "fair" or "reasonable" price. In the case of demand security, producing nations are instead preoccupied with "contained price volatility". This means that their goal is to keep the commodity prices within certain price

Table 2.4 Selected definitions of energy demand security

Author	*Definitions*
Bollino and Galkin (2021)	*The inclusion of exporters' viewpoints also allows a more comprehensive methodological approach to energy security research. Energy-exporting and importing economies face many of the same challenges and threats to their energy security, primarily issues related to domestic energy systems, physical security, and logistics. However, energy exporters face a separate range of economic challenges in the context of the new world paradigms of technology changes toward decarbonization, climate change mitigation and adaptation policies, and diffusion of renewable energy sources. We identify these challenges as follows. Energy exporters are exposed to global macroeconomic fluctuations that condition their export potential. An increasing competition from new emerging producers and new technologically developed substitutes can erode the energy exporters' market share. In addition, protectionist policies and sanctions, among others, constitute a pending menace in the global fuel markets. Some of the risks can be diversified across buyers, supply channels, fuels, and geographies; however, others are systemic, as demonstrated by the COVID-19 pandemic and subsequent plunge in global oil demand.* *While the physical security and stable flow of energy supplies affect both importers and exporters, their approaches to the economic component of energy security obviously differ. Energy exporters are also vulnerable to oil price shocks, (...), which led to a significant decrease in revenue. During such periods, energy exporters become increasingly concerned with the security of demand. This may lead to insufficient investment, particularly in the upstream sector, amplifying the magnitude of energy price cycles and their destabilizing impact on global energy markets.* *(...) suggests that the two major categories of energy security threats—physical supply disruption (such as armed conflict, piracy, terrorism, expropriation, and natural disasters) and economic (volume and price) instability—apply to both importers and exporters. However, exporters face a distinct set of challenges that require specific risk mitigation strategies. These include:* *– Negative macroeconomic dynamics (globally, and in importing economies)* *– Slowing demand for energy and specific fuels (globally, and in importing economies)* *– Downside price fluctuations in the global markets* *– Increasing competition, including from new exporters* *– Buyer-related risks including breach of contract and default* *– Protectionism, including tariff and non-tariff market access barriers* *– Sanctions, ranging from export embargoes to technological, financial, investment, and other collaboration restrictions* *– Shifts in legislation in energy-importing markets.*

(*Continued*)

Table 2.4 (Continued)

Author	*Definitions*
Boussena and Locatelli (2013)	*Russia's response to this concern over security is the "guarantee of gas demand" in the long term because it needs to make heavy investments to expand its export capacity.* *(...) There are two aspects to gas security, namely security of supply and security of demand. (...) On the one hand, it is felt that the supply security of the EU must take into account the "special Russian risk", while on the other, Russia wants to secure its long term investment through its European outlets.* *(...) Russia's objective to ensure security of demand. Means: vertical integration on European markets, long-term TOP contracts. System of governance: asset-swapping, bilateral relations, state-controlled companies with domestic competition but continuation of gas export monopoly, state control over access to hydrocarbon resources.*
Dike (2013)	*Energy demand security can be defined as the availability of a steady or regular demand for the energy exports (e.g., crude oil or gas) at competitive market prices (i.e., prices that can at least cover the production and transaction costs.*
Lee (2014)	*These diversification efforts are closely related to enhancing the country's energy security. (...) However, from the perspective of producers this concept implies security of demand.*
Novikau (2022)	*Since the most straightforward meaning of energy security for energy-importing countries is the adequate supply of energy at reasonable prices, and security of demand is often seen as the mirror image of security of supply, energy security for energy-exporting countries can be defined as adequate demand for energy at reasonable prices.*
Karatayev and Hall (2020)	*Energy security in resource-rich, energy-exporting countries is vulnerable to external shocks which can have profound and multiplier impacts on non-resource sectors, capital formation, environmental programmes, technology transfers, and overall economic growth.*
Konoplyanik (2005)	*(...) state of protection of the country (region), its citizens, society, state , economy from threats to sustainable fuel and energy supplies (...) under usual conditions (...) cover demand for fuel and energy resources (...) and under extreme conditions, (...) to guaranteed covering of minimal energy demand.*
Romanova (2013)	*Demand security covers economic and political aspects. Economic aspects include price stability, stability of oil and gas consumption, taxes in importing nations, stability of regulation and competition in export markets. Political aspects "are logical continuation of economic concerns" and include stable revenues for national budgets, development of new legal regime taking exporters' interests into account, objection to any form of politicization of energy relations.*
Ulatowski (2016)	*Energy demand security can be defined as stable export of energy resources at a reasonable price, which can guarantee exporters not only new energy investments but also economic growth. (Translation from Polish)*

(*Continued*)

Table 2.4 (Continued)

Author	*Definitions*
Ye et al. (2021)	*By comparison, energy-exporting countries could regard demand security as indivisible parts of their own national energy security. However, due to the abundance of resources in the exporting nations, there is a lack of understanding of the risks around energy security and accordingly often a policy vacuum.*

Source: Compiled by the author.

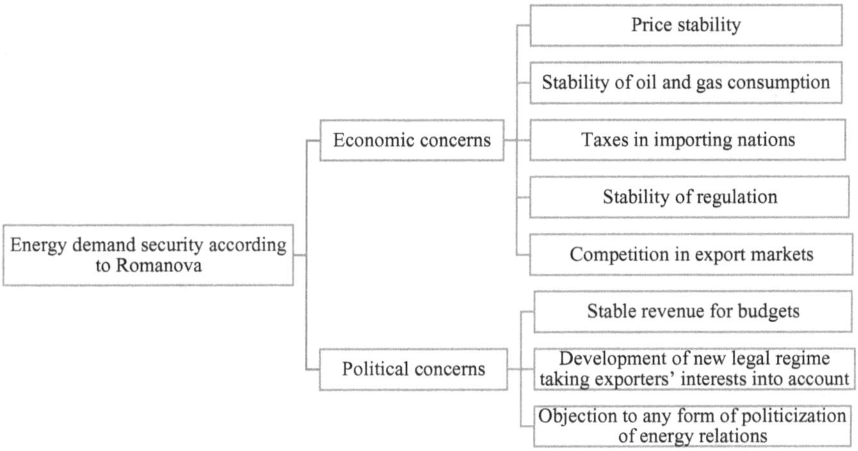

Figure 2.5 Energy demand security according to Romanova.

Source: Compiled by the author based on Romanova (2013).

bands. Exporters argue that energy prices are influenced more and more often by financial markets, which are "detached from supply and demand fundamentals" (Romanova, 2013). In common understanding, financial markets and especially energy-related derivatives destabilize oil markets.[12] Scientific investigations in that respect are inconclusive. There are some results contradicting the idea that derivatives destabilize the market (Fleming and Ostdiek, 1999), but there are also those supporting that argument, especially in the case of oil futures and spot prices (Lombardi and Van Robays, 2011; more on energy economics and financial markets can be found in Banks, 2000). Energy producers seek to design price-setting mechanisms that would guarantee stable income flows. As Romanova points out, long-term contracts with price mechanisms based on oil gave producers that comfort. However, with the growth of the LNG market and gas spot trading, prices became less and less predictable.

Stability of oil and gas consumption remains to be a key challenge for energy producers today. Romanova (2013) distinguishes two types of threats affecting that stability: short term and long term. The first group includes the outcomes of financial/economic crises in the world economy. Romanova uses the example of the financial crisis in 2008 when energy demand was significantly reduced. However, nowadays, with the coronavirus pandemic and its economic effects, similar challenges can be observed. That is why the category of short-term threats should be extended to wider economic crises as well. Long-term challenges are more complex. Romanova refers to the worldwide shift towards green economy. She argues that decarbonization, on the one hand, serves smaller, independent producers, but, on the other hand, it undermines the position of fossil fuel exporters. The former can easily phase into energy markets with smaller-scale investments, especially in the renewable sector, while the latter are not technically capable to relatively quickly reduce energy production. This is especially true for the natural gas sector. Firstly, natural gas can be to some extent substituted by renewables and, secondly, once a gas field is put into operation – it cannot be "shut down". Producers can either store excess production (up to their storage limit capacities) or flare/burn it at the site. She believes that this makes the supplier "a hostage of the consumer".

Another economic concern to energy demand security described by Romanova (2013) is tax burden in importing nations. She argues that duties levied on imported fuels distort prices for the final consumers and as a consequence discourage them from using these commodities. She claims that taxes imposed unilaterally on fossil fuels artificially increase the attractiveness of renewables. One can add that taxation policy is often a part of the wider energy policy strategies. Thus, decarbonization policy is accompanied by measures designed to discourage the use of some fuel types and encourage the use of others. That is why taxes on imported fuels should be treated as part of stability of regulation and, not as a sole, demand security component.

Stability of regulation is another economic concern of demand security described by Romanova (2013). She argues that this challenge is of special importance to exporters serving European markets. Liberalization processes, accompanied by unbundling principles and unconditional third-party access,[13] in her opinion, undermine the position of producing nations.

The last economic concern described by Romanova (2013) is the level of competition in export markets. She claims that suppliers would be more interested in exclusive contracts with final consumers. She also argues that unfair competition in export markets is exacerbated by discriminative taxation and instability of regulation.

Romanova's list of political concerns affecting demand security starts with the stability of revenues for budgets. One cannot escape the impression that this category should be treated as a type of economic concern. This is especially the case when Romanova (2013) claims that export revenues support the development of producing nations, especially social cohesion, education and modernization of economies. To sum up, one may argue that export revenues finance sustainable economic development of producing nations. However, Romanova adds that the export surplus serves more than just the economic goal. She believes that political stability of exporting nations "hinges on stability of oil and gas" revenues. This argument is especially interesting when confronted with her previous claim of suppliers being "hostages of consumers". It appears that exporters are worse off and their economic and political well-being is subjected to importers' whims. This idea seems to be flawed.

Another strictly political concern over demand security is the development of a new legal regime or adjustment of the present one to the interests of suppliers. Romanova (2013) does not give any exact examples of that but uses Russia's case to show how vocal this country has been so far in pursuing this path.

The last political concern is objection to politicization of energy relations. Romanova (2013) uses again the case of Russia to demonstrate that exporters are more interested in business-type energy relations. Thus, efforts of the European Union to meet natural gas demand by relying on alternative suppliers are perceived as political step. This way, Romanova overlooks the fact that including new suppliers is the simplest form of the diversification of energy imports, which is one of the limited tools in enhancing importers' supply security as highlighted by Vivoda (2009). That is why, energy import diversification has not much to do with politicization of energy relations. It is a pure business decision made with the goal to increase supply security and improve the negotiating position with other suppliers. Diversification may not be only focused on new supplying nations but also on new transporting facilities (new pipelines, commissioning new LNG terminals), transit routes, new forms of contracts (diversity in their length and contractual terms), and new companies supplying resources from one country. Poland is a perfect example of such activity in Central and Eastern Europe. This country has not only commissioned an LNG terminal but also secured contracts with LNG supplies from different countries (Norway, Qatar, the USA), with different companies from a single country (the USA), and under various contractual arrangements (spot and long-term contracts, free-on-board, ex-ship delivery).

Apart from mentioning demand security concerns, Romanova (2013) also proposes some measures aimed at addressing the above challenges. This approach resembles the way of thinking about energy supply security as proposed by Eggenhofer (2004). Even though Eggenhofer analysed supply security, he listed threats and later on proposed measures and costs that could be introduced in order to mitigate the risks. Romanova does not go that much into detail, proposing only countermeasures in a descriptive form, but still makes a valuable contribution to the demand security studies. She calls economic instruments "economic leverages" that suppliers use to defend their interests. These leverages include storage facilities and spare capacity, long-term contracts, control of transportation routes, efforts to correct the changes in the regulation of importing nations and broad-based diversification (of export markets, production, economy) (Figure 2.6).

Storage facilities and spare capacity are measures of a technical character. This means that either a producer is equipped with excess specific technological solutions or not. Storage facilities and spare capacity can be used in the short-term horizon to offset demand fluctuations and price volatility. However, they also constitute a considerable cost burden especially when left idle. Romanova (2013) points out that when they are used to smooth price volatility, they should be treated as global public good with the cost involved to be shared between producers and consumers.

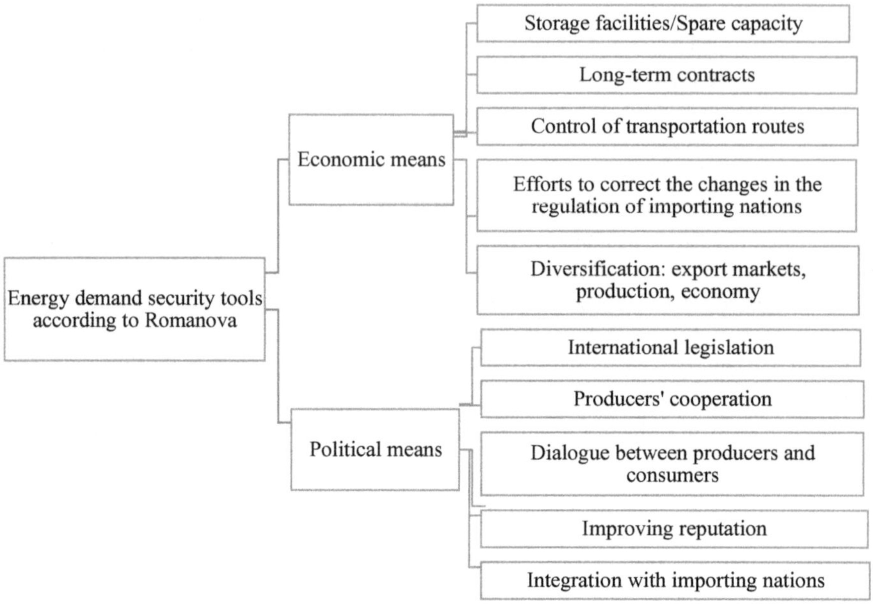

Figure 2.6 Energy demand security tools according to Romanova.

Source: Compiled by the author based on Romanova (2013).

However, she fails to consider storage facilities located at the premises of importing nations, financed by importers and used by consumers to safeguard against any supply disruptions. The International Energy Agency (IEA) (Jewell, 2011) confirms that the short-term storage capacities have built-in domestic resilience to respond to supply disruptions. That is why Romanova's and IEA's perspectives taken together may suggest that storage facilities are a tool for achieving short-term energy security, both for exporters and importers. In contrast to storage facilities, holding spare production capacity is only possible for producing nations. Indeed, it can be agreed that it is a money-consuming way of smoothing price volatility.

Extended duration of contracts is another economic tool for exporters to improve demand security. Producers are interested the most in long-term deals with guaranteed demand for resources. However, nowadays the length of agreements in natural gas trade has decreased significantly in line with the increasing commodity volumes traded in spot markets.[14] Producers often argue that long-term contracts are needed to safeguard return on high-cost infrastructural investments.

Romanova (2013) adds control of transportation routes as another type of economic tool to secure demand. She claims that it is the most efficient strategy in the natural gas business, where fixed infrastructure is too costly to be duplicated. Giving an example of Russia denying third-party access to its pipelines, Romanova tries to prove the success of that strategy. However, Russia's approach in that respect did not escape the criticism of the international community and as such is perceived as more of a political tool not only for controlling natural gas trade but also for pursuing foreign policy goals. That is why including control of transportation routes in the economic set of tools enhancing demand security is rather questionable.

The same refers to efforts of producers to offset or correct the changes in the regulation of consuming countries, especially when this puts producers at disadvantage. Romanova (2013) uses the example of the asset-swap strategy introduced, for instance, by Russia and Algeria. Asset swap is described as a situation in which companies from importing countries are invited to participate in the development of new gas fields in exporting nations and, in return, they offer the producer a share in the importing's nation distribution network. However, this approach is not legally allowed in countries with unbundling policies.

Probably, one of the most economic tools in the set proposed by Romanova (2013) is the strategy of diversification. It includes diversifying export markets, differentiating the structure of energy production and shifting economies away from energy-trade reliance. Geographical diversification of export markets is a strategy in which producers look beyond the existing demand. As Romanova points out, diversification of export markets is used, as only then consumers compete for resources. Diversification of energy production is an activity where upstream companies move away from their core business and divert to midstream activities or new energy sources. As an example, she presents the case of Algeria's Sonatrach company launching a business line in the solar panel sector. Even though Romanova very often provides different examples in her study, she overlooks cases of the European companies, such as Equinor. This firm not only partially diverted towards renewables but also changed the company's name in order not to be associated with fossil fuels (previously Statoil). The last trend in exporters' diversification has been decreasing the reliance of economies on trade in energy goods. Romanova claims that establishing oil and gas funds helps exporting nations to finance the modernization of their countries.[15]

Political means enhancing energy demand security include international legislation, producers' cooperation, dialogue between producers and consumers, improving producers' reputation and integration with importing nations. Romanova explains that these tools perform "an auxiliary function" to economic means and cannot be treated as a political weapon. However, a closer look at the set of political tools reveals their vague description. That is why they will be only briefly overviewed at this point.

International legislation and producers' attempt to influence it are the first political tool described by Romanova (2013). She argues that producers have tried to use international regulations to affect domestic legislation in importing nations. In particular, exporters have called for limiting importers' freedom to change their internal regulations. This strategy can be assessed as highly ambiguous, as producing nations, on the one hand, are very sensitive about their sovereign right to energy exploration and, on the other hand, they take or assume political measures aimed at restricting importers' liberty in the energy policy domain.

The truth is that producers very often use multilateral cooperation to improve their demand security. In the 21st century, this has been easier thanks to the emergence of exporting nations' new agreement. One of such new formats is the Gas Exporting Countries Forum (GECF) (Romanova, 2013).[16] This is an organization, often called an OPEC-like cartel, which sets itself the goal of deepening the dialogue between natural gas producers across the world. According to Romanova, GECF, unlike OPEC, has never had aspirations to control natural gas prices due to their regional character. However, after the emergence of GECF, Egypt called for a global and unilateral pricing scheme for natural gas. In the crude oil market, OPEC's activity has left no doubts about its price and volume control ambitions.

Dialogue is widely recognized by producers as a tool to enhance demand security. However, according to Romanova, exporters also engage in political discussions with importers. One of the international fora designed for such debates is the International Energy Forum, which is a neutral facilitator of dialogue between energy-producing and -consuming nations. In particular, it is a dialogue between OPEC (plus Russia) and IEA countries.

Energy producers have also attempted to improve their reputation as stable energy suppliers in an effort to dismiss continuous accusations that selected oil- and gas-exporting nations use energy trade as a geopolitical weapon. Another attempt to enhance demand security was an idea developed by Russia in 2010, according to which integration between Russia and the EU in the energy sector would eliminate threats to energy trade (Romanova, 2013).

Summing up Romanova's (2013) approach to demand security, one can claim that it follows the general supply security debate by separating the discussion into energy demand security challenges and ways used to improve demand security. It also offers a descriptive, easy-to-follow narrative manner of defining demand security. That is why, it is comprehensible and can be easily adopted in any research. At the same time, her study does not take into account pre-existing theoretical achievements in supply security. Thus, selected findings, as the one on diversification, are lacking such explanation. Her study would have been more persuasive if she had considered pre-existing findings. Romanova's angle, even though it separates economic and political perspectives, tends to mix them in some respects (e.g., taxation, regulations), so that the reader cannot see a clear delineation between the economic and political dimensions. Additionally, Romanova focuses mainly on the case of Russia, failing to consider other energy exporters. One possible explanation of that might be the fact that she focuses on the natural gas market, where Russia indeed plays a significant role. It is not expected that in a book published in 2013, the author would describe the case of the USA and shale gas exports, but Romanova still overlooks cases of long-standing natural gas exporters such as Norway or Qatar.

Unlike Romanova (2013), Bollino and Galkin (2021) look at a wider set of energy exporters in defining energy demand security. They refer to Russia, Iran and also Australia. Their approach includes developing countries (in-transition/emerging economies) and developed countries. That is why this research is valuable, as it depicts different types of economies. Like Romanova, Bollino and Galkin describe demand security by distinguishing challenges and tools used to improve it.

Energy demand security challenges include two main categories: physical supply disruption and economic (volume and price) instability. Apart from that,

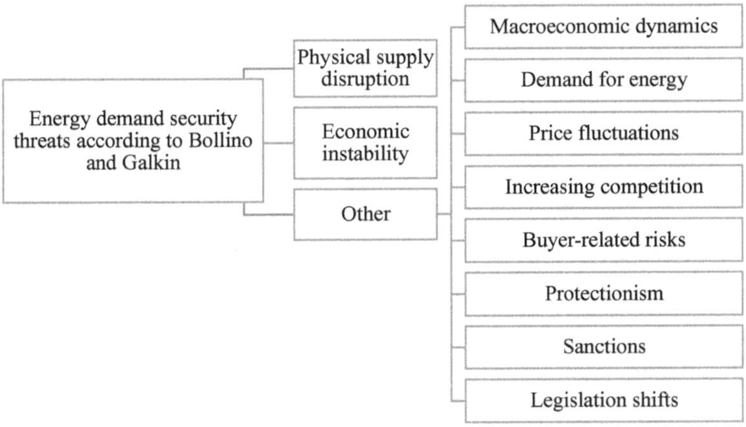

Figure 2.7 Energy demand security challenges according to Bollino and Galkin.

Source: Compiled by the author based on Bollino and Galkin (2021).

Bollino and Galkin (2021) distinguish a set of diverse challenges that cannot be attributed to any of the above categories (Figure 2.7).

The physical supply disruptions category includes threats to energy exporters connected with armed conflicts, piracy events, terrorism, expropriation, and natural disasters. Economic instability threats are also called volume and price instability. Although Bollino and Galkin (2021) do not provide a detailed explanation of that category, one may assume that these are challenges resulting from price volatility and demand/supply adjustments. The authors argue that the two above-mentioned categories of threats apply both to importers and exporters. To some extent, this idea resembles the supply security approach provided by the International Energy Agency (IEA, 2018) in which uninterrupted availability of energy sources is accompanied by their affordable price. The IEA's perspective on availability mirrors Bollino and Galkin's – physical supply disruption and volume instability, while affordability reflects price volatility. Naturally, IEA's standpoint represents the specific situation of importers while Bollino and Galkin's view represents more general conditions of exporters and importers.

The third category of challenges exporters face is not named. The authors only highlight that these are challenges requiring "specific risk mitigation strategies" (Bollino and Galkin, 2021). They add that this set of threats can be further classified by fuel type and geographical location criteria. The latter distinguish between domestic and international markets, adding also transit territories. The distinct challenges that exporters may face include, accordingly to the authors:

- negative macroeconomic dynamics observed, both on the global but also on the importing nation level,
- slowing demand for energy, both at the global but also at the importing nation level,

- downside price fluctuations in the global market,
- increasing competition from emerging exporters entering the market,
- buyer-related risks such as breach of contract or default,
- protectionism in the form of tariff and non-tariff trade barriers,
- sanctions including export embargoes, technological/financial, or investment restrictions,
- changes in legislation in energy-importing markets.

The authors provide a relatively detailed set of threats, as in their study they focus on minimizing risks and maximizing returns for the Gulf Cooperation Council countries. Therefore, precise risk assessment precedes empirical investigations, in which the authors use physical disruption risk and price volatility threat. It is unclear how Bollino and Galkin (2021) select other threats. Their study is silent about the selection criteria or the literature used for that purpose. One may expect that the authors applied a kind of heuristic technique to provide a selection of other risks. Using the heuristic method, a set of the above-mentioned challenges could be extended, in the opinion of this book's author, for instance, by

- contractual changes to existing export agreements, such as adjustment of the pricing formula forced by decisions of the international arbitrage communities, or
- political instability (turmoil) in importing nation (in the group of buyer-related risks),
- ground-breaking innovations that change the way specific energy resources are used without slowing energy demand and instead shift it to other applications, etc.

These are just few examples of challenges that are relevant to both price and volume volatility. An in-depth theoretical study in this respect could bring an even more detailed set of challenges.

Apart from listing threats, Bollino and Galkin (2021) present a list of policy tools that could be introduced to enhance energy security of exporters. These include a review of the domestic regulatory/policy environment to boost export capacity and competitiveness of exporters, taxation, domestic energy price incentives, diversification in foreign trade, contractual hedging, and vertical integration in global value chains (Figure 2.8).

The domestic regulatory environment has a potential to boost export capacity and competitiveness. A country's legislation can encourage companies to undertake new exploration and production (E&P) activities. This results in increased energy supply, the excess of which can be destined for exports. Additionally, Bollino and Galkin (2021) argue that only sufficient infrastructural investment levels in upstream and midstream projects guarantee physical security of supplies. They claim that these costly investments can be introduced through public-private partnerships. Additionally, the authors argue that policy-makers in energy-exporting countries should implement regulations on maintaining fuel stocks and managing spare capacity, as only then exporters will be able to quickly adjust to market changes.

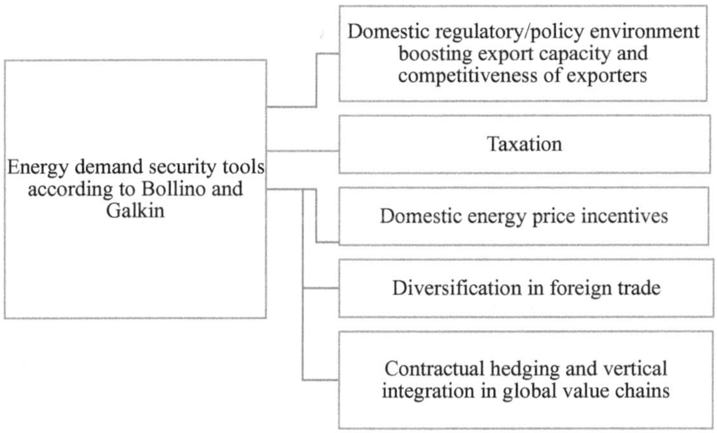

Figure 2.8 Energy demand security tools according to Bollino and Galkin.
Source: Compiled by the author based on Bollino and Galkin (2021).

Taxation is another policy tool enhancing demand security mentioned by Bollino and Galkin (2021). They argue that a well-designed tax system affects the entire export value chain from E&P through transportation to refining, storage, and export. The authors claim that stability of regulatory environment is crucial for long-term planning and development of energy-exporting industries.

Another policy tool affecting energy security of exporters can have dual effects for producing nations. Domestic energy price incentives can have both positive and negative impacts on exporters. If domestic prices converge with the global market, producers can generate additional revenue in the local market with lower risks than those faced in international markets. However, if domestic price incentives diverge from global markets, they reduce the availability of energy for export markets and decrease exporters' revenues. Additionally, in such circumstances, investments in the whole energy export value chain are inhibited. Thus, in the long term, a policy with domestic energy price incentives may harm energy-exporting industries.

Recognizing the importance of foreign trade to energy demand security, Bollino and Galkin (2021) highlight the central role of the diversification strategies both for importers and exporters. For exporters, diversification in foreign trade can take several forms, from the diversification of markets (often called buyer diversification) through the diversification of transit routes to the diversification of the exported products' portfolio. The diversification of markets reduces the dependence on a specific geographical market or country. The diversification of transit routes reduces the exposure to single logistical transit nodes and chokepoints. The diversification of the exported products' portfolio reduces the instability of export revenues resulting from changes in the global or regional commodity markets. This way of thinking corresponds with Romanova (2013).

Hedging is a tool similar to diversification. In general, hedging is a strategy in which an investor recognizing risks and potential losses from one investment secures it with another investment. In energy demand security, hedging refers mainly to contractual terms in energy agreements. It includes supply arrangements, pricing terms, and additional clauses. Supply arrangements refer to the length of the agreement between parties (long-term contract versus spot contract). Pricing terms describe the way in which the contract is settled. They may provide for fixed prices for the full contract duration or for variable prices linked to global/regional commodity benchmarks (prices at specific hubs).[17] Additional clauses define conditions of commodity delivery, such as free-on-board (FOB), cost, insurance, and freight (CIF), etc.

Vertical integration serving energy demand security refers to a situation in which investors acquire energy assets (or shares in assets) in foreign markets to control global/regional value chains. Vertical integration brings several benefits to companies. It allows for price management across the value chain, helps investors alleviate market access barriers and serves greater flexibility and scope of operations which in turn diversify revenue streams. Bollino and Galkin (2021) highlight that attempts to gain control over assets in importing nations might be perceived as a threat to consumer's supply security. Asset swaps, described also by Romanova (2013), are considered by Bollino and Galkin as a possible way to mitigate such supply security concerns. The authors provide an example of Russia's Gazprom and the EU market, when Gazprom was denied access to regional distribution companies but managed to swap assets in Austria and Germany. The swap involved Russian natural gas and condensate production assets for trading and storage assets, respectively, in Germany and Austria.

Apart from theoretical considerations, Bollino and Galkin (2021) provide a brief overview of energy demand security understanding in different countries and energy producers associations. A description of energy demand security perspectives in Russia, Iran, Australia, Nigeria, and in OPEC and GECF is available in Table 2.5 (in original order proposed by the authors).

It seems that the most sophisticated and detailed explanation of energy demand security among the countries analysed by Bollino and Galkin (2021) is offered by Russia. This demand security understanding includes both international and domestic aspects. Russia also follows the general trend in energy security studies, where threats or challenges are depicted. This approach is visible in demand security studies by Romanova (2013) and Bollino and Galkin (2021), and in supply security studies highlighted in Checchi, Behrens, and Eggenhofer (2009) and Eggenhofer (2004). In Russian strategy, all of these threats are foreign trade-related and include three categories: economic, political, and military challenges. Economic threats include changes in global economic growth, increased resource base, competition from new exporters, reduced demand in existing markets, and high entry barriers to new markets. Political challenges refer mainly to international regulatory changes, policy discrimination, introduction of sanctions, and security of energy transit. Military threats are not described in this book as they are beside its scope. This is a similar approach to that presented by Bohi and Toman (1996a), who, while describing energy security externalities, omitted military expenditures, suggesting that from the economic point of view they are irrelevant. The authors argue that it is impossible to separate military costs incurred for peacekeeping

Table 2.5 Selected approaches to energy demand security

Country/ organization	*Formal basis*	*Energy demand security understanding*
Russia	The Doctrine of Energy Security of the Russian Federation (2019)	"*energy security (...) ensures protection of the nation's economy and population from the national security threats in the energy domain, (...) and the export contracts and the international obligations of the Russian Federation are fulfilled.*"
Iran	Iranian Petroleum Act 1987	Energy security refers to four elements: economic security, physical security, environmental security, and absence of sanctions.
Australia	The National Energy Security Assessment of Australia (2011)	No precise concept presented.
Nigeria	National Energy Policy (2014, 2018)	No precise concept presented.
Canada	Energy Safety and Security Act (2016)	Focus on domestic issues.
OPEC	OPEC Statute (2012)	"*the necessity of securing a steady income to the producing countries; an efficient, economic and regular supply of petroleum to consuming nations; and a fair return on their capital to those investing in the petroleum industry.*"
GECF	GECF Long-Term Strategy (2017)	No precise concept presented, the only reference being to the organization's mission of "*supporting the security of supply and demand*".

Source: Compiled by the author based on Bollino and Galkin (2021).

purposes from those covered only for energy supply security reasons. That is why they highlight the existence of the category but do not research it further. It seems that the Russian approach to energy demand security stems from the country's experience in energy-trade relations with European countries. The specified energy demand security threats reflect the challenges Russia is facing in the EU.

An approach to energy demand security similar to Russia's is manifested by Iran. In the case of latter country, a clear reflection is also visible on the country's challenges in the international arena. Energy demand security in Iran consists of four building blocks: economic security, physical security, environmental security, and absence of sanctions. The last element is characteristic of Iran and its experience in economic relations on the global scale. It seems that energy demand security in Iran reflects the complexity of its economic situation. However, apart from that, the security idea refers also to economic security, which is understood as a mixture of stable (or increasing) energy prices and demand. Physical security pertains to protection provided to energy facilities and transit routes against any military or terrorist attacks. Environmental security is connected with mitigating negative impacts of the energy industry on the natural environment.

Unlike Russia's and Iran's, the Canadian and Nigerian way of thinking about energy demand security is rather inward-oriented. This means that both of these countries prioritize domestic issues over international concerns when it comes to energy demand security. In both countries, there is a visible focus on infrastructural arrangements, especially capacity building and research and development in the energy domain.

Australia, on the other hand, does not have any special category for energy demand security and seems to perceive its position in the international division of labour as an energy consumer rather than producer. That is why, its strategy includes an element of supply security defined by reliable and competitive energy supplies that support the development of the country's economy.

Definitely, apart from Russia, only the OPEC presents an elaborated view on demand security. The organization combines importers' and exporters' perspectives in its understanding of energy demand security. Consumers' view is represented by efficient and regular supply, while producers' standpoint is manifested in steady export incomes and fair returns on energy investments. Like the OPEC, the GECF recognizes both supply and demand security by giving it a central place in the organization's mission statement. In addition, the GECF also highlights revenues, market mechanisms, and objection to politicization of energy relations. That last element, as noted by Romanova (2013), forms a significant part in Russia's energy demand understanding. Not surprisingly, objection to politically motivated restrictions is integrated into the GECF's demand security understanding, as Russia is one of the most important members of the organization.

To sum up, there are few conclusions to be drawn from the analysis of energy demand security doctrines in various energy-exporting nations by Bollino and Galkin (2021). Firstly, as in energy supply security studies, energy demand security is highly contextual. According to this argument, brought forward for the first time by Winzer (2012), every country's energy security perspective is shaped by its energy mix, and its economic and political situation. It is very clear for Iran and Russia, where international concerns are integrated into the demand security concept. Secondly, in contrast to Frei's study (Frei, 2004), countries with different energy needs can share similar energy policy approaches, as proven by the cases of Canada and Nigeria. These countries are highly diverse in terms of their energy problems. Nigeria struggles with satisfying citizens with basic energy needs, while Canada focuses on reducing the negative impact of the energy industry on the natural environment. Yet, both countries share a similar approach to energy demand security by prioritizing the domestic market over the international one.

Recapitulating Bollino and Galkin's energy demand security definition (Bollino and Galkin, 2021), one may claim that their research fits into the general energy security studies in two dimensions. Firstly, it offers the IEA-style definition which is an idea based on physical supply and price volatility. Secondly, it presents demand security as a "risk and tools framework", which, as proved above, is also at the centre of supply security studies. The greatest advantage of that study over others is that it provides an enhanced list of demand security challenges and presents geographically and economically diverse demand security perspectives.

Other two studies that will be described below resemble the Bollino and Galkin (2021) approach to demand security. The similarity lies in the fact that Karatayev and Hall (2020) and Ye et al. (2021), like Bollino and Galkin, use definitions for the operationalization of empirical investigations. Additionally, Karatayev and Hall provide descriptions of energy demand security in various energy-exporting nations, similarly to Bollino and Galkin. However, Karatayev and Hall and Ye et al., in contrast to Bollino and Galkin, rely on a different theoretical framework for energy security. They refer to the so-called "4 As" approach (APERC, 2007), dominated by the geological availability of resources, geopolitical and geoeconomics accessibility of resources, acceptability of the use of certain resources, and affordability with regard to resource prices. This is a concept widely used in supply security research.

Karatayev and Hall (2020) employ that idea to assess demand security of energy-rich countries. The set of nations taken into consideration in their analysis includes Russia and Caspian region countries such as Azerbaijan, Iran, Kazakhstan, Turkmenistan, and Uzbekistan. The authors limit their definition of demand security to three dimensions: resources and dependency, intensity and sustainability, and cost and poverty (Figure 2.9).

The resources and dependency component mirrors APERC's (2007) availability and accessibility dimensions. It includes the availability of resources (oil, gas, and coal), primary energy production, supply of renewables (as percentage of total final energy consumption), and energy import dependency. The intensity and sustainability component in Karatayev and Hall's (2020) definition corresponds to APERC's acceptability criterion and consists of energy use per capita, CO_2 and NO_X emissions, water usage, volume of gas flared at production sites, and the grid efficiency indicator (percentage of energy loss). The cost and poverty section is linked to APERC's affordability dimension and is represented by electricity costs for industry and households, prices of gasoline, diesel fuel, and liquified petroleum gas, and energy poverty rates as percentage of population with little or no electricity access. Since Karatayev and Hall's approach serves mainly demand security operationalization, its definition is built on subjectively chosen indicators. But the authors enhanced their theoretical findings by referring to practical definitions presented in strategic documents of the countries in question. Since in the previous

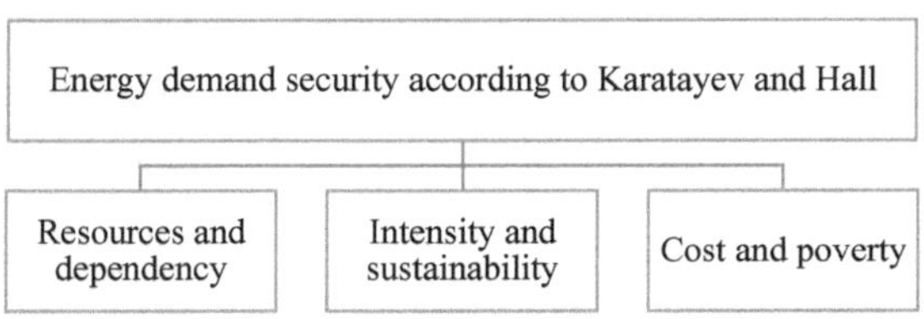

Figure 2.9 Energy demand security according to Karatayev and Hall.

Source: Compiled by the author based on Karatayev and Hall (2020).

Table 2.6 Selected approaches to energy demand security in the Caspian region

Country	*Strategic document*	*Definition*
Azerbaijan	State Programme for the Sustainable Use of Energy Resources and Energy Efficiency of End-Users for 2015–2020 (2015)	"*complex issue, where the main indicator of ES is the sufficiency and availability of primary energy resources for the needs of the country's economy.*"
Kazakhstan	Fossil fuel and power generation concept (2014)	"*the internal and external position of nation in which there are no threats to end-use consumers arising in the process of extracting, processing, transporting, trading and using energy resources.*"
Turkmenistan	National Sustainable Development Strategy (2012)	"*development of renewable and non-renewable resources for domestic economic use.*"
Uzbekistan	Energy Security Programme for 2016–2020 (2015)	"*National control of energy production, diversification of fuel and energy resources, involvement of renewable energy sources in national energy mix, and broad cooperation with neighboring countries in the field of sustainable water use.*"

Source: Compiled by the author based on Karatayev and Hall (2020).

parts Russia's and Iran's demand security perspectives have already been depicted based on Bollino and Galkin (2021), these two countries will be omitted at this point to focus on other Caspian region states (in alphabetical order): Azerbaijan, Kazakhstan, Turkmenistan, and Uzbekistan (Table 2.6).

The understanding of energy demand security in the above-mentioned countries is linked to their domestic economies. None of the definitions explicitly refers to demand security. One may get the impression that these concepts correspond to supply and not demand security. Again, as the cases of Canada and Nigeria described by Bollino and Galkin (2021), inward orientation prevails in energy security. However, in the above-mentioned Caspian group of countries, one nation's definition of demand security is slightly different from others'. It is Uzbekistan's idea in which energy demand security is depicted through tools used to enhance it. There is national control of energy production, in addition to diversification of fuel and energy resources (also in the domestic energy mix) and cooperation with neighbouring countries. Applying Romanova's (2013) and Bollino and Galkin's approaches to Uzbekistan's definition, one can find economic and political tools used to improve energy demand security of producers. That is why Uzbekistan's idea on demand security best reflects the country's position in the international division of labour, while Azerbaijan's, Kazakhstan's, and Turkmenistan's concepts correspond only to supply security concerns.

The approach based on APERC's "4 As" is also adopted by Ye et al. (2021). Like Karatayev and Hall (2020), the authors provide a theoretical framework which is later used to operationalize energy demand security. Security of exporters consists of four parts denoted as availability, accessibility, acceptability, and affordability (Figure 2.10).

As the authors focus on building an indicator for the natural gas market, their considerations specifically include that fuel type. That is why, in the availability dimension, there are natural gas reserves per capita and natural gas reserves-to-production ratio.[18] Accessibility includes natural gas net import/export diversification – presenting the contribution of international trade to domestic gas demand and the natural gas self-sufficiency ratio – describing the significance of the domestic resource production in the total gas consumption. Acceptability is represented through a set of energy environment-related indicators, such as concentration of $PM_{2.5}$ and energy-related CO_2 emissions per capita.[19] Affordability is captured by assessing the natural gas price in relation to GDP per capita and the ratio of net imports/exports to GDP (Ye et al., 2021). Extending this approach to markets other than natural gas is possible if gas reserves, gas imports/exports, and gas prices are substituted by other resources. This way, the framework adopted by Ye et al. can be easily adapted to any other energy commodity.

Ye et al. (2021) rightly claim that energy exporters regard their demand security as a part of national energy security. But at the same time, they highlight that abundance of resources does not motivate exporting nations to think about demand security risks. This passive approach by producers results in a lack of suitable "policy vacuums" that would integrate risks and policy responses. Even though Ye et al. do not admit that directly, by criticizing energy exporters, the authors indirectly point at the possible definitional path in demand security. Their argument would suggest that the "risk and tools framework" could provide a theoretical solution for demand security.

Another study describing energy demand security in a manner similar to that proposed by Karatayev and Hall (2020) and Ye et al. (2021) is the one published by Dike (2013). The similarity of these works lies in the fact that all of them focus on developing demand security measures. That is why the conceptualization of the phenomenon serves methods used to assess it quantitatively. Unlike the two mentioned above, Dike's study is more detailed in discussing the conceptual framework of demand security.

In his study, the author uses the IEA-like demand security definition by claiming that it is the "availability of a steady demand for the energy exports (e.g., crude oil or gas) at competitive market prices (i.e., prices that can at least cover

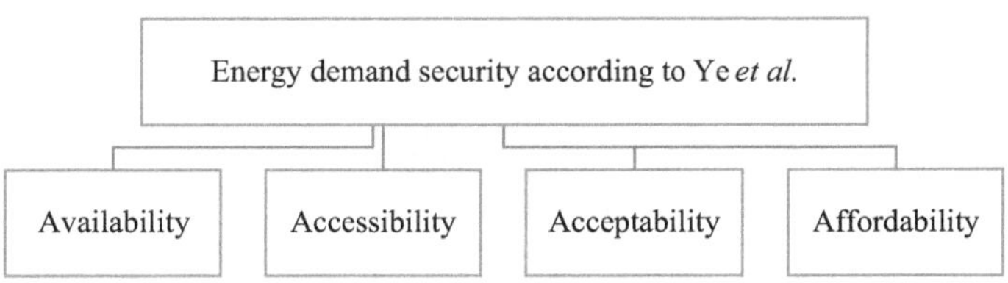

Figure 2.10 Energy demand security according to Ye et al.

Source: Compiled by the author based on Ye et al. (2021).

the production and transaction costs" (Dike, 2013, p. 594). Even though Dike factors in the physical supply and price component, while deepening the analysis he narrows it down to only the availability or non-availability of energy. It seems that physical supply lies at the heart of Dike's demand security considerations. He claims that security of energy-exporting nations, in contrast to energy-importing countries (Dike, 2013),[20] is affected by both economic and political factors. Determinants driving oil consumption can be regarded as the former, while unilateral environmental policy actions (such as the Kyoto Protocol) might be considered as the latter.

Dike's (2013) concept of demand security fits partially into the "risk and tools framework". He does not provide any exact details on risks apart from the claim that they are fuel-specific. The author is convinced that demand security risks for crude oil are different from natural gas risks. To some extent, this claim remains true, as oil and gas exhibit differences at least in price elasticity of demand, market character, and price-setting mechanisms. Strongly inelastic oil demand, global crude oil market, and global oil price-setting mechanisms do not correspond with relatively inelastic gas demand, regional gas markets character, and regional price-setting mechanisms.

Dike's (2013) demand security angle hinges upon demand shocks in energy markets. He advocates that oil demand shocks affect the supply of oil by producing nations. This way of thinking is different from the mainstream energy demand shock literature in which the volatility of oil prices influences macroeconomic performance of oil importers (e.g., Barsky and Kilian, 2004; Baumeister and Kilian, 2016) or in which exogenous or endogenous oil price determinants are investigated (e.g., Hamilton, 2009). This is what the literature calls "oil shock" (for more on the "oil shocks", see Hamilton, 2003, 2009, 2011; Kilian, 2008a, 2008b; or Kilian and Cheolbeom, 2009).

Dike (2013) distinguishes four building blocks in energy demand security: export dependence, transaction costs, economic dependence, and the monopsony factor (Figure 2.11). Export dependence is the value of energy exports in the total exports value. The larger this ratio, the higher demand security risks. The monopsony factor explains the share of imports of individual consumer (importing) nation in the country's total energy exports. The larger the ratio, the higher the monopsony power over an exporter and higher the demand risks. Transaction costs correspond to transport and infrastructural disruptions in energy export. The larger the distance between the exporter and the importer, the higher the energy demand risk. Similarly, the more countries are involved in exported energy transit, the higher the energy demand risk. Economic dependence is described through the contribution of exports to the producer's GDP. The more dependent the producing nation is on export in its GDP, the higher the demand security risks.

Summing up Dike's (2013) approach to demand security, it is worth highlighting that it is one of the first attempts to assess the phenomenon for OPEC countries. His conceptual framework serves the quantitative part of the study but also corresponds to the above-mentioned definitions of demand security. These general resemblance is visible especially in export and economic dependence, as it refers to an idea of stable export revenues and their importance for producing nations' budgets. Transaction costs correspond to transit countries' dependence. All of that assessed again in categories of risks. Dike's concept of energy demand security is a mix of "risk and tools framework", the IEA-like concept of physical supply and demand shocks.

Another interesting concept describing indirectly export demand security is Nowrouzi's idea (Nowrouzi et al., 2019). Even though in that work there is no exact definition of demand security, the authors perceive the phenomenon through the lens of associated risks. They focus on the case of Iran and, using portfolio theory, they assess the risks of gas export. Challenges are divided into two groups: systematic risks and non-systematic risks, which together form the total risk in the market (Figure 2.12).

Systematic risks are unpredictable risks pertaining to the whole market, which cannot be diversified. Sometimes this type of risk is called market risk or market volatility in portfolio theory. Non-systematic risks include specific risks arising due to special circumstances such as political instability of the importing/exporting nation. This type of risk can be addressed and compensated by, for instance, diversifying suppliers (switching to other countries). Nowrouzi et al. (2019) argue that any energy price changes and risk of cutting energy supplies can be regarded as non-systematic risks. In this sense, both supply and demand security risks might be considered as diversifiable. The authors take into consideration non-systematic

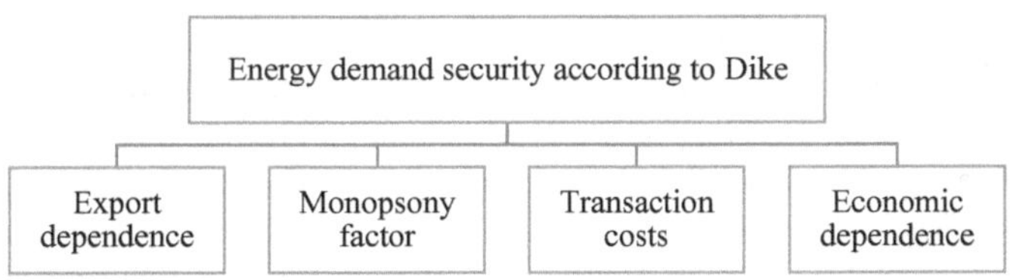

Figure 2.11 Energy demand security according to Dike.

Source: Compiled by the author based on Dike (2013).

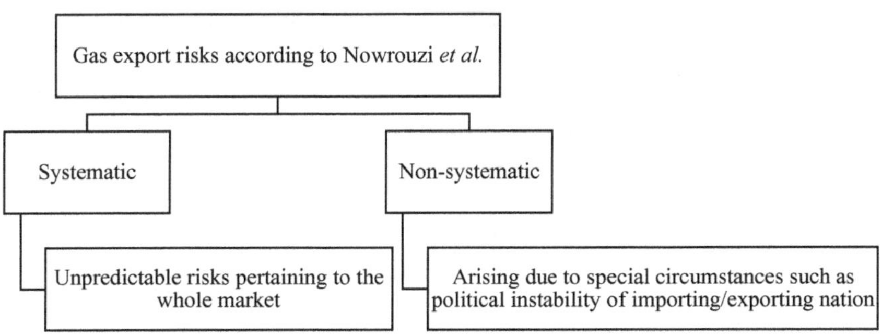

Figure 2.12 Gas export risks according to Nowrouzi et al.

Source: Compiled by the author based on Nowrouzi et al. (2019).

risks such as diversity of gas-importing countries, political risk of gas-importing nations, and the level of dependency risk of countries importing gas from Iran. They build a model for non-systematic risks which includes geopolitical factors, and so-called dependency risk consisting of adaptation capacity and system sensitivity (Figure 2.13). The higher the geopolitical and dependency risks, the higher is the non-systematic risk. The higher the system sensitivity and the lower the adaptation capacity, the higher the dependency risk. To sum up, the higher the geopolitical and dependency risks due to price changes and energy import reduction, the higher the non-systematic risk for gas export revenues.

Geopolitical factors refer to gas export volumes, export portfolio diversity, and political risk of the importing nation. The higher the export volumes, or the lower the export diversity, and the higher the political instability of importer, the greater geopolitical risks are involved. The higher the geopolitical risks to price changes and import volume reduction, the higher the risk the system faces.

Adaptation capacity reflects the ability of the system to adapt to changes such as price shock or disruption in natural gas imports. In other words, it is the system's ability to balance shock. One may expect that the higher the adaptation capacity to price changes and reduction in demand, the lower the risk the system faces. Adaptation capacity includes domestic alternative energy sources (relative to primary energy), gas supplier diversity, domestic gas production, gas availability per gas demand, energy exports (relative to primary energy). The authors do not explain the exact influence of each risk type on adaptation capacity. They only give an example of domestic gas production related to domestic gas consumption and argue that this risk shows the extent to which domestic gas production can respond to energy demand in the case of a system change. They believe that the higher the ratio of domestic gas production to domestic gas consumption, the greater the adaptation capacity of the system. In a similar manner, one may draw conclusions referring to remaining adaptation capacity risks. The higher the ratio of domestic alternative energy sources (renewables, nuclear) to primary energy, the greater the adaptation capacity of the system, as additional supply of energy smooths shocks. Similarly, the higher the diversity of gas suppliers (assuming that there are numerous companies engaged in E&P activities in the country) and gas availability, the greater the adaptation capacity. In other words, the more diversified sources of

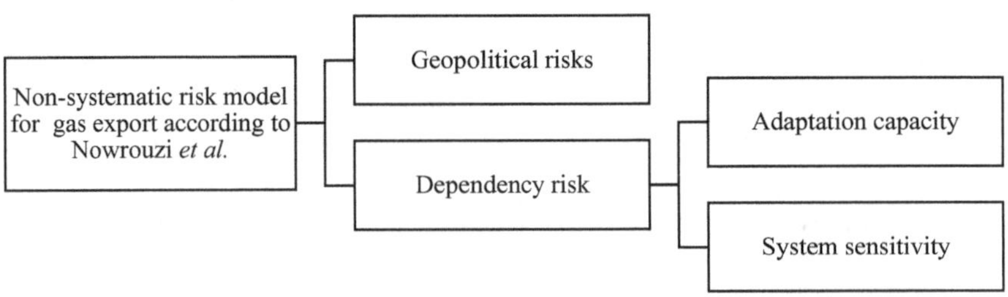

Figure 2.13 Non-systematic risk model for gas export according to Nowrouzi et al.

Source: Compiled by the author based on Nowrouzi et al. (2019).

supply of exported fuels, the greater the chance that the system will balance the shock. Finally, concluding on energy export and its relation to adaptation capacity remains problematic. Since the authors do not offer any clear explanation, one may expect the same direction of changes as in the examples given above. However, it is not clear how high a ratio of energy exports related to primary energy could improve the system's adaptation capacity. One may expect that the higher the ratio, the lower the ability of the system to balance the shock, as huge reliance on foreign trade makes the system prone to external shocks. One possible explanation behind the positive relationship between energy exports/primary energy and adaptation capacity is that the authors considered a variety of exported products, ranging from commodities (such as crude oil, natural gas, coal) to their processed forms (such as petrochemical products). In such a situation, one may expect that the higher the diversity of exported products relative to primary energy, the greater adaptation capacity, as the system is not reliant on a single export product.

System sensitivity depicts the degree to which changes in the external environment influence natural gas supply, such as price changes and import volume reduction. The authors expect that the higher the system's sensitivity to price changes and reduction in energy imports, the greater the risk the system faces. System sensitivity includes gas consumption in relation to primary energy, energy intensity (use of energy per unit of GDP), GDP per capita, CO_2 intensity (amount of emissions per unit of energy used) and gas imports related to gas demand. As with adaptation capacity, the authors explain only a chosen variable's influence on system sensitivity. They show it using the example of energy intensity. The authors argue that the higher energy intensity, the greater the system's sensitivity, as an inefficient energy structure increases the dependency risk. In a similar manner, one may draw conclusions referring to remaining risks. The higher the ratio of gas consumption to primary energy, the higher the system's sensitivity, as less of the resource can be directed for export. The higher the ratio of gas imports to gas demand and CO_2 intensity, the greater the sensitivity of the system, as high import reliance and carbon-burdened economy decrease the capability to manage external shocks. Finally, drawing conclusions on GDP per capita and its relation to system sensitivity remains problematic. Since the authors do not provide any clear explanation, one may expect the same direction of changes as in the examples given above. However, it is not clear how a high GDP per capita increases the system's sensitivity or, in other words, its ability to cope with external shocks. One may expect that the higher the GDP, the lower the system's sensitivity, as wealthier economies can possibly withstand any price shocks and import volume decreases better than others. Still, since no argumentation is provided by the authors, the last conclusion remains only an assumption.

To sum up the approach of Nowrouzi et al. (2019), it is worth mentioning that it offers a systemized framework for risk classification. Dividing it into systematic and non-systematic risks according to the portfolio theory brings two conclusions. First, since systematic risks cannot be mitigated, there is no policy option that would contain them. Thus, any efforts within these types of risks might be aimed at their careful observation and analysis. Secondly, non-systematic risks can be mitigated by certain economic and policy measures. These might be aimed at geographical diversification of the energy export structure, limiting the number of politically instable importers, and improving the domestic energy system's capacity to contain any possible shocks. Interestingly, the above-mentioned proposals correspond to the tools used to enhance the energy security of exporters. That is why the approach taken by Nowrouzi et al.'s fits into the "risk and tools framework" described above.

The study by Nowrouzi et al. (2019) is designed for empirical purposes and, as such, it offers relatively limited theoretical explanations. It would have been even more useful if the authors had described or, at least listed, a selection of systematic risks. One may expect that such systematic risks include also shocks in the global economy, such as the COVID pandemic, shock-induced global economic slowdown, global financial crises, global energy price changes, global policy regulations aimed at decarbonizing economies, and reducing CO_2 emissions. As is visible, these systematic risks might fit into the demand security risk classifications prepared by Romanova (2013) or Bollino and Galkin (2021). This may prove that the analysis on demand security risks, even though differently named, evolves around the same categories of threats for exporters.

The study by Nowrouzi et al. (2019) focuses on the case of Iranian gas exports, while Boussena and Locatelli (2013) put Russian gas exports in the centre of the analysis. These authors compare perspectives of the supply security of the EU and demand security of Russia. They argue that while the EU takes into account the "special Russian risk" among its supply security concerns, Russia tries to secure its long-term investments through European outlets in its demand security quest.[21] Boussena and Locatelli highlight that demand security for Russia in the European markets is inherently connected with market liberalization, which creates a risk for suppliers. They argue that it generates uncertainty about the future natural gas demand hindering investment processes. The authors list aspects which threaten demand security from the supplier point of view (here, Russia). These include climate policy and uncertainties related to contractual arrangements. Climate policy increasing the use of renewable resources reduces natural gas demand, decreasing volumes of imported fuels at the same time. Ambiguities referring to contractual arrangements include contract duration, take-or-pay clauses and price indexation schemes. From the point of view of the exporter, long-term contracts are crucial for investment pay-offs, while from the point of view of the importer they constitute a market entry barrier for potential players. Additionally, the less flexible contract conditions are, the higher bargaining power the exporter wields and conversely, the more elastic contract clauses are, the higher the importer's bargaining power becomes. The authors argue that due to this dual and justified standpoint, demand security can complement supply security only when institutional changes are introduced both on the exporter's and the importer's side. On one hand, for the importer to satisfy security of supply, the exporter would have to comply with existing energy market regulations in importing nations and, on the other, the importer would in return have to offer access to downstream and upstream investments in importing nations. Apart from that reconciling solution for importers and exporters, Boussena and Locatelli (2013) describe demand security in terms of means and system of governance (Figure 2.14).

The ultimate goal for exporters is to ensure demand security. It can be achieved with means such as vertical integration and long-term contracts. As mentioned above, regulations in importing nations (especially in the EU) do not allow vertical integration due to the unbundling principle. However, companies find their ways to circumvent regulations by employing asset-swapping strategies. For Boussena and Locatelli (2013), these arrangements fall into the category of governance. Unlike vertical integration, long-term contracts are not forbidden by law. Contracts with take-or-pay clauses are especially interesting for exporters. As will be presented in next chapters, in the 21st century importers have been discouraged by market conditions from committing themselves to long-term contracts. Instead of that, they have more often turned towards spot contracts. For this reason, the above means available to exporters might not be introduced in every importing nation's market due to the regulations in place or prevailing market conditions.

The system of governance includes asset swapping described above, bilateral relations, state-controlled companies engaged in hydrocarbon exploration, production, and transmission, and state-controlled hydrocarbon production. Apart from bilateral relations, the remaining three aspects of the system of governance are of an economic character. Asset-swapping is a business strategy, and maintaining government control over companies and resources is a kind of economic policy that the country pursues. One may argue that state-controlled enterprises extend the country's policy interests, which is always a possibility. Bilateral relations are a purely political factor built into the system of governance that may further exporter's interests.

To sum up the approach adopted by Boussena and Locatelli (2013), one may claim that this is a country-specific analysis, as it focuses on Russia only and presents mainly demand security threats Russia faces in the European market. However, this leads again to the conclusion that energy demand security is, like supply security, a highly contextual phenomenon (Winzer, 2012).

Other literature focusing on demand security includes works by Lee (2014) and Novikau (2022). The former describes Turkmenistan's quest to diversify its export routes, while the latter is more of a theoretical investigation into demand security. Lee admits that from energy producers' perspective demand security is an applicable idea instead of supply security. The author looks at the possibilities of enhancing demand security of Turkmenistan by diversifying its sources of demand. Lee

Means	System of governance
• Vertical integration • Long-term contracts	• Asset swapping • Bilateral relations • State-controlled companies • State-controlled resources

Figure 2.14 Energy demand security of Russia according to Boussena and Locatelli.

Source: Compiled by the author based on Boussena and Locatelli (2013).

believes that diversification efforts are the way to enhance energy demand security. Additionally, it can be positively influenced by reducing exporting nations' vulnerability to economic pressure resulting from export dependence, decreasing the impact of possible import disruption, and providing opportunity for compensating lost demand. Lee does not describe the additional solutions in detail; however, one may expect that reducing the impact of high reliance of export on the producer's economy depends on diversifying the structure of GDP, avoiding possible import disruptions refers to infrastructure-related investments and compensating for lost demand relies on alternative demand sources/routes. Lee's framework for energy demand security is a descriptive way of phenomenon's explanation. The author devotes more attention to political issues connected to Turkmenistan's position in the geopolitical energy arena which are beyond the scope of this book. What may appear as the most interesting conclusion from Lee's paper is that it highlights widely recognized diversification as energy demand security tool. This again proves that energy demand security is in line with the energy supply security framework and as such should be analysed in a similar manner. Novikau supports this claim by arguing that energy demand security is a mirroring concept to energy supply security. He argues that demand security is as legitimate concept in energy security studies as the idea of supply security. He also adds a descriptive definition of energy demand security, which, according to his opinion, means ensuring the continuity of demand at fair prices or adequate demand for energy at reasonable prices. Again, physical continuity of demand and fair prices emerge in these concepts. One may assume that Novikau's energy demand security idea resembles the IEA's supply security definition. This makes it similar to the studies by Dike (2013) and Bollino and Galkin (2021).

2.2.3 Reflective discussion on conceptual approaches

Summing up theoretical considerations on energy demand security, there are a few conclusions to be made. One is of methodological importance, while the other three are of theoretical significance. Firstly, energy demand security research is embedded in the energy supply security framework. Even though it is not visible at the first glance and authors do not refer directly to that concept, they do intuitively use ideas, nomenclature, and schemes of analysis used in supply security studies. Secondly, theoretical frameworks used in demand security research refer to "risks and tools", the "4 As" approach, and the IEA-like definition. This variety of concepts, next to the results of the scope review mentioned in Chapter 1, prove that the demand security research is still at an early stage of development. The majority of research on supply security referring to similar theoretical frameworks dates back to the beginning of the 21st century. Additionally, the use of the above-mentioned ideas in demand security research is an evidence of the interdisciplinarity of the studies. The most popular definitions are those that offer greater generalizability potential. Thus, such concepts can be used by engineers, economists, lawyers, and political scientists. Thirdly, risks related to energy demand security can be categorized as systematic and non-systematic. Such an effort allows phenomena which are importer-independent to be excluded, which thus might not be addressed. Instead, specific risks call for deeper analysis and carefully designed mitigation and adaptation strategies. Fourthly, the existing literature on demand security is relatively silent on exporters' vulnerability to demand security risks. Some research effort explaining this idea is provided by Nowrouzi et al. (2019) in the form of system sensitivity and adaptation capacity measures, but no theoretical conclusions on the sources of vulnerability are presented.

One may conclude that energy demand security is a concept mirroring that of energy supply security. Energy supply security "quietly slipped into the energy lexicon without any meaningful discourse about its meaning or assumptions" (Chester, 2010) and so did demand security by "entering discourse uncritically" (Novikau, 2022). At this stage of research, demand security strongly resembles supply security (Table 2.7). The source of risks in both cases is in international trade in energy commodities; for producing nations, it is export, while for consuming countries it is import.

Export of energy resources may be associated with two types of risks for energy exporters: systematic and non-systematic risks (Table 2.8). Among those that cause the entire system to malfunction, the following can be distinguished: price fluctuations in energy markets, geopolitical stability of importing nations, and global legislation changes undermining the use of exported fuels. Price volatility negatively affecting producing nations includes both price decreases and price increases. In the short term, price drops may affect exporters economic situation, but in the long term sustained price spikes may discourage importers from the use of expensive commodities and increase the competitiveness of alternative energy sources. Geopolitical stability in the world markets is a systematic type of risk, as it affects all market players supplying energy. So does global legislation that undermines the use of exported fuels. Thus, any regulation decarbonizing economies on a global scale might be perceived as systematic risk. That is why, the regulatory framework supporting energy transition as indicated by Bellos (2018) constitutes a systematic risk.

However, some of these challenges, if referred only to the selected importing nations, might be regarded as non-systematic risks. Legislation changes in energy consumers' markets prohibiting or discouraging from the use of certain fuels, geopolitical instability of a specific consumer, and slowing energy demand due to a country's economic downturn can be treated as market-specific risks, provided that they are limited to a geographical area. Apart from that, there are other non-systematic risks including protectionism in the form of tariff and non-tariff trade

Table 2.7 Energy demand and supply security as mirroring concepts

Energy demand security	*Criterion*	*Energy supply security*
Resource export	Source of risk/challenge	Resource import
Price and physical demand	Channels of influence	Price and physical supply
Diversification	Means/tools to enhance	Diversification

Source: Compiled by the author.

Table 2.8 Energy demand systematic and non-systematic risks

Systematic energy security risks for exporters	*Non-systematic energy security risks for exporters*
Price stability, political concerns, stability of regulation (Romanova, 2013)	Taxes in importing nations, competition in export markets (Romanova, 2013)
Economic instability, macroeconomic dynamics, demand for energy, price fluctuations, legislation changes, negative macroeconomic dynamics observed on the global level, slowing demand for energy on the global level (cf. Bollino and Galkin, 2021)	Changes in legislation in energy-importing markets, physical supply disruption, protectionism in the form of tariff and non-tariff trade barriers, sanctions including export embargoes, technological/financial or investment restrictions, increasing competition from emerging exporters entering the market, buyer-related risks such as breach of contract or default but also contractual changes in existing export agreements, such as adjustment of the pricing formula forced by decisions of international arbitration communities, changes in legislation in energy-importing markets, negative macroeconomic dynamics observed on the importing nation level, slowing demand for energy on the importing nation level (cf. Bollino and Galkin, 2021)
Ground-breaking innovations changing the way the specific energy resources are used and not slowing energy demand but rather shifting that to other applications etc.	Transit risk, lack of investments

Source: Compiled by the author.

barriers, sanctions including export embargoes, technological/financial or investment restrictions, increasing competition from emerging exporters entering the market, buyer-related risks such as breach of contract or default, and taxes in importing nations or physical supply disruption. Not all of them affect market players in the same manner. For instance, changed competition in the importing market may be especially challenging for incumbent players, while trade policy measures affect all players. Trade policy measures, regardless of their form, constitute a trade barrier and hinder or withhold existing trade flows. On the other hand, buyer-related risks may affect specific or all importers. If these challenges refer to contractual changes in existing export agreements, such as adjustment of the pricing formula forced by decisions of international arbitration communities, then they relate only to specific importers. But if other consumers decide to follow suit against the exporter – buyer-related risks may affect all importers having trade ties with the exporter. This way, buyer-related risks might be extended through judiciary precedent from an individual case to all consumers of exported products. Breach of contract or the importer's default reduces the credibility of the importing nation or causes existing trade ties to cease and affects only a specific trade relationship. Taxes in importing nations may be the source of price discrimination against specific fuels or suppliers. Interestingly, physical supply disruption may be regarded as non-systematic risk, as it refers to specific trade flows and certain infrastructural connections. Stable or instable revenues for budgets, even though mentioned by Romanova (2013) as a threat, are rather an effect of threats that have been realized. In this sense, budget instability is a result of threats that have not been mitigated. Taking systematic and non-systematic risks together, it is visible that the price component in energy demand security falls into the category of systematic challenges, while its another inherent dimension – physical supply disruption – falls within the non-systematic risk category. Energy prices, and specifically price-setting mechanisms in energy contracts, are subjected to global (in the case of crude oil) or regional (in the case of natural gas) price benchmarks. They follow similar worldwide trends and as such constitute a systematic risk for the global energy markets. But, as mentioned above, physical supply disruption may refer only to a specific transport, transit, or route risk which is of a local not global character.

Here arises the question of the transit risks and their influence on demand security. Even though these have been rather indirectly described above as a demand security risks, they are added to the group of non-systematic risks, as transit challenges are connected with a specific country, region, means of transport, or even pipeline route. Including transit risks among demand security challenges contradicts to some extent an idea of the Energy Charter Secretariat (2015), according to which transit security constitutes part of supply security. However, since transit is a significant section of export and import flows, it might be regarded as a common aspect of both concepts. Apart from the above risks described in the literature, both systematic and non-systematic challenges may include additional challenges. In the group of systematic risks, one may add ground-breaking innovations changing the way specific energy resources are used without slowing energy demand and instead shifting it to other applications. Such innovations are usually supported by research and development (R&D) investments. As noted by Bohi (1994), R&D in the development of "cost-effective alternative energy sources and less energy-intensive technologies may be strongest tools (over the longer term) for countering any market power exerted by energy exporters". What might be another possible non-systematic risk is the lack of investments carried out by exporters and aimed at increasing the resource base, production capacity, technological endowment, and transport potential. These aspects, similarly to R&D activities by importing nations, exhibit long-term structural consequences for exporters.

The "risk and tools" approach additionally depicts the ways in which exporters can enhance their demand security. These measures can be divided into political and economic means. Since political aspects are beyond the scope of this book, at this point they are only listed without any detailed discussion. Based on the above-mentioned literature, political means include international legislation, producers' cooperation, dialogue between consumers and producers (or their bilateral relations), activities aimed at improving producers' reputation, integration with importing nations. This group can be expanded by adding Romanova's (2013) economic tools such as efforts to correct the changes in the regulation of importing nations but also Bollino and Galkin's (2021) domestic regulatory environment aimed at boosting export capacity and competitiveness of export. It seems that regulatory aspects remain more in the policy or lobbying area, which is an important institutional framework but beyond the economic dimension.

The main economic tool behind demand security improvement is diversification, which is also a basic instrument improving supply security (Adelman, 1993). In demand security studies, diversification might be divided into three groups: transport-related, contract-related, and asset-related instruments (Figure 2.15).

Transport-related tools include export routes, means of transport, consuming countries, and transit countries. The diversification of export routes refers to using different pipeline arteries (land, offshore) or sea routes to deliver resources to consumers. The choice of the means of transport in the case of natural resources, especially hydrocarbons, is relatively limited. Both oil and gas can be carried by pipelines or tankers. Including both of these means of transport in the export portfolio further increases the flexibility of exporters to adjust to any sudden changes such as pipeline or liquification/regasification terminal malfunction or terrorist or piracy (for waterborne commodities) attacks. Exporters may also opt for greater diversity in the consuming countries' portfolio. This way, producing nations decrease their dependence on consumers, enhance their energy policy choices, and diversify

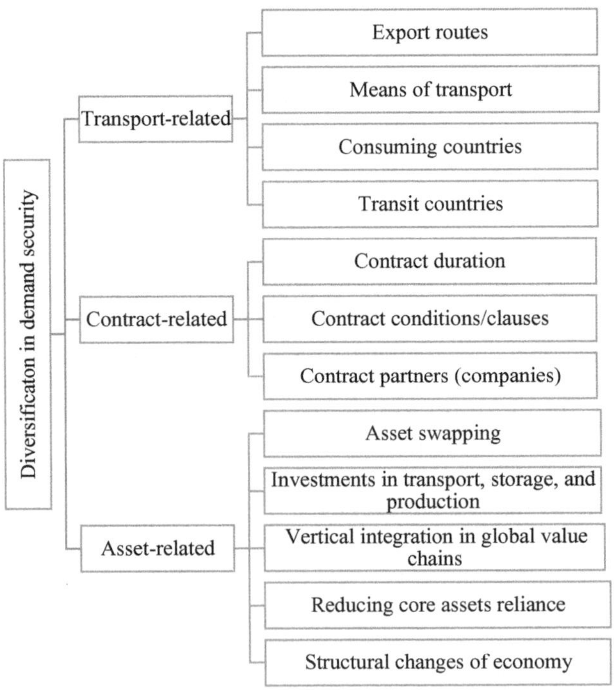

Figure 2.15 Diversification in demand security.

Source: Compiled by the author.

the geographical structure of export revenues. The diversification of transit countries works in a similar way. It decreases exporters' reliance on specific export routes and offers the possibility of optimizing transit fee burdens.

Contract-related tools refer to measures introduced in contractual arrangements with the goal to ensure demand security. These refer mainly to contract duration, contract conditions/clauses, and contract partners (companies). Even though exporters may be interested the most in having long-term contracts, it is recently visible that, especially in the LNG market, the significance of short-term, spot sales increases. Combining a variety of long- and short-term commitments provides exporters with greater flexibility in achieving profits from sudden price changes (especially price spikes). Spot sales offer instant and higher profit margins. The diversification of contract conditions and clauses refers to a variety of flexible delivery and pricing solutions integrated in sales agreements. These provisions include take-or-pay, destination/delivery and review clauses along with price-setting formulas. Exporters might be interested in including in contracts maximum possible quantities that have to be imported or paid, relatively flexible dates for contract evaluation to offset contractual uncertainty, and destination (territorial diversion) clauses that restrict possible competition of a buyer with the seller's other partners or in the seller's other markets. Diversifying contract partners pertains to companies importing commodities. Exporters might be interested in keeping arrangements with as many firms from a single country as is possible, as this increases the seller's bargaining power.

Asset-related instruments refer to ways in which exporters diversify their business (at the micro level) and economic activity (at the macro level). At the micro level, such diversification includes asset-swapping, investments in transport, storage and production, vertical integration in global value chains, and reducing core asset reliance, while at the macro level, it pertains to the economy's structural changes. Asset-swapping, next to vertical integration in global value chains, is a way to diversify the portfolio of business activity. Asset-swapping is a method used in regions, where, due to unbundling principles, integration across the value chains is not possible. Both of the methods are designed to increase control over the value chain. Vertical integration in global value chains additionally attenuates the opportunistic behaviour of contract partners (Joskow, 2003), which is of special importance in the case of demand security. Any asset diversification efforts would not be possible without cost-effective investments in energy transport, storage, and production. In the long term, these activities influence the exporter's production capacity, transmission, and stockpiling possibilities. Apart from that, exporters facing global decarbonization trends integrate their exiting asset portfolios with less carbon-intensive assets, such as renewables. This way, producers mitigate systematic risks and optimize their future profit structure. A similar influence is exerted on exporters' economies at the macro level by changes in the economic output structure. Through this effort, producing nations reduce their budget reliance on energy-exporting industries and move towards a more diverse GDP structure.

Diversification is a long-term strategy and, thus, diversification tools can be described as tools enhancing energy demand security in the long term, as all of the above-mentioned activities require time (at least a year) (Figure 2.16). However, there is also a possibility for producers to influence demand security in the short term. It can be achieved through maintaining spare production and transport capacities. Keeping a spare capacity margin allows production and transmission to be increased whenever import or price disruption happens. Within the spare capacity margin, producers may enhance their demand security in the short-term horizon. However, keeping such reserve is burdened with high investment and maintenance costs; that is why not every exporter can afford to use it.

The above synthetized approaches to demand security include various supply security approaches. However, they do not refer to the most recognized economic understanding of the phenomenon which was brought by Bohi and Toman (1996b). Based on their work on energy security externalities, a similar approach can be applied to demand security externalities (Figure 2.17) (for more on supply security externalities, see Nyga-Łukaszewska, 2020b). However, it is essential to make reservation that just as energy supply security create pecuniary externalities, so can energy demand security. Thus, the below depicted set of external effects is of theoretical nature and distinguishing between their technological or pecuniary character would require additional empirical studies similar to those of Bohi and Toman (1996b). Thus, this book's author suggests such research effort as an interesting future research step. Yet, in this book, due to its goal, such empirical

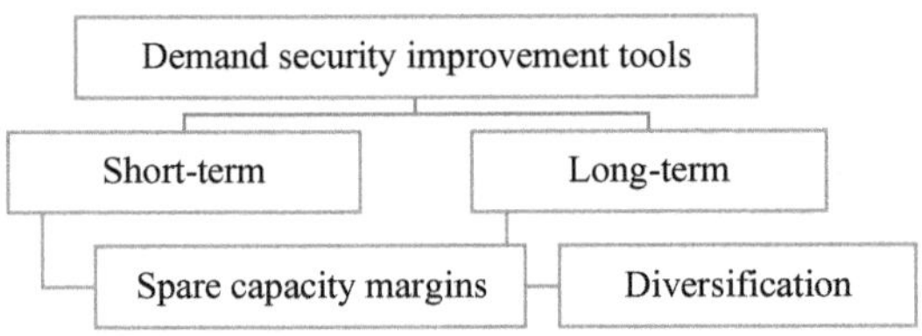

Figure 2.16 Demand security improvement tools according to time perspective.

Source: Compiled by the author.

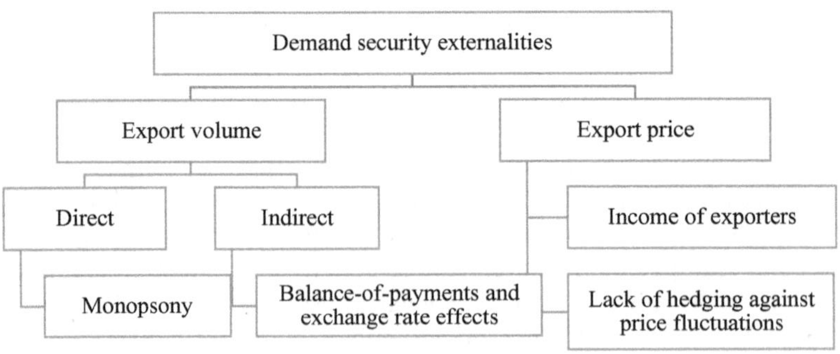

Figure 2.17 Demand security externalities.

Source: Compiled by the author.

study goes beyond the assumed framework. The rationale behind describing demand security in the externalities' perspective in this book include the novelty of such an approach and the relevance of the phenomenon for public policy. Since the former has already been depicted in this book with the use of theoretical analysis of energy demand security phenomenon, the latter requires additional explanation. Pecuniary (monetary) externalities (Scitovsky, 1954) affect markets differently than technological (so-called real) ones. Monetary external costs are influencing prices of products or production factors, while real – result in inefficient resources' allocation. That is why pecuniary externalities are signal of market efficiency and technological – market failure. Regardless of that public policies are designed to equally compensate for both – as Holcombe and Sobel (2001) convince. Thus, from the public policy point of view, society should be protected from adverse consequences of various externalities. Taking into consideration meaningful role of energy policy in the public policy of exporting nations driven by key position of energy exports' in budgetary incomes, one may expect that analysing options of externalities' internalization (even pecuniary ones) in these countries might be an important research direction, which brings theory closer to economic practice.

Demand security externalities can be broken down into export volume and export price externalities. The former can be further divided into direct and indirect externalities. Export volume externalities can be observed in the long and medium terms, while export price externalities can be treated as short-term price shock adjustments.

Direct externalities, in the case of exporters, may refer to the market power that the importer can exercise against an exporter. It refers to the ability to alter market prices of energy resources through changes in the quantities of purchased commodities. In the case of exporters, such a situation can be described as monopsony. A single buyer – monopsonist – has the ability to influence the prices of products sold by exporters. Indirect externalities refer to effects related to inflation or the balance of payments.[22] However, it is relatively difficult to imagine the situation in which low energy prices can result in inflationary pressures on producing nations. In the case of importing nations, all externalities are associated with high energy costs;[23] thus, for exporting countries, externalities mainly result from low oil prices. That is why inflation as a result of rising oil prices is challenging for importing nations but will not be included in the analysis of exporting nations.[24] Our main focus is the balance of payments as an indirect energy demand externality. Low prices of exported energy have an unfavourable effect on the merchandise trade balance, which could in turn negatively affect the exchange rate of the exporter's domestic currency. In general, one may claim that the merchandise trade deficit leads to a current account deficit and balance-of-payments deficit (assuming no change in capital flows), resulting in the excess of supply of the exporter's domestic currency in foreign exchange markets and a deteriorating exchange rate of the exporter's currency. To some extent, these negative effects might be balanced by increased competitiveness of other (than energy) exported products. As the domestic currency exchange rate would depreciate, the country's exports would become more competitive. That is why, the exports' structure and share of energy commodities may determine whether and to what extent the exporter can be affected by low energy prices. Another factor influencing the exporter's terms of trade (cf. Marion and Svensson, 1986) and domestic currency exchange rate may be the structure of the country's foreign currency reserves. The more foreign currencies of importing nations the producer holds, the more active the exporter would be in fighting their depreciation (Krugman, 1983), but one cannot expect this to happen to the detriment of domestic currency. That is why, the exact result would depend on the importers' portfolio and the currencies in which energy is bilaterally traded (usually EUR, USD).

Export price externalities are short-term externalities associated with adjustment to rapid fluctuations in prices. Their effects may be visible for exporting nations in two ways. First, through reduced national income, and second, as a result of lack of hedging strategies against price fluctuations. The first type of price externalities may be observed when decreased prices reduce export revenues and as a result contribute to decline in potential national income. Bohi and Toman (1996b) admit that even though they treat reduced national income as an externality, it is not an externality *per se*. They add that a possible loss in national income is an externality only to the extent that wealth transfer is exacerbated by existing market failures.[25] The second type of price externalities refers to the private sector and its efforts to hedge against energy price volatility. With exporting nations, this might pertain to companies involved in the production, exploration, and transportation of energy but also to firms supplying the energy industry with services, goods, and technologies. For exporter, the hedging strategy might include keeping physical inventories, maintaining excess production capacity, and conducting financial transactions securing against future energy price drops. Energy price adjustments may vary from one producing region to another. That is why their character is relatively local. These costs depend on the size of price changes and volume of energy produced. However, macroeconomic costs can also be observed on the country scale in the form of GDP curtailment. Energy shocks induced by exported energy price drops can effect real and potential GDP. Assuming that all production factors are fully employed in the economy, an energy price decrease would negatively influence real GDP. In exporting nations, this can be seen in the reduction of output of energy-exporting and producing industries as well as all service and goods providers supplying energy-exporting industries, combined with a decrease in export revenues. A decline in potential GDP may be (assuming full employment of all production factors), as suggested by Bohi and Toman, treated as a loss in the producer surplus in a partial equilibrium model of energy markets.

Externalities are inherently connected with internalization possibilities (Stiglitz and Rosengard, 2015). Bohi and Toman (1996b) provide a selection of internalization possibilities for supply security externalities. Extending that approach to energy demand security externalities, one may think of the following set of internalization options (Figure 2.18): financial mechanisms that guarantee long-term profits from energy exports, such as sovereign wealth funds (SWFs), hedging strategies against energy price fluctuations (inventories, excess in production capacity,

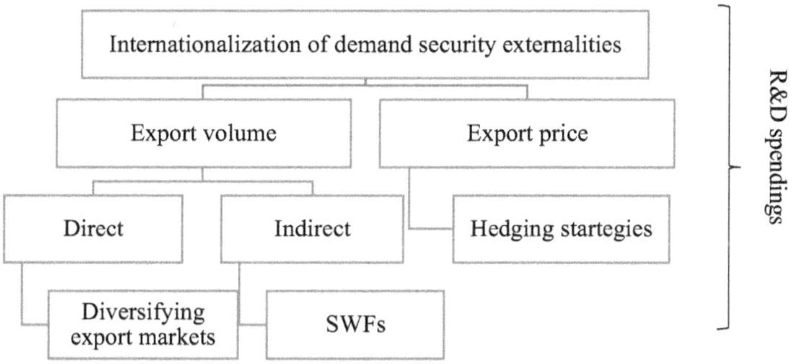

Figure 2.18 Demand security externalities internalization.

Source: Compiled by the author.

energy-based financial instruments), and R&D spendings aimed at increasing the variety of applications of existing energy sources and diversifying export markets. SWFs and export market diversity address indirect and direct export volume externalities, while hedging strategies deal with export price volatility. R&D spending may be regarded as a type of an "umbrella" type of internalization strategy because they address export volume and price externalities. However, there is additional layer of the analysis of R&D spendings. They constitute positive externality in case of energy security (cf: Bohi and Toman, 1996b), but at the same time create further externalities themselves. Even though Bohi and Toman (1996b) focus on energy supply security, they deliver the argument suitable for energy demand security discussion. The authors convince that R&D aimed at cost-effective, alternative energy sources and energy-saving technologies can significantly reduce market power of exporters in the long-term perspective. That is why R&D in energy sector has double meaning – as an effect of energy security externalities and as a cause for further externalities.

To sum up, energy demand security is still a relatively novel research field. Its analysis relies on lessons from supply security studies, including the most commonly used concepts of the "4 As" framework, resource (here) export dependency, and risk analysis approach. The contemporary demand security studies overlook, however, the perspective of energy security externalities, and possibilities of their internalization. While recognizing that is it not the latest research perspective on energy security, its achievements might become useful for the explanation and clarification of the economic approach to demand security.

2.3 Methods of assessing energy demand security

Analysis of energy demand security measures is not that popular as in the case of energy supply security. In the group of measures analysing demand security, one can distinguish sets of simple measures presented by Romanova (2013), complex indices such as the Risky Energy Export Demand Index (REED) delivered by Dike

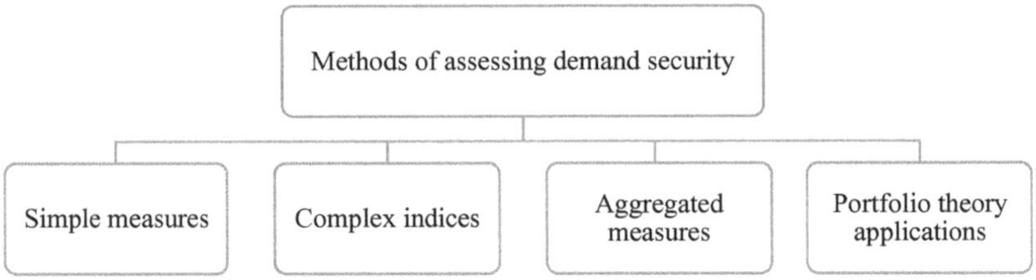

Figure 2.19 Methods of assessing demand security.

Source: Compiled by the author.

(2013), or aggregated measures such as those presented by Karatayev and Hall (2020), Ye et al. (2021), and methods relying on the portfolio theory provided by Bollino and Galkin (2021) and Nowrouzi et al. (2019) (Figure 2.19).

2.3.1 Simple measures

Since the description of Romanova's (2013) and Karatayev and Hall's (2020) energy demand security definition in previous chapters inherently also included a presentation of simple metrics used to assess the phenomenon, at this point only a reflective discussion on their applicability will be presented. For the clarity of the investigation, it is worth highlighting that Karatayev and Hall's approach is mentioned at this point and later in the aggregated measures' section as authors provide a set of simple indicators aggregated statistically.

Romanova (2013) embeds a few indicators in the demand security definition for assessing the phenomenon. They include both measurable categories, such as fuel storage capacity, the level of spare production capacity (energy extraction/processing), securing the sale of commodities with long-term contracts, controlling raw material transport routes, diversifying markets and export products, as well as immeasurable ones, e.g., counteracting legislative changes in raw material-importing countries which are negative from the exporter's point of view. At the same time, these are instruments that the supplier can use to ensure its energy security.

When assessing the possibilities of exporters to apply the above-described instruments to ensure demand security, it can be noticed that their use is not always possible or profitable. It is relatively easy for an exporter to ensure their security by concluding long-term contracts with "take-or-pay" clauses, which oblige the importer to pay for the unused quantity of the resource. This is also the case with the diversification of markets and export products. Exporters, wishing to reduce the risk related to the concentration of operations in a selected geographic market or in the oil and gas industry, invest in alternative regions of the world or other market segments, including energy. Such a strategy can be observed, *inter alia*, in the case of Russian or Algerian companies. In search for alternatives to gas supplies to European markets, the Russians turned to Asian markets. In turn, Algeria's

Sonatrach invested in renewable energy sources to diversify its business portfolio (Romanova, 2013). As an example from markets other than energy, Romanova (2013) mentions investments of oil and gas-based sovereign wealth funds in financial markets. The classification of sovereign wealth fund (SWF) investments under the category of alternative forms of investment seems debatable, as the ultimate goal of SWFs is to stabilize revenues from oil and gas exports over time, and not to reduce the risk of the domestic energy industry.

The above-mentioned energy storage capacity and spare capacity margins also pose several risks as a demand security measurement method. Firstly, they can be useful only in short periods (days, months) of price or demand fluctuations. Secondly, they constitute the exporter's additional investment cost which makes future investments less profitable. Thus, there is doubt about how they can be assessed from the longer time perspective along with discounted future cash flows.

On the other hand, while the control of energy export routes by exporters is effective, it is rather difficult to achieve. It is effective, as it prevents parties other than the exporters from using the transmission infrastructure. Nevertheless, it turns out to be difficult to apply due to the progressive liberalization of energy markets (e.g., in Europe) and the obligatory third-party access to the existing infrastructure. One example of seeking to maintain control over the routes for transporting raw materials is Russia's strategy, which, even in the WTO accession negotiations, refused other suppliers the right to access its gas pipelines. Thus, this method may be difficult to apply in the assessment of energy demand security of exporters supplying, among others, European customers.

Most of the above-mentioned methods of assessing the energy security of suppliers is relatively easy to observe and evaluate at the very first glance. Gas or oil storage facilities have a specific capacity, and the capacity reserve is a measurable value, similar to SWF investments or involvement in new market segments. Most of this information is reported by listed companies in their reports submitted to regulators. However, extending the analysis to a longer time horizon or discounting for future cash flows make the estimation more complicated. Still, recognizing these obstacles is a first step towards creating more comprehensive demand security measures.

2.3.2 Complex indices

Dike (2013) presented a comprehensive approach enabling a quantitative estimation of the energy security of exporters. Using the example of the OPEC countries, Dike quantified the security of demand for the cartel members separately for the oil and natural gas markets. In order to do this, he created the REED index (Risky Energy Export Demand). In terms of methodology, the construction of the index corresponds to similar measures assessing the security of energy supply for importers such as the REES (Risky External Energy Security) and CERE (Contribution to EU Risk Exposure) indicators prepared by Le Coq and Paltseva (2008). REED is a combination of the REES and CERE approaches including such measures as dependence on energy exports, the importer's market power, transaction costs, or the share of exported fuel in the exporter's GDP.

$$REED = \left\{ \left[\left(\frac{Vex_i^{x+y}}{Vex_i^{\text{total}}} \right) \times \left(\frac{Qim_{a,\, b,\, c,\, ..z}}{Qex_{OPEC}} \right)^2 \times D \times \left(\frac{Vex_i^{x+y}}{GDP_i} \right) \right] \right\} \qquad (1)$$

where:

Vex_i^{x+y} – value of the country's oil and natural gas exports *i* (in Dike's research, it was an OPEC member state),

Vex_i^{total} – total export value of country *i*,

$Qim_{a,\, b,\, c,\, \ldots z}$ – value of countries' *a*, *b*, *c*, …, *z* oil and natural gas imports from country *i*,

Qex_{OPEC} – value of oil and natural gas exports of OPEC countries,

D – transaction costs (for *distance*),

Vex_i^{x+y} – value of oil and natural gas exports of country *i*,

GDP_i – GDP of country *i*,

$$D = \begin{cases} 1, \text{ if distance between captials of importing exporting nations } \leq 1{,}500 \text{ km} \\ 2, \text{ if distance between captials of importing exporting nations } \leq 4{,}000 \text{ km} \\ 3, \text{ if distance between captials of importing exporting nations } > 4{,}000 \text{ km} \end{cases}$$

The first of the components of the REED index is the share of revenues from oil and gas exports in the total value of a country's (exporter's) exports. The importer's market power is presented by analysing the possibility of a monopsony. It is assessed by calculating an index which is the sum of the squares of the shares of individual importers in the total oil and gas exports from OPEC countries. The measure constructed this way refers to the classic form of the Herfindahl-Hirschman Index. The third component of the REED measure consists of transaction costs, which are assessed in relation to the possibility of supply disruption. Dike (2013) confirmed, citing Le Coq and Paltseva (2008), that the greater the distance between the capitals of an exporter and an importer, the higher the risk of supply disruptions. Dike argues that the risk increases with the number of borders that are crossed during energy transport. Therefore, he recognizes that the risk of an increase in transaction costs arises when the said distance becomes greater than 1,500 km. Otherwise, transaction costs will not increase. The limit of 1,500 km is the range of trade between European countries. As Le Coq and Paltseva suggested, within the EU the risk of energy supply interruption is the lowest. Along with moving away from the borders of the Community, the risk grows, although it is of a non-linear nature. Le Coq and Paltseva balanced distance in their REES index with the political stability of the supplier. This approach was based on the assumption that even export from countries far away from the EU may carry a low risk of supply disruption if the exporting country is politically stable. The REED index, contrary to the REES and CERE measures, does not assess the political stability of the importer or transit countries. It may be argued, on the one hand, that the less politically stable an importer is, the higher the risk of his insolvency; on the other hand, the less politically stable the transit countries are, the greater the chance of supply disruption. It also seems that the political stability of the transit countries is of equal importance to the importers. The last component of the REED index is that reflecting the importance of oil and gas export from the perspective of a country's GDP. The higher the values of the REED index, the greater the risk to the exporter's energy security.

2.3.3 Aggregated measures

Aggregated measures include methods assessing demand security with the use of normalization procedures, decision-making tools (such as the analytical hierarchy process) or statistical methods aimed at reducing the dimensionality of large data sets to find strong patterns (such as the principal component analysis). In all of these methods, the authors rely on simple indicators which are then transformed statistically into larger aggregated measures.

Karatayev and Hall (2020), similarly to Romanova (2013), presented simple measures broken down into three categories: resources and dependency, intensity and sustainability, and cost and poverty. All the metrics used to construct the above categories are measurable and relatively easily accessible in various international databases. For example, reserves of resources (in physical units) from the first category, energy use per capita (USD per kg oil equivalent) from the second dimension, and energy poverty rates (percentage of population having no or little access to electricity) in the third category can be accessed through either the World Bank database, the International Energy Agency statistics, or the Eurostat database – depending on the geographical scope of the analysis. This way Karatayev and Hall's approach offers high applicability. The authors suggest that for international comparisons, the three categories described above should be normalized. To do that, they applied the *Z*-score approach which had been used in a number of previous energy supply security studies (e.g., Brown and Sovacool, 2007; Brown et al., 2014). This method of normalization treats simple metrics included in the measurement as diverse units and turns them into those resulting in a dimensionless quantity that indicates how many standard deviations a particular analysed unit (e.g., country) is below or above the assumed benchmark level (e.g., for an analysed group of countries) (Lobova et al., 2019). *Z*-score is calculated for every indicator and every data point included in the analysis. It may take the following form:

$$Z-\text{scored}_x = \frac{\text{Absolute value}_x - \text{Mean value}_x}{\text{Standard deviation}_x} \quad (2)$$

where:

$Z-\text{scored}_x$ – is the normalized value of indicator x at a certain data point,
Absolute value_x – is the absolute value of indicator x at a certain data point,

Mean value_x – is the mean value of indicator x at a certain data point,
Standard deviation_x – is the standard deviation of indicator x at a certain data point.

Obtained Z-scores are then summed for individual years, with an equal weight given to each indicator and a total energy security score provided for each analysed unit (e.g., country) at every data point (e.g., in each year). As Obadi and Korcek (2020) suggest, imposing Z-score normalization makes it possible to distinguish between "common cause" variation (when all countries experience similar shifts) and "special cause" variation (when a country's actions and situations result in a distinct change in energy security). However, the Z-score method of normalizing indicator values has also its weaknesses. Karatayev and Hall (2020) see these limitations and highlight that the Z-score method does not provide information on the relative importance of each indicator. That is why they suggest applying the analytical hierarchy process (AHP) to order and rank each indicator in a quantitative and qualitative manner. This methodology has already been used in supply security studies (Ren and Sovacool, 2015) for the natural gas market (Madzarevic et al., 2018). Possibly another way of objective assessment of individual indicators is offered by the principal component analysis (PCA) used in supply security studies by Radovanovic, Filipovic, and Pavlovic (2017) or Erahman et al. (2016) or Li, Shi, and Yao (2016). Wang and Zhou (2017) go even beyond that and develop a new evaluation technique based on subjective and objective weight allocation methods (SOWA).

Ye et al. (2021) presented another composite index assessing demand security called Natural Gas Security Index (NGSI). This measure employs, in a conceptual manner, similarly to Dike (2013), the supply security perspective captured by the "4 As" approach depicted earlier in this book. The NGSI looks at the "4 As" idea in a quantitative manner but also exhibits how well countries manage trade-offs among availability, accessibility, acceptability, and affordability of energy. Since all indicators in each of the four dimensions have been depicted in the theoretical part, at this point an explanation and discussion is offered with a methodological approach. In the first step of the procedure, similarly to Karatayev and Hall (2020), the indicators are normalized. The authors use the min-max normalization method, arguing that it is more intuitive and offers all normalized data as positive numbers. The formula takes the following form:

$$Z_{ic} = \frac{\text{Max}\left(X_i\right) - X_{ic}}{\text{Max}\left(X_i\right) - \text{Min}\left(X_i\right)} \tag{3}$$

where:

Z_{ic} – is the standardized result of indicator i for country c, calculated according to the mean and standard deviation of a sample of n countries,
X_{ic} – raw data of indicator i for country c,
$\text{Max}\left(X_i\right)$ – maximum of X_i,
$\text{Min}\left(X_i\right)$ – minimum of X_i.

This formula already accounts for the possibility of negative indicators in the net import/export diversification, annual median $PM_{2.5}$ concentration, per capita energy-related CO_2 emissions, etc.

The second step of the procedure includes two stages. In the first stage, relevant indicators (out of the analysed group) are identified, and in the second one a weighting methodology is introduced. The selection of indicators is performed with the use of the Delphi method, which is followed by designing a questionnaire in which experts assess the relative importance of the indicators. Thereafter, data is analysed through the AHP procedure. Finally, the NGSI takes the following form:

$$NGSI_c = \sum_{j}^{n} W_i \times Z_{ic} \quad (4)$$

where:

$NGSI_c$ – Natural Gas Security Index for country c,
W_i – weight of indicator i,
Z_{ic} – the standardized result of indicator i for country c, calculated according to the mean and standard deviation of a sample of n countries,
n – number of analysed countries.

2.3.4 *Portfolio theory applications*

The portfolio theory approach, just like the method depicted above, has also been used in estimating energy supply security. Portfolio theory was introduced, for the first time in economics, in 1952 by Markowitz (1952) in finance to assess a portfolio of assets with a maximized expected return for a given level of risk. According to the theory, the rate of return and risk should not be estimated individually for each asset but with reference to its contribution to the whole portfolio's expected return and risk. In energy research, the most popular use of the portfolio theory is associated with the electricity generation mix (Awerbuch, 2006; Awerbuch et al., 2006; Bazilian and Roques, 2008) where it is more convenient to optimize portfolio-generating costs as opposed to the portfolio return. That is why, the expected portfolio-generating cost is weighted against the average of the risks of the individual technology costs (Awerbuch and Yang, 2007). In energy security studies, portfolio theory has been applied to estimate the portfolio of imported oil (Bigerna, Bollino, and Galkin, 2020) considering the quantity of oil imports and the risk associated with this quantity. This is a novel approach since the majority of studies on supply security refer to physical supply, whereas Bigerna, Bollino, and Galkin (2020) combine the supply approach with risk. The results of the study prove that energy security of an individual importer should be analysed from the perspective of the structure of its import portfolio instead of analysing the risks associated with suppliers, import routes, or potential disruptions. The authors suggest that increasing the share of oil imports even from the most reliable and stable suppliers could be detrimental to the overall import portfolio.

In demand security studies, the portfolio approach was used by Nowrouzi et al. (2019) and Bollino and Galkin (2021). Nowrouzi et al. offered a definitely more comprehensive approach than Bollino and Galkin, explaining in detail every step of the analysis and its rationale. As a result of the portfolio approach, they built an index called Gas Exports Non-systematic Risk (GENSR). As highlighted in the theoretical part, Nowrouzi et al. focused on non-systematic risks such as geopolitical risk and import dependency on natural gas (Figure 2.20).

The Geopolitical Index combines the political risk indicator for selected gas importers and the Herfindahl-Hirschman Index (squared share of exports to each country via different modes of transport: pipelines or LNG). The political risk indicator stems from the PRS Group indicators for political risk for countries. The Geopolitical Index takes the following form:

$$\text{Geopolitical Index}\left(GI\right) = \sum_{k}\sum_{T} P_{t,k}^{2}\left(1 - PRR_k\right) \tag{5}$$

with:

$$P_{t,k} = \frac{V_{t,k}}{V_{\text{total}}} \tag{6}$$

$$V_{\text{total}} = \sum_{t}\sum_{k} V_{t,k} \tag{7}$$

where:

Geopolitical Index $\left(GI\right)$ – is the geopolitical index of political stability for country k,
k – analysed country,
t – transmission method: pipeline, LNG,
$P_{t,k}$ – share of natural gas exports to country k based on transmission method t,
PRR_k – political risk of country k (PRS Group),
$V_{t,k}$ – volumetric gas exports of exporting nation to country N with the use of transmission method t,
V_{total} – total volumetric gas exports of exporting nation to country N.

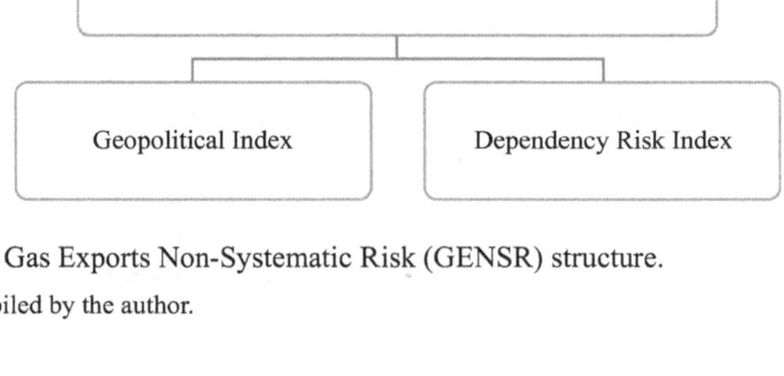

Figure 2.20 Gas Exports Non-Systematic Risk (GENSR) structure.

Source: Compiled by the author.

The Geopolitical Index ranges from 0 to 1. When the GI is getting closer to 1, the level of diversity of gas export portfolio decreases and export is dependent on one country. When the index approaches 0, export diversity is the highest. Additionally, the greater the value of PRR_k, the higher the political stability of importing nation k.

The Dependency Risk Index is built using the entropy aggregation method. The respective indicators, taken into consideration (and described in the theoretical part), have been normalized using the min-max normalization method, and then the entropy of information has been calculated. The Dependency Risk Index takes the following form:

$$\text{Dependency Risk Index } (DRI) = \sum_{j=1}^{n} w_j P_{ij} \tag{8}$$

where:

$$w_j = \frac{1 - e_j}{\sum_{j=1}^{n} (1 - e_j)} \tag{9}$$

$$P_{ij} = \frac{X_{ij}}{\sum_{i=1}^{m} (1 - e_j)} \tag{10}$$

$$e_j = \frac{-1}{Ln(m)} \sum_{i=1}^{m} P_{ij}\, Ln(P_{ij}) \tag{11}$$

$$X_{ik} = \frac{x_{ik} - \min(x_{ik})}{\max(x_{ik}) - \min(x_{ik})} \tag{12}$$

$$\text{or } X_{ik} = \frac{\max(x_{ik}) - x_{ik}}{\max(x_{ik}) - \min(x_{ik})} \tag{13}$$

X_{ik} – normalized indicators for dependence representing a either negative or positive relationship with the degree of dependency, creating the matrix of the numbers X_{ij} $(m \ x \ n)$ – taking values between 0 and 1, with 0 indicating the least dependence and 1 – the most dependence,

i – gas-importing nations,

j – indicators included in consideration,

m – number of selected countries,

n – number of selected indicators,

P_{ij} – ratio formed based on the X_{ij} matrix,

e_j – entropy of information,

w_j – weight of each calculated indicator.

Combining GI and DRI, the GENSR index takes the following form:

$$GENSR = 1 - \left(1 - (GI)\prod_{k}\left(1 - V_{\text{total},\,k}\frac{\left[1 - \frac{\sum_{t} V_{k,t} DRI_{k,t}}{V_{\text{total},k}}\right]}{V_{\text{total}}}\right)\right) \tag{14}$$

where:

$$V_{\text{total}} = \sum_{t}\sum_{k} V_{t,k}$$

$$V_{\text{total},k} = \sum_{t} V_{t,k}$$

Replacing GI with equation 5 gives GENSR in the following form:

$$GENSR = 1 - \left(1 - \left(\sum_{k}\sum_{T} P_{t,k}^{2}\left(1 - PRR_{k}\right)\right)\prod_{k=1}^{N}\left(1 - V_{\text{total},\,k}\frac{\left[1 - \frac{\sum_{t} V_{k,t} DRI_{k,t}}{V_{\text{total},k}}\right]}{V_{total}}\right)\right) \tag{15}$$

In Nowrouzi et al.'s (2019) approach, the GENSR function is supposed to minimize the risk of a portfolio with several constraining conditions. Optimization of a country's export portfolio includes constraints such as expected level of return, constraints on the capital return rate, export capacity, and export plans. The expected level of profits equals the value of gas exports minus fuel and operation and maintenance costs. It takes the following form:

$$\sum_{k}\sum_{t}\left(V_{k,t}\, P_{t}\right) - \sum_{k}\sum_{t}\left(OM_{k,t} + F_{k,t}\right) \geq E_{exp} \tag{16}$$

where:

$P_t = V_t / V_{\text{total}}$,

V_t – volumetric gas exports from Iran using transmission method t,

V_{total} – total gas exports of Iran,
$OM_{k,t}$ – operation and maintenance costs of transmission method t to country k,
$F_{k,t}$ – fuel costs of transmission method t to country k,
E_{exp} – expected export expenditures.

Constraints on the capital return rate refer to the internal rate of return as an important determinant of investments. It is assumed that the internal rate of return of an investment project for transmission to country k with transmission method t exceeds the expected internal rate of return. The formula describing this limitation takes the following form:

$$IRR_{k,t} \geq IRR_{exp} \tag{17}$$

where:

$IRR_{k,t}$ – that internal rate of return of an investment project for transmission to country k with transmission method t,
IRR_{exp} – expected internal rate of return.

Export capacity limitation refers to export programmes designed for a specific time horizon (e.g., five, ten years, etc.). It is assumed that export capacity in each importing country and transmission mode will be lower than the total export capacity. The formula describing this limitation takes the following form:

$$\sum_{k}\sum_{t} V_{k,t} \leq V_{\text{total}} \tag{18}$$

Export programme constraints are described by the exporter's commitments to exporting specific amounts of energy to selected countries. Additionally, the authors include in this limitation a set of scenarios under which the export plan is implemented. It is assumed that the sum of gas volumes exported to different countries by various modes of transport equals volumetric commitments of energy exports to a specific country. The formula describing this limitation takes the following form:

$$\sum_{t} V_{k,t} = V_{k,c} \tag{19}$$

where:

$V_{k,c}$ – export programme reflecting export commitments to country k using transmission method t.

Additionally, the scenario approach to reflect on export commitments assumes that the rate of energy exports in a specific scenario to a selected country with the use of a transmission method is greater than the sum of gas volumes exported to that country by this mode of transport. The formula describing this limitation takes the following form:

$$\sum_{t} V_{k,t} = V_{k,s} \tag{20}$$

where:

$V_{k,s}$ – ratio of energy exports in scenario s to country k with the use of transmission method t.

Including the constraints described above and minimizing the portfolio risk, GENSR will take the form of minimized objective function as follows:

$$\text{Min.}\left[1-\left(1-\left(\sum_{k}\sum_{T} P_{t,k}^{2}\left(1-PRR_{k}\right)\right)\prod_{k=1}^{N}\left(1-V_{\text{total},\,k}\,\frac{\left[1-\frac{\sum_{t} V_{k,t} DRI_{k,t}}{V_{\text{total},k}}\right]}{V_{\text{total}}}\right)\right)\right] \tag{21}$$

For minimizing the above objective function, mathematical programming models are usually used, such as GAMS. As suggested by Nowrouzi et al. (2019), the optimal portfolio model suggests the lowest risk level with expected natural gas export rates.

Bollino and Galkin (2021) also use the portfolio theory to assess demand security; however, their approach is far less transparent than that offered by Nowrouzi et al. (2019). That is why at this point it is only described as a portfolio method without any detailed investigation into the method. Bollino and Galkin (2021) apply the portfolio theory to selected Gulf Cooperation Council Countries constructing portfolios which represent trade-offs between maximizing returns (measured by energy export growth or energy export prices) and minimizing risks (captured in the form of standard deviation of return variables). They built two portfolio frontiers for selected countries. Both are characterized by returns, one on oil export volume growth and the other on oil export prices. The first frontier is measured by the historical export data for individual buyers. This portfolio shows a trade-off between export growth and concentration of importers. Lower risk is associated with higher diversification of importing nations. The second frontier is measured by the average monthly energy price received by the exporter. The portfolio shows combinations of a high expected return with high concentration on few importing nations and a low expected return on a more diversified structure of importers. These portfolios refer to two aspects of demand security: one is about minimizing the risk while securing export demand, and the other pertains to obtaining favourable price terms.

However, even though Bollino and Galkin (2021) use the portfolio approach, apart from that they offer an interesting discussion on possible simple measures that can be used to assess demand security. Since all of them refer to international trade, from the point of view of the focus of this book, it is essential to mention them at least briefly. The authors argue that the prime methods differentiating between supply and demand security are foreign trade indicators. These can refer to trade dependency, markets and supply chains, and foreign trade strategies.

The prime measure for trade dependency is balance in energy trade (usually expressed in physical units of energy – bcm, bbl, or toe, etc.) or the ratio of reliance of exporting economies on export revenues (usually measured as a ratio of export values to macroeconomic indicators such as GDP). The authors add that for energy exporters the influence of export on the current account balance or total sales (measured as value added) of the energy sector may be equally important. Apart from the above, payment history, current and potential tariff, and non-tariff trade barriers would also matter for both exporters and importers. According to Bollino and Galkin (2021), each trade relationship should be discounted by risk factors specific to energy export routes and modes of transport (pipeline versus maritime transport).

To assess the influence of markets and supply chains on demand security, Bollino and Galkin (2021) recommend using the Herfindahl-Hirschman Index (HHI) as a common measure of market concentration. This method provides information on export diversification. They suggest the index should be in the following form:[26]

$$HHI = \sum_{i=1}^{n} x_{ik}^2 \qquad (22)$$

where:

i – energy-importing nation from exporter k,
n – number of importing nations,
X_{ik} – market share of importer i from exporting nation k.

In this form, the index takes values lower than 1,500 – when the market is competitive or between 1,500 and 2,500 – when the market enjoys relative competition and values above 2,500 indicating high concentration. The authors suggest that the HHI is not a perfect measure, as it does not capture costs associated with managing additional consumers/markets which might involve additional transactional costs.

Describing foreign trade strategies, Bollino and Galkin (2021) refer to policy tools aimed at guaranteeing demand security. As they have been depicted in the theoretical section, they are omitted at this point.

To sum up, even though energy demand security is a younger concept than supply security, it has already used the latest assessment methods from the supply security research field. This includes complex or aggregated measures along with the portfolio approach. Even though all of them rely on simple indicators referring to the economy/trade structure or energy mix, one cannot escape the impression that an in-depth discussion on the sense and applicability of selected measures is missing. The approaches described above rightly rely on the achievements of supply security studies, trying to adjust and adapt them to the demand security perspective. Unfortunately, they omit a part of the reflective and, sometimes, critical debates on whether or not it is reasonable to use specific indicators (as done for supply security in, e.g., Boehringer and Bortolamedi, 2015). In addition, all the demand security measures presented above are quantitative in their nature, whereas supply security studies have already successfully combined quantitative measures with a qualitative approach applied (e.g., Sovacool and Mukherjee, 2011; Biresselioglu et al., 2017a, 2017b), even though the latter approach was criticized (Cherp, 2012). Moreover, comparing demand security to supply security studies reveals that the former lack one of the most popular approaches in measurement based on trade concentration and diversification perspectives (Neumann, 2004). Apart from basic references to the Herfindahl-Hirschman Index, there is no detailed literature on whether and how these achievements could be used in demand security assessment. This is the case although, from the point of view of the international trade structure, importers' concentration and dispersion measures should be at the centre of the demand security analysis. It can be concluded that demand security measurement studies have so far been lacking diversity in measurement methods and methodological approaches. It seems that studies on demand security have grown prematurely, ignoring detailed but rudimentary analysis on the selection and importance of measures included in complex and aggregated indicators.

2.4 Energy demand security in selected theoretical approaches (neoclassical) of international economics

The uneven geographical distribution of resources means that they are not only located but also controlled, e.g., in the course of production, by a relatively small group of countries. This way, resource-producing countries have the opportunity to exert pressure on resource-importing countries. However, it seems that the most important feature of natural resources is their depletability. This applies in particular to non-renewables, such as gold, salt, but also crude oil or hard coal. For this reason, the state policy in the field of fuel resources management significantly affects the degree of deposit depletion. Another feature related, in this book's author opinion, indirectly to natural resources is the fact that their production, consumption, and transport generate external effects. Most often they are negative and take the form of external costs. The position of the mining industry in the country's economy, in turn, is of particular importance to resource-exporting countries. This concerns both the dependence of GDP on export revenues and its concentration around a few resources. As the WTO emphasizes, this is most evident in the case of trade in energy resources (WTO, 2010). The last of the characteristics of resources mentioned by the WTO is their susceptibility to price fluctuations, which translates into investment and production decisions.

International trade in energy resources is the area of economic activity that constitutes a reference point in the concept of energy security. The remoteness of resource production centres from the places of their consumption creates the need to import them. The purchase of resources from foreign suppliers poses a number of threats to the importer's economy but, on the other hand, it translates into the exporter's dependence on income from the sale of resources.

The very concept of energy security is not clearly defined in the scientific literature. Due to the high level of interdisciplinarity of this phenomenon, researchers, having different conceptual instruments, provide different definitions of it. Presenting a single, universal, and widely used definition of energy security is a challenge. As estimated by Ang, Choong, and Ng (2015), more than 100 different definitions of the phenomenon emerged between 2001 and 2014. For the purposes of this analysis, an approach to energy security is adopted, in which the most prominent role is attributed by the International Energy Agency (IEA, 2004) to energy imports. According to the IEA, energy security in the traditional supply-side dimension is primarily related to the availability of energy at a "reasonable price" while minimizing the negative impact on the natural environment. In this view, the dominant subject of energy security is the energy-importing country. It is worth noting here the growing interest in the perspective of energy exporters, which results from dependence on exports and related revenues. Thus, demand security concept used below is a mirror reflection of supply security idea delivered by the IEA but referring to energy exporters. In the following text, the analysis focuses on the perspective of energy commodity trade in the context of selected trade theories.

2.4.1 Factor endowment theory and its extensions

International trade theory includes "a set of generalizations about the development of trade and the associated benefits" (Misala, 2003). Theoretical concepts can be divided into several groups depending on the criteria analysed.[27] The most popular way of analysing international trade theory is the chronological approach, which is related to the question of the author's affiliation with the mercantilist, classical, neoclassical, or contemporary school. The below analysis refers to that criterion by including selected neoclassical approaches taking into account the premises of trade development. This investigation refers to factor endowment theory, neo-factor proportion theories and concepts based on them relating to natural resources (Figure 2.21).[28] Specifically, this analysis refers to four key propositions, as suggested by Jones (1956), describing the properties of the standard Heckscher-Ohlin (H-O) model with two goods and two production factors. These are Heckscher-Ohlin theorem, Stolper-Samuelson, Factor-price equalization, and Rybczyński theorem. Apart from that, analysis includes also neo-factor explanations of the Leontief's paradox where natural resources play role. This does not mean, however, that other concepts would not have at least intuitive potential to apply to

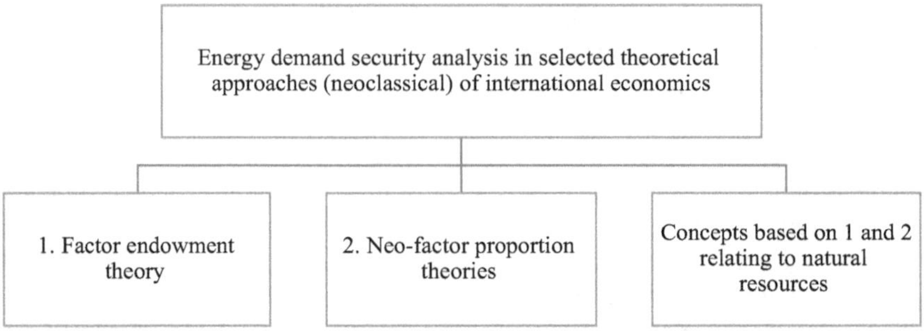

Figure 2.21 Energy demand security analysis in selected theoretical approaches (neoclassical) of international economics.

Source: Compiled by the author.

the analysis of energy security. These omitted ideas include, for instance, intra-industry trade,[29] differences in technology endowment,[30] environmental externalities influencing international trade,[31] "new" new trade theory,[32] or even the specific factors theory, closely connected to Heckscher-Ohlin theorem.[33]

The group of theories that gave rise to modern international economics includes the neoclassical resource endowment theory with its extensions. The core of the concept was independently developed by Heckscher and Ohlin and expanded by Samuelson. The factor endowment theory is also referred to as Heckscher-Ohlin model or H-O model. The theory conception date can be taken to be the earliest date of its development: 1919 (Heckscher, 1919) or 1933 (Ohlin, 1933). The formal framework for H-O model was brought by Jones (1956). It is a concept based on the classical assumptions of the Ricardian model, in which there are two countries, two commodities, two homogeneous, perfectly divisible and internationally comparable factors of production necessary to produce each of the commodities.[34] At the same time, it is assumed that the endowment of countries with factors of production is different. In addition, it is expected that one of the commodities is more labour-intensive, and the other is more capital-intensive. Both countries have identical production technology, there is perfect competition and customers have identical tastes that do not change over time. What is more, consumers maximize their utility function and have full freedom to choose different variants of goods. In addition, it is assumed that there are no tariff and non-tariff barriers in international trade, and there is excellent mobility of factors of production within the country and none between the countries. However, transport costs are not taken into account. H-O's claim is that a country abundantly endowed with a factor of production exports that good whose production requires the intensive use of that factor (e.g. Caves, Frankel, and Jones, 1993; Misala, 2003; Van Marrewijk, Ottens, and Schueller, 2012; Salvatore, 2013; Melitz, Obstfeld, and Krugman, 2018). In particular, more on H-O theory and its extensions can be found in Baldwin (2008).

As Samuelson noted, such intensive use of a factor abundant in a country can affect its price by increasing the demand for this factor of production and the associated increase in price. At the same time, a decrease in the production of a good for the production of which a rare factor is used causes a decrease in demand for this factor, leading to a decrease in its price. As a consequence of international exchange, the prices of factors of production are equalized between countries according to the Heckscher-Ohlin-Samuelson theorem (Samuelson, 1948, 1949). In addition, the movement of the prices of factors of production initiated by international trade affects the incomes of the owners of the factors of production. According to the Stolper-Samuelson (Stolper and Samuelson, 1941) theorem, there is an increase in the real income of the owners of the abundant factor and a decrease in the real income of the owners of the rare factor (e.g. Caves, Frankel, and Jones, 1993; Misala, 2003; Budnikowski, 2006; Van Marrewijk, Ottens, and Schueller, 2012; Salvatore, 2013; Melitz, Obstfeld, and Krugman, 2018). Stolper-Samuelson theorem did not escape the criticism. For instance, Davis and Mishra (2006) convince that theory is invalid as in case of Latin American, labour-abundant countries, where after trade liberalization, wage inequality rose instead of decreasing as the theorem would have suggested. Thus, authors suggest announcing "Stolper-Samuelson dead".

2.4.1.1 Rybczyński theorem and Dutch disease

The factor endowment theory is the basis of the so-called Rybczyński (1955) theorem according to which in a small country, under conditions of constant relative prices, an increase in the endowment of one factor of production, with the level of the other unchanged, leads to an increase in the good consuming primarily the factor whose endowment increases, and to a decrease in the production of a good in which a factor of production is needed whose endowment does not change.

Drawing on the Rybczyński theorem, Opp, Sonnenschein, and Tombazos (2009) built the reverse Rybczyński theorem (Figure 2.22). Model shares the same assumptions as traditional H-O: general equilibrium model with two countries (home and foreign), two goods (x and y), two production factors (capital: K and labour: L), relative factor endowments are different in two countries, one good being labour-intensive and other capital-intensive (x is labour intensive and y is capital intensive), consumer preferences are homothetic thus no goods are inferior in either country, returns to scale are constant, there are no transport costs and there is perfect competition and trade barriers do not exist. Opp, Sonnenschein, and Tombazos reject the Rybczyński's small country hypothesis. They also modify assumptions of the H-O model by introducing taste-bias towards exportable good. This assumption seems to have meaningful consequences for the model's conclusions. Homothetic preferences indicate that if the price of home-produced good falls (here: x), the home country must sacrifice more of that commodity to purchase foreign product (here: y), and if home-produced good has low elasticity of substitution in consumption, it is forced to reduce its consumption of the home and foreign product in order to maintain equilibrium. If such low elasticity of substitution is the case for both countries, which additionally prefer exportable products, then, as Opp, Sonnenschein, and Tombazos (2009, p. 140) convince, "*in a neighborhood of equilibrium*

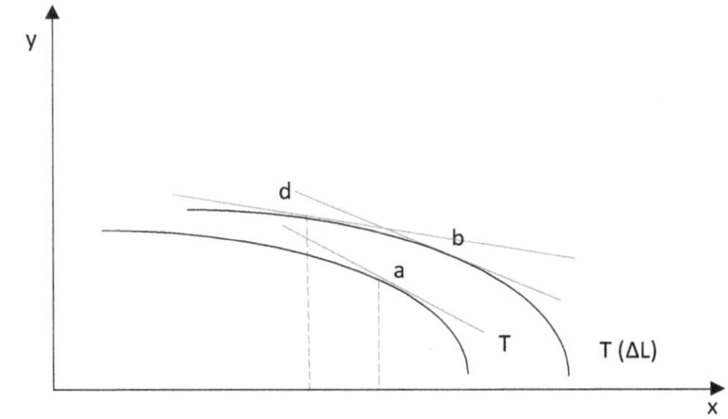

Figure 2.22 Reverse Rybczyński theorem – graphical summary.

Source: Compiled by the author based on Opp, Sonnenschein, and Tombazos (2009).

a small decrease in price reduces the home country's consumption of x more than it increases the foreign country's consumption of that commodity." Under reverse Rybczyński conditions, it is assumed that elasticity of substitution in consumption in two countries is zero. Thus, price effects in equilibrium are even stronger. These price effects are responsible for ruling out Rybczyński's result concerning the output of x and y even when preferences are homothetic. Opp, Sonnenschein, and Tombazos (2009, p. 142) claim that "*outputs, consumption, prices, and welfare change as a result of changes in the factors of production.*" Alike in Rybczyński marginal rate of transformation in the production of x and y is constant. Thus, an increase in labour (ΔL) moves production possibilities schedule from T to $T(\Delta L)$. Initial equilibrium supply (a) with T comes with profit maximization at p (price at the equilibrium level). The incremental labour increase (ΔL) increases the supply of x more than demand at p. With homothetic consumer preferences and lack of inferior goods in either country, increase in labour in the home country results in an excess supply of x at the initial equilibrium p and so the price of x must fall relative to the price of y. The reduction in price required to restore equilibrium is sufficiently large leading to a reduction in the equilibrium production of x in the home country. These movements can be observed in a simplified graphical model in Figure 2.23. Movement from a to b is considered Rybczyński effect associated with the rise in labour pool in home country, while change from b to d is a price effect (decrease) resulting from the labour increase. As Opp, Sonnenschein, and Tombazos (2009, p. 140) argue, "*'net' movement from a to d represents a decrease in the home production of the labour intensive good (x) and an increase in the production of the capital intensive commodity (y); thus 'Reverse Rybczyński'*". This means that an increase in the supply of one factor of production leads, instead of an increase in the use of a good that makes intensive use of this factor, to a reduction in the production of that commodity, and at the same time to an increase in the production of a good in the production of which this factor of production is used less intensively.

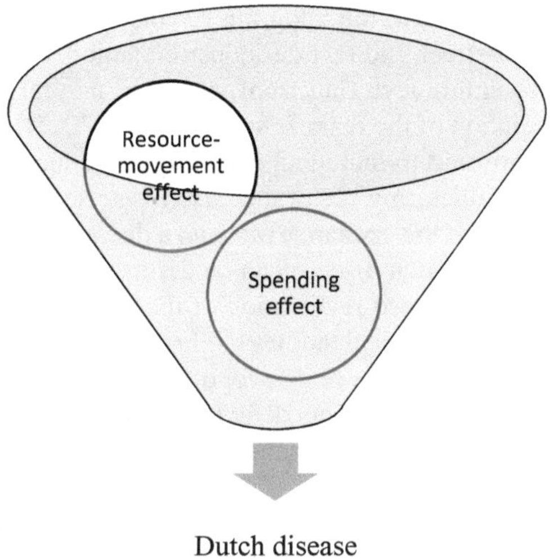

Figure 2.23 Dutch disease graphical summary.

Source: Compiled by the author based on Corden and Neary (1982).

The authors additionally prove that with the removal of the small country assumption, on the one hand, and introduction of preferences (in each country) towards an exported commodity on the other, so-called immiserizing growth may occur. If p decreases at a substantial rate as a result of the increased home endowment of L, then this can cause factor growth to be immiserizing. As the authors themselves point out, the results of their deliberations should not be expected to be of general application. The Rybczyński and Stolper-Samuelson theorems are commented up by Robinson and Torvik (2013), demonstrating that Bhagwati's (1958) immiserizing growth is the best proof of that.[35] Bhagwati's immiserizing growth model presented in 1958 describes a situation in which an economic growth occurs in a large country as a result of an increase in the production capacity of the exported good, characterized by low price elasticity of demand. As a result of the change in trade relations in international markets, the country in question is experiencing an immiserizing growth through a shift to a lower social indifference curve.

The Rybczyński (1955) theorem became the basis for explaining the phenomenon of the Dutch disease, which was first observed in the Netherlands after the discovery of the Groeningen gas field. The concept was brought for the first time in a theoretical manner by Corden and Neary in 1982[36] and has been often analysed by scientists. Interesting summaries of these developments can be found in Mien and Goujon (2022) or Nuelle and Davis (2018).

Corden and Neary (1982) noticed that an increase in production prices or resource prices causes the de-industrialization of a country. The Dutch disease leads to the de-industrialization of the economy. De-industrialization can take two forms: direct and indirect. Direct de-industrialization refers to a shift in production towards the natural resources sector, which results in factor inputs moving away from the rest of the economy to the booming sector. That is why it is sometimes called factor movement effect. Indirect de-industrialization, or the spending effect, refers to additional spending resulting from increased natural resource revenues, which leads to appreciation of the real exchange rate (WTO, 2010). The symptoms of the Dutch disease are said to include a decrease in production, real wages, and employment in the manufacturing sector, but also a deterioration in the balance of the trade, an appreciation of the exchange rate and a decrease in the country's international competitiveness. Dutch disease can be defined in the fixed exchange rate systems as "the resource-induced revaluation of the real exchange rate" (Paldam, 2013). Even though some empirical studies confirm exchange rate appreciation as a consequence of the Dutch disease (e.g., Mogotsi, 2002; Kutan and Wyzan, 2005; Mironov and Petronevich, 2015), others deny it (e.g., Pegg, 2010; Mainguy, 2011). As Cherif (2013) points out, the appreciation of the exchange rate is not always a factor accompanying the Dutch disease.[37] Cherif makes no explicit reference to the resource sector in his research and instead seeks to capture differences between countries by looking at the technological distance between them. Nor does the author make reference to income from resource exports, as was the case in the original study by Corden and Neary, and instead substitutes this category with payments to the country from abroad, which affect wage levels in both analysed countries. This way, as Cherif argues, under the conditions of monopolistic competition and growing benefits of scale, a gap emerges not only in wage levels but also in labour productivity between the analysed countries. Cherif shows that, paradoxically, a country can become rich thanks to the discovery of oil, improving the standard of living of its inhabitants, but being at the same time technologically backward in relation to countries deprived of natural resources. The situation of such an exporter deteriorates significantly when the resource deposits are depleted or their prices fall in the long term. This has a negative impact on internal consumption and the welfare of the country. Thus, the mechanism described above offers an alternative explanation of what is known as the "resource curse" or the "paradox of plenty". The resource curse is often identified with the Dutch disease. Nevertheless, the curse is associated with a lower level of economic development in countries rich in natural resources compared to those poor in resources. Mien and Goujon (2022) suggest that resource curse should be analysed as an inherently growth-reducing phenomenon and the Dutch disease as a driver of structural transformation.

Based on the work of Corden and Neary (1982), the Dutch disease can be summarized in two effects spending and resource movement (Figure 2.23). The first refers to an increased income of domestic factors from the resource booming sector and increased private and public spendings. The second effect pertains to flow of the capital and labour to booming natural resource sector. This movement is accompanied by adjustment mechanisms.

In Corden and Neary's (1982) study, increased exports of natural resources led to the appreciation of the exchange rate and they crowded out of international trade other products offered by the country concerned. Krugman (1987)[38] adds that a sector crowded out of the domestic market moves abroad and is unlikely to return to the same market in future, after favourable conditions for the development of resource exports. In Krugman's view, as well as in Sachs and Warner's (1995) opinion, only in such a situation can the term "disease" be applied to assess this phenomenon.[39] Interestingly, Collier et al. (2010) argue that the crowding-out effect does not need to happen. The authors claim that in Keynesian economy circumstances, when there are underemployed resources, additional demand can be met by putting into use resources that are already underemployed.

Robinson and Torvik (2013) argue that whether or not a resource curse will occur in a country depends on the quality of institutions. In doing so, they refer to the results of research by Mehlum, Moene, and Torvik (2006), testing how the abundance of natural resources affects economic growth determined by the quality of institutions in a country. The authors give the example of Norway, which was one of the poorest countries in Europe in 1900, and now belongs to the group of the richest countries. Economic growth in Norway is the result of the exploitation of natural resources such as wood, fish, and energy from water (hydroelectric power plants), and in recent years also from non-renewable resources such as oil and natural gas. Norway is considered one of the least corrupt countries in the world.

In the study by Mehlum, Moene, and Torvik (2006), institutions are described in the spirit of North's approach, *inter alia*, through the level of bureaucratic procedures, rule of law, or the probability of breach of contract by government. It turned out that countries with grabber-friendly institutions are more susceptible to the resource curse than those with producer-friendly institutions. The results of the study have, thus, shown that in countries with high-quality institutions, natural resources stimulate economic growth, as is the case, for example, in Botswana, Chile, or Malaysia; in countries with low-quality institutions, natural resources are hampering economic growth, such as Cameroon, Mexico, and Venezuela.

Conclusions from research by Mehlum, Moene, and Torvik (2006) are of a breakthrough nature, as previous research confirmed, in the spirit of the Dutch disease theorem, an absolutely negative impact of the abundance of natural resources on countries' economic growth. These studies include research by Krugman (1987) and Sachs and Warner (1995). However, other empirical simulations are not that conclusive about the Dutch disease effects for a booming economy. In contrast to Bruno and Sachs (1982), Sachs and Warner (1995), and Stijns (2003), who, using different methods and methodological approaches, confirmed the existence of negative effects of the resource boom for the home economy, Rambaldi, Hall, and Brown (2006) found no direct or indirect evidence for the resource curse. Hutchison (1994) is less clear, having found little evidence for the Netherlands and the UK but confirmed the Dutch disease effects for Norway in the short term. Only later did Brunstad and Dyrstad (1997) acknowledge the Dutch disease effects for Norway, but limiting them solely to factor movement and excluding spending effects. Interestingly, Alexeev and Conrad (2009) found that the resource boom indeed induces high-growth rates at the beginning of the extraction period and slower as the resource depletes. Thus, they suggest including that time perspective in empirical research on the Dutch disease phenomenon.

Empirical investigation on the resource-rich countries suspected of experiencing the Dutch disease includes cases of Azerbaijan (Hasanov, 2013), Russia (Oomes and Kalcheva, 2007; Mironov and Petronevich, 2015; Ito, 2017), or countries in the Middle East and North Africa region (Aspergis et al., 2014) as well as developed countries such as Australia (Koitsiwe and Adachi, 2015), Canada (Beine, Bos, and Coulombe, 2012), or the USA (Allcott and Keniston, 2017). In the case of Canada, it was checked (Beine, Bos, and Coulombe, 2012) whether the increase in oil prices in 2002–2008 and the related increased production of oil from oil sands in the Canadian province of Alberta led to the development of symptoms of the Dutch disease. It turned out that in that period Canada experienced an increase in nominal GDP per capita, a simultaneous appreciation of the Canadian dollar against the US dollar and a decline in the share of the manufacturing sector in the Canadian economy. Completely different symptoms appeared in the USA (Allcott and Keniston, 2017), where, as a result of the increased production of unconventional hydrocarbons, a faster increase in wages in the oil and gas industry was noticed, but this was not at the expense of the manufacturing sector, whose share in the national economy increased, and additionally was accompanied by an increase in labour productivity. Russia seems to be one of the most interesting examples in the analysis of the Dutch disease symptoms due to its economic transformation and rich energy resources. Research conducted by the International Monetary Fund (IMF) (Oomes and Kalcheva, 2007) analysed the value of the Russian rouble, the development of the manufacturing/services sector, and real wages in Russia in the late 1990s and at the beginning of the new century. It turned out that although the rouble appreciated rapidly during that period, the exchange rate was undervalued until 2002. It was also noticed that the rouble exchange rate did not rise higher than the equilibrium rate. The IMF estimated that the 1% increase in oil prices led (over the period under review) to a 0.5% appreciation of the rouble. With regard to the situation of the manufacturing sector, the regression of which could be a symbol of de-industrialization, the IMF noted that, although growth in that sector was weaker than in other sectors of the economy, and employment was declining, this could be the effect of the transformation of the Russian economy towards an economy dominated by the service sector, as at the same time the importance of the service sector has grown. Over the analysed period, real wages continued to rise in the Russian economy. To sum up, the IMF confirms that the symptoms observed in Russia point to the Dutch disease, as there has been a sharp appreciation of the rouble, the production of the manufacturing sector has decreased and there has been an increase in wages. Nevertheless, it is difficult to assess to what extent this is due to the impact of the Dutch disease, and to what extent it is the effect of the transformation of the Russian economy after the 1998 crisis.

2.4.1.2 Heckscher-Ohlin models with natural resources

In the 1970s and 1980s, the H-O model became the basis for research taking into account exhaustible natural resources. In accordance with the assumptions of the model, it still included two factors of production, two industries: resources and manufacturing, the difference being that one of the factors of production was an exhaustible natural resource. In the majority of models, it was land (apart from traditional labour) (e.g., Kemp and Suzuki, 1975; Kemp and Long, 1979). According to Osei and Lapan (1995), H-O models created in the 1970s and 1980s with a resource as one of the factors of production were a response to doubts about whether the models and theorems used so far (Rybczyński, Stolper-Samuleson, traditional H-O model) well capture the specificity of non-renewable resources.

In this strand of research, the following studies can be distinguished: Long (1974), Kemp and Suzuki (1975), Ono (1982), Vousden (1974), and Kemp and Long (1979, 1982). As emphasized by Vousden (1974), concepts taking into account natural resources were mainly of a microeconomic character (e.g., Hotelling's work) and focused mainly on determining the optimum level of resource extraction.

Vousden (1974) proposes a macroeconomic approach, in which the perspective of non-renewable natural resource is considered from the point of view of selection of the optimal way of managing the resource. The research question to which an answer is being sought in these works is what an optimum pattern of consumption, production, and export should look like in the economy. It is about, among other things, how the import and export of raw material should be shaped over time, taking into account its non-renewable nature and in the production of which of the goods (commodity/labour/capital-intensive) the country should specialize. As Vousden notes, the choice of the optimal approach from the point of view of the country depends on how the terms of trade are formed, as well as what the social indifference curve looks like for a particular country. The author distinguishes three cases, differing from each other in the relations of prices of both commodities and the combination of goods satisfying consumers. The first of these concerns a situation in which a resource-intensive product is relatively cheaper and preferred by society. The optimal choice in this case should be associated with the initial export of the resource, which should be replaced after a short time by imports and supplemented by domestic production. In the case of resource depletion, there should be a complete specialization in the production of labour-/capital-intensive goods and import of the resource.

The second scenario concerns a situation in which society prefers to consume a labour/capital-intensive good or when a resource is relatively expensive. The optimal choice in this case concerns the export of the resource due to favourable terms of trade in world markets until its stock is depleted. Then complete specialization in the production of the labour/capital-intensive good follows without international exchange of the resource. The third situation is one in which society shows no preference for any of the goods, neither resource-intensive nor labour-/capital-intensive. The optimal choice in this case is the export of part of the resource, as long as its stock is large. Then, when the resource becomes a rare factor of production, part of it is imported, and when its stock is exhausted, it is all imported.

The example of Vousden's (1974) model is one of the first H-O models with a resource as a factor of production. At the same time, it is a dynamic model, which takes into account resource endowment changing over time. With the passage of time, the assumptions in the analyses undertaken were changed, but invariably these were formalized theoretical analyses that captured the phenomenon in model form. The use of the H-O model with a resource as a factor of production did not escape criticism. Harris (1981) pointed out that the H-O model with the use of a resource in a static approach, that is, without taking into account its stock changing over time, was incorrect. At the same time, he mentioned several notable examples in this strand of analysis, including studies by Vousden (1974) and Kemp and Suzuki (1975).

2.4.1.3 Leontief's paradox and neo-factor theories

Not only did the H-O theorem, along with developments and generalizations in the form of elaborate models with resources, made direct or indirect references to energy resources. Such references can also be found in attempts to explain what is known as Leontief's paradox (Leontief, 1953),[40] which is empirical verification of the H-O theorem. In the 1940s, Leontief, applying the input-output method sought to find out whether, according to the H-O theory, capital-intensive goods prevailed in exports from the USA, a country relatively well endowed with capital. It turned out that, contrary to the H-O theorem, the USA exported labour-intensive goods, using the country's relatively rare factor of production, and imported capital-intensive goods, the production of which involved a relatively greater use of a factor abundant in the country.

Apart from the Leontief's explanation of the H-O theorem, there have been various attempts to do it. Their synthetic summary is available, for instance, in, Salvatore (2013) or Helpman (1999). Attempts at explaining this paradox included studies fitting in with the so-called neo-factor theories. As Misala (2003) notes, there are three groups of neo-factor theories. The first of them treats natural resources as the third factor of production, next to labour and capital. The second ignores natural resources but considers the complexity of the labour and capital factors. The third group comprises synthetic theories that treat natural resources as an additional factor of production, but at the same time take into account the complexity of other factors of production. Here, the representative concepts that fall within the first and last group of these theories will be discussed.

Among the three-factor theories explaining Leontief's paradox, a concept put forward by Vanek (1959) deserves special attention. He noted that the inclusion of natural resources in the analysis means that Leontief's paradox does not occur. According to Vanek's (1959) estimates, the USA, as a country relatively well endowed with capital and labour, exports capital- and labour-intensive goods, and imports resource-intensive goods, as a country relatively poorly endowed with natural resources. Gandolfo (2014) cites the example of oil production in Arab countries, the USA, and Venezuela, and argues that the same companies with the same equipment and human resources will perform better in Arab countries and Venezuela than in the USA, due to the abundance of oil deposits. Vanek claims that capital and natural resources can be treated as "strictly complementary" factors (Misala, 2003, citing Vanek, 1963). Such a thesis harmonizes with the results of research by Hillman and Bullard (1978), in which, more specifically, energy resources and capital form technologically complementary factors of production. The authors built a composite index from them, which was an approximation of the endowment of the American economy with capital and energy resources. Comparing the US labour endowment and the capital index along with energy, they concluded that the USA was a relatively labour-rich country with low energy/capital endowment. The results of these studies conducted for the US economy in 1963 and 1967 confirmed what Vanek had written about Leontief's paradox.

Another group of neo-factor theories are synthetic theories, which include multi-factor theories that take into account natural resources. This part of the concept is based on the achievements of Hufbauer and Keesing, who explained the existence of Leontief's paradox by referring to the heterogeneity of labour resources in the USA (Misala, 2003). They believed that labour as a factor of production is a composite of simple labour and human capital. Leontief's paradox was explained by the relatively abundant occurrence of human capital in the USA. In the group of multi-factor theories, apart from the complexity of labour and capital, natural resources are taken into account. Concepts that fit in with this strand of research are described by Baldwin (1971) or Hartigan (1981). Both concepts include resources in the analysis, beside heterogenous labour. Drawing on data from the US economy for 1958 and 1962, Baldwin (1971) noticed that the inclusion of natural resources in the analysis reduced the paradox but did not eliminate it completely from the results obtained. On the other hand, according to Hartigan (1981), the inclusion of natural resources completely eliminates the paradox.

Studies extending the H-O model form an abundant source of literature (an in-depth study of Leontief's paradox, and the H-O, H-O-S models can be found, e.g., in Borkakoti, 1998). There are many extensions of the model, involving not only the inclusion of other factors of production but also other countries (Heckscher-Ohlin-Vanek, H-O-V). Among the models of this type, a model proposed by Leamer in 1984 can be distinguished, which Baldwin refers to among the first attempts, beside his own work of 1979, to verify the H-O theory under the conditions of many countries and many factors of production (Baldwin, 2008).

In his 1984 study,[41] Leamer takes into account data for 60 countries for the years 1958 and 1975. He considers ten aggregates of traded commodities, including two natural resources (one of them being crude oil), four agricultural commodities (e.g., cereals and meat), four processed products (e.g., machinery and chemicals). The last, 11th category of goods are non-traded goods. In parallel, Leamer takes into account 11 factors of production, including capital, three types of labour involving different skills, four types of soil dependent on climate conditions, three types of natural resources, including coal, oil, and the minerals category (Feenstra, 2004). The conclusion of this analysis denies the existence of Leontief's paradox, confirming instead that the main trade streams are explained by the H-O model (Baldwin, 2008).

Summing up, the issue of energy demand security echoes in these trade theories which are, on the one hand, related to the diversified endowment in factors of production and, on the other hand, to the impact of the export of resources on the economies of exporting countries. In the factor endowment theory and neo-factor concepts constituting fundamental theories of trade, particular attention is paid to issues related to differences in endowment with factors of production, which, in the case of energy (fossil) resources, is the result of diverse geological conditions in the world. Naturally, only countries that have resources can become their exporters, and at the same time countries importing resources can supplement foreign purchases with domestic extraction if respective minerals are available in their territory.

Concepts based on the factor endowment theory are an interesting area of analysis from the point of view of natural resources. Although in the most commonly discussed issues the problem of energy does not appear directly (apart from the Rybczyński theorem), it is a permanent feature in many references to the H-O model. Dynamic H-O models that take into account natural resources are in turn a source of information on optimal decisions for the export and import of resources. In addition to their formalized character, the considerations that are the subject of these studies have predominantly a theoretical dimension, which may pose a difficulty in their empirical application. However, their dynamic character, which takes into account the specificity of energy resources, deserves a positive assessment. In this book's author opinion, this is a direct reference to Hotelling's research.

Neo-factor theories take into account natural resources, including minerals such as oil or coal. This is particularly the case with studies that focus on explaining Leontief's paradox. They point to the important role of resources in reducing the alleged paradox or its complete elimination. They confirm the complementarity of capital and energy (Velthuijsen and Worrell, 2002) as factors of production, which is of major significance from the point of view of selection of a specific energy production technology.

The clearest reference to energy issues can be seen in the following subjects: the Dutch disease, immiserizing growth, or the resource curse. These are descriptive concepts derived from the Rybczyński theorem, which show the consequences of exploitation and export of energy resources. This approach corresponds most closely to the issue of energy security. However, while diversified endowment with factors of production concerns both the exporter and the importer of energy, the consequences of foreign sales of resources are an inherent feature of the exporter.

Negative long-term effects of persistent dependency on revenue from energy resource exports are called by Nyga-Łukaszewska (2019) a peculiar paradox of the exporter's energy security. Arguing that monocultural export combined with high incomes, in the long term and with persistently high energy prices pose a threat to the exporter because, on the one hand, it discourages the exporter from transforming the economy and, on the other, encourages importers to look for alternative, cheaper energy sources. At the same time, such a negative situation from the exporter's point of view is positive for the importer. It can, therefore, be concluded that this is a zero-sum game.

2.4.2 Trade policy-related aspects and their potential use

Trade policy, next to trade theory, constitutes an important part in the analysis in international economics. Trade policy use in the energy market studies (in general) or even demand security seems to be instinctive. This intuitive contribution seems to be even more relevant for the strategic trade policy in particular. Thus, it is essential to check if, from the theoretical point view, strategic trade policy might be applied to the energy demand security analysis. In order to answer that question, author investigates, on the one hand, which type of the competition natural gas market fits into and thus which strategic trade policy models might be applied and, on the other, whether and how natural gas market might be suitable for introducing strategic trade policy instruments.

A closer look at the international natural gas market proves that it fits rather Cournot than Bertrand competition framework. It is highlighted in works of Egging and Gabriel (2006); Hamie, Hoayek, and Auer (2021); Haurie et al. (1987); Hulshof, van der Maat, and Mulder (2016); and Jansen et al. (2012). According to Hulshof, van der Maat, and Mulder (2016) and Jansen et al. (2012), natural gas market characteristics in Cournot configuration include relatively homogeneous good – gas, international prices set above marginal costs, and limited number of suppliers. Hulshof, van der Maat, and Mulder (2016) add that even though there are quality differences between natural gas in terms of its calorific values, they are mirrored in the international prices of commodity and thus natural gas can be treated as homogeneous good.

Following the logic that international natural gas market fits into Cournot competition framework, one cannot apply strategic trade policy models based on Bertrand scheme. That is why Eaton and Grossman's (1986) model with tax on exports increasing social welfare is not included in further analysis. The same applies to models including Stackelberg competition, for instance, Harris' (1985) framework with voluntary export restraints. Further considerations on strategic trade policy and energy demand security in the natural gas market include only Cournot-based frameworks.

Brander and Spencer's (1985) model regarding the use of export subsidies as a mean to increase national welfare is one of the most popular Cournot competition frameworks. Model assumes Cournot duopoly with firms operating in different countries and producing homogeneous goods sold only in the third country market. As long as competition and good requirements hold true in case of the natural gas market, the last assumption on sales destinations seems invalid in the energy markets in general and natural gas market in particular. In most of the cases, energy companies produce and sell products in domestic and foreign markets. This is true regardless of the ownership structure of the company in question. Nationally owned companies, constituting majority of energy producers in the world markets, are even obliged by government policies to meet firstly domestic demand and only later foreign markets. This is the result of the strategic approach to energy resources and domestic energy supply security. However, dual operations of energy companies in domestic and foreign markets undermine appropriate use of Brander-Spencer model in the analysis of energy demand security in the natural gas market. Adding to this the fact that Brander-Spencer framework focuses on export subsidies, which are not common in the natural gas market; it seems that this model cannot be included in the further analysis.

Other Brander and Spencer (1985) model extensions removing some of the original assumptions seem not to be valid either. The first group of such models includes these with free market entry and exit barriers and resulting from it changed number of market participants which builds oligopoly instead of duopoly (Venables, 1985; Horstman and Markusen, 1986; Markusen and Venables, 1988; Wild, 1997). Energy markets, and natural gas markets in particular, are considered to hold relatively high entry and exit barriers regardless of the market segment (upstream, midstream, downstream) (Juris, 1998). The former include formal (regulatory) requirements – usually in the form of licensing procedures or capacity allocation auctions; high capital requirements – connected with significant financial outlays needed to start (infrastructural) investments; technological requirements – resulting from having an access to specific technology critical for company to operate; last but not least – political requirements – according to which some companies may be favoured for operating in some markets over the others. The exit barriers refer to expensive capital assets companies hold for energy operations, severance packages for high skilled workers, and – removing, if applicable, environmental footprint, that might have occurred as a consequence of companies' operations. High entry and exit barriers exclude the above models from further investigation. Second group of models different than Brander-Spencer assumptions consists of frameworks referring to information asymmetry either between governments and companies (Qiu, 1994, 1995) or just between companies (Collie and Hviid, 1992, 1993). In energy markets, especially the upstream and midstream segments of energy-producing countries, governments have knowledge about sector's structure, it's technological characteristic, approximate levels of profitability of market participants but also supply and demand (price) elasticities for sold products. Similarly, even companies operating in different countries can approximately assess with the help of engineering expertise the level of approximate marginal costs of their rivals. That is why Brander and Spencer models with information asymmetry are not appropriate for energy demand security analysis in natural gas markets. The third group of models with other than Brander-Spencer assumptions includes these frameworks that pertained to producers' influence (lobbying) on governments. These are unproductive profit-seeking behaviours or attempts to encourage policy-makers to introduction of trade policy instruments that favour single group of producers (Bletschacher and Klodt, 1992; Moore and Suranovic, 1993). Even though, intuitively, one may expect that especially in energy industry lobbying of fossil fuel producers (in fossil fuel-producing countries) may be of special significance in times of global decarbonization processes and GHG reduction efforts, still the above frameworks – just as two above-mentioned groups of models – strictly rely on the Brander-Spencer assumption of third country sales which make it unuseful for energy demand security considerations.

Interestingly, the idea of possible use of strategic trade policy in the analysis of the situation of oil-exporting countries was mentioned by Rynarzewski (2005). Intuitive similarity of oil and gas might suggest using the strategic trade policy framework for the analysis of energy demand security in the international gas markets. In order to answer the question of possible use of the strategic trade policy in the gas demand security studies, one should start with description of the natural gas industry according to Spencer's (1998) conditions underlying introduction of the successful strategic trade policy instruments.

Spencer (1998) developed several aspects describing the specific industry branch. These factors predetermine whether the strategic trade policy will be successful or not. The above determinants include six different characteristics. The first determinant describes industry profitability and entry barriers. Spencer suggests that industries offering additional returns and entry barriers should be targeted in the pursuit of the successful strategic trade policy. Additional returns refer either to profits or greater returns to workers. These returns should exceed the total cost of the trade policy instrument that has been used to develop it (originally Spencer describes export subsidy). Moreover, industry should exhibit substantial barriers to entry for at least a period of time. The second determinant refers to restrictions in sales of foreign firms. It is assumed that the successful strategic trade policy instrument use is accompanied not only by increased domestic exports but also a significant reduction in the output levels of rival foreign companies or a decrease in future investment outlays of rival foreign firms. The third characteristic refers to domestic and foreign industry concentration levels. Spencer suggests that successful trade policy should target these domestic industries producing for exports, in which concentration levels are comparable or even higher than in the rival foreign industry. It is expected that greater domestic industry concentration, resulting from the introduction of the strategic trade policy instrument (export subsidy), will lead to a stronger foreign sales reduction. Similar effects might bring an increase in a number of domestic beneficiaries of the strategic trade policy instrument. The fourth determinant pertains to factor prices. It is assumed that successful targeting of the domestic industries destined for the introduction of the trade policy instruments should not lead to a strong increase in factor prices. This is possible when three conditions are met. Firstly, when the industry does not have strong trade unions, which by demanding higher wages, neutralize positive effects (such as increased price competitiveness of goods produced by domestic exporting industries) resulting from the introduction of the trade policy instrument. Secondly, factor prices are not destined to increase much when worker incomes are partially based on profit-sharing mechanisms within the company. Thirdly, targeting of domestic exporting industries does not bear the negative price effect if key inputs are not in fixed supply. Dixit and Grossman (1984) suggest that such an input might be scientists or engineers critical for the undisrupted business operations. Spencer clarifies that this might be a problem in the short term. In the long term, inputs are not in the fixed supply. With time the labour pool of human capital, such as engineers and scientists, might be increased by additional trainings or/and influx of skilled migrants. However, it all additionally depends on the substitution effect between capital and labour in a respective industry branch. Possibly the higher is the capital-labour substitution effect, the less chance that wage increase demands will neutralize positive trade instrument consequences. The fifth determinant refers to the cost advantage that domestic exporting industries have over foreign rival firms. Spencer highlights that domestic exporting industries have a better potential in using advantages of trade policy instrument especially when they have already enjoyed fundamental cost advantage relative to the foreign competition. This cost advantage may result from the access to cheaper raw materials, better location characteristics, or better-trained workers. These fundamental cost advantages are naturally reinforced by scale and learning effects from increased production levels. The above-mentioned five characteristics refer to a specific strategic trade policy instrument which is an export subsidy. The sixth one refers to a R&D subsidy which, similarly to the fifth determinant, has the potential to generate a fundamental cost advantage. The sixth determinant pertains to knowledge spillover effects and product lifecycle. It is assumed that successful trade policy should target those industry branches in which, on the one hand, there is knowledge transfer from foreign to domestic companies and not in the opposite direction (from domestic to foreign firms) and, on the other, the exported product is at an early stage of development or production rising additional barriers of entry for potential foreign rivals.

Analysing Spencer's (1998) conditions for choosing the optimal industry sector suitable for introducing strategic trade policy instruments, in the context of energy sector and natural gas industry in particular, one may highlight few aspects. Firstly, energy sector enjoys higher concentration in the domestic than in the foreign markets. Usually, there is a single or a limited number of energy producers or suppliers. It is a result of treating energy sectors by governments as sensitive industry branches. Secondly, domestic energy companies due to conducive (if there are such) geological conditions have access to cheaper raw materials. Even if deposit location does not justify prolonged commercial production, such fields are kept as a possible source of future energy production. Good geological conditions bring economies of scale and learning for domestic energy-producing companies. Thirdly, economies of scale are imprinted in the energy industry performance in various value chain stages. However, they are the most visible in the transport and transmission of natural gas, which by design is a large-scale operation (Austvik, 2000). Three of the above-depicted aspects describe characteristics of energy industry and none of them results in the introduction of strategic trade policy instruments.

That is why, even though energy sector exhibits some characteristics that make it suitable match for introduction of strategic trade policy instruments, subsidies in energy sector cannot be treated as export subsidies in a way that Spencer (1998) understands them. Energy subsidies, or their type—fossil fuel subsidies, are mainly production or consumption subsidies. In both cases, they affect domestic supply of fuels. Fossil fuel consumption subsidies in net exporting countries discourage private investments in the energy sector and as a result are considered to reduce economic growth (Barany and Grigonyte, 2015). That is why their contribution to social welfare is rather debatable. Production subsidies, even though, different from export subsidies have an indirect trade impact. It is especially visible in the case of crude oil producers, as oil is the most subsidized fossil fuel (IEA, 2022). Production subsidies granted to fossil fuel producers apart from price and output effects indirectly influence trade. Price effect is visible in the lowered price of produced crudes while output effect is visible in the increased output of crudes. Trade impact covers three different effects. First is called import substitution effect. It is connected with resulting from granted subsidy, greater ability of domestic producers to meet the domestic demand. Second effect refers to subsidy-induced increased export ability that allows the producer to increase his share in the world market of exported products. Third effect pertains to reduced competitiveness of alternative to exported fuels resulting from the subsidy use (Moerenhout and Irschlinger, 2020). Summing up, fossil fuel subsidies cannot be treated as export subsidies. Interestingly, the gas sector is not subjected to the heaviest subsidization by governments from all fossil fuels. Surprisingly, more suitable match for export subsidies are renewables. However, export subsidies in general are still considered prohibited subsidies by the World Trade Organization especially when subsidy favours a recipient of export sales over its domestic sales (Verkuiji et al., 2017).

Wrapping up, possibility of use of strategic trade policy in energy demand security analysis covering natural gas markets, even though intuitively remains appropriate, with detailed model investigations loses its relevancy. Main reasons behind it include natural gas market specifics (such as, using production instead of export subsidies, selling products both in domestic and foreign markets, exhibiting high entry and exit barriers), which do not allow to use the Brander-Spencer model as well as it's extensions.

Notes

1 An interesting approach to the internal and external dimensions of energy security is presented by Luciani (2004), who puts forward the thesis about the equal impact of domestic and foreign threats on energy security. Mitchell (2002) speaks in the same vein, referring to the British miners' strike in 1974 to confirm the correctness of the presented views – as an element of national threat to the continuity of energy supplies (Mitchell, 2002; Luciani, 2004).
2 Differences between traditionally understood externalities and energy security externalities are explained in Section 2.2.3.
3 Military expenditures are described further in the chapter.
4 Market power, most often analysed in relation to monopolistic competition, is the manner of behaviour of the buyer or the seller that allows them to influence the functioning of the market. Cf. Nojszewska (2010).
5 Originally, authors referred to the crude oil market and military presence in the Middle East.
6 Research published in 2010.
7 Equations kept in original form as presented by Hedenus, Azar, and Johansson (2010).
8 The authors chose the crude oil market for several reasons. First, it is not competitive due to the presence of OPEC. Second, due to the fact that oil is traded on international markets, there is one global price for this commodity. Third, oil prices are part of the price clauses on the basis of which natural gas prices are calculated. Fourth, the crude oil market has experienced interruptions in the supply of this commodity in the past. Fifth, oil prices in Europe are subject to high taxes, which makes them an interesting subject for research (Hedenus, Azar, and Johansson, 2010).
9 Explanation of this will be provided in subsequent chapters.

10 WTO rules applicable to trade in goods refer also to trade in energy. These are export control measures but also freedom of transit. For the WTO members, import and export of energy resources have to comply with

> GATT 1994 provisions on tariffs, non-tariff measures and non-discriminatory principles. For resources exporting WTO Members, the following measures taken by importing WTO Members will affect their export earning[s]: (1) whether the import tariffs in energy resources are bounded under Article II of the GATT 1994; and (2) whether such resources are subject to discriminatory taxes or measures. For resources importing WTO Members, on the other hand, the following measures taken by exporting members will affect the security of supply on energy resources: (1) whether export tariffs and other charges can be raised; and (2) whether export restriction measures can be adopted at will and unpredictably.
>
> Shih (2009)

Additionally, in energy trade, especially for the types requiring pipelines and transmission grids, the principle of freedom of transit applies as provided in Article V of the GATT 1994. More on energy security and WTO regulations can be found in Shih (2009).

11 Especially pipeline parts beyond the producers' territories.
12 Most financial instruments are oil-based.
13 Third-party access will be described in subsequent chapters.
14 Changes in the length of contracts will be described in detail in subsequent chapters.
15 Sovereign wealth funds will be described in detail in subsequent chapters.
16 GECF will be described in detail in subsequent chapters.
17 Between these two solutions, there are a variety of so-called hybrid solutions combining elements of fixed and variable pricing schemes (Bollino and Galkin, 2021).
18 The R/P index will be explained in detail in subsequent chapters of this book.
19 $PM_{2.5}$ – atmospheric dust/pollution with a diameter less than 2.5 μm.
20 Dike believes energy security of importing nations is only affected by economic factors (Dike, 2013).
21 Boussena and Locatelli offer an interesting comparison of the European and Russian perspectives, but since supply security is not of interest in this book, this aspect is omitted.
22 An interesting article answering the question whether oil prices still drive inflation nowadays (21st century): Renou-Maissant (2019).
23 Additionally, as proven by Al-Qenaie (2016), high inflation in oil-exporting countries is an effect of high oil prices, low money growth, high exchange rates, and low population growth.
24 For educational purposes, at this point high inflation rates in producer countries are not taken into consideration. However, it has to be admitted that high oil prices, inducing high-inflation rates, can be harmful for energy producers in the long-term horizon as consuming nations can divert to other energy sources and technologies.
25 A possible market failure might include a drop in real wages and resulting employment reduction (Bohi and Toman, 1996a).
26 HHI formula is presented at this point as Bollino and Galkin's (2021) work offer portfolio theory applications to demand security analysis. However, HHI is a part of other demand security measures, for instance: Dike (2013), Nowrouzi et al. (2019), and Ye et al. (2021). Its description at this point results only from the logic of the measurement methods' aggregation. Wider analysis on HHI relevance for energy security studies from the economic point of view and its methodological challenges (e.g. normalization) can be found in Nyga-Łukaszewska (2013). Description of the general HHI can be found in Hirschman (1980).
27 More on criteria in: WTO (2010).

28 Wider description on that topic available in Polish only can be found in Nyga-Łukaszewska (2020a).

29 One of such ideas is the concept of intra-industry trade (Grubel and Lloyd, 1975). It will not be applied in the study of trade in energy resources, despite the fact that in many countries of the world there is simultaneous export and import of natural resources, including energy resources. This is indicated by the values of the Grubel-Lloyd index presented by the WTO (2010). It turns out that the indicator reached high values (closer to 1) for fuels and processed petroleum products. In the group of petroleum products, in 2008, the index reached 0.73 in the USA, 0.93 in the EU (27), and 0.84 in Japan. By comparison, in the fuel group, the indicators ranged from 0.96 in the EU for the briquette or coal categories and 0.81 for coal in China. One possible explanation of that might be either the index calculation methodology or spatial differences in resource use within larger countries. Firstly, the WTO included indices at 3-digit SITC level, which involves relatively high data aggregation. That is why differentiating at lower levels of aggregation may bring different results. Secondly, in larger economies, there may be areas which export resources and other areas which import them. The WTO (2010) proves that by providing an example of bilateral trade in electricity (secondary energy) between Canada and the USA and claiming that while in 2006 the Ontario province imported electricity from the USA, Quebec exported the same product to the USA. Another example of using primary energy sources is Poland's international trade in coal. On the one hand, Poland exports coal from the Upper Silesia region, but on the other hand, the country imports it to regions located close to its eastern border. In the case of Poland this is a result of differences in price and quality of imported and domestically produced resource (Nyga-Łukaszewska, Aruga, and Stala-Szlugaj, 2020). As natural gas is more homogenous product than different coal and crude oil types, to lesser extent it can be subjected to intra-industry trade.

30 Differences in technology endowment (Vernon, 1966) and the resulting innovativeness of countries (Hirsch, 1975; Sohns, 1976) may determine the development of resource extraction in one country and its lack in another, as was the case during the shale revolution caused by the dissemination of the hydraulic fracturing technology in the USA. As a result, the position of the USA in international energy markets shifted from being natural gas importer to natural gas exporter. That has multidimensional consequences (economic, geopolitical) for energy demand security. However, their analysis due to complexity of the effects deserves a separate study as, for instance, provided by: Medlock, Jaffe, and Hartley (2011), Kobek, Ugarte, and Aguilar (2015) and Shirazi, Ghasemi, and Šimurina (2021). First two of these studies apart from the narrative geopolitical analysis (Kobek, Ugarte, and Aguilar, 2015) also deliver formalized perspective by using dynamic spatial general equilibrium model – Rice World Gas Trade Model (RWGTM) Medlock, Jaffe, and Hartley (2011). The third one – by Shirazi, Ghasemi, and Šimurina (2021) – applies the Markov switching model and dynamic network connectedness measures to explore the impact of the North American shale gas technology on behavioral regimes and spillover effects of natural gas trade cycles, regarding the US energy security.

31 Similarly to differences in technology endowment, this study also omits one of the most important features of natural resources and their effects on international trade – environmental externalities, both those defined as flow and stock. Energy-related environmental externalities influencing international trade are multidimensional and depend on the presence of asymmetric information on resource availability, availability of cost-reducing technologies, discovery of new resources and not well-defined property rights (WTO, 2010). Asymmetric information on resource availability is connected with the development of a backstop technology – an idea introduced by Nordhaus (1973). Backstop technology can encourage exporters to overestimate their resource base and incentivize importers to increase their bargaining power. As a result,

exporters will increase resource production to either lower its price or lend credibility to overestimated resource stocks. In either case, resource production is above the social optimum leading to environmental damage. Availability of cost-reducing technologies and discovery of new resources have a similar impact on environmental externalities. In the short term, technological advances, just as a newly tapped resource base, decrease resource prices and drive up its consumption, increasing environmental pollution. In the long term, the rising value of the resource still in the ground and diminishing returns on resource exploration will increase resource prices. From the point of view of environmental externalities, the amount of pollution generated due to the availability of cost-reducing technologies or discovery of new resources depends on the length of short-term increase in resource demand. Apart from the above-described negative effects of technologies on environmental externalities, cost-reducing technologies may also have a positive impact. Carbon-abatement technologies reducing air pollution resulting from resource production can reduce the amount of GHG emissions. The last factor affecting the relationship between trade and environmental externalities is the quality of protection of property rights. If they are not well protected, resource owners will be incentivized to speed up resource extraction above social optimum levels in order to quickly lock in profits (WTO, 2010). To sum up, speeding up resource extraction induced by different factors is always detrimental to the environment. For energy security, this means increasing resource supply and driving prices down. However, much of that depends on whether energy resources are substitutable and, as a consequence, if import of one fuel can be replaced by foreign deliveries of another. If substitutability does exist, and a highly emissive resource is substituted (e.g., coal) by a less emissive resource (e.g., natural gas), then changed international trade flows can help mitigate potential air pollution and, thus, at least partially reduce environmental externalities.

32 Currently, the dynamically developing trend in the empirical and theoretical literature described synthetically, for instance, by Brodzicki (2016), referred to as "new" new trade theory (NNTT) may probably be less applicable to energy demand security analysis. This is due to the fact that in this theoretical trend, companies, not states, are the main subject of analysis. The reason is that "new" new trade theory (Bernard and Jensen, 1999; Bernard et al., 2003; Melitz, 2003; Hagemajer and Kolasa, 2008; Mayer and Ottaviano, 2008; Michałek, 2010) assumes that not all companies in a given country with a certain comparative advantage in international markets will become exporters. This heterogeneity of enterprises is at the centre of the analysis of this theoretical thread. On the other hand, in the case of energy security, the subject of the analysis is generally state because resource-exporting companies are usually partly or wholly owned by entities representing the state.

33 Specific factors theory is sometimes called a special case of the H-O theory. It assumes that labour is mobile, while capital and land – immobile (fixed). These assumptions are true especially for the short run, while in the long run, accordingly to H-O model all production factors are mobile between industries. Specific factors theory was introduced by Jones (1971) and Samuelson (1971) in the 1970s of the 21st century.

34 First attempt to relax these assumptions is visible in Deardorff (1982), where author introduces into the analysis more than two commodities, factors of production and countries.

35 As an example, contradicting the Stolper-Samuelson theorem, Robinson and Torvik refer to the discovery of diamond deposits in South Africa: Kimberly in 1873 and Johannesburg in 1886. In the first half of the 20th century, gold prices increased significantly and the terms of trade in South Africa improved. In South Africa, a system of incentives has been created for workers willing to work in the mines. Gold mines are a labour-intensive industry. According to the Stolper-Samuelson theorem, wages in mines should have increased gradually due to the increase in gold prices. In fact, in 1970 they were

20% lower than in 1911. This way, in the intensively developing export industry, there was a decline in real wages, contrary to the Stolper-Samuelson theorem. The authors took into consideration wages of Black mine workers. Robinson and Torvik (2013).

36 The term "Dutch disease" was introduced by journalists in 1977 in "The Economist". The Economist (1977).

37 Cherif does not rely in his work on the neoclassical H-O model; nevertheless, referring to this idea here seems to be justified even though it does not fit in methodologically with neoclassical concepts but rather refers to new trade theories (Krugman-Helpman model). The rationale for including Cherif's work here arises from its results, which describe the symptoms of the Dutch disease in a slightly different way than before.

38 Krugman's (1987) work is only synthetically mentioned at this point as his model relies on the Ricardian approach. Krugman (1987) introduced a model of the Dutch disease with manufacturing sector productivity gains, referred to as the learning-by-doing effect. This is an extension of the Ricardian approach in which Krugman assumes that labour requirements change over time.

39 Sachs and Warner (1995) add that disease can be claimed only when shrinking manufacturing sector effects spill over towards the rest of the economy.

40 The issue of using the terminology of "paradox" is debatable, as many authors have indicated that in fact such a structure of US exports and imports is not a paradox. Cf. Misala (2003).

41 In contrast to the results of Leamer's (1984) study is the 1987 study by Bowen, Leamer, and Sveiskaukas from the same year – 1987. In this case, the H-O-V model was also used, this time for 1967 data from 1967 with 12 factors of production from 27 countries. However, the results obtained did not confirm Leamer's earlier conclusions (Borkakoti, 1998). Further attempts to verify the H-O-V model were made by Trefler in 1993 and 1995. In the first work, the author admits the existence of differences in the productivity of factors of production between countries, based on Leontief's original statement in 1953 that the USA is a country in which labour is an abundant factor when its productivity is taken into account. Trefler examined 33 countries for ten different factors of production. These factors did not include natural resources. Trefler argued that oil and coal are to a large extent traded internationally. Therefore, citing Leamer (1984), Trefler decided that they could not be treated as non-transferable factors of production on an international scale (Trefler, 1993). Instead, Trefler focused on seven types of labour, capital, pastures, and arable land. The result of the research is the claim that the differences in the productivity of labour factors correspond to the differences in their prices. This discovery leads him to confirm the validity of the H-O-V model in explaining trade streams. In his 1995 study, Trefler likewise examines nine factors of production in 33 countries (1983 data) (Trefler, 1995). The regularity observed by him that rich countries are poorly endowed with most of the factors of production, while poor countries are well endowed, does not harmonize with the H-O-V model. The author calls this part of trade (unexplained by the H-O-V model) "missing trade" and attributes its occurrence to the effects associated with the consumption of goods according to Armington's (1969) theory and differences in technology endowment. Feenstra (2004) considers the latter as a kind of return to the Ricardian model, which explains the development of trade through differences in technology endowment. As pointed out by Feenstra (2004), researchers provide many other explanations for the development of trade on the basis of H-O-V models. These include growing economies of scale, geographical and climate issues, or social capital. According to Feenstra, it remains an active strand of research that attracts many supporters and will continue to do so in future. The H-O concept itself, in its original form, despite many assumptions that are no longer useful for the analysis of international trade (Gawlikowska-Hueckel, 2016), may be relevant to the study of global trade streams (Umiński, 2012), and in particular those resulting from the input-output specialization, as Zielińska-Głębocka (2012) notes.

References

Abdullah, F.B. et al. (2020) 'Energy security indicators for Pakistan: an integrated approach', *Renewable and Sustainable Energy Reviews*, 133(2), p. 110122. doi:10.1016/j.rser.2020.110122.

Adelman, M.A. (1993) 'Security of Eastern Hemisphere fuel supply', in *The economics of petroleum supply*. Cambridge, MA: MIT Press, pp. 469–472.

Alexeev, M. and Conrad, R. (2009) 'The elusive curse of oil', *The Review of Economics and Statistics*, 91(3), pp. 586–598. doi:10.1162/rest.91.3.586.

Allcott, H. and Keniston, D. (2017) *Dutch disease or agglomeration? The local economic effects of natural resource booms in modern America*. NBER Working Paper 20508. Cambridge: National Bureau of Economic Research, pp. 1–76.

Al-Qenaie, J. (2016) 'Causes of Inflation across Main Oil Exporting Countries'. SciencesPo. Available at: https://www.sciencespo.fr/kuwait-program/wp-content/uploads/2018/05/KSP_Paper_Award_Fall_2016_AL-QENAIE_Jawan.pdf (Accessed: 22 January 2022).

Ang, B.W., Choong, W.L., and Ng, T.S. (2015) 'Energy security: definitions, dimensions and indexes', *Renewable and Sustainable Energy Reviews*, 2015(42), pp. 1077–1093. doi:10.1016/j.rser.2014.10.064.

APERC (Asia Pacific Research Centre) (2007) *A quest for energy security in the 21st century. Resources and constraints*. Tokyo: Institute of Energy Economics.

Armington, P.S. (1969) 'A theory of demand for products distinguished by place of production', *IMF Staff Papers*, 16, pp. 159–178.

Arnold, S. and Hunt, A. (2009) *National and EU-level estimates of energy supply externalities*. CEPS Policy Brief 186, Brussels: Centre for European Policy Studies. Available at: http://aei.pitt.edu/10815/1/1834-1.pdf (Accessed: 9 February 2018).

Aspergis, N. et al. (2014) 'Dutch disease effect of oil rents on agriculture value added in Middle East and North African (MENA) countries', *Energy Economics*, 45, pp. 485–490. doi:10.1016/j.eneco.2014.07.025.

Augustis, J. et al. (2015) 'Dynamic model based on Bayesian method for energy security assessment', *Energy Conversion and Management*, 2015(101), pp. 66–72. doi:10.1016/j.enconman.2015.05.002.

Austvik, O.G. (2000) *Economics of natural gas transportation*. Forskningsrapport HIL, Research report no 53, Lillehammer: Lillehammer College. Available at: http://www.kaldor.no/energy/hilrap2000-08.pdf (Accessed: 25 May 2022).

Austvik, O.G. (2016) 'The energy union and security-of-gas supply', *Energy Policy*, 96, pp. 372–382. doi:10.1016/j.enpol.2016.06.013.

Awerbuch, S. (2006) 'Portfolio-based electricity generation planning: policy implications for renewables and energy security', *Mitigation and Adaptation Strategies for Global Change*, 11(3), pp. 693–710. doi:10.1007/s11027-006-4754-4.

Awerbuch, S. and Yang, S. (2007) 'Efficient electricity generating portfolios for Europe: maximising energy security and climate change mitigation', *European Investment Bank Papers*, 12(2), pp. 8–37.

Awerbuch, S. et al. (2006) *Full-spectrum portfolio and diversity analysis of energy technologies, managing enterprise risk: what the electric industry experience implies for contemporary business*. doi:10.1016/B978-008044949-4/50046-5.

Azzuni, A. and Breyer, C. (2020) 'Global energy security index and its application on national level', *Energies*, 13(10), p. 2502. doi:10.3390/en13102502.

Badea, A.C. et al. (2011) 'Composite indicators for security of energy supply using ordered weighted averaging', *ESREL 2009 Special Issue*, 96(6), pp. 651–662. doi:10.1016/j.ress.2010.12.025.

Baldwin, R. (1971) 'Determinants of the commodity structure of U.S. trade', *American Economic Review*, 61(1), pp. 126–46.
Baldwin, R. (2008) *The development and testing of Heckscher-Ohlin trade models.* Cambridge, MA: Massachusetts Institute of Technology.
Banks, F. (2000) *Energy economics: a modern introduction.* 1st edn. Boston, MA: Springer.
Barany, A. and Grigonyte, D. (2015) *Measuring fossil fuel subsidies.* ECFIN Economic Brief 40. Brussels: European Commission's Directorate-General Economic and Financial Affairs (ECFIN). doi: 10.2765/85991.
Barsky, R. and Kilian, L. (2004) *Oil and the macroeconomy since the 1970s.* NBER Working Paper 10855. Cambridge: National Bureau of Economic Research. Available at: http://www.nber.org/papers/w10855 (Accessed: 29 March 2018).
Baumeister, C. and Kilian, L. (2016) 'Lower oil prices and the U.S. economy: is this time different?' *Brookings Papers on Economic Activity*, 2, pp. 287–336.
Bazilian, M. and Roques, F. (2008) 'Introduction: analytical approaches to quantify and value fuel mix diversity', in Bazilian, M. and Roques, F. (eds.), *Analytical methods for energy diversity & security.* Oxford: Elsevier (Elsevier Global Energy Policy and Economics Series), pp. xxv–xlii. doi:10.1016/B978-0-08-056887-4.00018-4.
Beccue, P. and Huntington, H.G. (2005) *Oil disruption risk assessment.* Energy Modeling Forum Special Report 8. Stanford: Stanford University Press.
Beccue, P.C. et al. (2018) 'An updated assessment of oil market disruption risks', *Energy Policy*, 115, pp. 456–469. doi:10.1016/j.enpol.2017.12.013.
Beine, M., Bos, C.S., and Coulombe, S. (2012) 'Does the Canadian economy suffer from Dutch disease?' *Resource and Energy Economics*, 34, pp. 468–492. doi:10.1016/j.reseneeco.2012.05.002.
Bellos, E. (2018) 'Sustainable energy development: how can the tension between energy security and energy transition be measured and managed in South Africa?' *Journal of Cleaner Production*, 205, pp. 738–753. doi:10.1016/j.jclepro.2018.08.196.
Bernard, A.B. and Bradford Jensen, J. (1999) 'Exceptional exporter performance: cause, effect, or both?' *Journal of International Economics*, 47(1), pp. 1–25. doi: 10.1016/S0022-1996(98)00027-0.
Bernard, A.B. et al. (2003) 'Plants and productivity in international trade', *American Economic Review*, 93(4), pp. 1268–1290. doi:10.1257/000282803769206296.
Bhagwati, J. (1958) 'Immiserizing growth: a geometrical note', *The Review of Economic Studies*, 25(3), pp. 201–205. doi:10.2307/2295990.
Bigerna, S., Bollino, C.A., and Galkin, P. (2020) 'Balancing energy security priorities: portfolio optimization approach to oil imports', *Applied Economics*, 53(5), [Preprint], pp. 555–574.doi:10.1080/00036846.2020.1808573.
Biresselioglu, M.E. et al. (2017a) 'Establishing an energy security framework for a fast-growing economy: industry perspectives from Turkey', *Energy Research & Social Science*, 27(May), pp. 151–162. doi:10.1016/j.erss.2017.03.007.
Biresselioglu, M.E. et al. (2017b) 'Interpreting Turkish industry's perception on energy security: a national survey', *Renewable and Sustainable Energy Reviews*, 67(January), pp. 1208–1224. doi:10.1016/j.rser.2016.09.093.
Bletschacher, G. and Klodt, H. (1992) *Strategische Handels- and Industriepolitik. Theoretische Grundlagen, Branchenanalysen und wettbewerbspolitische Implikationen.* Tuebingen: J.C.B. Mohr (Paul Siebeck).
Blyth, W. and Lefevre, N. (2004) *Energy security and climate change. Policy interactions.* Paris: International Energy Agency.

Boehringer, C. and Bortolamedi, M. (2015) 'Sense and no(n)-sense of energy security indicators', *Ecological Economics*, 119(November), pp. 359–371. doi:10.1016/j.ecolecon.2015.09.020.

Bohi, D.R. (1994) *Energy security externalities and fuel cycle comparisons*. Oak Ridge: Oak Ridge National Laboratory. Available at: https://inis.iaea.org/collection/NCLCollectionStore/_Public/35/052/35052308.pdf?r=1&r=1 (Accessed: 25 February 2019).

Bohi, D.R. and Toman, M.A. (1996a) 'Empirical evidence on energy security externalities', in *The economics of energy security*. Boston, MA: Kluwer Academic Publishers, pp. 31–58.

Bohi, D.R. and Toman, M.A. (1996b) *The economics of energy security*. Boston, MA: Kluwer Academic Publishers.

Bollino, C.A. and Galkin, P. (2021) 'Energy security and portfolio diversification: conventional and novel perspectives', *Energies*, 14(14), p. 4257. doi:10.3390/en14144257.

Borkakoti, J. (1998) *Trade: causes and consequences. An empirical and theoretical text*. London: Macmillan, pp. 98–210.

Boussena, S. and Locatelli, C. (2013) 'Energy institutional and organisational changes in EU and Russia: revisiting gas relations', *Energy Policy*, 55, pp. 180–189. doi:10.1016/j.enpol.2012.11.052.

Bożyk, P. (2008) *Międzynarodowe stosunki ekonomiczne. Teoria i polityka*. Warszawa: Polskie Wydawnictwo Ekonomiczne.

Bożyk, P. and Nyga-Łukaszewska, H. (2013) 'Pojęcie i miary bezpieczeństwa energetycznego', in Bożyk, P. (ed.), *Bezpieczeństwo energetyczne Polski w ujęciu autonomicznym i zintegrowanym z Unią Europejską*. Warszawa: Akademia Finansów i Biznesu Vistula, pp. 9–26.

Brander, J.A. and Spencer, B.J. (1985) 'Export subsidies and international market share rivalry', *Journal of International Economics*, 18(1–2), pp. 83–100. doi:10.1016/0022-1996(85)90006-6.

Brodzicki, T. (2016) 'Nowa nowa teoria handlu', in Gawlikowska-Hueckel, K. and Umiński, S. (eds.), *Analiza handlu zagranicznego Polski w świetle najnowszych koncepcji teoretycznych*. Warszawa: Wydawnictwo Naukowe Scholar, pp. 104–110.

Brown, M.A. and Sovacool, B.K. (2007) 'Developing an "energy sustainability index" to evaluate energy policy', *Interdisciplinary Science Reviews*, 32(4), pp. 335–349. doi:10.1179/030801807X211793.

Brown, M.A. et al. (2014) 'Forty years of energy security trends: a comparative assessment of 22 industrialized countries', *Energy Research & Social Science*, 4, pp. 64–77. doi:10.1016/j.erss.2014.08.008.

Brown, S.P.A. and Huntington, H.G. (2013) 'Assessing the US oil security premium', *Energy Economics*, 38, pp. 118–127. doi:10.1016/j.eneco.2013.03.010.

Brown, S.P.A. and Huntington, H.G. (2015) 'Evaluating US oil security and import reliance', *Energy Policy*, 79, pp. 9–22. doi:10.1016/j.enpol.2015.01.001.

Bruno, M. and Sachs, J. (1982) 'Energy and resource allocation: a dynamic model of the "Dutch disease"', *The Review of Economic Studies*, 49(5), pp. 845–859. doi:10.2307/2297191.

Brunstad, R.J. and Dyrstad, J.M. (1997) 'Booming sector and wage effects: an empirical analysis on norwegian data', *Oxford Economic Papers*, 49(1), pp. 89–103.

Budnikowski, A. (2006) *Międzynarodowe stosunki gospodarcze*. Warszawa: Polskie Wydawnictwo Ekonomiczne.

Cabalu, H. (2010) 'Indicators of security of natural gas supply in Asia', *Energy Policy*, 38, pp. 218–228. doi:10.1016/j.enpol.2009.09.008.

Caporaso, J. (1978) 'Dependence, dependency, and power in the global system: a structural and behavioral analysis', *International Organization*, 32(1), pp. 13–43. doi:10.1017/S0020818300003842.

Carbaugh, R. (2012) *International economics*. 14th edn. Boston, MA: Cengage Learning.
Cardoso, F.H. and Faletto, E. (1979) *Dependency and development in Latin America*. Berkeley, CA: University of California Press.
Caves, R., Frankel, A., and Jones, R. (1993) *International trade and finance: an introduction*. 6th edn. New York, NY: Harper and Collins College Publishers.
Checchi, A., Behrens, A., and Eggenhofer, C. (2009) *Long-term energy security risks for europe: a sector-specific approach*. CEPS Working Paper No. 309. Brussels: Centre for European Policy Studies. doi:10.2139/ssrn.1334620.
Cherif, R. (2013) 'The Dutch disease and the technological gap', *Journal of Development Economics*, 101(C), pp. 248–255. doi:10.1016/j.jdeveco.2012.10.010.
Cherp, A. (2012) 'Defining energy security takes more than asking around', *Energy Policy*, 48, pp. 841–842. doi:10.1016/j.enpol.2012.02.016.
Cherp, A. and Jewell, J. (2013) 'Energy security assessment framework and three case studies', in Dryer, H. and Trombetta, M.J. (eds.), *International handbook of energy security*. Cheltenham: Edward Elgar Publishing, pp. 146–173. doi:10.4337/9781781007907.00018.
Cherp, A. and Jewell, J. (2014) 'The concept of energy security: beyond the four As', *Energy Policy*, 75, pp. 415–421. doi:10.1016/j.enpol.2014.09.005.
Chester, L. (2010) 'Conceptualising energy security and making explicit its polysemic nature', *Energy Policy*, 38(2), pp. 887–895. doi:10.1016/j.enpol.2009.10.039.
Ciborski, J. (2006) 'Bezpieczeństwo energetyczne', in Kuciński, K. (ed.), *Energia w czasach kryzysu*. Warszawa: Wydawnictwo Difin, pp. 127–146.
Cohen, G., Joutz, F., and Loungani, P. (2011) 'Measuring energy security: trends in the diversification of oil and natural gas supplies', *Energy Policy*, 39(9), pp. 4860–4869. doi:10.1016/j.enpol.2011.06.034.
Collie, D.R. and Hviid, M. (1992) *Export subsidies as signals of competitiveness*. Economic Research Papers 268511. University of Warwick – Department of Economics. Coventry: University of Warwick. doi:10.22004/ag.econ.268511.
Collie, D.R. and Hviid, M. (1993) 'Export subsidies as signals of competitiveness', *The Scandinavian Journal of Economics*, 95(3), pp. 327–339. doi:10.2307/3440359.
Collier, P. et al. (2010) 'Managing resource revenues in developing economies', *IMF Staff Papers*, 57(1), pp. 84–118.
Constantini, V. and Gracceva, F. (2004) *Social costs of energy disruptions*. FEEM Working Papers 116. Milano: Fondazione Eni Enrico Mattei.
Corden, M. and Neary, P. (1982) 'Booming sector and de-industrialisation in a small open economy', *The Economic Journal*, 92(368), pp. 825–848. doi:10.2307/2232670.
Ćwiek-Karpowicz, J. (2016) 'Postrzeganie i definiowanie bezpieczeństwa energetycznego w warunkach kryzysu na Ukrainie', *Polityka Energetyczna- Energy Policy Journal*, 19(1), pp. 137–148.
Czerpak, P. (2006) 'Bezpieczeństwo energetyczne', in Żukrowska, K. (ed.), *Bezpieczeństwo międzynarodowe: teoria i praktyka*, pp. 122–128. Warszawa: Oficyna Wydawnicza SGH.
Davis, D.R. and Mishra, P. (2006) 'Stolper-Samuelson is dead, and other crimes of both theory and data', in Harrison, A.E. (ed.), *Globalization and poverty: NBER conference report*. Chicago: University of Chicago Press, pp. 87–107. Available at: https://www.nber.org/system/files/chapters/c0111/c0111.pdf (Accessed: 10 March 2023).
Davis, M. et al. (2005) *Ukraine – the impact of higher natural gas and oil prices*. 38602. Washington, DC: World Bank. Available at: http://documents.worldbank.org/curated/en/838301468173971844/Ukraine-The-impact-of-higher-natural-gas-and-oil-prices (Accessed: 9 February 2018).

Deardorff, A.V. (1982) 'The general validity of the Heckscher-Ohlin theorem', *The American Economic Review*, 72(4), pp. 683–694.

Dike, J.C. (2013) 'Measuring the security of energy exports demand in OPEC economies', *Energy Policy*, 60, pp. 594–600. doi:10.1016/j.enpol.2013.05.086.

Dixit, A.K. and Grossman, G.M. (1984) *Targeted export promotion with several oligopolistic industries*. Discussion Paper 71. Woodrow Wilson School of Public and International Affairs. Princeton: Princeton University.

Dos Santos, T. (1970) 'The structure of dependence', *American Economic Review*, 60(2), pp. 231–236.

Eaton, J. and Grossman, G. (1986) 'Optimal trade and industrial policy under oligopoly', *Quarterly Journal of Economics*, 101(2), pp. 383–406. doi:10.2307/1891121.

Eggenhofer, C. (2004) *Market based options for security of energy supply*. INDES Working Paper [Preprint]. Brussels: Centre for European Policy Studies.

Eggenhofer, C. and Lege, T. (2001) *Security of energy supply. A question for policy or the markets?* CEPS Working Papers [Preprint]. Brussels: Centre for European Policy Studies.

Egging, R.G. and Gabriel, S.A. (2006) 'Examining market power in the European natural gas market', *Energy Policy*, 34(17), pp. 2762–2778. doi:10.1016/j.enpol.2005.04.018.

Energy Charter Secretariat (2015) *International Energy Security. Common Concept for Energy Producing, Consuming and Transit Countries*. Available at: https://energycharter.org/fileadmin/DocumentsMedia/Thematic/International_Energy_Security_2015_en.pdf (Accessed: 2 May 2018).

Erahman, Q.F. et al. (2016) 'An assessment of Indonesia's energy security index and comparison with seventy countries', *Energy*, 2016(111), pp. 364–376. doi:10.1016/j.energy.2016.05.100.

Erdal, L. (2015) 'Determinants of energy supply security: an econometric analysis for Turkey', *Ege Akademik Bakis*, 15(2), pp. 153–163. doi:10.21121/eab.2015217981.

Feenstra, R. (2004) *Advanced international trade. Theory and evidence*. Princeton: Princeton University Press.

Fleming, J. and Ostdiek, B. (1999) 'The impact of energy derivatives on the crude oil market', *Energy Economics*, 21(2), pp. 135–167.

Frank, A.G. (1970) 'The development and underdevelopment', in Rhodes, R.I. (ed.), *Imperialism and underdevelopment*. New York, NY: Monthly Review Press, pp. 4–17.

Frei, C.W. (2004) 'The Kyoto Protocol – a victim of supply security? or: if Maslow were in energy politics', *Energy Policy*, 32(11), pp. 1253–1256. doi:10.1016/j.enpol.2003.12.012.

Gandolfo, G. (2014) *International trade theory and policy*. 2nd edn. Berlin: Springer Verlag.

Garcia-Gusano, D., Iribarren, D., and Garrain, D. (2017) 'Prospective analysis of energy security: a practical lice-cycle approach focused on renewable power generation and oriented towards policy-makers', *Applied Energy*, 2017(190), pp. 891–901. doi:10.1016/j.apenergy.2017.01.011.

Gawlikowska-Hueckel, K. (2016) 'Przegląd teorii handlu', in Gawlikowska-Hueckel, K. and Umiński, S. (eds.), *Analiza handlu zagranicznego Polski w świetle najnowszych koncepcji teoretycznych*. Warszawa: Wydawnictwo Naukowe Scholar, pp. 76–87.

GEI (2018). *International index of energy security risk*. Washington, DC: Global Energy Institute/US Chamber of Commerce. Available at: https://www.globalenergyinstitute.org/sites/default/themes/bricktheme/pdfs/energyrisk_intl_2018.pdf (Accessed: 30 June 2018).

Gillessen, B. et al. (2019) 'Natural gas as a bridge to sustainability: infrastructure expansion regarding energy security and system transition', *Applied Energy*, 251, 113377. doi:10.1016/j.apenergy.2019.113377.

Gracceva, F. and Zeniewski, P. (2014) 'A systemic approach to assessing energy security in a low-carbon EU energy system', *Applied Energy*, 123, pp. 335–348. doi:10.1016/j.apenergy.2013.12.018.

Greene, D.L. and Leiby, P.N. (2006) *The oil security metrics model*. Oak Ridge: Oak Ridge National Laboratory.

Grubel, H.G. and Lloyd, P.J. (1975) *Intra-industry trade: the theory and the measurement of international trade in differentiated products*. New York, NY: John Wiley and Sons.

Gupta, E. (2007) 'Assessing the relative geopolitical risk of oil importing countries', in *Energy security in Europe*, Proceedings from the conference 'Energy Security in Europe', pp. 207–225. Lund: Centre for European Studies, Lund University.

Gwiazda, A. (1985) *Międzynarodowa współzależność ekonomiczna we współczesnym świecie*. Warszawa: Państwowe Wydawnictwo Naukowe.

Hagemajer, J. and Kolasa, M. (2008) *Internationalization and economic performance of enterprises: evidence from firm-level data*. NBP Working Paper 51. Warsaw: National Bank of Poland.

Hamie, H., Hoayek, A., and Auer, H. (2021) 'Modeling post-liberalized European gas market concentration—a game theory perspective', *Forecasting*, 3(1), pp. 1–16. doi:10.3390/forecast3010001.

Hamilton, J. (2003) 'What is an oil shock?' *Journal of Econometrics*, 113, pp. 363–398. doi:10.1016/S0304-4076(02)00207-5.

Hamilton, J. (2009) 'Causes and consequences of the oil shock of 2007–08', *Brookings Papers on Economic Activity* (Spring) [Preprint]. Available at: https://www.brookings.edu/wp-content/uploads/2016/07/2009a_bpea_hamilton-1.pdf (Accessed: 20 July 2021).

Hamilton, J. (2011) *Historical oil shocks*. NBER Working Papers, 16790. Cambridge: National Bureau of Economic Research, pp. 1–52. doi:10.3386/w16790.

Harris, R. (1981) 'Trade and depletable resources: the small open economy', *The Canadian Journal of Economics*, 14(4), pp. 649–664.

Harris, R.G. (1985) 'Why voluntary export restraints are voluntary', *Canadian Journal of Economics*, 18(4), pp. 799–809. doi:10.2307/135091.

Hartigan, J. (1981) 'The US tariff and comparative advantage: a survey method', *Weltwirtschaftliches Archiv*, 117(1), pp. 65–107. doi:10.1007/BF02696578.

Hasanov, F. (2013) 'Dutch disease and the Azerbaijan economy', *Communist and Post-Communist Studies*, 46, pp. 463–480. doi:10.1016/j.postcomstud.2013.09.001.

Haurie, A. et al. (1987) *A stochastic dynamic Nash-Cournot model for the European gas market*. Technical Report G-86-24. Montréal: GERAD, Ecole des Hautes Etudes Commerciales.

Heckscher, E. (1919) 'The effect of foreign trade on the distribution of income', *Ekonomisk Tidskrift*, 21, pp. 497–512 [Printed in: *Readings in the theory of international trade*, Ellis, H.S. and Metzler, L.A. (eds.). Philadephia, PA: Blakiston].

Hedenus, F., Azar, C., and Johansson, D.J.A. (2010) 'Energy security policies in EU-25—the expected cost of oil supply disruptions', *Energy Policy*, 38(3), pp. 1241–1250. doi:10.1016/j.enpol.2009.01.030.

Helpman, E. (1999) 'The structure of foreign trade', *The Journal of Economic Perspectives*, 13(2), pp. 121–144.

Hillman, A. and Bullard, C. (1978) 'Energy, the Heckscher-Ohlin theorem, and U.S. international trade', *The American Economic Review*, 68(1), pp. 96–106.

Hirsch, S. (1975) 'The product cycle model of international trade: a multi-country cross-section analysis', *Oxford Bulletin of Economics and Statistics*, 37(4), pp. 305–317.

Hirschman, A.O. (1980) *National power and the structure of foreign trade*. Los Angeles, CA: University of California Press.

Holcombe, R. and Sobel, R. (2001) 'Public policy toward pecuniary externalities', *Public Finance Review*, 29(4), pp. 304–325.

Horstman, I.J. and Markusen, J.R. (1986) 'Up to the average cost curve inefficient entry and the new protectionism', *Journal of International Economics*, 20(3–4), pp. 225–247. doi:10.1016/0022-1996(86)90020-6.

Hulshof, D., van der Maat, J.P., and Mulder, M. (2016) 'Market fundamentals, competition and natural-gas prices', *Energy Policy* 94, pp. 480–491. doi:10.1016/j.enpol.2015.12.016.

Huntington, H.G. (2004) 'Shares, gaps and the economy's response to oil disruptions', *Energy Economics*, 26(3), pp. 415–424.

Hutchison, M. (1994) 'Manufacturing sector resiliency to energy booms: empirical evidence from Norway, the Netherlands, and the United Kingdom', *Oxford Economic Papers*, 46(2), pp. 311–329.

IEA (2004) *Security of supply in open markets*. Paris: International Energy Agency.

IEA (2018) *What is energy security?* Available at: https://www.iea.org/topics/energysecurity/whatisenergysecurity/ (Accessed: 29 March 2018).

IEA (2022) *Energy subsidies*. Available at: https://www.iea.org/topics/energy-subsidies (Accessed: 25 June 2022).

Iskra, W. (2004) *Miedzynarodowe stosunki gospodarcze*. Warszawa: Fundacja Innowacja.

Ito, K. (2017) 'Dutch disease and Russia', *International Economics*, 151, pp. 66–70.

Jansen, J.C., van Arkel, W.G., and Boots, M.G. (2004) *Designing indicators of long-term energy supply security*. Energy Research Centre of the Netherlands. Petten: Energy Research Centre of the Netherlands - ECN. Available at: https://www.ecn.nl/publicaties/PdfFetch.aspx?nr=ECN-C--04-007 (Accessed: 29 June 2018).

Jansen, T. et al. (2012) 'A modified Cournot model of the natural gas market in the European Union: mixed-motives delegation in a politicized environment', *Energy Policy* 41, pp. 280–285. doi:10.1016/j.enpol.2011.10.047.

Jewell, J. (2011) *The IEA Model of Short-term Energy Security (MOSES)*. Paris: International Energy Agency. Available at: https://www.iea.org/media/freepublications/oneoff/moses_paper.pdf (Accessed: 29 June 2018).

Johansson, B. (2013) 'A broadened typology on energy and security', *Energy*, 2013(53), pp. 199–205. doi:10.1016/j.energy.2013.03.012.

Jones, C.R., Kaklamanou, D., and Lazuras, L. (2017) 'Public perceptions of energy security in Greece and Turkey: exploring the relevance of pro-environmental and pro-cultural orientations', *Energy Research & Social Science*, 2017(28), pp. 17–28. doi:10.1016/j.erss.2017.04.002.

Jones, R.W. (1956) 'Factor proportions and the Heckscher-Ohlin theorem', *The Review of Economic Studies*, 24(1), pp. 1–10. doi:10.2307/2296232.

Jones, R.W. (1971) 'A three-factor model in theory, trade and history', in Bhagwati, J. et al. (eds.), *Trade, balance of payments and growth*. Amsterdam: North-Holland, pp. 3–21.

Joskow, P.L. (2003) 'Vertical integration', in Menard, C. and Shirley, M. (eds.), *Handbook of new institutional economics*. Berlin, Heidelberg: Springer-Verlag, pp. 319–348.

Juris, A. (1998) *The emergence of markets in the natural gas industry*. Policy Research Working Papers. Washington, DC: World Bank. doi:10.1596/1813-9450-1895.

Karatayev, M. and Hall, S. (2020) 'Establishing and comparing energy security trends in resource-rich exporting nations (Russia and the Caspian Sea region)', *Resources Policy*, 68(October), p. 101746. doi:10.1016/j.resourpol.2020.101746.

Kemp, M. and Long, N. (1979) 'International trade with an exhaustible resource: a theorem of Rybczyński type', *International Economic Review*, 20(3), pp. 671–677.

Kemp, M. and Long, N. (1982) 'Rybczyński's theorem in a context of exhaustible resources: the case of time-contingent prices', *International Economic Review*, 23(3), pp. 699–710. doi:10.2307/2526384.

Kemp, M. and Suzuki, H. (1975) 'International trade with a wasting but possibly replenishable resource', *International Economic Review*, 16(3), pp. 712–732.

Kilian, L. (2008a) 'A comparison of the effects of exogenous oil supply shocks on output and inflation in the G7 countries', *Journal of the European Economic Association*, 6(1), pp. 78–121. doi:10.1162/JEEA.2008.6.1.78.

Kilian, L. (2008b) 'The economic effects of energy price shocks', *Journal of Economic Literature*, 46(4), pp. 871–909. doi:10.1257/jel.46.4.87J.

Kilian, L. and Cheolbeom, P. (2009) 'The impact of oil price shocks on the U.S. stock market', *International Economic Review*, 50(4), pp. 1267–1287. doi:10.1111/j.1468-2354.2009.00568.x.

Kisel, E. et al. (2016) 'Concept of energy security matrix', *Energy Policy*, 2016(95), pp. 1–9. doi:10.1016/j.enpol.2016.04.034.

Knox-Hayes, J. et al. (2013) 'Understanding attitudes toward energy security: results of a cross-national survey', *Global Environmental Change*, 2013(23), pp. 609–622. doi:10.1016/j.gloenvcha.2013.02.003.

Kobek, M.L.P., Ugarte, A., and Aguilar, G.C. (2015) 'Shale gas in the United States: transforming energy security in the twenty-first century', *Norteamérica*, 10(1), pp. 7–38. doi:10.20999/nam.2015.a001.

Kocaslan, G. (2014) 'International energy security indicators and Turkey's energy security risk score', *International Journal of Energy Economics and Policy*, 4(4), pp. 735–743.

Kocaslan, G. (2020) 'A critique of energy security measurement', *Uluslararası İktisadi ve İdari Bilimler Dergisi*, 6(2), pp. 37–51. doi:10.29131/uiibd.832430.

Koitsiwe, K. and Adachi, T. (2015) 'Australia mining boom and Dutch Disease: analysis using VAR method', *Procedia Economics and Finance*, 30, pp. 401–408. doi:10.1016/S2212-5671(15)01307-6.

Konoplyanik, A. (2005) 'Energy security and the development of international energy markets', in Barton, B. et al. (eds.), *Energy security. Managing risk in a dynamic legal and regulatory environment*. Oxford and New York, NY: Oxford University Press, pp. 47–83.

Krikštolaitis, R. et al. (2022) 'Analysis of electricity and natural gas security. A case study for Germany, France, Italy and Spain', *Energies*, 15(3), p. 1000. doi:10.3390/en15031000.

Krugman, P. (1983) 'Oil shocks and exchange rate dynamics', in Frenkel, J.A. (ed.), *Exchange rates and international macroeconomics*. Chicago: University of Chicago Press, pp. 259–284. Available at: http://www.nber.org/chapters/c11382.pdf (Accessed: 3 October 2017).

Krugman, P. (1987) 'The narrow moving band, the Dutch disease, and the competitive consequences of Mrs. Thatcher: notes on trade in the presence of dynamic scale economies', *Journal of Development Economics*, 27(1), pp. 41–55. doi:10.1016/0304-3878(87)90005-8.

Kruyt, B. et al. (2009) 'Indicators for energy security', *Energy Policy*, 37(6), pp. 2166–2181. doi:10.1016/j.enpol.2009.02.006.

Kutan, A.M. and Wyzan, M.L. (2005) 'Explaining the real exchange rate in Kazakhstan, 1996–2003: is Kazakhstan vulnerable to the Dutch disease?' *Exchange-Rate Economics in Transition Countries*, 29(2), pp. 242–255. doi:10.1016/j.ecosys.2005.03.009.

Labandeira, X. and Manzano, B. (2012) 'Some economic aspects of energy security', *European Research Journal*, 15, pp. 47–64.

Leamer, E. E. (1984). *Sources of comparative advantage: Theory and evidence*. Cambridge, MA: MIT Press.

Le Coq, C. and Paltseva, E. (2008) *Measuring the Security of External Supply in the EU*. Available at: https://www.hhs.se/contentassets/5205d56daf0945d891b6d2b92cdf78dc/2008-measuring-the-security-of-external-energy-supply.pdf (Accessed: 22 October 2016).

Lee, Y. (2014) 'Opportunities and risks in Turkmenistan's quest for diversification of its gas export routes', *Energy Policy*, 74, pp. 330–339. doi:10.1016/j.enpol.2014.08.003.

Leiby, P.N. et al. (1997) *Oil imports: an assessment of benefits and costs*. Oak Ridge: Oak Ridge National *Laboratory*. Available at: https://pl.scribd.com/document/103470100/LeibyEtAl1997-Oil-Imports-an-Assessment-of-Costs-and-Benefits-ORNL6851 (Accessed: 29 March 2018).

Leontief, W. (1953) 'Domestic production and foreign trade: the American capital position re-examined', *Proceedings of the American Philosophical Society*, 97(4), pp. 332–349.

Li, Y., Shi, X., and Yao, L. (2016) 'Evaluating energy security of resource-poor economies: a modified principle component analysis approach', *Energy Economics*, 2016(58), pp. 211–221. doi:10.1016/j.eneco.2016.07.001.

Lobova, S.V. et al. (2019) 'Energy security performance: a dataset on the member countries of the Commonwealth of Independent States, 2000–2014', *Data in Brief*, 26, 104450. doi:10.1016/j.dib.2019.104450.

Loeschel, A., Moslener, U., and Ruebellke, D.T.G. (2010) 'Indicators of energy security in industrialised countries', *Energy Policy*, 2010(38), pp. 1665–1671. doi:10.1016/j.enpol.2009.03.061.

Lombardi, M.J. and Van Robays, I. (2011) *Do financial investors destabilize the oil price?* Working Paper Series 1346. Frankfurt: European Central Bank, pp. 1–40. Available at: https://www.ecb.europa.eu/pub/pdf/scpwps/ecbwp1346.pdf (Accessed: 22 January 2022).

Long, N. (1974) 'International borrowing for resource extraction', *International Economic Review*, 15(1), pp. 168–183.

Luciani, G. (2004) *Security of supply for natural gas markets. What is it and what is it not?* INDES Working Paper No. 2. Brussels: CEPS.

Madzarevic, A. et al. (2018) 'Assessment of vulnerability of natural gas supply in Serbia: state and perspective', *Energy Policy*, 121, pp. 415–425. doi:10.1016/j.enpol.2018.06.037.

Mainguy, C. (2011) 'Natural resources and development: the gold sector in Mali', *Resources Policy*, 36(2), pp. 123–131. doi:10.1016/j.resourpol.2010.10.001.

Mansson, A., Johansson, B., and Nilsson, L.J. (2014) 'Assessing energy security: an overview of commonly used methodologies', *Energy*, 2014(73), pp. 1–14. doi:10.1016/j.energy.2014.06.073.

Marion, N. and Svensson, L. (1986) 'The terms of trade between oil importers', *Journal of International Economics*, 20(1–2), pp. 99–113.

Markowitz, H. (1952) 'Portfolio selection', *The Journal of Finance (The Journal of the American Finance Association)*, 7(1), pp. 77–91. doi:10.1111/j.1540-6261.1952.tb01525.x.

Markusen, J.R. and Venables, A.J (1988) 'Trade policy with increasing returns and imperfect competition: contradictory results from competing assumptions', *Journal of International Economics*, 24(3–4), pp. 299–316. doi:10.1016/0022-1996(88)90039-6.

Mayer, T. and Ottaviano, G.I. (2008) 'The happy few: the internationalization of European firms', *Intereconomics*, 43(3), pp. 135–148. doi:10.1007/s10272-008-0247-x.

Medlock, K.B., III, Jaffe, A.M., and Hartley, P. (2011) *Shale gas and US [U.S.] national security*. Houston, TX: James A. Baker III Institute for Public Policy Rice University. Available at: https://www.bakerinstitute.org/media/files/Research/ccecf6b6/EF-pub-DOEShaleGas-07192011.pdf (Accessed: 12 May 2022).

Mehlum, H., Moene, K., and Torvik, R. (2006) 'Institutions and the resource curse', *The Economic Journal*, 116(508), pp. 1–20. doi:10.1111/j.1468-0297.2006.01045.x.
Melitz, M.J. (2003) 'The impact of trade in intra-industry reallocations and aggregate industry productivity', *Econometrica*, 71(6), pp. 1695–1725. doi:10.1111/1468-0262.00467.
Melitz, M.J., Obstfeld, M., and Krugman, P.R. (2018) *Ekonomia międzynarodowa*. Warszawa: Wydawnictwo Naukowe PWN.
Michałek, J. (2010) *Eksport a rozwój gospodarczy: co może wynikać dla Polski z nowej-nowej teorii hadlu i analizy wymiany na poziomie firm*. Unpublished manuscript. Warszawa: Uniwersytet Warszawski.
Mien, E. and Goujon, M. (2022) '40 Years of Dutch disease literature: lessons for developing countries', *Comparative Economic Studies*, 64(3), pp. 351–383. doi:10.1057/s41294-021-00177-w.
Mironov, V.V. and Petronevich, A.V. (2015) 'Discovering the signs of Dutch disease in Russia', *Resources Policy*, 46, pp. 97–112. doi:10.1016/j.resourpol.2015.09.007.
Misala, J. (2003) *Współczesne teorie wymiany międzynarodowej i zagranicznej polityki ekonomicznej*. Warszawa: Oficyna Wydawnicza SGH.
Mitchell, J. (2002) *Renewing energy security*. London: Royal Institute of International Affairs.
Moerenhout, T. and Irschlinger, T. (2020) *Exploring trade impacts of fossil fuel subsidies*. Winnipeg: International Institute for Sustainable Development.
Mogotsi, I. (2002) 'Botswana's diamonds boom: was there a Dutch disease?' *South African Journal of Economics*, 70(1), pp. 128–155. doi:10.1111/j.1813-6982.2002.tb00041.x.
Moore, M.O. and Suranovic, S.M. (1993) 'Lobbying and Cournot-Nash competition. Implications for strategic trade policy', *Journal of International Economics* 35(3–4), pp. 367–376. doi:10.1016/0022-1996(93)90025-S.
Neumann, A. (2004) *Security of supply in liberalized European gas markets*. Frankfurt: Viadrina Universitaet.
Neumann, A. and Hirschhausen, C. (2006) *Long term contracts and assets specificity revisited: an empirical analysis of producer-importer relations in the natural gas industry*. DIW Discussion Papers, 552 [Preprint]. Berlin: Deutsches Institut für Wirtschaftsforschung.
Nojszewska, E. (2010) *Podstawy ekonomii*. Warszawa: Wydawnictwa Szkolne i Pedagogiczne.
Nordhaus, W. (1973) 'The allocation of energy resources', *Brookings Papers on Economic Activity*, 4(3), pp. 529–576.
Novikau, A. (2022) 'Rethinking demand security: between national interests and energy exports', *Energy Research & Social Science*, 87, 102494. doi:10.1016/j.erss.2022.102494.
Nowrouzi, A. et al. (2019) 'Optimizing Iran's natural gas export portfolio by presenting a conceptual framework for non-systematic risk based on portfolio theory', *Energy Strategy Reviews*, 26, p. 100403. doi:10.1016/j.esr.2019.100403.
Nuelle, G.M. and Davis, G. (2018) 'Neither Dutch nor disease? Natural resources booms in theory and empirics', *Mineral Economics*, 31(1), pp. 35–59. doi:10.1007/s13563-018-0153-z.
Nyga-Łukaszewska, H. (2013) *Bezpieczeństwo dostaw gazu ziemnego do Polski w świetle członkostwa w Unii Europejskiej i uzależnienia od importu tego surowca z Rosji*. PhD dissertation. Warszawa: Oficyna Wydawnicza SGH.
Nyga-Łukaszewska, H. (2018a) 'Bezpieczeństwo energetyczne Polski w latach 2010–2016 w świetle prostego modelu importu netto', *Ekonomia Międzynarodowa*, 24, pp. 117–132. doi:10.18778/2082-4440.24.01.
Nyga-Łukaszewska, H. (2018b) 'Rewolucja łupkowa a bezpieczeństwo energetyczne USA w latach 2007–2015', *International Entrepreneurship Review*, 4(1), pp. 23–37. doi:10.15678/PM.2018.0401.02.

Nyga-Łukaszewska, H. (2019) *Bezpieczeństwo energetyczne na międzynarodowym rynku gazu ziemnego*. Warszawa: Oficyna Wydawnicza SGH.

Nyga-Łukaszewska, H. (2020a) 'Bezpieczeństwo energetyczne w ekonomii międzynarodowej: analiza zjawiska na gruncie teorii obfitości zasobów i wybranych koncepcji neoczynnikowych', in Bednarz, J. and Markiewicz, M. (eds.), *Wyzwania gospodarki globalnej*. Gdańsk: Wydawnictwo Uniwersytetu Gdańskiego, pp. 131–154.

Nyga-Łukaszewska, H. (2020b) 'Energy security externalities – phenomenon description', *Polityka Energetyczna – Energy Policy Journal*, 23(1), pp. 19–36. doi:10.33223/epj/116334.

Nyga-Łukaszewska, H., Aruga, K., and Stala-Szlugaj, K. (2020) 'Energy security of Poland and coal supply: price analysis', *Sustainability*, 12(6), p. 2541. doi:10.3390/su12062541.

Obadi, S.M. and Korcek, M. (2020) 'Quantifying the energy security of selected EU countries', *International Journal of Energy Economics and Policy*, 10(2), pp. 276–284. doi:10.32479/ijeep.8847.

Ohlin, B. (1933) *Interregional and international trade*. Cambridge, MA: Harvard University Press.

Ono, H. (1982) 'Note on "international trade with an exhaustible resource: a theorem of Rybczyński type"', *International Economic Review*, 23(1), pp. 165–170. doi:10.2307/2526470.

Oomes, N. and Kalcheva, K. (2007) *Diagnosing Dutch disease: does Russia have the symptoms?* IMF Working Paper WP/07/102. Washington, DC: International Monetary Fund, pp. 1–34.

Opp, M.M., Sonnenschein, H.F., and Tombazos, C.G. (2009) 'Rybczyński's theorem in the Heckscher–Ohlin world – anything goes', *Journal of International Economics*, 79(1), pp. 137–142. doi:10.1016/j.jinteco.2009.05.005.

Osei, E. and Lapan, E. (1995) *The generalized H-O model with different natural resource intensities*. Economic Staff Paper Series 253. Ames: Iowa State University. Available at: http://lib.dr.iastate.edu/econ_las_staffpapers/253 (Accessed: 3 March 2020).

Paldam, M. (2013) 'The political economy of Dutch disease: a survey', in *Constitutional economics and public institutions*. Cheltenham: Edward Elgar Publishing, pp. 179–196. Available at: https://EconPapers.repec.org/RePEc:elg:eechap:14863_10. Doi: 10.4337/9781781003978.00020 (Accessed: 13 March 2023).

Pirani, S. and Yafimava, K. (2016) *Russian gas transit across Ukraine post-2019 – pipeline scenarios, gas flow consequences, and regulatory constraints*, Oxford: Oxford Institute for Energy Studies. Available at: https://api.semanticscholar.org/CorpusID:217771012 (Accessed: 13 March 2023).

Pegg, S. (2010) 'Is there a Dutch disease in Botswana?' *Resources Policy*, 35(1), pp. 14–19. doi:10.1016/j.resourpol.2009.07.003.

Podbregar, I. et al. (2020) 'The international energy security risk index in sustainable energy and economy transition decision making—a reliability analysis', *Energies*, 13(14), p. 3691. doi:10.3390/en13143691.

Qiu, L.D. (1994) 'Optimal strategic trade policy under asymmetric information', *Journal of International Economics*, 36(3–4), pp. 333–354. doi:10.1016/0022-1996(94)90007-8.

Qiu, L.D. (1995) 'Strategic trade policy under uncertainty', *Review of International Economics*, 3(1), pp. 75–85. doi:10.1111/j.1467-9396.1995.tb00053.x.

Radovanovic, M., Filipovic, S., and Pavlovic, D. (2017) 'Energy security measurement – a sustainable approach', *Renewable and Sustainable Energy Reviews*, 68(2), pp. 1020–1032. doi:10.1016/j.rser.2016.02.010.

Rambaldi, A., Hall, G., and Brown, R. (2006) *Re-testing the resource curse hypothesis using panel data and an improved measure of resource intensity*. Contributed paper prepared for presentation at the International Association of Agricultural Economists Conference, Gold Coast, Australia, August 12–18, 2006. Queensland: International Association of Agricultural Economists. Available at: https://EconPapers.repec.org/RePEc:ags:iaae06:25289 (Accessed: 3 March 2020).

Ren, J. and Sovacool, B.K. (2014) 'Quantifying, measuring, and strategizing energy security: determining the most meaningful dimensions and metrics', *Energy*, 76, pp. 838–849. doi:10.1016/j.energy.2014.08.083.

Ren, J. and Sovacool, B.K. (2015) 'Prioritizing low-carbon energy sources to enhance China's energy security', *Energy Conversion and Management*, 92, pp. 129–136. doi:10.1016/j.enconman.2014.12.044.

Renou-Maissant, P. (2019) 'Is oil price still driving inflation?' *The Energy Journal*, 40(6), pp. 199–220. doi:10.5547/01956574.40.6.pren.

Robinson, J. and Torvik, R. (2013) 'Institutional comparative statics', in Acemoglu, D., Arellano, M., and Dekel, E. (eds.), *Advances in economics and econometrics*. Tenth World Congress, Volume II: Applied Economics. Cambridge: Cambridge University Press, pp. 97–134.

Romanova, T. (2013) 'Energy demand: security for suppliers?' in Dyer, H. and Trombetta, J. (eds.), *International handbook of energy security*. Cheltenham: Edward Elgar, pp. 239–249.

Rybczyński, T.M. (1955) 'Factor endowment and relative commodity prices', *Economica*, 22(88), pp. 336–341. doi:10.2307/2551188.

Rynarzewski, T. (2005) *Strategiczna polityka handlu międzynarodowego*. Warszawa: Polskie Wydawnictwo Ekonomiczne.

Sachs, J. and Warner, A. (1995) *Natural resource abundance and economic growth*. NBER Working Paper Series, 5398. Cambridge: National Bureau of Economic Research. doi:10.3386/w5398.

Salvatore, D. (2013) *International economics*. 11th edn. New York, NY: Wiley & Sons. Available at: https://ccsuniversity.ac.in/bridge-library/pdf/Dominick-Salvatore-International-Economics.pdf (Accessed: 11 March 2023).

Samuelson, P.A. (1948) 'International trade and the equalisation of factor prices', *The Economic Journal*, 58(230), pp. 163–184. doi:10.2307/2225933.

Samuelson, P.A. (1949) 'International factor-price equalisation once again', *The Economic Journal*, 59(234), pp. 181–197. doi:10.2307/2226683.

Samuelson, P.A. (1971) 'Ohlin was right', *The Swedish Journal of Economics*, 73(4), pp. 365–384. doi:10.2307/3439219.

Scitovsky, T. (1954) 'Two concepts of external economies', *Journal of Political Economy*, 62(2), pp. 143–151. doi:10.1086/257498.

Shih, W.C. (2009) 'Energy security, GATT/WTO, and regional agreements', *Natural Resources Journal*, 49(2), pp. 433–484.

Shirazi, M., Ghasemi, A., and Šimurina, J. (2021) 'The impact of the North American shale gas technology on the US' energy security: the case of natural gas', *International Journal of Sustainable Energy*, 41(7), pp. 1–22. doi:10.1080/14786451.2021.1979002.

Šimić, G. et al. (2021) 'Fuzzy logic approach in energy security decision-making: "ES-ecFuzzy" software application', *Soft Computing*, 25, pp. 10813–10828. doi:10.1007/s00500-021-05976-y.

Sohns, R. (1976) *Theorie der internationalen Arbeitsteilung*. Stuttgart: Gustav Fischer Verlag.

Sovacool, B.K. and Mukherjee, I. (2011) 'Conceptualizing and measuring energy security: a synthesized approach', *Energy*, 2011(36), pp. 5343–5355. doi:10.1016/j.energy.2011.06.043.

Spencer, B.J. (1998) 'What should trade policy target?' in Krugman, P.R. (ed.), *Strategic trade policy and the new international economics*. 8th printing. London: MIT Press, pp. 69–91.

Staśko, D. and Kaliski, M. (2006) 'Bezpieczeństwo energetyczne', in *Bezpieczeństwo energetyczne w gospodarce paliwowej Polski*. Kraków: Wydawnictwo Instytutu Gospodarki Surowcami Mineralnymi i Energią PAN, pp. 107–163.

Stavytskyy, A. et al. (2021) 'Methodology for calculating the energy security index of the state: taking into account modern megatrends', *Energies*, 14(12), p. 3621. doi:10.3390/en14123621.

Stern, J. (2002) *Security of European natural gas supplies. The impact of import dependence and liberalization*. London: Royal Institute of International Affairs.

Stiglitz, J. and Rosengard, J. (2015) *Economics of the public sector*. 4th edn. New York, NY: W.N. Norton & Company, Inc.

Stijns, J.-P. (2003) 'An empirical test of the Dutch Disease hypothesis using a gravity model of trade', *International Trade*, p. 0305001. Available at: https://ideas.repec.org/p/wpa/wuwpit/0305001.html (Accessed: 20 March 2022).

Stolper, W.F. and Samuelson, P.A. (1941) 'Protection and real wages', *The Review of Economic Studies*, 9(1), pp. 58–73. doi:10.2307/2967638.

Sumskis, V. and Giedraitis, V. (2015) 'Economic implications of energy security in the short run', *Ekonomika*, 94(3), pp. 119–138. doi: 10.15388/Ekon.2015.3.8791.

The Economist (1977) 'The Dutch disease', *The Economist*, 26 November, pp. 82–83.

Trefler, D. (1993) 'International factor price differences: Leontief was right!' *Journal of Political Economy*, 101(6), pp. 961–987

Trefler, D. (1995) 'The case of the missing trade and other mysteries', *The American Economic Review*, 85(5), pp. 1029–1046.

Ulatowski, R. (2016) *Analiza porównawcza polityki energetycznej importerów i eksporterów surowców energetycznych na przykładzie Niemiec i Arabii Saudyjskiej – perspektywa geoekonomiczna*. Warszawa: Wydawnictwo Naukowe Scholar.

Umiński, S. (2012) *Rozważania and naturą, przyczynami oraz konkurencyjnością działalności eksportowej w ujęciu regionalnym dla Polski*. Gdańsk: Wydawnictwo Uniwersytetu Gdańskiego.

Van Marrewijk, C., Ottens, D., and Schueller, S. (2012) *International economics*. 2nd edn. New York, NY: Oxford University Press.

Vanek, J. (1959) 'The natural resource content of foreign trade, 1870–1955, and the relative abundance of natural resources in the United States', *The Review of Economics and Statistics*, 41(2), pp. 146–153.

Vanek, J. (1963) *The natural resource content of foreign trade, 1870–1955*. Cambridge: Cambridge University Press.

Velthuijsen, J. and Worrell, E. (2002) 'The economics of energy', in van der Bergh, J. (ed.), *Handbook of environmental and resource economics*. Cheltenham: Edward Elgar Publishing, pp. 177–196.

Venables, A.J. (1985) 'Trade and trade policy with imperfect competition: the case of identical products and free entry', *Journal of International Economics*, 16(1–2), pp. 1–19.

Verkuiji, C. et al. (2017) 'Tackling fossil fuel subsidies through international trade agreements', *Climate Strategies*, November, London: Climate Strategies. Available at: https://climatestrategies.org/wp-content/uploads/2017/11/CS-Report_FFS-2017.pdf (Accessed: 25.05.2022).

Vernon, R. (1966) 'International investment and international trade in the product cycle', *Quarterly Journal of Economics*, 80(2), pp. 190–207. doi:10.2307/1880689.

Vivoda, V. (2009) 'Diversification of oil import sources and energy security: a key strategy or an elusive objective?' *Energy Policy*, 2009(37), pp. 4615–4623. doi:10.1016/j.enpol.2009.06.007.

Vousden, N. (1974) 'International trade and exhaustible resources: a theoretical model', *International Economic Review*, 15(1), pp. 149–167.

Wang, Q. and Zhou, K. (2017) 'A framework for evaluating global national energy security', *Applied Energy*, 2017(188), pp. 19–31. doi:10.1016/j.apenergy.2016.11.116.

WEC (2017). *World Energy Trilemma Index 2017*. London: World Energy Council. Available at: https://trilemma.worldenergy.org/reports/main/2017/2017%20Energy%20Trilemma%20Index.pdf (Accessed: 30 June 2018).

Wild, J. (1997) *Strategische Handelspolitik. Alternative Instrumente bei oligopolitischen Wettbewerb*. Frankfurt: Peter Lang GmbH.

Winzer, C. (2012) 'Conceptualizing energy security', *Energy Policy*, 2012(46), pp. 36–48. doi:10.1016/j.enpol.2012.02.067.

Wright, P. (2005) 'Liberalisation and the security of gas supply in the UK', *Energy Policy*, 2005(33), pp. 2272–2290. doi: 10.1016/j.enpol.2004.04.022.

WTO (2010). *World Trade Report 2010*. Geneva: World Trade Organization. Available at: https://www.wto.org/english/res_e/publications_e/wtr10_e.htm (Accessed: 20 May 2013).

Wysokińska, Z. (1995) *Dynamiczne współzależności wymiany handlowej krajów Europy Środkowej i Wschodniej w świetle teorii integracji i wymiany międzynarodowej*. Łódź: Wydawnictwo Uniwersytetu Łódzkiego.

Yafimava, K. (2011) *The transit dimension of EU energy security: Russian gas transit across Ukraine, Belarus, and Moldova*. Oxford: Oxford Institute for Energy Studies/Oxford University Press. Available at: https://EconPapers.repec.org/RePEc:oxp:obooks:9780199599226 (Accessed: 20 May 2023).

Ye, R. et al. (2021) 'Natural gas security evaluation from a supply vs. demand perspective: a quantitative application of four As', *Energy Policy*, 156, p. 112425. doi:10.1016/j.enpol.2021.112425.

Zeng, S., Streimikiene, D., and Balezentis, T. (2017) 'Review and comparative assessment of energy security in Baltic States', *Renewable and Sustainable Energy Reviews*, 2017(76), pp. 185–192. doi:10.1016/j.rser.2017.03.037.

Zielińska-Głębocka, A. (2012) *Współczesna gospodarka światowa, Przemiany innowacje, kryzysy, rozwiązania regionalne*. Warszawa: Wolters Kluwer.

3 Energy security in the global gas market and its determinants

3.1 Global gas market

Natural gas has many applications. It can be used, among others, to produce electricity, heat, and chemicals. Like any other energy commodity, it features specific characteristics in economics. First, natural gas is a primary energy source, which can be converted into secondary energy, thus contributing to the generation of electricity or heat. Like any commodity, it is characterized by low price elasticity of supply and demand, especially in the short term. It is caused by a long investment cycle, high capital intensity of investments and a high share of fixed costs in the total extraction costs. Due to all these features, the supply does not react flexibly to price changes (except for the spare capacity margin). This means that in periods of falling prices, the production of energy remains at a slightly changed level. The low price elasticity of demand is associated with a significant number of substitutes for natural gas in almost every application. In the production of electricity or heat, coal, uranium, crude oil, or renewable energy sources can be used alternatively, in transport – from crude oil, and in the processes of chemical synthesis – from coal.

Natural gas was the energy resource with the highest consumption growth dynamics in the world among all fossil fuels (2017–2016). It turns out that the demand for crude oil grew (year on year) at the rate of 1.6%, whereas for coal, it grew at 1% and for natural gas at 3%. The only fuel for which the demand grew even faster were renewable energy sources (6% y/y) (BP, 2017). With the COVID-19 pandemic, natural gas saw the smallest decrease in demand (2020–2019: crude oil −8.9%, coal −3.8%, nuclear −4%, natural gas −2.1%), opposite to changes in the dynamics of renewable energy consumption (2020–2019: 6%) (BP, 2021).

Natural gas met one-fourth of the world's primary energy consumption (Figure 3.1). It was used equally often by developed countries and developing countries, which represent countries outside the OECD group. A similar trend to that of natural gas was observed in the case of crude oil and renewable energy. By comparison, it is worth noting that coal was consumed mainly in developing countries and nuclear energy in developed countries. This is evidenced by the statistics of the share of individual groups of countries in primary energy consumption in 2020 (Table 3.1).

DOI: 10.4324/9781003052241-4

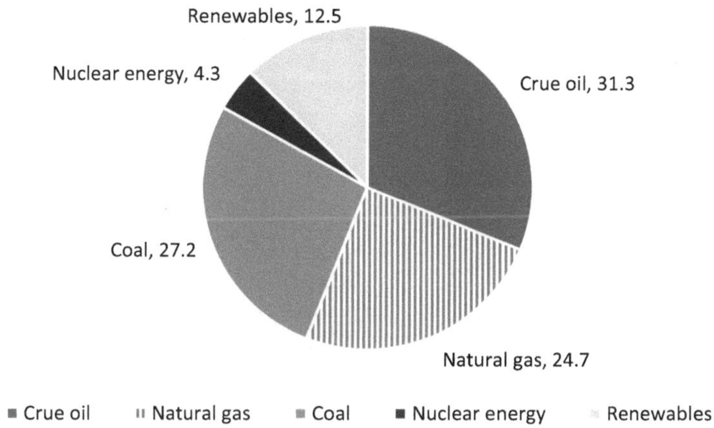

Figure 3.1 World energy mix 2020 (share of respective energy types in %).

Source: Compiled by the author based on BP (2021).

Table 3.1 Share of OECD and non-OECD countries in respective fuel use in 2020 (in %)[a]

	Crude oil (%)	*Natural gas (%)*	*Coal (%)*	*Nuclear energy (%)*	*Renewables (%)*
OECD (including EU)	45	46	18	70	45
Non-OECD	55	54	82	30	55
EU	11	10	4	25	14

Source: Compiled by the author based on BP (2021).

[a] As EU counts into OECD, columns do not add up to do 100%.

According to the Massachusetts Institute of Technology, natural gas may become a transition fuel on the way to the era of low-emission fuels (MIT, 2011). Due to the fact that its combustion is associated with lower harmful air emissions than other fossil fuels, it is an alternative to coal and crude oil. Due to the growing popularity of this fuel and the uneven distribution of natural gas resources in the world, some countries have to import it. This way, the international natural gas market was created, described both by trade flows being a function of the supply and demand for natural gas, the price of the commodity, and producer organizations.

3.1.1 Global natural gas supply

Natural gas deposits are located mainly outside the OECD countries (approx. 71% of the world's natural gas resources in 2020 – BP, 2021). The largest documented natural gas resources in the world are located in three countries, respectively: Russia, Iran, and Qatar (Table 3.2). The share of Russia and Iran in the world's natural

Table 3.2 World's biggest natural gas reserve holders at the end of 2020

Country	*Natural gas reserves (tcm)*	*World share (%)*	*R/P* [a]
Russia	37.4	20.0	58.6
Iran	32.1	17.3	128.0
Qatar	24.7	13	144.0
Turkmenistan	13.6	7	230.7
USA	12.6	7	13.8
China	8.4	4	43.3
Venezuela	6.3	3	333.9
Saudi Arabia	6.0	3	53.7
UAE	6.1	3.3	98.5
Nigeria	5.5	3	110.7

Source: Compiled by the author based on BP (2021).

[a] R/P (ang. *resources to production*) it is the ratio of resources to the current level of their extraction. It shows how many years the current resources would last if the current level of their extraction were to be maintained.

gas resources is comparable and amounts to approximately 17–20%. Qatar has a 13% share of the world's natural gas resources. Turkmenistan and the USA (7% share each in global deposits) and China (4%) have smaller resources on a global scale. Among the countries with rich natural gas deposits are the countries of Africa: Nigeria, Algeria, Egypt, and Libya, as well as Australia, Indonesia, Canada, and Norway. At the end of 2020, the European Union as a whole had deposits that gave it a total share of 0.2% in the world's resources of natural gas. Based on the analysis of the distribution of natural gas resources in the world, it is possible to see their geographical concentration in the Middle East (approx. 40% of the world's resources) and Russia (20% of the world's resources).

Taking into account the level of the R/P ratio (resources to production), which reflects the relation of natural gas resources to the current level of gas production, it can be noted that a country with the largest deposits (in absolute terms) and the largest share in its global resources does not necessarily have the highest R/P ratio. This index approximately shows for how many years the documented reserves of the commodity will last if the current level of its production is maintained. Iraq is an example of a country with the above-mentioned index above 300, as the country's resources will be sufficient for another 336 years. This is due not only to the rich resource base, but above all to the low level of domestic production, which oscillated around 10 bcm of natural gas per year (2020). By comparison, Poland, which has significantly smaller natural gas resources, i.e., 0.1 tcm (2020), with an annual extraction of about 4 bcm, was characterized by an R/P ratio of about 18 (2020) (Table 3.2).

Particularly noteworthy is the distinction between conventional and unconventional natural gas resources. The presence of unconventional deposits does not coincide geographically with conventional deposits. Unconventional resources of natural gas include shale gas, tight gas, and coal bed methane. Unconventional gas, just like conventional gas, is a mixture of hydrocarbons (mainly methane,

Table 3.3 Shale gas reserve holders 2016[a]

Country	*Shale gas reserves (tcm)*
China	31.6
Argentina	22.7
Algeria	20.0
USA	17.6
Saudi Arabia	17.0
Canada	16.2
Mexico	15.4
Australia	12.2
South Africa	11.0
Poland	4.1
Turkey	0.7

Source: Compiled by the author based on World Energy Council (2016).

[a] Latest available data.

as well as ethane, propane, and butane) and nitrogen. The feature that distinguishes both types of natural gas is the type of rock from which their deposits come. In the case of conventional gas, these are porous rocks covered with a layer of impermeable rocks, and in the case of unconventional deposits, these are only impermeable rocks (Poprawa, 2018). Due to the fact that in both domestic and international statistics, the specification of resources and production of unconventional gas types is negligible, the following considerations use shale gas as an example and, where possible, data on all types of unconventional gas.

As depicted in Table 3.3, countries with the richest shale gas deposits are China, Argentina, Algeria, the USA, and Saudi Arabia. In China, the most promising fields are Sichuan and Tarim, located, respectively, in the south and north-west of the country (Gao, 2012). In Argentina, the Vaca Muerte field is promising, as is Ghadames in Algeria (the eastern part of the country, on the border with Tunisia and Libya), and several smaller fields in the central part of the country, with the Timimoun field being the largest (Boersma, Vandendriessche, and Leber, 2015). In the USA, the most abundant fields are Barnett (North Texas), Fayetteville (Arkansas), Haynesville (East Texas/North Louisiana), Woodford (Oklahoma), Eagle Ford (South Texas), Marcellus and Utica (North Appalachia) (EIA, 2017).

Natural gas extraction in the world coincides with the regions of its occurrence (Table 3.4). A great majority of them are non-OECD countries (62% share in the global production of natural gas in 2020 – BP, 2021). The largest producer of natural gas in the world in 2020 was the USA, which achieved over 24% share in the global production of this commodity with its production of approximately 914 bcm. The second largest producer of natural gas was Russia, which produced about 638 bcm of natural gas accounting for 17% of the world's production of this commodity. Production in both of these countries accounts for less than half of the world's natural gas production. Apart from the USA and Russia, major world producers of natural gas with comparable output were Iran (251 bcm), China

Table 3.4 World's biggest natural gas producers in 2020

Country	*Natural gas production (bcm)*	*Share in the world production (%)*
USA	914	24
Russia	638	17
Iran	251	7
China	194	5
Qatar	171	4
Canada	165	4
Australia	142	4
Saudi Arabia	112	3
Norway	111	3
Algeria	81	2

Source: Compiled by the author based on BP (2021).

(194 bcm), and Qatar (171 bcm). Production in other countries included in the group of large natural gas producers (Norway, Saudi Arabia, Canada, and Australia) ranged around 100 bcm in 2020.

Figures showing gas production from unconventional deposits (see the Appendix, Figures A.1–A.7) were prepared on the basis of IEA data obtained both from companies (e.g., Cedigaz) and statistics from selected countries (e.g., USA, Canada).[1] The USA, Canada, Argentina, and China play the leading role in the production of shale gas in the world. Shale gas production in the USA was incomparably greater than in other regions of the world. According to IEA estimates, around 380 bcm of this commodity was extracted in that country in 2014. This accounted for more than half of the national production of natural gas (733 bcm in 2014 – BP, 2017). Commercialization of shale gas extraction in the USA was possible, *inter alia*, thanks to abundant and geologically easily accessible resources of this commodity. Canada is another country with advanced shale gas production amounting to 6 bcm in 2014. This volume was incomparably smaller than that of US production. Argentina and China are other countries where shale gas production started. In 2014, shale gas production in these countries oscillated between 0.3 and 1.3 bcm, respectively. A significant difference in the production of shale gas between the USA and other countries results from the fact that the USA started its commercial production in 2007 (first records from the official statistics of the American Energy Information Administration), while China did not do so until 2012 (Nyga-Łukaszewska, 2017).

Similar trends were visible in the world production of tight gas, as the countries of North America played a dominant role. The advantage of the USA in this case was much smaller than in the production of shale gas. According to IEA estimates, the USA produced 127 bcm of tight gas in 2014, and Canada 73 bcm. The production of this commodity in China amounted to 17 bcm, and in Argentina 2 bcm. Russia's production in the same year amounted to 20 bcm of tight gas. It is the only type of unconventional gas production in which Russia was significantly involved.

The production of coal bed methane (CBM) was slightly different than shale and tight gas.[2] This type of unconventional gas is associated with coal seams. For this reason, methane from coal beds is produced mainly by countries which are also major global coal producers. This group includes, respectively, the USA, China, and Australia. In 2014, China was the world's largest producer of coal (3,873 mt), while the USA, with a production of 907 mt, and Australia, with 504 mt, were among the top producers of this commodity (BP, 2017). According to the IEA, the largest CBM production in 2014 was recorded in the USA, China, and Australia. As with other types of unconventional gas, production in the USA was higher than in other countries. However, this difference was the smallest among all types of unconventional resources. In 2014, the USA produced 37 bcm of CBM, China – 14 bcm, and Australia – 7 bcm.

3.1.2 World demand and prices for natural gas

Demand for energy, including natural gas, is the amount of product that buyers are willing to buy for a certain price. Bhattacharyya (2011) suggests that there are subtle differences in this way of thinking about energy demand. A different understanding of energy demand is related to the difference between the reported (*ex-ante*) energy demand and its consumption (*ex-post*). Energy demand may include the amount of energy that is not used later. Therefore, it is not equal to energy consumption (Bhattacharyya, 2011). Being aware of this difference, in the course of further considerations, its consumption is considered to be an equivalent of the demand for natural gas.

Contrary to the share of non-OECD countries in the global resources and extraction of natural gas in the natural gas consumption, dominance of this group of countries is not so strong. Natural gas consumption in 2020 was comparable in the OECD countries and those outside the group (respectively: 46% and 54% of the global consumption of natural gas). The group of countries with the highest consumption of natural gas includes mainly countries that are significant producers of natural gas. This applies to the USA, Russia, China, Iran, Canada, and Saudi Arabia.

The country with the highest consumption of natural gas in the world is also its largest producer – the USA (Table 3.5). In 2020, 832 bcm of natural gas was used there, compared to 914 bcm of natural gas extracted from domestic deposits. The demand for natural gas from the Russian economy, in the amount of 411 bcm, accounted for a tenth of the global demand for the commodity. China's natural gas consumption tripled between 2010 and 2020. In 2010, China consumed 111 bcm of natural gas annually, and in 2020 as much as 331 bcm. By comparison, back in 2000, the country used 25 bcm of gas per year. Such a dynamic increase in demand results both from the high rate of economic growth and the increasingly frequent replacement of coal with natural gas (Gao, 2012).

In the case of Iran, almost all of the gas produced is consumed domestically (251 bcm – production, 233 bcm – consumption in 2020). Significant recipients of this commodity are the electricity sector (26% of total consumption) and industry (27%). If sanctions on Iranian natural gas exports are lifted, the importance of this industry in Iran is expected to increase (EIA, 2022a). In Saudi Arabia, as in Iran,

Table 3.5 World's biggest natural gas consumers in 2020

Country	*Natural gas c onsumption (bcm)*	*Share in world natural gas consumption (%)*
USA	832	22
Russia	411	11
China	331	9
Iran	233	6
Canada	113	3
Saudi Arabia	112	3
Japan	104	3
Germany	86	2
Mexico	86	2
United Kingdom	73	2

Source: Compiled by the author based on BP (2021).

the country's entire natural gas resource is allocated to the Saudi economy and electricity production (EIA, 2022c).

In Japan, as in Iran and Saudi Arabia, a significant proportion of natural gas (34%, 2019) (EIA, 2022b) is used to generate electricity. Nevertheless, with time, it is expected that the decommissioned nuclear reactors will be gradually put back into operation (due to the accident at the Fukushima-Daichii power plant), and, therefore, the consumption of natural gas in electricity production will decrease. Contrary to the Arab countries, in Japan all natural gas used in the country is imported.

Among the world's major consumers of natural gas, the United Kingdom deserves greater attention. The high consumption of natural gas in that country is part of the tradition associated with its developed hydrocarbon mining. Nevertheless, between 2000 and 2014, both the production of natural gas and its consumption in the United Kingdom gradually decreased. On the other hand, in 2015–2016, a slight upward trend was observed and continues today (EIA, 2022d). Natural gas continues to be one of the main sources of electricity production in the country. Due to the reduction of coal consumption in power plants and its replacement with natural gas, it is predicted that its consumption may increase in the future (EIA, 2018).

The UK is one of the most important natural gas markets in the world. The British Heren National Balancing Point (Heren NBP) is, next to the American Henry Hub, one of the few hubs in the world where reference prices for natural gas are recorded. The Japanese market and especially natural gas prices imported to Japan are also one of such regional price hubs. Heren NBP prices are the most representative natural gas prices for the European market, as are Henry Hub prices for the American market and Japan's prices for the Asia Pacific market.

Comparing the prices of natural gas on the British, American, and Asian markets, it can be seen that the historically lowest natural gas prices at the Heren NBP have given way to the American resource (Figure 3.2). Since 2008, natural gas prices at the American Henry Hub have been among the lowest in the world. This

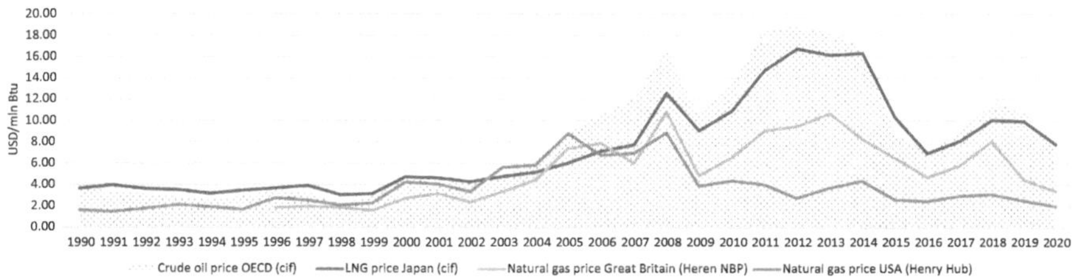

Figure 3.2 Natural gas prices in selected hubs and crude oil prices in OECD countries between 1990 and 2020.

Source: Compiled by the author based on BP (2021).

* Natural gas prices in the United Kingdom (Heren NBP) are available since 1996.

is the effect of the continued oversupply of natural gas on the US market caused by the exploitation of shale deposits. The opposite tendency is observed in the Asia Pacific market. The price of natural gas has recently increased in that region. It was record high in 2012 (USD 16.75/mBtu). Then, as a result of the tsunami, there was a disaster at the Fukushima Daiichi nuclear power plant and all nuclear reactors in Japan were shut down. Deficit energy demand was covered by its production from power plants fired with imported natural gas.

Apart from the regional hubs determining the reference prices of natural gas in the world, (current) prices of this commodity are also quoted on selected world exchanges (e.g., NYMEX). Nevertheless, in the case of most of the long-term contracts for the sale of natural gas, crude oil prices are usually the main component of the so-called price formulas. Therefore, all prices, including those recorded in hubs, are similar to oil prices in OECD countries (Figure 3.2). The strongest correlation between the prices of crude oil and those of natural gas is found in the Japanese and British markets. In the period of 1990–2020, the Pearson correlation coefficient for both variables was 0.97 and 0.93, respectively. The American market sees a slightly weaker correlation of crude oil and natural gas prices. In the years 1996–2020,[3] the Pearson coefficient in this case was 0.43. The comparison of the correlation coefficients of crude oil and natural gas prices in relation to the American, Asian, and European markets confirms how profound changes took place in the natural gas market in the USA.

3.1.3 *World trade in natural gas*

Due to the geographic concentration of natural gas resources and extraction, most countries have to import it. International trade in natural gas can take one of two forms depending on the mode of transport. The first is related to the transport of natural gas by pipelines (by sea or land), the second – by tankers (by sea).

In terms of the volume of international trade in natural gas, pipelines are the dominant means of transport in this case. In 2020, approximately 756 bcm of natural gas and 488 bcm of liquified natural gas (LNG) (BP, 2021) were sold abroad via

Table 3.6 World's biggest natural gas importers 2020 (bcm)

Country	*Pipeline imports*
Germany	102
Italy	51
USA	68
Mexico	54
China	45
	LNG imports
Japan	102
China	94
South Korea	56
India	36
Taiwan	25

Source: Compiled by the author based on BP (2021).

gas pipelines. The annual growth rates of both markets in the period 2009–2019 were significantly different. In the case of the gas pipeline market, it was around 2%, and in the case of the LNG market, it was around 7%. This confirms the dynamic development of the liquid gas market, which, unlike the pipeline market, offers greater flexibility in terms of the direction of supply. Pipelines permanently connect the importer, exporter, and the transit country, while LNG tankers are free to change routes and destination points of supply of commodities.

Most of the trade in natural gas via pipelines takes place within Europe (Table 3.6). In 2020, approximately 447 bcm of natural gas was purchased this way in the region. The second largest market was North America, where approximately 144 bcm was imported via pipelines from abroad in the same year. It is worth noting, however, that in the case of the North American market, most of the imports are traded between the USA, Canada, and Mexico. In Europe, the largest importers of natural gas supplied via pipelines are Germany and Italy, which in 2020 thus purchased 102 bcm and 51 bcm of gas, respectively. In the case of Germany, imports were at a level similar to the pre-pandemic period (100 bcm in 2016), while in Italy they decreased significantly (from 60 bcm in 2016) (BP, 2017). In the rest of the world, trade in pipeline gas was smaller. The largest amount of gas, apart from Europe, was sold via pipelines from Turkmenistan to China – around 45 bcm in 2020 (compared to 30 bcm in 2016). The largest suppliers of gas via pipelines were (2020), as before the COVID-pandemic, Russia (198 bcm) and Norway (107 bcm) (Table 3.7). Russia has dominated gas supplies by pipelines to the largest importers in Europe. In 2020, it was responsible for 56 bcm of gas delivered to Germany and 20 bcm sold to Italy. At that time, both countries also used natural gas from Norway (31 bcm to Germany) and Algeria (31 bcm to Italy), respectively. In the case of the USA, pipeline deliveries were made entirely from Canada to Mexico entirely from the USA. China purchased more than half of the gas imported via gas pipelines from Turkmenistan (28 bcm).

Table 3.7 World's biggest natural gas exporters 2020 (bcm)

Country	*Pipeline exports*
Russia	198
Norway	107
USA	76
Canada	68
Turkmenistan	32
	LNG exports
Australia	106
Qatar	106
USA	61
Russia	40
Malaysia	33

Source: Compiled by the author based on BP (2021).

Natural gas is transported through pipelines over shorter distances than by LNG tankers. Currently, the largest importer of LNG in the world is the Asia region (Table 3.6). The largest LNG importers (2020) include Japan (102 bcm), China (94 bcm), South Korea (56 bcm), India (36 bcm), and Taiwan (25 bcm). The imports of LNG to China are noteworthy, having increased significantly in recent years. In 2016, China purchased 53 bcm (BP, 2017), while in 2020 it was already over 90 bcm of gas. Among European countries, the largest recipients of LNG at the same time were Spain (21 bcm) and France (20 bcm). In turn, the largest exporters of LNG in the world in 2020 were (Table 3.7) Australia (106 bcm) – which, compared to 2016, almost doubled its sales of gas from 56 bcm (BP, 2017), Qatar (106 bcm), the USA – which joined the group of the largest LNG exporters in recent years (61 bcm), and Malaysia (33 bcm). LNG sales, unlike pipeline gas, are global in nature. Qatar and Australia supply LNG mainly in the Asia Pacific region, while the USA and Russia share their LNG supplies relatively evenly between Europe and Asia. In the case of Qatar and Australia, the volume of LNG delivered to a single recipient is much greater than in the case of the USA and Russia. The largest LNG recipients from Australia (Japan – 41 bcm, China – 40 bcm) or Qatar (India – 14 bcm, South Korea – 13 bcm) contract significantly larger amounts of gas than the largest US trading partners (South Korea – 8 bcm, Japan – 6 bcm), and Russia (China – 7 bcm, France – 5 bcm). Interestingly, the customers of the above exporters are the same, with only the quantities differing. To sum up, the structure of supplies of American and Russian LNG is significantly more diversified than that of Australian or Qatari gas.

It is worth noting that the trade in natural gas delivered via pipelines compared to that delivered by LNG tankers is rather local in nature. Most transactions take place within the regions: Europe, America (North or South), and Asia. In the case of LNG, the opposite is true – trade in liquid gas is global.

3.1.4 Organization of the world natural gas market

The organization of the market is understood as its structure, number of participants, nature of competition, and entry barriers. Due to the fact that some of these aspects are described in the sections on supply, demand, and price, only the main organization of natural gas producers will be presented here. The rationale for this approach is that it determines the nature of competition in the natural gas market.

The most important organization associating producers in the natural gas market is the Gas Exporting Countries Forum (GECF). GECF was established in 2001 in Tehran. Its members were then Algeria, Brunei, Indonesia, Iran, Malaysia, Oman, Qatar, Russia, Turkmenistan and, as an observer, Norway. By 2018, out of the founding countries, only Algeria, Iran, Qatar, and Russia had remained in the organization. Oman became an observer member. The GECF has expanded to add new members, including Nigeria and Venezuela. Since the organization was founded, the group of observer countries has also changed significantly. Currently, apart from Norway, this status is also enjoyed by Angola, Azerbaijan, Iraq, Malaysia, Oman, and Peru (Table 3.8).[4] The difference between GECF member and observer countries refers to their voting right. According to article 6 of the GECF Statue (2008), member countries can attend the ministerial meetings and vote, while observer can only attend and even participate in a discussion but without the voting privilege. The ministerial meeting, as article 9 of the GECF Statue (2008) stipulates is a "*supreme governing body of the Forum*". Any gas-exporting

Table 3.8 GECF members and observers (14 March 2022)

No.	*GECF members*
1	Algeria
2	Bolivia
3	Egypt
4	Equatorial Guinea
5	Iran
6	Libya
7	Nigeria
8	Russia
9	Qatar
10	Trinidad and Tobago
11	Venezuela
GECF observers	
12	Angola
13	Azerbaijan
14	Iraq
15	Malaysia
16	Norway
17	Oman
18	Peru
19	United Arab Emirates

Source: Compiled by the author based on GECF (2021).

country may become member providing that in the former case: accepts the GECF Statue and its candidacy is approved by the three-fourths of members at a ministerial meeting. The observer-candidate country has to be a gas-exporting state that submits a request to the Secretariat of the Forum to become GECF observer. Such request is subjected to voting during the ministerial meeting. In order to become an observer, candidate country needs to be approved by the three-fourths of members at a ministerial meeting.

In 2020, the GECF countries (members and observers) controlled approximately 62% of the world's natural gas resources, the majority of which was located in the member states (88%). The largest deposits of natural gas were in three countries: Russia, Iran, and Qatar (in this order). Among the observers, Iraq had the largest resources (approx. 3,700 bcm) corresponding to the smallest resources among the member countries (e.g., Algeria – approx. 4,500 bcm). As the GECF expanded, its resource base and production was gradually increasing (GECF, 2021).

Natural gas production in the GECF countries (members and observers) accounted for 44% of gas production in the world in 2020. The observer countries accounted for approximately 23% of this. The undisputed leader in the GECF in terms of natural gas production was Russia, which produced approximately 644 bcm of gas in 2020. Iran, ranking second, produced around 330 bcm, and Qatar, third – 211 bcm. Among the observer countries, Norway had the highest production of natural gas, having produced about 148 bcm in 2020 (Figure 3.3). The production volume in the GECF countries in 2020 was comparable to the 2019 production.

In terms of natural gas exports (via pipelines), there is much greater polarization between the GECF member countries and the observers (Figure 3.4). In 2020, both

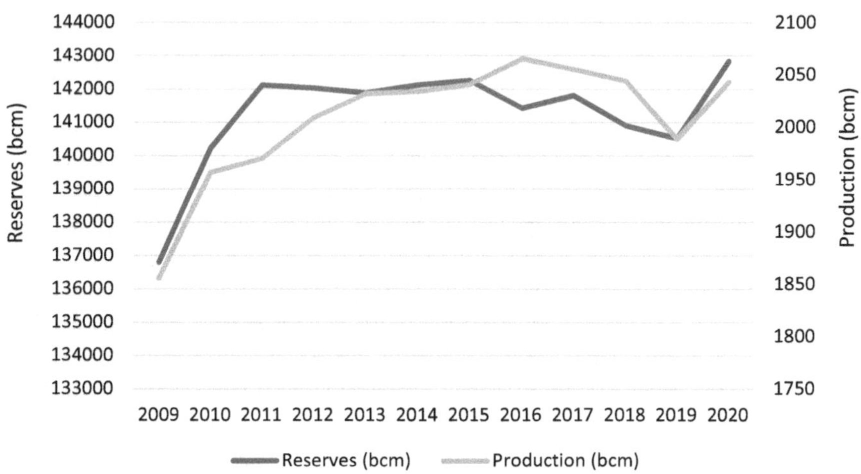

Figure 3.3 GECF members' and observers' natural gas reserves and production (bcm) between 2009 and 2020.

Source: Compiled by the author based on GECF (2021).

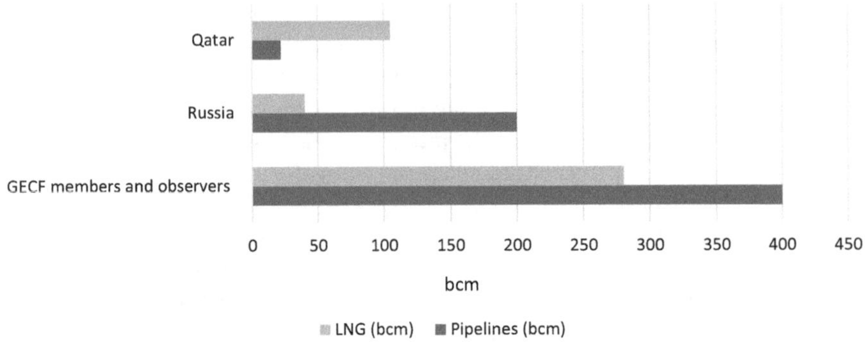

Figure 3.4 GECF members' and observers' share in natural gas exports in 2020 by different modes of transport.

Source: Compiled by the author based on GECF (2021).

groups of countries had a total share of 52% in the global exports of natural gas, split between 36% for the member states and the remaining 16% for the observer countries. Among the GECF member states, Russia remains the undisputed leader with exports (2020) at the level of 199 bcm, and in the group of observers, Norway exports around 107 bcm of natural gas (GECF, 2021). The export volumes of both of the above countries in 2019 were similar to the 2020 levels.

In terms of LNG exports, the GECF countries had an approximately 58% share in its global exports (2020). However, in this gas trade segment, the share of observer countries was small and amounted to approximately 24% of GECF exports. The largest LNG exporter in the group of observers in 2020 was Malaysia (around 32 bcm), the sales volume of which can be compared to Russia's (around 40 bcm) or Nigeria's (around 31 bcm). Qatar was by far the largest LNG exporter not only in the GECF but also in the world, with about 105 bcm of liquid gas sold in 2020 (GECF, 2021).

The establishment of the GECF sparked a discussion in the scientific community about its role in the global natural gas market. Discussions are fuelled mainly by the fact that the GECF constitutes a strongly diverse group of countries with regard to their natural gas exports, production capacity, and GDP per capita (Figure 3.5). Heterogeneity in these aspects makes the GECF, often referred to as the "gas cartel", an interesting research topic. Therefore, what has become the main subject of the scientific debate is the possibility of influencing the global prices of natural gas by the organization. In order to properly assess the impact of the GECF on global gas prices, it is necessary to analyse the stability of the international cartel.

"An international cartel is an agreement between producers to divide the market in order to obtain a monopolistic profit and to evenly distribute losses between producers in the period of decline in demand" (Budnikowski, 2006, p. 246). The mechanism of operation of an international cartel acting as a monopolist (or centralized cartel) can be described using microeconomic instruments (Figure 3.6). In an equilibrium situation in a market with perfect competition, the equilibrium

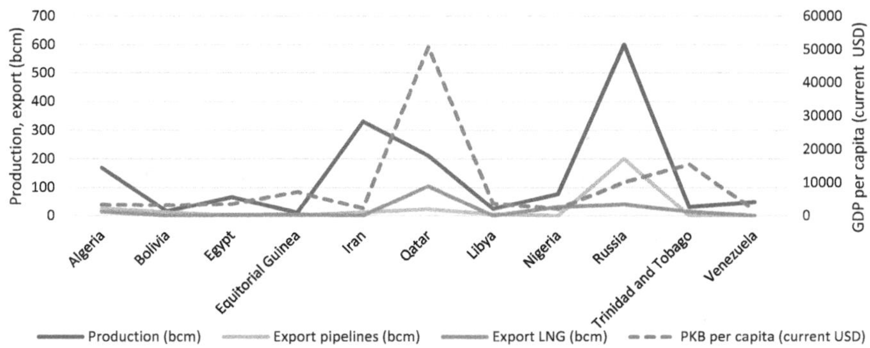

Figure 3.5 Natural gas production and exports in the GECF member countries (in bcm) and their GDP per capita (current USD) in 2020.

Source: Compiled by the author based on GECF (2021).

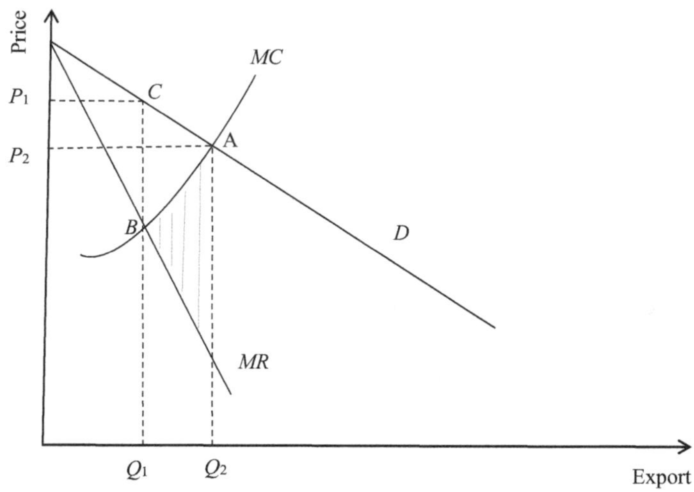

Figure 3.6 Profit maximization in the international cartel.

Source: Compiled by the author based on Salvatore (2011).

point (*A*) is the intersection of the demand (*D*) curve with the marginal cost (*MC*) curve.[5] At point *A*, the equilibrium price is P_2 and the quantity is Q_2. In the case of imperfect competition, the total supply in the market is reduced to the amount of Q_1, which guarantees the alignment of the marginal profit (*MR*) with the marginal cost (*MC*). Under these conditions, the price is P_1 and it is higher than the equilibrium price under perfect competition. The main objective of the cartel is, therefore, to set the price at $MR = MC$ on the one hand and, on the other hand, supply at a level lower than the demand resulting from that price level. The increase in the total profits of the exporters of commodity (as a cartel) is given by the dashed area in the figure. The reason for this increase is connected with restricting total exports of commodity to Q_1 which as a result eliminated all exports for which the marginal cost (*MC*) exceeded the marginal profit (*MR*). That is why total profits are higher by the sum of those differences (Salvatore, 2011).

According to Buckley and Casson (2021), international cartels have three areas of activities: the regulation of trade, the pooling of existing resources, and the provision of shared resources. Regulation of trade includes price-fixing, quantity-fixing, or capacity-fixing. Price-fixing refers to setting the minimum prices and quantity-fixing involves setting maximum production quotas. Capacity-fixing involves reduction of the spare capacity and reinforcing limits on production. Pooling of existing resources includes revenue pools, profit pools, and patent pools. A revenue and profit pools aggregate the revenues or profits of all members and divides them between the participants usually according to their market shares. However, with profit pools higher-cost producers might be better compensated. In the patent pools, all members collect patented technologies so they can produce a full range of products and thus dominate their own local markets. The provision of shared resources includes joint funding of industry research facilities, technical education for employees, benchmarking (pooling information on costs), representation of industry interests and the financing of stock-piles in recessions to buffer fluctuations in supply and demand. Cartels combine these motives but also change them over time.

The challenge for international cartels is their stability, both internal and external. A cartel remains internally stable when none of its participants finds it profitable to take action against other members of the grouping, e.g., to cheat. External stability is defined as a situation where none of the companies outside the cartel can find it profitable to join it. A cartel is stable if it meets both of these conditions (Prokop, 2009).[6] Additionally, Budnikowski (2006) points to several factors determining the stability of an international cartel:

- low price elasticity of demand for a given good,
- low price elasticity of supply from producers outside the cartel,
- a small number of producers with similar production potential and motives for reducing supply.

The low price elasticity of the demand for a given good means that it has no close substitutes and that it plays an important role in meeting specific needs. On the other hand, the low price elasticity of the supply of producers from outside the cartel means that even small changes in the prices of a given good will not encourage other producers to produce it. From a practical point of view, the most difficult condition to meet is the internal structure of the cartel. This is due to the international diversity of production capacities and the reasons why countries decide to reduce production. Accordingly, it is assumed that the more similar the production functions of enterprises, and thus the costs, are, the easier it is to obtain a stable agreement. Prokop (2009) also adds that in oligopolistic industries exhibiting price leadership with the number of companies in the industry less than and/or equal to five, all companies will be part of a stable cartel, while in an industry with a larger number of companies (regardless of which), only three of them will form a stable cartel.

The above-described cartel stability conditions will be used next to assess the possibility market power being exerted by the GECF in the international gas market.[7] The application of the price elasticity criterion of the demand for natural gas makes it possible to notice that natural gas, unlike crude oil, has many substitutes. In each of natural gas uses, it has an alternative fuel. For transport purposes, natural gas in the form of compressed natural gas (CNG) is substituted with refined crude oil. A wide range of substitute fossil fuels, both solid (coal) and liquid (crude oil), are used in the municipal and housing sector, where gas is used to prepare meals or for heating purposes. The range of substitutes for natural gas is significantly increasing when it comes to natural gas used for electricity production. In addition to the above-mentioned fuels, natural gas remains competitive in this respect in comparison with renewable energy sources and nuclear energy. The fuel with relatively fewest substitutes is natural gas used in the production of chemical fertilizers. In this case, it can be replaced with coal.[8]

The criterion of the price elasticity of supply of producers from outside the cartel clearly indicates that the countries which do not belong to the GECF are not significant producers, exporters of natural gas. The exception is the USA, which has allocated the oversupply of natural gas for export and, therefore, revolutionized the international trade in LNG. The strength of the GECF could be additionally weakened by observer countries, which are significant players (Norway) in the segment of gas exports via pipelines. Assuming that all observers are outside the cartel, and their position is additionally strengthened by the role of the USA in the natural gas market, it could turn out that the price elasticity of these producers' supply is quite high, which works to the detriment of the GECF.[9]

Another criterion determining the stability of a cartel is its internal structure. The large variation in GDP per capita implies different expectations of producers as to the pace of achieving export profits. Poorer countries, due to their significant social needs, will tend to be more focused on achieving quick profits in the short term (such as Nigeria). In turn, rich countries will be interested in maintaining stable budget revenues in the long run (such as Qatar).

An important issue from the perspective of not only the cartel's stability but also the effectiveness of its impact on the international market is the participation of the producer who could assume the role of a swing producer (in the case of the OPEC, this role has been assumed and is performed by Saudi Arabia, which maintains spare production capacity). It is an exporter that is able to "flood" the market with additional supply of a commodity in order to influence the world prices. In the case of the GECF, it is difficult to speak of a single leader due to the segmentation of the export market. While Russia dominates the pipeline gas market, Qatar holds the leading position in the LNG segment. Lack of cooperation between these countries prevents the cartel from having an effective impact on the international natural gas market.

The GECF is also not favoured by the regionalization of trade in natural gas, and thus the lack of a uniform, global price of this commodity. The GECF does not limit the production and sale or stocks of natural gas in order to influence the level of its prices in the world markets (contrary to the OPEC's recent export quota policy). In this way, the organization does not regulate the trade or pool-existing resources. At this point, the GECF rather acts as a provider of pooled (shared) resources in the limited form. It refers mainly to representation of shared interests, lobbying activities, or benchmarking the information on costs. The GECF does not even use stock-piling policy or buffer-measures to influence the supply and demand in times of recession. Hence the organization denies using "hard" cartel-specific provisions such as price and quantity fixing and instead of that focuses only on the "soft" cartel-typical measures such as limited pooling of shared resources. In this way, it might be called "soft" cartel-like organization in the natural gas market aiming at representation of shared interests.

To sum up, the GECF, beside pooling shared resources in a limited scope, has little chance of influencing the international gas market. That results from the limitations related to the characteristics of natural gas, which translate into the structure of international trade in this commodity, and the relatively high flexibility of supply of producers from outside the cartel (including the observer countries and the USA). These arguments are supported by existing empirical research. Wagbara (2007) wonders if and how the GECF can influence gas markets in the future. He answers that question by comparing the GECF with the OPEC with the use of collusion theory (cartel theory). The author concludes that the GECF can influence the market through price, contract, and fiscal mechanisms. Specifically, this can be achieved through unification of gas prices across all GECF members with Russia leading the pack, re-introduction of destination restriction clauses to LNG contracts or unanimously imposing a flat-rate tax on importers (per cm of imported gas) to determine prices. Wagbara (2007) adds, however, that the success of the above-mentioned actions depends heavily on market and geopolitical conditions (a comparison of the OPEC and the GECF can be also found in Nyga-Łukaszewska, 2009). The more inconducive to the GECF they are, the greater the possibility that the GECF will fail as successful cartel. Historical volatility of global markets (economic downturn starting in 2008–2009, shale gas revolution, COVID-pandemic) in recent years has proved that the possibility of the GECF's success is rather limited. Gabriel et al. (2010) also check that by analysing possible future gas cartels and their effects on gas markets in a number of regions across the world. By applying the World Gas Model, they conclude that if the GECF is expanded to the Caspian and Middle Eastern countries, Europe experiences losses in 2030 amounting to USD 91.4 bn in lost consumer surplus and gas consumption decreased by 21%. By contrast, thanks to shale gas production, North America sees no changes in prices, consumption, and production in such scenario. The situation alters when the unconventional gas resource base in the United States is diminished, as then only the North American market is affected by changes in gas prices and consumption while the rest of the world remains unaffected.

3.2 Determinants of energy security in the international natural gas market

Energy security is presented in theoretical terms from the point of view of importers and exporters. Therefore, only for the clarity of the analysis, in the section devoted to the factors determining energy security in the international natural gas market, a similar approach will be used where possible. This approach in theoretical dimension refers to arguments delivered in Chapter 2 according to which supply and demand security might be treated as mirroring concepts and thus analysed, to a certain extent, within similar criteria. However, taking into account this book's focus, aspects concerning exporters are given more central place in this chapter.

Determinants of energy security have been divided into two groups. The division of factors is a reflection of theoretical concepts relating to the way of understanding this phenomenon. The first group includes factors behind the volume of natural gas being traded in international markets. The second group takes into account the determinants of the price of the commodity in world markets.

3.2.1 Determinants of the volume of trade in natural gas

Factors determining the volume of natural gas include the resource and infrastructure base, non-price terms of trade contracts, and energy policy. All of these elements are medium- and long term, which means that their impact is visible over a period of more than one year.[10]

3.2.1.1 Resource and infrastructure base

Abundant energy resources play a dual role in the energy security of importing countries. Firstly, they allow domestic energy needs to be met without having to purchase resources abroad, which makes the country energy self-sufficient (such a state can be called a kind of energy autarky). Secondly, the domestic resource base may, in a situation where the import of energy commodities is complementary, reduce the volume of imported resource, which brings about an improvement in the trade balance.

The index used by the IEA, which is the ratio of the total production of primary energy in the country to its total consumption, may provide an approximation of energy self-sufficiency. Nevertheless, the use of such a measure would require the acquisition of internationally comparable data. Due to the different geographical scope of databases and the use of different units, it is reasonable to present a measure that will cast more light on the phenomenon and enable its comparison on an international scale. Such functions seem to be fulfilled by an indicator used by the World Bank. The measure in question represents the ratio of net energy imports to the energy consumed in the country. The World Bank's database (World Bank, 2014) covers almost all countries and additionally offers data aggregated to the level of geographical regions (e.g., Europe, Asia), groupings (e.g., European

Union, euro area), or the level of economic development.[11] The latest full data collected in the World Bank databases comes from 2014.

The net energy import ratio shows primarily whether a country is a net importer or exporter of energy. Positive values of the measure characterize exporters, while negative values characterize importers. In an indirect way, the indicator is also an approximation of the resource base held. It can be assumed that countries that are net energy importers have an insufficient fuel base for their own needs in terms of both quantity and type. The resources held may be negligible or different in qualitative terms from those the economy needs.[12]

Among the net energy-exporting countries, Arab countries hold the leading position (Figure 3.7). In the World Bank statistics, this group is represented by the members of the League of Arab States. It includes countries such as Algeria, Iraq, Kuwait, Libya, Oman, Saudi Arabia, Qatar, and the United Arab Emirates. The rich resource base and developed export infrastructure mean that the net import index in 2014 assumed negative values in the region, ranging at approximately –164% of the energy consumed in this group of countries. Other groups of countries classified as net energy exporters in the world saw a much lower rate of net energy imports (in relative terms). This group included sub-Saharan African countries, the least developed countries (or LDCs, according to the UN nomenclature) and the region of Africa further south of the Sahara. In this area, there are countries such as Angola, Equatorial Guinea, and Nigeria, which are heavily dependent on income from hydrocarbon exports. In sub-Saharan African countries, the net import rate accounts for 48% of energy consumption. The same indicator was slightly lower, at –33%, for the group of least developed countries. It is a group of countries that includes partly the countries of sub-Saharan Africa (excluding Nigeria and South Africa), nine countries of Asia, four in Oceania, and Haiti in America. Although

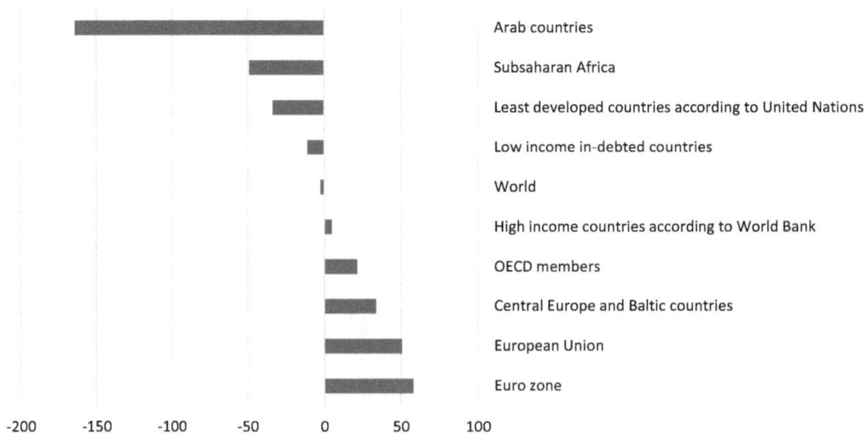

Figure 3.7 Net energy imports in 2014 in selected world regions (% of energy use).*

* Latest available data.

Source: Compiled by the author based on World Bank (2014).

African countries accounted for a significant part of the group of indebted low-income countries (30 out of 37 countries) in 2014, as classified by the World Bank, their net import ratio stood at 10% of energy consumed. This is due to the fact that there were no significant energy exporters in that group.[13]

The world's largest net energy importers in 2014 were the following countries (Figure 3.8): the eurozone, the EU, Central Europe (Baltic States),[14] the OECD,

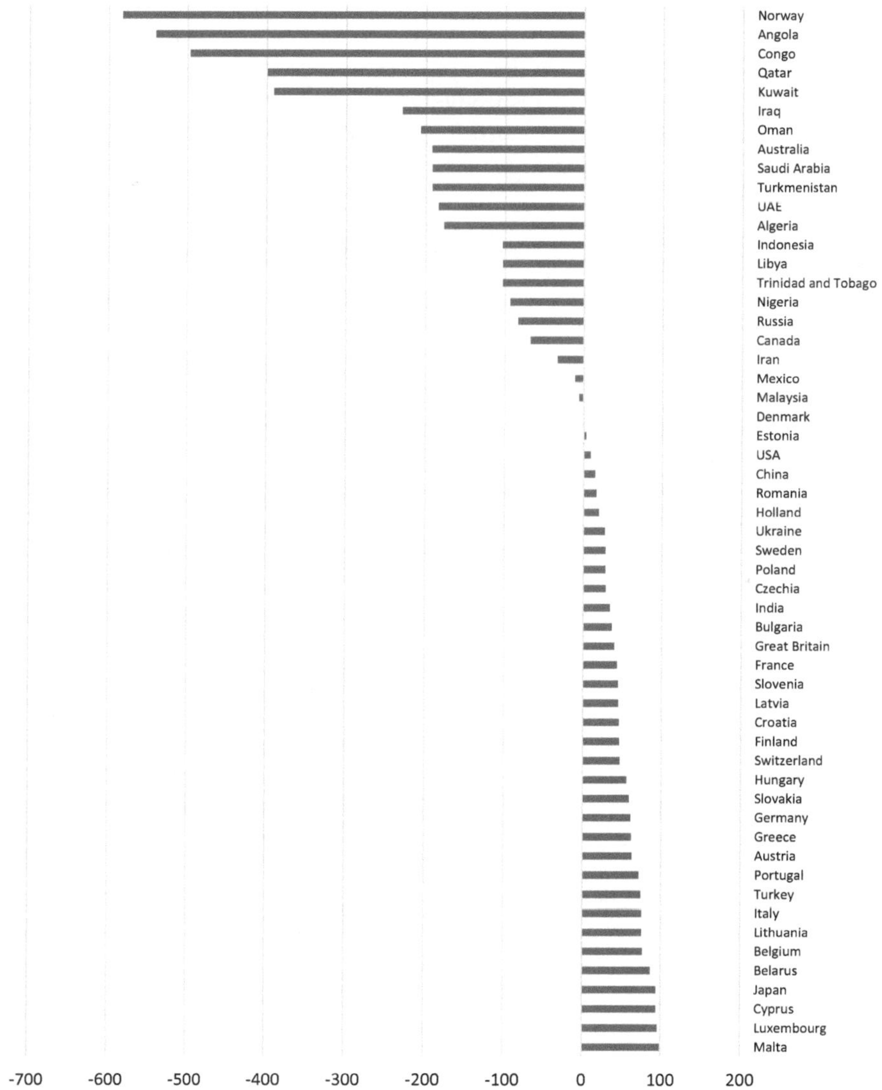

Figure 3.8 Net energy imports in 2014 in selected countries (% of energy use).*

* Latest available data and countries' names as in the World Bank database.

Source: Compiled by the author based on World Bank (2014).

and high-income countries (according to the World Bank nomenclature). The dominant role in this group was played by the euro area countries and the European Union, which in 2014 were characterized by a net energy import ratio of 57% and 50%, respectively. The geographical structure of both groups is responsible for the convergence of statistics. The countries of Central Europe and the Baltic States depend less on energy imports than the eurozone countries and the EU. This is due to the fact that some of them remain at the same time significant energy exporters, such as Czechia or Poland. The OECD countries and high-income countries,[15] as broadly defined by the World Bank, are two further groups of net energy importers. They were characterized by a net energy import ratio in 2014, at the level of 23% and 10% of energy consumed, respectively. The low rate in the group of high-income countries is due to the fact that they include important global exporters of resources, respectively, such as Saudi Arabia, the United Arab Emirates, Kuwait, Oman, or Norway.

The last-mentioned country also has the world's highest (in relative terms) rate of net energy imports in relation to its consumption (−582% in 2014). Given that Norway is a net exporter of primary and secondary energy, it can be assumed that Norwegian energy exports are nearly six times higher than its consumption. Equally high rates were recorded in 2014 for Angola and Congo, at −540% and −496%, respectively. Such a high rate observed in both economies is not only the effect of a significant role of hydrocarbon export but also of low-energy consumption in those countries. The African continent was characterized by a relatively constant and unchanging share of its countries in global primary energy consumption. Both in 2008 and 2016, the countries (excluding Algeria, Egypt, and South Africa) had a total share of approximately 1% in global primary energy consumption (BP, 2017). One of the factors contributing to the low level of energy consumption in these countries is the lack of infrastructure necessary for the production and distribution of energy. Angola and Congo belong to the group of countries with limited access to electricity for residents. According to the World Bank, in 2014 about 40% of the Angolan population and about 51% of Congolese citizens had access to electricity (World Bank, 2018). In countries such as Norway, the USA, or Poland, the entire population has access to electricity. The degree of electrification in 2014 presented in the case of Angola and Congo is a big change from what could be observed in these countries in the early 1990s. In 1990, the same rates were 11% for Angola and 0.1% for Congo.

An analysis of the group of net energy-exporting countries shows that it is dominated by countries with a significant share in the world's fuel resources and their production. The ratio of exported energy to its domestic consumption ranges between 400% and −5%. The vast majority of these countries are developing nations or in-transition/emerging economies (e.g., Iraq, Iran, Nigeria, Russia). The exceptions in the group of net energy exporters are Australia and Canada. In the case of Australia, the net energy export ratio stood at −192% in 2014, while in the case of Canada it was 68%.

Australia owed its position in the global energy market mainly to the export of coal and natural gas. Canada was included in this group primarily due to trade in energy commodities with the USA. Therefore, in the case of Canada, its role in the global energy market can hardly be considered significant.

All these net energy-exporting countries share a similar perspective on energy security. For (net) energy exporters, energy security is important in the context of demand security. The second group of countries are countries oriented towards security of supply, as they show net energy imports. The economies most dependent on fuel imports in 2014 were small countries such as Malta (−98% of energy consumed), Luxembourg (−96% of energy consumed), and Cyprus (−94% of energy consumed), and Japan (−94% of energy consumed). In the case of the group of small economies, their relatively high net energy import ratio resulted from a low level of energy consumption (on a global scale) and it being met entirely with imports. Comparing the situation of Malta, Luxembourg, and Cyprus with Japan's, it can be seen that despite a similar indicator of net energy imports, there were differences between them in absolute terms.

Japan was one of the world's largest energy consumers. For many years (1990–2016), it ranked fourth or fifth among the world's largest energy consumers. It trailed only the USA, China, Russia, and periodically India. Analysing the data since 1990, it can be observed that Japan has not changed this position or periodically assumed the role of the world's largest energy importer, which was the case, e.g., in 1990–1992 (Enerdata, 2018). The large volume of energy imports in Japan (422 Mtoe) was due to the role it played in individual fuel markets. In 2016, Japan was the world's largest importer of LNG in the liquefied gas market, whereas in the oil market – it was one of the three largest, and in the coal market one of the four largest global importers of these resources (EIA, 2022b).

As a highly developed country, Japan is a representative example of the entire group of net energy importers. Apart from, respectively, Belarus, Ukraine, India, and China, most of the energy-importing countries are economically developed countries (e.g., respectively, Belgium, Italy, Germany, Sweden, and the USA). The position of both India and China in net energy imports at 34% and 15% of energy consumption, respectively, was due to the relatively high rate of economic development and insufficient domestic resource base. Both countries were significant coal producers (2016: China –46% share in global coal production, India –9%) (BP, 2017); nevertheless, they covered their deficit demand for oil and natural gas[16] with deliveries from abroad. Both China and India are among the world's largest oil importers. In 2015 and 2016, China led the pack of oil importers, while India ranked third. The fast-growing automotive industry in those countries, as well as an absorptive domestic market, drove demand for crude oil. In the case of natural gas imports, China was among the five largest global importers of this resource. As for India, due to the low importance of natural gas in the country's economy (6% share in the primary energy balance in 2015) (EIA, 2016) and substantial domestic production of this resource, the country imported more than 20 bcm of gas annually, which represented approximately one-third of the natural gas imported to China (BP, 2017).

Compared to China and India, Belarus had a significantly higher net import ratio, which accounted for 86% of the country's energy consumption. This was due to the dependence of the Belarusian economy on imported fuels. Hydrocarbons came entirely from Russia. In 2016, out of 17 bcm of natural gas consumed by Belarus, 16.6 bcm was purchased from Russia (BP, 2017). A similar situation occurred in the oil market. Of the 24 mt of crude oil processed in Belarusian refineries, 22–23 mt came from Russia (Czerniewicz, 2015).

In the case of Ukraine, net imports accounted for about 27% of the energy consumed in the country, which means that more than one-fourth of the energy demand came from abroad. Ukraine's situation differed from that of Belarus, as the former relied more on domestic fuel resources. This applied to both coal and natural gas (Table 3.9).

Table 3.9 Transit of Russian natural gas through Ukrainian territory in 2014[a]

Country	*Export quantity in 2014 (bcm)*
100% of imported gas transited through Ukraine	
Italy	21.7
Hungary	5.4
Czechia	4.8
Slovakia	4.4
Austria	4.2
Bulgaria	2.8
Greece	1.7
Serbia	1.5
Romania	0.5
Slovenia	0.4
Bosnia and Herzegovina	0.2
Croatia	0.2 (2013 data)
Macedonia	0.1
Total	47.86
Part of imported natural gas transiting Ukraine	
Turkey	27.3
Poland	9.1
France	7.6
Total	48.2
None of imported natural gas transiting Ukraine	
Germany	40.3
United Kingdom	15.5
Netherlands	4.7
Finland	3.1
Lithuania	2.5
Latvia	1.1
Denmark	0.4
Estonia	0.4
Switzerland	0.3
Total	68.3

Source: Compiled by the author based on Pirani and Yafimava (2016).

[a] Latest available data.

Domestic coal and crude oil covered about three-quarters of the country's consumption of these fuels (EIA, 2015; BP, 2017), and Ukrainian natural gas accounted for approximately a half of the demand for the resource (18 bcm of 37 bcm). If Ukraine's net import rate were estimated for 2015 or 2016, the results would probably be higher. The reason was the increased imports of hard coal in 2015–2016, the production of which was largely based in the east of Ukraine (EIA, 2015).[17]

From the point of view of energy security, Ukraine and Belarus play a dual role as energy consumers and as transit countries. For both of these groups, according to the theoretical considerations presented in Chapter 2, the perspective of security of resource supply is important. Although this study does not focus on the role of transit countries, this topic does deserve attention and the major countries performing such a function in the international natural gas market should be identified. To this end, the example of Europe and the supply of Russian natural gas will be used, as the continent, as indicated previously, relies mostly on the supply of natural gas through pipelines, and Russia is one of the most significant suppliers in that market. The transit countries for Russian gas to Europe, apart from Ukraine and Belarus, referred to above, also include Austria, Slovakia, Romania, and Poland. Austria's Baumgarten is a transit point for Russian gas transported to Italy or France. Gas reaches Austria through the territory of Slovakia. For its part, Romania is a transit country for Russian gas destined for the southern markets: Bulgaria, Turkey, Greece, and Macedonia. Poland is a transit country in the case of gas supplied to the German market.

Ukraine is the most important country in the context of Russian gas transit. In 2014, approximately 62.2 bcm of natural gas purchased by European countries (including Turkey and Moldova) was transported through the territory of Ukraine (Pirani and Yafimava, 2016). Recipients who rely entirely on Russian resources transported through Ukraine include Italy, Austria, Hungary, Bulgaria, Czechia, and Slovakia, as well as other countries. In total, it was about 48 bcm of gas in 2014. A similar volume of gas was exported to countries which, apart from transit through Ukraine, could also use other routes for transporting Russian gas. These were Turkey, Poland, and France. In 2014, Germany, the United Kingdom, the Netherlands, Finland, and Lithuania were independent of gas transport through Ukraine. With Russian-Ukrainian conflict of 2022, gas transit through the Ukrainian territory became even more important issue of international interest. Between 2021 and 2024, Russian gas transit through Ukraine was to amount 40 bcm/year. But in 2022, as Cahil and Palti-Guzman (2023) report, transit reached 18.7 bcm. Russian gas destined for European countries enters Ukrainian territory with two points: Sudzha and Sokhranivka. As the Sokhranivka gas transit point is located in the occupied Luhansk Region of eastern Ukraine, Ukraine's Gas Transmission System Operator in May 2022 was forced to declare *force majeure* with immediate gas transit hold up. Before the invasion and till May 2022, gas transit through Sudzha and Sokhranivka amounted to 110 mcm/daily. Since May 2022, Sudzha has been carrying around 40 mcm of gas daily,[18] as Statista (2023) reports.

The role of transit countries in ensuring energy security reflects the importance of infrastructure factors. Of particular importance in this respect is also the number of national transmission system entry points available for the imported resource in the country. From the perspective of the importing country, the most desirable situation is one in which it can benefit from the supply of gas transported not only by pipelines but also by ships. In addition, the diversification of supply routes within a specific mode of transport is also of great importance.

Poland is an example of a country that has been in such a situation since 2014. Imported natural gas reaches Poland through the LNG terminal in Świnoujście, as well as through two entry points to the national transmission system: one in Kondratki and the other in Drozdowicze but also number of interconnectors at Polish borders. Natural gas is transported to the Kondratki entry point through the territory of Belarus, and to Drozdowicze through the territory of Ukraine. Although natural gas is imported via both entry points from a single supplier (Russia), there is a diversity of supply routes of pipeline transport. Such diversification proved to be particularly important during the gas crisis in 2009, when the volume of Russian natural gas supplied through the territory of Ukraine decreased. At that time, the import of natural gas to Polland via the Kondratki entry point increased.

Among the countries of Western Europe, France is a country (significant importer) with natural gas imports diversified in terms of the infrastructure involved. The country uses both LNG supplies and pipelines. LNG is received at four terminals (two being located in Marseille: Fos-Cavaou and Fos-Tonkin, one in the Loire region – Montnoir-de-Bretagne, and one in Dunkirk – Loon-Plage). Pipeline gas (including Russian gas) is supplied via two different routes. As in the case of Poland, they run across the territory of Ukraine or Belarus (Table 3.10).[19]

From the legal point of view, energy transit, similarly to the energy trade, falls into the jurisdiction of the World Trade Organization and General Agreement on Tariffs and Trade in particular. Thus, there are no specific legal regimes devoted only to energy trade issues or its transit specifically. One of the legal attempts to establish a framework for energy trade, and transit in particular, is the Energy Charter Treaty and its Trade Amendment (1998). Treaty's trade provisions comply with the rules and practices of the World Trade Organization (WTO) such as non-discrimination, transparency, and a commitment to the progressive liberalization of international trade (Energy Charter, 2023a). But Energy Charter Treaty is not a universally accepted act. Its decisions are binding for signatories states.[20] As of 2023, in this group, were such natural gas producers as Norway, the Netherlands, or Turkmenistan and transiting countries like Ukraine. Belarus, which is next to Ukraine, is an important transit state for the Russian gas, had in 2023 suspended application status (Energy Charter, 2023b).

Apart from the lack of a single, legal regime governing only energy transit issues, complexity of energy transit also refers also to its characteristics. Firstly, energy transmission is restricted and, beyond spare capacity margin, limited to the physical capacity of the infrastructure. Secondly, transmission and distribution infrastructure might be controlled by incumbent players creating monopoly with restricted grid access. Thirdly, infrastructure is fuel-dedicated, which means that it cannot be used for transport of other energy types, e.g., gas pipelines used for electricity transport.[21] Fourthly, energy transportation infrastructure construction

Table 3.10 Number of transit countries (borders crossed) and routes of Russian gas deliveries in 2014[a]

Country	*Number of transit countries (crossed borders)[b]*	*Russian gas delivery routes*
Austria	2	Ukraine–Slovakia, Slovakia–Austria
Bosnia and Herzegovina	3	Ukraine–Hungary, Hungary–Serbia, Serbia–Bosnia and Herzegovina
Bulgaria	3	Ukraine–Moldova, Moldova–Romania, Romania–Bulgaria
Czechia	1	Germany–Czechia
Denmark	3	Belarus–Poland, Poland–Germany, Germany–Denmark
Estonia	0	Import directly from Russia
Finland	0	
France	4 3	Ukraine–Slovakia, Slovakia–Austria, Austria–Germany, Germany–France or: Belarus–Poland, Poland–Germany, Germany–France
Greece	4	Ukraine–Moldova, Moldova–Romania, Romania–Bulgaria, Bulgaria–Greece
Netherlands	3	Belarus–Poland, Poland–Germany, Germany–Netherlands
Lithuania	1	Belarus-Lithuania
Latvia	0	Import directly from Russia
Macedonia	4	Ukraine–Moldova, Moldova–Romania, Romania–Bulgaria, Bulgaria–Macedonia
Germany	2 0 2 (1)[b]	Belarus–Poland, Poland–Germany Greifswald (German coast) Greifswald, Czechia-Germany
Poland	1 1	Belarus–Poland Ukraine–Poland
Romania	2	Ukraine–Moldova, Moldova–Romania
Serbia	2	Ukraine–Hungary, Hungary–Serbia
Switzerland	3 2 (1)[b] 3 (2)[b]	Belarus–Poland, Poland–Germany, Germany–Switzerland Greifswald, Germany–Switzerland Greifswald, Czechia–Germany, Germany–Switzerland
Turkey	4 0	Ukraine–Moldova, Moldova–Romania, Romania–Bulgaria, Bulgaria–Turkey Samsun (Turkish coast)
Hungary	1	Ukraine–Hungary
Great Britain	4 4	Belarus–Poland, Poland–Germany, Germany–Belgium, Belgium–United Kingdom Belarus–Poland, Poland–Germany, Germany–Netherlands, Netherlands–United Kingdom
Italy	3	Ukraine–Slovakia, Slovakia–Austria, Austria–Italy

Source: Compiled by the author based on Pirani and Yafimava (2016).

[a] Latest available data.

[b] In the majority of cases, the number of transit countries is the same as number of borders crossed. The exception is natural gas reaching Europe via the Nord Stream gas pipeline through the point in Greifswald to Germany and Switzerland. At those entry points, the number of crossed borders is greater by 1 than the number of transit countries.

is money- and time-consuming. Fifthly, energy and gas transit, in particular, are politically sensitive.[22]

As Yegorov and Wirl (2010) suggest that transport constraints and political externalities resulting from opportunistic political behaviour can lead to the extortion of rent by transit countries. Gas transit creates game theory situations where conflict arises – according to Yegorov and Wirl – on the one hand due to geopolitical tensions (2010) and on the other due to the fact that there is surplus that can be shared between producing and transit country (2009). Analysis of the gas transit from the game theory point of view is presented, among others, in Chyong and Hobbs (2014), Hubert and Ikonnikova (2004), Hubert and Suleymanova (2008), Hubert and Ikonnikova (2011), Von Hirschhausen, Menihart, and Pavel (2005), Yegorov and Wirl (2009, 2010), and Schulte and Weiser (2019). Majority of these works analyses transit in the context of Ukraine[23] and gas deliveries from Russia. The exception is Schulte and Weiser (2019) who investigate Turkish market power as a transit country and Yegorov and Wirl (2010) who look at the case of the Russian transit (from Turkmenistan).

The latter suggest that gas transit apart from creating games also build externalities. They give an example of natural gas producer and consumer separated by a third country (transit country) that is neither producer nor consumer. If a transit country is a rent seeker or just destructor of the pipeline, then externality arises, as the right of producer and consumer is violated by the third state. The authors also distinguish between games with a transit country as a net gas exporter (such as the case of Turkmen gas transits through Russia) and with a transit country as a net gas importer (such as Turkey). From the point of view of this book's angle – the net gas exporter case fits the demand security discussion more than perspective of the importing country, which falls into the category of the supply security. Yegorov and Wirl (2010) provide an example of the case of Russia's transit from Turkmenistan to Europe. They suggest that such a situation is far more complex compared to transit through net importing country (such as Ukraine). According to results of their research, edge producer (Turkmenistan) has to compensate transit country (Russia, net gas exporter) not only for the use of its pipelines but also for undermining trade condition through the influence on market prices in final destination country (EU). Yegorov and Wirl convince that bargaining power of transit countries can be reduced or even eliminated by amendments to international law. One may expect that the above-mentioned Energy Charter Treaty and its Trade Amendment might fit into this role. However, as Yegorov and Wirl notice since geopolitics also influences such legal decisions, they might not yield economically efficient legal implementations. The authors conclude that game structure depends on geopolitical aspects and international law.

Political instability in the transit countries and the balance of power for each transit route are next to gas dependency (net imports from the single supplier), diversification of transit routes from a given supplier or risk of pipeline rupture, parts of Transit Risk Index (TRI) constructed by Le Coq and Paltseva (2012). This relatively rare quantitative perspective in transit risk studies, assesses transit risk from the security of supply dimension. Thus, only due to its uniqueness, index deserves attention in the investigation of the demand security in the natural gas market. Analysis for TRI is carried out for European markets supplied with natural gas from Russia and transiting Ukraine. The authors extend the index to many supplying countries in the form of the Transit Risk Index in case of Multiple suppliers (TRIM). As Le Coq and Paltseva notice, TRIM estimation is rather limited by the unavailability of data. The authors admit that in the case of European countries, they failed to obtain complete data on exact transit routes for all gas suppliers.

Summing up, transit risks result from rent-seeking, politically motivated opportunistic behaviour which builds externalities and game situations. Transit risks are exacerbated by the characteristics of energy as a product transported via fixed infrastructure with capacity constraints and limited storage options and features attributed to energy investments as a highly capital-intensive projects with long-term period of return. Lack of a single and universally accepted and legally binding regime applicable to transit conflicts by majority of the biggest natural as producers/transiting states creates additional difficulties. Thus, any investment commitment of the producer is accompanied by the desire to ensure future demand. On the other hand, transit states depending on their position in the international gas market may have different goals. These expectations are the highest when transiting state is a net gas exporter.

3.2.1.2 Non-price terms of contract

Among the non-price terms of contract determining energy security, it is worth taking into account, first of all, the duration of the trade contract and elements of price formulas affecting the amount of the imported resource.

Trade contracts can take the form of both short-term and long-term contracts. The former serve more often to diversify supplies or to meet periodically increased demand for natural gas. They enable the consumer of energy commodities to benefit from greater flexibility of supply and price arbitrage. However, long-term contracts play a special role in building energy security, which is why the considerations presented here will mainly concern this type of contracts.

The role of long-term contracts is one of the currents of institutional economics research focused in particular on transaction costs. It is recognized, after Williamson (1983), that this type of trade contract reduces the risk of opportunistic behaviour by trading partners. On the basis of energy market analyses, the issue of long-term contracts was taken up by researchers such as Crocker and Masten (1991), Masten and Crocker (1985), Hubbard and Weiner (1991), and Mullerhin (1986), Parsons (1989), as well as by Neumann and Hirschhausen (2004) and Le Coq (2004). These are analyses that concern the coal market (Joskow, 1988) and the natural gas market (Neumann and Hirschhausen, 2004). As pointed out by Creti and Villeneueve (2004), the natural gas market provides an ideal setting for transaction cost analyses. This is due to the high initial capital expenditure on both the seller's and the recipient's sides.

Trade agreements may take the form of long-term or short-term contracts. Accurately determining the duration of a contract and classifying it into one of the two categories mentioned above is difficult. With the passage of time, the duration of trade contracts between partners is constantly decreasing (this applies to both the pipeline gas and LNG supply market). Until a few years ago, a 25-year contract was considered a long-term contract, while today even a 15-year contract is considered a long-term one (Neumann and Hirschhausen, 2004). This trend is particularly visible in the natural gas market, where short-term spot contracts have become popular due to the dynamic development of the LNG market. Contracts with terms longer than 15 years are a less common arrangement, but they are still used. An example of such an agreement is Azerbaijan's 2013 contract with European customers, signed for 25 years. In the opinion of Franza (2014), long-term contracts will prevail for new, capital-intensive investment projects, while shorter 10–15-year contracts will result from the renegotiation of existing contracts or the conclusion of new supply contracts within the existing infrastructure.

In the natural gas market, despite the changes taking place, long-term trade contracts are still used. This is due to the theory of transaction costs. Investments in infrastructure related to the import of natural gas are intended only for this commodity and cannot be used to transport oil or coal. In addition, the construction and maintenance of transport infrastructure is a large cost. For these reasons, both the exporter and the importer seek to minimize or reduce opportunistic behaviour (Chyong, 2015). It can be concluded that, for the same reasons, long-term contracts are an element that guarantees energy security in the long term from the point of view of both the energy importer and the exporter. In the case of the former, the long-term contract ensures energy supply, in the case of the latter – the sale and profitability of the long-term investment.

One of the ways of sharing the risk between the supplier and recipient of energy commodities related to the investment in infrastructure for energy transport is the application of the take-or-pay (or minimum bill) principle (Hubbard and Weiner, 1991). It is a non-quantifiable element of the price formula on the basis of which natural gas is sold. According to this clause, the importer is obliged to pay for the commodity amount specified in the contract, even if it does not take delivery of the commodity due to reduced demand from the domestic market.[24] The take-or-pay principle is included among the conditions determining the volume of imported commodity because by definition the importer is obliged to purchase a certain amount of natural gas.[25]

An economic interpretation of the take-or-pay principle is presented by Creti and Villeneueve (2004) and Hartley (2013) after them. Creti and Villeneueve take into account in their considerations the Crocker and Masten (1985) model, which leads them to the conclusion that the take-or-pay clause can be written as follows:

$$\gamma = \frac{\delta}{y} = \frac{y-s}{y} = 1 - \frac{s}{y} \qquad (1)$$

where:

γ – take-or-pay clause – as a percentage,

δ – financial penalty imposed on the buyer failing to take delivery of a specified quantity of the commodity,

y – payment to the supplier for a contractually specified quantity of the commodity,
s – value of the alternative quantity of the commodity bought from another supplier.

Creti and Villeneueve introduce the notions of commodity value dependent on the random demand shock (θ) – $v(\theta)$ and payment to its seller – y. The authors argue that the buyer will not be interested in taking delivery of the commodity in two situations. First, if $y > v(\theta)$, which means that the value of gas is lower than the demanded payment. Second, if $s > v(\theta)$, i.e. when the alternative to the purchase of the contracted commodity is more attractive than the value of the gas being bought would indicate. Termination of the contract with the supplier will not be beneficial to the buyer in a situation where $s < v(\theta) < y$, that is, when, on the one hand, less is paid for the commodity than as provided in the contract and, on the other hand, alternatives are less attractive (Creti and Villeneueve, 2004). Creti and Villeneueve (2004) also notice that under take-or-pay contracts, the supplier may impose penalty (δ) on the buyer for failing to take delivery of the contracted quantity of the commodity. The penalty is the difference between payment to the supplier (y) and the value of an alternative quantity of the commodity purchased from another supplier (s). Thus, $\delta > 0$.

The take-or-pay clause (γ) takes values greater than zero and is given as a percentage. When there are no alternatives available ($s = 0$), the value of $\gamma = 100\%$. The more valuable the alternatives, the lower values the take-or-pay clause takes. For example, the value of the take-or-pay clause for the Ukraine–Russia relationship is 80% (Matuszak and Kardaś, 2017).

Due to dynamically changing market conditions, importers are increasingly asking exporters to refrain from demanding payment for the commodity that has not been taken. An example is the situation of RWE Transgaz supplying gas to the Czech market. In 2012, the company won a commercial dispute with Gazprom before an Austrian court. As a consequence, RWE Transgaz did not pay the Russian supplier for failure to take delivery of contracted gas (Reuters, 2012). A similar effect arises from the 2017 decision of the Stockholm court of arbitration on a dispute of Ukraine's Naftogaz with Gazprom. The court rejected the Russian supplier's claims under the take-or-pay clause against Ukraine. The claim concerned the amount of USD 56 bn and covered the cost of untaken gas in 2009–2017 (Matuszak and Kardaś, 2017).

A feature that lends flexibility to long-term take-or-pay contracts is the reduction of the take-or-pay liability or allowing the importer to take the disputable quantity of the commodity in subsequent years. The former arrangement occurs rarely, as it involves measurable losses for the exporter. In 2012, Gazprom reduced the take-or-pay volume for the Italian company Eni from 85% to 75% and for the Bulgarian company Bulgargaz from 90% to 80% (Franza, 2014). The latter arrangement, which postpones the obligation to take delivery of the commodity, is more popular. The quantity of gas which can be taken later is called annual deficiency. Contracts specify both the maximum period within which the buyer is obliged to use untaken gas (usually three to five following years), and the maximum quantity of the commodity (take or pay bank) that can be managed this way (usually 15% of the take-or-pay volume) (Zajdler, Hara, and Staniłko, 2012).

Another feature of contracts that affects the volume of gas available on the market is the application of broad-based territorial restrictions on the use of imported commodity. It may take different forms, including export ban or the obligation to use gas at a certain destination (destination clause) (European Commission, 2015).

The objective the exporter pursues by using such mechanisms is to limit price arbitrage between individual markets. From the importer's perspective, this situation leads to a restriction of competition in the market and, in an extreme situation, an oversupply of the commodity in the domestic market. Milder forms of territorial restrictions are the mechanisms of profit splitting (between the seller and the buyer), use restrictions (restriction on decision-making as to how the possible profit from the sale of the commodity will be used by the importer), or market sharing (applying different prices for individual customers in the same market) (Waloszyk, 2014).

Territorial restrictions are applied in Gazprom's contracts with customers, e.g., in Central and Eastern Europe (Bulgaria, Czechia, Estonia, Hungary, Latvia, Lithuania, Poland, Slovakia) and Southern Europe (Serbia). In 2012, the European Commission initiated proceedings against Gazprom aimed at limiting the use of such practices. It was argued that Gazprom used unfair practices against member states from the Central and Eastern Europe region, which prevented the development of a single energy market in the European Union. In consequence of the proceedings (Vavilov, 2015) Gazprom removed all kind of territorial restrictions from contracts with importers in Hungary (export ban and destination clause), Slovakia and Chechia (territorial restrictions), and export ban clauses in contracts with buyers in Bulgaria and Poland (European Commission, 2017a). Similar provisions were removed by the Russian supplier as early as 2004, e.g., from a contract with Austrian buyers (Stern, 2005).

Territorial restrictions are not only the domain of the Russian supplier. In 2004, the European Commission initiated proceedings against EU companies: French GDF and Italian Eni, similar to those against Gazprom. The agreement between the companies concluded in 1997 concerned the transport by GDF of gas purchased by Eni in northern Europe and delivered through the territory of France to Switzerland. GDF introduced a clause in the contract according to which the Italian company could not resell part of the gas in France. This was declared by the European Commission (2004) to be contrary to EU regulations.

3.2.1.3 Energy policy

As highlighted in the previous chapter, regulatory policy within the energy market remains one of the key aspects influencing energy demand security. Energy policies' impact on demand security has a cross-cutting character. Firstly, it refers to energy policies along the energy supply chain, starting with the producers, through transit territories' regulations ending with policies of the consuming nations. Each of those market participants might have different expectations concerning energy but without a doubt, any legislation changes in either of above-mentioned impacts reversely others. Secondly, energy policies are not limited solely to the national level. They can be drafted on the regional but also global scale thus affecting not only energy producers. Thirdly, the impact of energy policies on the volumes of traded energy might be direct or indirect. Looking from the perspective of the energy producer/exporter, any home policy lifting ban on energy exports will immediately boost export volumes while global decarbonization trends will shift the demand from fossil fuels towards renewables. Recognizing the possibility of the multivariate influence of energy policy on energy exporters, this book's author attempts to present only selected policy initiatives admitting that their choice is subjective. However, being aware of the variety and complexity of energy policies and pursuing book's goal, author does her best to, at least, signal these issues conceding that their comprehensive and deep analysis, in the demand security context, deserves greater scientific attention.

Focusing mirror of all these cross-cutting issues is the energy policy of the European Union. One of such policy initiatives, which is unique at the global scale is energy market integration in the European Union. This entirely regional initiative can be called a type of economic integration related to the energy market. Its objective is to integrate energy markets into one supranational economic body. The process of energy integration in the EU takes place with the involvement of the European institutions, in particular the European Commission. Therefore, it cannot be regarded as real integration. It is forced by EU regulations and economic policy preferring cross-border interconnectors.

The Energy Union project was launched in the EU in 2015. It is a response to the gas crisis of 2009 (Pach-Gargul, 2016). One of the objectives of the Energy Union is to ensure energy security for countries dependent on natural gas imports, in particular from one direction. The Energy Union is to include the harmonization of energy policy not only in the natural gas and electricity markets[26] but also with regard to climate policy.[27]

Energy Union builds on the achievements of the three energy packages introduced in the EU. These regulations date back to 1996 when the first package was introduced. Between 1996 and 2009 (when the last package was adopted), gas market became liberalized, gas transmission was separated from its distribution, national energy regulators were established, and consumers gained free choice to choose gas suppliers. The community achieved substantial progress in diversyfing away from reliance on the dominant supplier – Russia. It is visible in various initiatives, including

- established bi-directional capacity – allowing to transport gas in both directions at all EU cross-border interconnections (Heidecke et al., 2022),
- newly built cross-border interconnectors linking Central (e.g., interconnector Poland-Slovakia, mid-2022) and South-East Europe (e.g., interconnector GreecBulgaria, late 2022) and Baltic states (e.g., interconnector Poland-Lithuania, mid-2022) with the rest of Europe (Heidecke et al., 2022),
- introducing network codes for transmission/transit of gas in the EU which made allocation of the capacity at interconnection points more consistent and transparent (Łoskot-Strachota, 2020).

Energy Union concept, to some extent, accompanies EU's efforts to become a world leader in the decarbonization efforts. Their latest elaboration has been presented in the "European Green Deal" (European Commission, 2023) and following regulatory check-up "Fit for 55" package (European Council, 2023). Even though energy issues are of vital importance in the "European Green Deal" ("Green Deal"), the strategy includes a wider policy approach including, for instance, farming, biodiversity, or sustainable finance.[28] Naturally climate neutrality cannot be achieved without energy sector engagement. Clean energy transition aiming at reducing greenhouse gas emissions is, among others, designed to ensure secure and affordable energy supply for the EU. Through prioritizing energy efficiency, wider use of energy sources other than fossil fuels (e.g., such as renewables, hydrogen), promoting sustainable and smart mobility, member states are encouraged to contribute to ambitious net-zero future. It is expected that the above actions will re-design EU energy consumption patterns. On the other hand, "Green Deal" will also affect relationships with key energy exporters such as Russia, Algeria, the USA, or Saudi Arabia (Leonard et al., 2021). Siddi (2021) adds that energy transition will pose a major challenge especially to these "hydrocarbon producers and trade relationships that rely disproportionately on the hydrocarbon economy", such as Russia, for which trade in fossil fuels is vital from economic and geopolitical perspective. It has been estimated by Makarov, Chen, and Paltsev (2020) that only Paris Agreement commitments (−40% GHG emissions by 2030), would drive Russian gas exports down by 6% compared to business-as-usual scenario, thus reducing GHG emissions by 55% before 2030, would increase gas exports' drops. The ultimate goal of reduced fossil fuel use is determined by new infrastructural and technological investments and closer energy cooperation within EU in times of energy supply crises. Thus, indirectly, the European energy policy either in the form of Energy Union, energy packages, or "Green Deal" assumptions, will impact energy demand security of EU energy partners.

COVID-pandemic reinforced EU decarbonization policy, as a way to help economy revive after lockdowns. Yet, the Russian invasion in Ukraine (2022) imprinted the EU energy policy even stronger. The community not only announced plans on full withdrawal from the imports of Russian fossil fuels but also speeded up plans on new infrastructural projects. The plan called "REpowerEU" was presented in May 2022 and assumes, among others, voluntary common purchases of gas, LNG, massive scaling-up and speeding-up of renewable energy, and reducing fossil fuel consumption. It is estimated that by 2030 only these actions might save the industry sector up to 35 bcm of natural gas by 2030 (apart from what has already been envisaged by the "Green Deal" and "Fit for 55") (European Commission, 2022). Additionally, war in Ukraine, re-launched LNG projects that had been previously suspended or abandoned. These refers to either expansion of existing facilities or construction of new ones. List of such projects includes, among others: expansion of Krk terminal in Croatia, new floating LNG terminal in France (La Havre), Germany (Wilhelmshaven), Greece (Thrace LNG, Argo FSRU), Ireland (Shannon LNG FSRU, Mag Mell FSRU), Italy (FSRU 1 and 2 – SNAM), the Netherlands (Eemshaven FSRU), and also onshore LNG terminals in Germany

(Brunsbuettel LNG terminal, Stadte LNG terminal), Italy (Porto Empedocle LNG), and offshore LNG gravity-based structure (GBS) – Porto Levante in Italy (Heidecke et al., 2022). Thus, existing policies aiming at rebalancing geographical structure of EU gas imports have been recently reinforced and targeted directly against one of the suppliers – Russia. In this case, extreme geopolitical events evoked energy policy exacerbation by importer and its consequences will affect demand security of Russia.

Apart from the regional energy policy examples, one may consider also national cases, which represent individual countries' approach towards energy issues. At this point this book's author would like to draw the reader's attention to the energy initiatives undertaken within energy policy of Lithuania and the USA. The choice of these two countries is subjective and results from their uniqueness in the global scale. Lithuanian example proves that even as energy-importing nation, country can undertake policy initiatives excluding certain suppliers. The American case show, on the other hand, how existing regulations can increase energy exports and make a country a global energy market player. Thus, from the point of view of energy demand security, two presented below energy policy initiatives influence the investigated phenomenon. The Lithuanian policy initiative – in a negative, the US – in a positive manner for energy exporters.

Lithuania, as a member of the EU follows the same regulations as other Community countries. However, energy issues are partially legally exempted from the EU jurisdiction according to paragraph 2 of article 194 of the "Treaty of the Functioning of the European Union" (2012). This exemption refers to "Member State's right to determine the conditions for exploiting its energy resources, its choice between different energy sources and the general structure of its energy supply" (*Treaty of the Functioning*..., 2012, p. 135).[29] In accordance with the Treaty, late December 2022 Lithuania passed an amendment to existing "Law of the Republic of Lithuania on Natural Gas No. VIII-1973" (2022), which came into force with the beginning of 2023. Amendment refers, among others, to the functioning of the LNG import facility in Lithuania. According to the paragraph 3 of article 46 of the law,

> The LNG terminal operator may not allocate and/or use LNG terminal capacity or part of it to supply liquefied natural gas from countries that, according to the National Security Strategy, pose a threat to the national security of the Republic of Lithuania and the safeguarding of national security interests.
>
> Law of the Republic... (2022)

As of 2023, the group of the discussed countries includes Russia and Belarus. The only exceptional case is a transit of Russian gas from mainland to the Kaliningrad region. However, also in this case there is a disclaimer that transited gas quantities shall not exceed the amount needed by the region. Timing of the introduced amendment is not coincidental. It is a result of the Lithuanian's government decisions which followed Russian invasion in Ukraine in 2022. This energy policy initiative of the Lithuanian government shows how by regulatory means an importing nation can fully reject the presence of the exporter on its gas market. From the point of view of the exporting country, such policy initiative results in a market loss. It is only export-not transit-restricted as Lithuania has long-term transit contract with Russia which expires in 2026 (Pietkova, 2022). That also shows the unique transit importance for the exporting nation. The peculiarity of this transit case refers to the supply security of exporter's own exclave – Kaliningrad.

The US case is different from the Lithuanian in two ways. Firstly, now the USA is an energy-exporting nation and secondly, its regulatory approach was used to increase volumes of the gas sold into international markets. It was possible thanks to the shale gas exploration which made the country global energy market player influencing the quantities of the resource available for sale and developing and maintaining the price pressure. Shale gas production surplus could have been directed from domestic to international markets in the form of LNG thanks to gas export regulatory policy. This approach includes close cooperation between the Department of Energy (DOE) and the Federal Energy Regulatory Commission (FERC). DOE, under the "Natural Gas Act" (1938, with amendments) grants company willing to export domestically produced gas authorization to export it. Approval is based upon the criterion of the US public interest. If export project meets the US public interest, approval is granted, otherwise – it is not. It is assumed that all projects aiming at the gas export to the FTA (free trade agreement) countries are serving public interest. In case of the non-FTA states, DOE investigates in detail several criteria, including economic, geopolitical, and environmental impact of the project. In practice, DOE approval has to be granted to all projects with exports of gas to other countries than Australia, Bahrain, Chile, Colombia, Costa Rica, Dominican Republic, El Salvador, Guatemala, Honduras, Israel, Jordan, Korea, Mexico, Morocco, Nicaragua, Oman, Panama, Peru, and Singapore.[30] Once the project is authorized by the DOE, it is assessed by the FERC. FERC, based on the "Natural Gas Act" (1938, with amendments) provisions, has the jurisdiction over the siting, construction, and operation of LNG export facilities in the USA and thus leads the environmental impact assessment of the project in accordance with "National Environmental Policy Act" (1969, with amendments). Obtaining the DOE's and the FERC's approval allows gas exports. Regulating gas exports contributed to increase of the American gas supply in the international markets making the USA top LNG exporter in the world in the first half of 2022 (EIA, 2022e) and main LNG supplier in Europe amidst the Russian-Ukrainian conflict (2022) (EIA, 2023). The US case shows how energy regulatory procedures can adjust the quantity of the gas in the international market. By authorizing gas exports to non-FTA countries, the USA had not only increased gas sell but also secured number of contracts. From the point of view of the exporting nation, such activity positively contributes to the demand security. At this point worth mentioning is also the fact that shale gas fever and associated oil production encouraged the USA to lift a 40-year ban on oil exports introduced in the midst of the oil crises of the 70s of the 20th century.

Regardless of that, the US and Lihuanian examples, even though different, share something in common. They are proofs that energy policy is inherently linked not only to economic policy of the country but also to geopolitical developments. As gas market and trade has been politicized recently, gas strategy of an individual country is an emanation of country's political preferences and choices in the international market.

Apart from brief description of selected EU/individual countries' energy policy initiatives and their potential influence on demand security, it is also worth looking at how this nexus can be empirically investigated. An interesting way of investigating energy demand security and energy policy nexus delivers Voudouris (2013). He offers conceptual framework addressing energy security and energy policy in terms of diversifying energy exports for net energy producers.[31] Voudouris uses the ACEGES (Agent-based Computational Economics of the Global Energy System) model to explore the future export and production/potential of crude oil for selected countries. Even though his 2013 analysis is limited to oil from Saudi Arabia, Russia, and Iraq, his later research from 2014 (Voudouris et al., 2014) proves model's usefulness for the natural gas market.

The ACEGES model was introduced (2010) and extended (2011) by Voudouris (2010, 2011). It is an agent-based model for the energy policy exploration. According to the model, the global energy market is a complex but adaptive system of interacting agents (countries), who do not necessarily possess perfect rationality and information. Model output might be, for instance, gas production based on assumptions concerning upstream investment incentives such as, among others, prices, taxes, or subsidies. ACEGES outputs feed the SPT (Stochastic Portfolio Theory) framework. SPT is used to analyse the energy trade. As a result, SPT suggests possible energy trade flows between countries through the export portfolio of the exporting countries. The portfolio is determined by a certain weight, which is a proportion of portfolio's export assigned to a particular country. In other words, the SPT mathematically analyses given global gas market characteristics to construct the energy exports portfolio. In this way the SPT framework addresses energy security aspects, while ACEGES accommodates energy policy questions. To better understand the model's potential use, let's consider an example: the USA optimal export portfolio weight for Poland might be 0.2 (zero would mean that there are no exports to Poland). With time and changing global gas market conditions, this weight might alter. An example of such change might be substituting nuclear energy in Japan with natural gas as a consequence of the Fukushima nuclear power plant failure. Rebalancing of the portfolio weights has to be accommodated by the US/Japan diplomatic initiatives. ACEGES scenarios fuelled by SPT framework help to answer the question how diplomatic initiatives might influence export portfolios (cf.: Voudouris, 2013).

The ACEGES with the SPT as its integral part might serve as a valuable and insightful option of investigating energy policy influence over energy security of exporters in the natural gas market. However, by 2023, there has been no (or at least not commonly available) publication describing such an empirical attempt. Thus, the ACEGES model with the SPT remains a conceptual framework for future use. Regardless of that, one has to admit that the model's perspective on the demand security in the light of trade flows makes it an interesting tool for the analysis of this phenomenon from the point of view of international energy economics.

Summing up, regional energy policy initiatives and individual countries' approaches contribute to the demand security in the gas market. In case of the EU, it can be concluded that the ultimate objective for the community is to become at least partially independent of dominant third-country suppliers. Political turmoil resulting from the Russian-Ukrainian conflict (2022) resulted in unprecedented policy steps undertaken by the importing nations. As a result, Lithuania rejected Russian gas for domestic needs. The USA gained on the Ukrainian war securing demand for its LNG for coming years. Regulatory procedures authorizing non-FTA gas exports, that had already been used, made it happen. In this way, by created policy pressure strengthened by political rationale incumbent exporters are threatened by the loss of the demand. Investigating energy policy and demand security link might be carried out with a described novel agent-based approach.

3.2.2 Determinants of natural gas prices

Factors influencing the price of natural gas, in addition to the demand and supply discussed earlier, include the price terms of trade contracts, energy subsidies, and sovereign wealth funds. All these are medium- and long-term elements.

3.2.2.1 Price terms of contract

The price at which resources are sold are a significant element of trade contracts. Due to trade secrets, which include the prices of resource supplies under long-term contracts, the economic viability of imports will be presented on the basis of selected aspects related to the formation of natural gas prices.[32]

Natural gas is sold under long-term contracts on the basis of price formulas. They take the form of net-back pricing or replacement value – in international trade, or the cost-plus pricing or net-forward pricing method[33] – in domestic gas trade. The net-back pricing formula appeared with the discovery of the Dutch Gröningen field and it is nowadays the most popular method of forming natural gas prices (in various variants). According to the formula, the price of the resource is determined on the basis of its market value from the buyer's perspective and in relation to other competitive fuels used in the importer's market. One of the elements of the resource pricing mechanism discussed is the value of competing fuels (replacement value) and the net-back value to delivery point. The net-back pricing mechanism is as follows:

$$\text{Net back pricing mechanism} = \left(\text{replacement value; indexation}\right) + \left(\text{net back value to delivery point}\right) + \left(\text{review}\right). \quad (2)$$

The value of competing fuels is determined on the basis of the prices of other products. These may be light fuel oil (LFO), heavy fuel oil (HFO), gas, coal, or electricity price. The inflation rate is an additional element in pricing formulas of this type. As Konoplyanik (2010) points out, the share of individual products used in the pricing formula varies depending on the fuel supplier. At the beginning of the 20th century,[34] pricing under Russian, Dutch, and Norwegian contracts was based on light fuel oil (50%) and heavy fuel oil (30%). Another component taken into account in pricing at the time under contracts with Norway and the Netherlands was inflation (2.7% and 0.9%, respectively) (Konoplyanik, 2010).

In recent years, there has been a gradual shift from the inclusion of oil prices in long-term contracts in favour of natural gas prices. According to various estimates, between 2012 and 2013, in Europe, the indexation of long-term contracts taking into account the prices of natural gas at hubs accounted for 30% (in 2013, according to Gazprom) through 45% (in 2012, according to the International Gas Union – IGU) to 53% (in 2013, according to IGU) of the total gas used in Europe (Franza, 2014).

Indexation based on the price of gas can be partial or full. Gazprom offers partial indexation performed mainly on the basis of prices from the Dutch hub Title Transfer Facility (TTF).[35] For the first time, the company introduced this type of indexation in a contract with the UK's E.ON in 2010. Gazprom agreed to 15% indexation using spot prices of natural gas. In the course of proceedings pending before courts of arbitration, the Russian supplier provided such an option for other buyers (e.g., RWE). In contracts with Italy's Eni and Poland's PGNiG, Gazprom uses the indirect indexation principle, which takes into account gas prices on the spot market. When oil-indexed gas prices exceed those of indexed to natural gas prices, indexation shall be applied taking into account gas plus the exporter's premium. In a reverse situation, where gas prices calculated on the basis of natural gas prices are higher than for crude oil, indexation using gas prices minus the exporter's discount is used (Franza, 2014).

Important determinants of the price of natural gas in contracts are the so-called price review clauses. Price review is a mechanism that, in the case of long-term contracts, allows the contracting parties to adjust to changing market conditions based on the price review clauses set out in the contracts. The contracts provide for a predetermined number of inspections. Most often they are preceded by mandatory price negotiations (which take three to six months). The price change achieved as a result of such a review may be retroactive, which means that it is calculated from the moment the contracting party requests a review. In the event of disagreement, the dispute between the counterparties is settled through international arbitration. Disputes are dealt with by courts of arbitration in New York, Geneva, Paris, or Stockholm.

Price review clauses are a mechanism for making long-term contracts more flexible. This is evidenced by a study conducted by Crocker and Masten (1991) on a sample of 659 natural gas contracts in the USA in 1982. The authors proved that the flexibility of commodity prices sold (e.g., in the form of a price review clause) is the greater, the longer the duration of the trade contract. They indicate the uncertainty of both parties as to the market situation during a long-term contract as the cause of this relationship.

Clauses providing for price review first appeared in gas contracts in the 1980s as gas extraction started from the Norwegian Troll field. The popularization of clauses took place at the beginning of the new century as a result of the liberalization of the natural gas market in Europe and the related decline in the price of this commodity. The years 2008–2010 saw another breakthrough, when as a result of the economic crisis, the demand for natural gas decreased and at the same time its supply increased as a consequence of the increase in shale gas production in the USA. In the same period, the liberalization of the natural gas market was in progress in the EU, the volume of gas sold at European gas hubs was growing, as was competition in the European natural gas market. At the same time, as a result of favourable conditions in the international market, periodic price reviews were carried out in contracts for the purchase of natural gas. As a consequence, the prices of natural gas purchased by Austria, Bulgaria, Germany, Italy, the Netherlands, Poland, and Romania dropped. In the second decade of the new century, as a result of a further increase in the liquidity of European natural gas markets, the process of gradual replacement of crude oil with natural gas in long-term contracts began.

Indexing contracts based on gas prices from major European hubs means that the market reacts less than in the case of crude oil to changing conditions in the international market. In the future, this would mean that price review clauses are not needed. Exceptions could be made for those importers where prices at gas hubs would reflect changing conditions in their domestic market. Price review clauses could also work in future in the non-liberalized Asian market, where indexation to oil prices still prevails (Anway and von Mehren, 2017).

The flexibility of long-term contracts with regard to price review clauses is reflected by the fact that they have traditionally taken place every three years, whereas recently this time has been shortened. An example is the negotiations between Italy's Eni and Gazprom in 2012, as a result of which the importer secured the right to request a price review at any time (Franza, 2014). Another element that makes contracts more flexible is the method of calculating the delay on the basis of which the final price of the commodity is calculated in the formula. Previously, the so-called "12.0.6" rule was in force, which meant that the price was indexed to the average price of oil for the last 12 months, effective immediately after the end of that period (0) for the next six months (6). The final price calculation and validity periods are now being shortened so that they take the form of "6.0.3" or "3.0.3" rule. This means that the calculation of the final price takes into account the average price of oil over the last six or three months, respectively, and is applicable immediately after the end of that period for the following quarter (Franza, 2014).

3.2.2.2 Energy subsidies

The impact of energy subsidies on energy security is primarily related to increasing the availability of energy for domestic entities. Since subsidies are a form of (mainly monetary) support, they are included in the category of price conditions.

Subsidies, also called subventions or grants, are a form of transfer from public authorities to domestic entities, which are not accompanied by transfers of funds in the opposite direction (Nojszewska, 1995). Subsidies may take different forms. They include:

- monetary subsidies, which represent the direct transfer of funds to selected entities, and
- hidden subsidies, which provide support in the form of preferential loan conditions, tax exemptions, or reliefs.

The former type of subsidies now tends to be used increasingly less often. Indirect forms of support to domestic entities are more common.

Subsidies are also classified, among other things, in terms of the (OECD, 2013):

- target – may concern both beneficiaries: producers or consumers, as well as factors of production or a specific product (energy source);
- instrument – monetary transfers, tax exemptions, under-pricing of public services, and products;
- purpose – regional development, energy conservation, etc.

The fourth element is the pathway of benefit, that is, whether the subsidy is direct (in the form of monetary transfer), or indirect (in other forms). It seems that it is secondary to the type of instrument used and, therefore, does not deserve separate classification.

Subsidy beneficiaries may be both producers and consumers. In the case of the former, there are subsidies to domestic production and export subsidies.[36] Consumer subsidies are usually financed from budget (on-budget) and take the form of quasi-fiscal instruments, such as electricity tariffs at a price lower than the supply cost. These types of subsidies are easy to identify. Subsidies earmarked for producers are more problematic as most of them are funded off-budget, which makes their identification more difficult (OECD, 2013).

Subsidies are one of the non-tariff trade measures regulated by the WTO and its predecessor General Agreement on Trade and Tariffs (GATT). Uruguay Round (1986–1994) resulted in adoption (1995) of the Agreement on Subsidies and Countervailing Measures (SCM Agreement), which redrafted the original GATT understanding of subsidies (Michałek, 2004).

The SCM Agreement regulates the provision of subsidies, and countervailing measures used to offset injury caused by subsidized imports. Contemporary definition of the subsidies under SCM regime includes, as Michałek (2004) highlights, three elements. Firstly, a financial contribution, secondly government or any public body support, and thirdly granting a benefit (SCM Agreement, 1995 with amendments). Each of these conditions has to be met for the subsidy to exist. Financial contribution includes grants, loans, and equity infusion or loan guarantees, fiscal incentives such as tax credits but also situations when a government provides goods or services other than general infrastructure, or purchases goods or the government makes payments to a funding mechanism, or entrusts or directs a private body to carry out above highlighted activities, which are usually carried out by governments. A benefit emerges when compared to standard market situation, such profit would not be achieved. A subsidy that falls into jurisdiction of the SCM Agreement has to be specific. It means that a subsidy has to be granted to an enterprise, group of enterprises (enterprise specificity), sector of the industry, industry/industries (industry specificity), or targets producers in specified parts of its territory for subsidization (regional specificity) (WTO, 2023). Only such specific subsidies can be subjected to the SCM provisions.

The SCM Agreement distinguishes two types of the subsidies: prohibited (part II of the SCM Agreement) and actionable (part III of the SCM Agreement). The latter are subjected to the WTO general rules (e.g., multilateral dispute settlement procedure with Dispute Settlement Understanding and Body involved) or the SCM countervailing measures. In the group of prohibited subsidies, there are export and local content subsidies. Actionable subsidies, including for instance, production subsidies, are not prohibited and can be challenged if they adversely affect interests of other WTO member states. Such negative impact includes three types of effects. First one refers to the injury domestic industry experiences as a result of subsidized imports. Second pertains to serious prejudice which arises as a result of adverse effects (e.g., export displacement) in the market of the subsidizing member or in a third country market. Third includes nullification or impairment of benefits accruing under the GATT 1994. Nullification or impairment arises when the improved market access resulting from the tariff reduction is undercut by subsidization. Difficulty lies in demonstrating the above-mentioned adverse effects (Michałek, 2004; WTO, 2023).

Summing up, a countervailing measure may not be imposed unless subsidized imports, injury to a domestic industry, and a causal link between the subsidized imports and the injury are determined (WTO, 2023). There are groups of countries that are exempted from the general SCM regulations on subsidies as WTO admits in article 27.1 of the SCM that "subsidies may play an important role in economic development programmes[37] of developing country Members" (SCM Agreement, 1995, with amendments, p. 257). Thus, export subsidies are not prohibited in case of least-developed countries (LDCs), WTO members with a GNP per capita of less than USD 1,000 per year which are listed in Annex VII to the SCM Agreement, and other developing countries. As WTO (2023) suggests, the lower a member's level of development, the more favourable the treatment it receives with respect to the subsidies disciplines.

Energy subsidies are a specific type of government transfers. Their beneficiaries are energy producers or consumers, but there are also transfers provided to support a specific energy source. However, defining an energy subsidy poses a great deal of difficulties. This is evidenced by the fact that there are many divergences between the main international organizations in the perception of the substance of subsidies (Piotrowski, 2015). Such institutions include the IMF, the OECD, and even the OECD's energy agenda – the IEA.

According to the OECD definition (von Moltke, McKee, and Morgan, 2017), an energy subsidy is "any measure that keeps prices for consumers below market levels, and for producers above market levels". Piotrowski (2015) believes that the OECD definition is broad and includes both direct monetary transfers and tax exemptions or reliefs. This author emphasizes that in this approach the energy subsidy cannot be a subsidy for energy consumption. This is a basic measure used in developing countries. In his opinion, this is associated with the fact that, in OECD statistics, the amount of energy subsidies is the smallest compared to the estimates of other international organizations.

The International Energy Agency recognizes as energy subsidies such government transfers to the energy sector that reduce production costs, increase prices obtained by producers and lower prices paid by consumers (IEA, 2014). As Piotrowski (2015) points out, the amount of subsidy is calculated on the basis of an analysis of the difference in fuel prices in international markets and for end users.

In that author's opinion (Piotrowski, 2015), the most complex definition of energy subsidies is used by the International Monetary Fund. The IMF's terminology seems to refer mainly to theoretical aspects. Clements et al. (2013) present subsidies broken down into support for producers and for consumers. Calculation of the subsidy amount is performed in different ways, depending on whether or not the product concerned is traded in international markets. For internationally traded goods, the transfer represents the difference between the price of the commodity in international markets (reference price) and the price for end users. In the other case, when non-traded goods are involved, such as electricity, the basis is the cost of production increased by distribution costs and return on capital ("price-gap" approach).[38]

Energy subsidies take various forms (Table 3.11). These can be both the simplest direct subsidies, preferential tax policy, as well as business regulation or supporting

Table 3.11 Types of energy subsidies

		The way the subsidy works		
Type of government intervention	*Example*	*Lowers cost of production*	*Raises cost of production*	*Lowers price to consumer*
Direct monetary transfer	Grants to producers	X		
	Grants to consumers			X
	Low-interest, preferential loans to producers	X		
Preferential tax policy	Rebates of exemptions on royalties, sales taxes, and tariffs	X		
	Tax credit	X		X
	Accelerated depreciation allowances on energy equipment	X		
Trade barriers	Quotas, embargoes, technical restrictions		X	
Energy-related services provided by government below cost	Investment in energy infrastructure	X		
	Spending on energy research and development	X		
Regulation of the Energy sector	Sales guarantees	X	X	X
	Price control		X	
	Market entry barriers		X	

Source: Compiled by the author based on UNEP (2004).

the energy sector by providing services at a lower than market price. Energy subsidies also include trade barriers, mainly non-tariff barriers, which, like administrative sales assurance, price controls, and restrictions on access to the energy market, increase the cost of energy production. All other energy subsidies reduce either production costs or prices for consumers. The mechanism of non-tariff barriers and administrative regulation leads to an inefficient allocation of resources, resulting in an increase in commodity prices.

What can also be called energy subsidies, as in other areas of activity, are low-interest preferential loans or deferral of tax payment, as well as accelerated depreciation write-offs for equipment. Nevertheless, government transfers also include a type of subsidy highly specific to the energy industry. This concerns the extraction and exploration of fuels. In this respect, any reduction or exemption from the obligation to pay royalties (mining licence fee) is treated as a subsidy. Another type of subsidy, equally specific to that market, is the reduction or exemption from sales tax on extracted resources.

For example, in 2015, in the USA, an exemption from production fees was applied for those quantities of natural gas that were emitted into the atmosphere or burned on site at the drilling rig. It is estimated that this way about USD 70 m was not paid into the US budget in 2015. In addition, approximately USD 288 m was transferred to energy companies in the form of a tax subsidy. This is due to the fact that geological and geophysical survey expenses enjoy an accelerated two-year depreciation period. Another tax preference is the modified method of calculating income tax for listed companies that obtain at least 90% of their gross income from the extraction of exhaustible natural resources or real estate. Such companies did not pay traditional corporate income tax (CIT) in the USA. The annual value of this subsidy was estimated at USD 342 m in 2015 (US Government, 2016).

Based on the type of energy (object criterion) that is subsidized, subsidies can be divided into subsidies for fossil fuels and subsidies for renewable energy sources (RES). These are two different varieties of subsidies that arouse much controversy. On the one hand, supporters of RES question the legitimacy of granting aid to coal mines or companies extracting hydrocarbons; on the other hand, the coal/oil lobby opposes support for wind farms. Energy subsidies for renewable and non-renewable fuels can take various forms, as already mentioned (Table 3.11). Among the most commonly used subsidies for RES are the so-called feed-in tariffs, which impose the obligation to purchase electricity produced from a specific source (RES), at a fixed price for a certain period of time.

Energy subsidies are mainly domestic production subsidies. The purpose of such subsidies, in particular those supporting domestic fuel production, is to protect employment in the sector or reduce the volume of exports. These are indirect subsidies, which are mostly financed off-budget (UNEP, 2004).

In the opinion of Bhattacharyya (2011), energy subsidies for producers have become a domain of developed countries, and those intended for consumers are specific mainly to developing countries. Bhattacharyya argues that in developed countries, domestic fuel production is supported (e.g., Germany) for employment protection reasons, and in developing countries, to protect the poorest social groups. This view contradicts the opinion expressed by the WTO (2006), which, citing the example of Brazil and Nigeria, showed that energy subsidies in developing countries can also aim at industrialization by keeping energy prices low for domestic energy-intensive companies.

Due to the wide variety of ways of defining and estimating energy subsidies, the statistics showing their size also differ. Differences result, among others, from including different energy retail and reference prices and different ways of calculating subsidies for power generation/industry and housing. This means that the IMF's estimates of subsidies significantly exceed those of the IEA (Figure 3.9). The IMF estimates that in 2018 the total amount of subsidies for the energy sector (including the electric power industry) amounted to about USD 337 bn, while according to the IEA it was about USD 185 bn. According to the IMF, energy subsidies reached USD 5.9 tr in 2020, accounting for 6.8% of global GDP during that period and are projected to continue to grow (Parry, Black, and Vernon, 2021).

Differences in the way subsidies are estimated by the IMF and the IEA are also evident in the comparison of subsidies in different groups of countries depending on their place in the international division of labour in the energy market (Figure 3.10). It is true that the countries that export energy, in the opinion of both institutions, are groups of countries providing much more subsidies than importers, but the scale of these differences varies. According to the IMF, in 2018, the total amount of subsidies in the group of exporters was more than twice as large (USD 272 bn) as in the group of exporters according to the IEA (USD 123 bn). In the statistics on importers, the IMF and the IEA give similar amounts of subsidies in 2018 at approximately USD 60 bn.

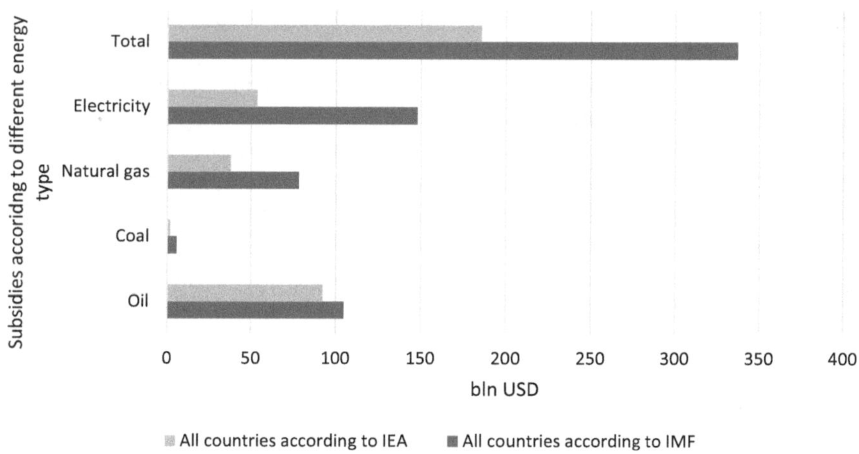

Figure 3.9 Comparison of IEA and IMF subsidy estimates for 2018 (USD bn).

Source: Compiled by the author based on Parry, Black, and Vernon (2021).

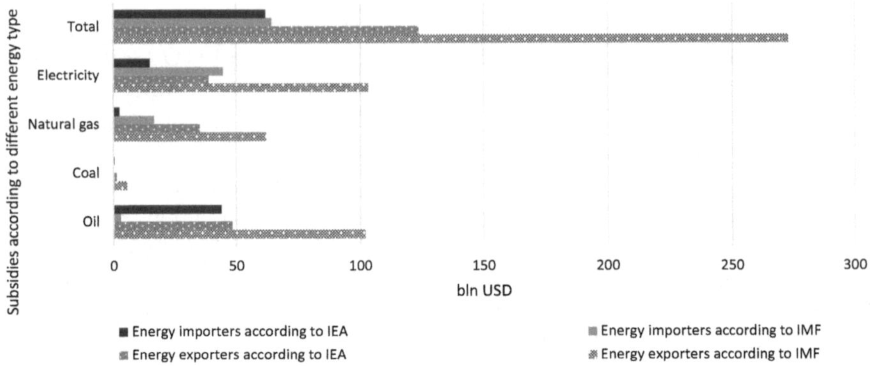

Figure 3.10 Comparison of IEA and IMF subsidy estimates for different energy types in energy-exporting and importing nations in 2018 (USD bn).

Source: Compiled by the author based on Parry, Black, and Vernon (2021).

In energy-exporting countries, the hydrocarbon and electric power industries were by far the most heavily subsidized in 2018 (according to the IMF and the IEA). In energy-importing countries, the main beneficiaries were the electric power industry (according to the IMF) and the oil industry (in the IEA's opinion). According to the IMF, the country providing the most subsidies in 2018 was Russia with about USD 67 bn, of which approximately USD 42 bn went to the gas industry, and, according to the IEA – China, which directed most of the total of USD 26 bn in energy subsidies (about USD 22 bn) to the oil industry. By comparison, in the IEA statistics, in the same year, Russia granted about USD 15 bn in energy subsidies, of which USD 7 bn went to hydrocarbons and USD 8 bn to the electric power industry. In turn, according to the IMF statistics, China granted about USD 14 bn in energy subsidies in 2018, of which almost all went to the electric power industry (Parry, Black, and Vernon, 2021).

Dead-weight losses associated with subsidies are visible in economic, environmental, and social effects. The economic impact is manifold. First, subsidies reduce revenues to the government budget, making fiscal policy more difficult to implement. Second, they have a negative impact on the trade balance[39] due to the increase in prices (by subsidy costs) of exported or imported fuels. Third, in the long run, subsidies reduce the innovation and efficiency of domestic energy companies and reduce the country's attractiveness to foreign investors. Fourth, they artificially create a competitive advantage of some fuels over others. An example would be the preference for RES at the expense of fossil fuels. This way, fuel consumption patterns change. The scope and pace of this change are dictated by the complementarity and substitutability of fuels. To sum up, it can be concluded, as the World Bank has done, that subsidies are an opportunity cost of lost export profits for energy-exporting countries, and for energy-importing countries – a budgetary burden. In the case of the former group of countries, subsidies have a particularly positive effect when domestic energy companies have a limited export potential. On the other hand, for the other group of countries, subsidies further improve the system of foreign exchange reserves (World Bank, 2010).

The resulting environmental impact is shown in Figure 3.11. It illustrates the relationship between price, fuel quantity, and environmental pollution. It is assumed that the increased supply of fuels (usually fossil fuels) leads to environmental pollution. Therefore, the introduction of a subsidy for producers to each unit of fuel causes a shift in the supply curve from S to S_{ps}. This, in turn, causes a decrease in fuel prices from P to P_{ps}, an increase in its supply from Q to Q_{ps}, and an increase in environmental pollution from E to E_{ps}. The introduction of a subsidy for consumers has a similar effect. Increasing fuel consumption by each subsidized fuel unit causes a shift of the demand curve from D to D_{cs}, a decrease in fuel price from P to P_{cs}, an increase in its supply from Q to Q_{cs}, and an increase in environmental pollution from E to E_{cs}. It is clear that irrespective of the type of subsidy, its environmental impact is the same. The exact impact of the subsidy depends on the price flexibility of supply and demand. The less sensitive they are to price changes, the less impact the subsidy has on environmental pollution (UNEP, 2004).

The social impacts include a shift in subsidy spending from socially relevant areas such as health, education, and infrastructure. In this sense, subsidies increase the polarization of societies, as their main beneficiaries are the upper and middle classes. Energy subsidies also discourage energy saving, which seems counterproductive in the context of global trends towards energy efficiency. In the long term, such an inefficient allocation of resources has a negative impact on social welfare (World Bank, 2010; Rentschler and Bazilian, 2017).

The links between energy subsidies (regardless of their recipient) and energy security are evident in the reasons for which subsidies are granted. Energy security is, apart from job creation, a form of protection of the national economy against external competition – one of the basic motives for granting government subsidies (Koplow, 2004; Rentschler and Bazilian, 2017). This is particularly evident in the case of subsidies involving coal. In countries with rich coal resources and developed infrastructure generating electricity from this fuel, subsidizing mines is an argument for energy security. In addition, in such cases, the subsidies are justified by referring to the above-mentioned general economic interest, job protection, and also social aspects. The latter matters the most in countries where significant coal production comes from several mines employing considerable number of local society. The rationale for the improvement of energy security is also invoked with subsidies for RES. This is due to the fact that RES are in a sense a "domestic" source of energy – and its use is not associated with the import of fuels from abroad. This is particularly important for countries that import energy commodities for electricity production. In such countries, RES become a substitute for imported fuels. Due to energy subsidies, electricity generated from RES is more competitive in terms of price compared to other fuels and enjoys privileges in access to distribution and transmission infrastructure. This way, subsidizing domestic energy sources affects not only its prices but also increases energy supply, which in turn translates into energy independence/self-sufficiency.

The most extensive insight into energy security and related subsidies is presented by D'Agostino (2013). Referring to the multi-dimensional concept of energy security (APERC, 2007), the author concludes that energy subsidies affect security through the financial criterion. They enable access to total energy or access

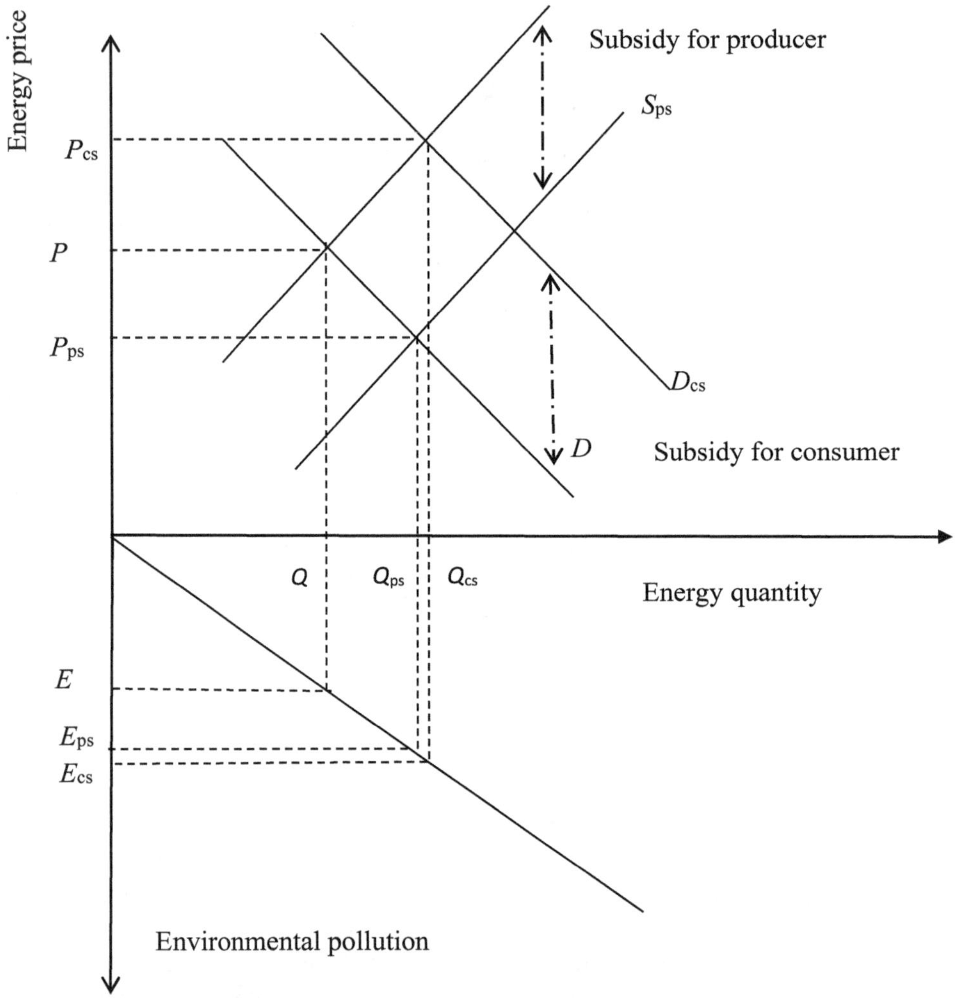

Figure 3.11 Environmental impact of fossil fuel subsidies.

Source: Compiled by the author based on UNEP (2004).

to modern energy services. These are mainly the poorest consumers who, in the absence of support, would be excluded from energy consumption. This way, energy subsidies close the gap in access to energy.

Price shocks in energy markets are another channel of impact of energy subsidies on security (Murshed, 2017). This reasoning refers to the World Bank's definition of energy security (Davis et al., 2005), according to which the phenomenon is described by the impact of changes (among other things) in energy prices on macroeconomic variables (e.g., GDP). Murshed (2017), giving the example of Bangladesh, rightly argues that rapid changes in energy prices are particularly difficult for developing countries. This is because such economies are struggling to absorb supply shocks.

In sum, energy subsidies can take different forms, but regardless of their type they have similar influence over energy market. They reduce either production costs or prices for consumers. Energy subsidies for producers have become a domain of developed countries, and those intended for consumers are specific mainly to developing countries. In energy-exporting countries, majority of subsidies cover hydrocarbons, among which there is natural gas.

3.2.2.3 Sovereign wealth funds

Sovereign wealth funds (hereinafter: SWFs), often referred to as national funds or investment funds, are institutions established and administered by the general government and tasked with the management of financial assets.

Economic theories underpinning the creation of SWFs include concepts developed by Hotelling (1931) and Hartwick (1977). They are elements of the theory of sustainable development, which focuses on the issue of managing economic rent from the extraction of non-renewable resources, called in short resource rent. According to Hartwick's rule, the resource rent should be used for investment other than natural resources without specifying what investments this concerns. Following this rule enables countries to accumulate savings so that they can continue to develop/build wealth even after the non-renewable resources have been exhausted. However, the World Bank, followed by the OECD, points out that resource-rich countries do not comply with the Hartwick rule and do not accumulate savings, which makes them poorer every year. As the OECD emphasizes, respect for this rule can protect individual countries from the effects of what is known as a resource curse. In this sense, SWFs are the government's response (in the field of economic policy) to the risks associated with the negative effects of the Rybczyński theorem, the Dutch disease, and immiserizing growth.

According to the criterion of purpose proposed by the International Monetary Fund (Al-Hassan et al., 2018), for which SWFs have been created, they can be divided into those mainly motivated by:

- stabilization of state revenues – and their protection against rapid changes in commodity prices in international markets,
- accumulating savings for future generations, resulting from the adoption of the principle that today's non-renewable resources are transformed into financial assets immune to price changes,

- development of the state and support for priority socio-economic projects, including infrastructure,
- accumulation of a reserve for future government pension expenses.

A different classification of SWFs concerns the source of capital, which is used for their creation. According to this criterion, the following categories are distinguished (after Baran, 2012):

- commodity SWFs, for which the sources of capital are enterprises exporting natural resources, both state-owned and private (through taxation)
- non-commodity SWFs, which feed government foreign exchange reserves, budget surplus, national savings, or proceeds of privatization.

According to IMF's definition (Al-Hassan et al., 2018), commodity-based sovereign wealth funds are special purpose funds that are owned by the general government. They are created for macroeconomic purposes. The role of SWFs is to hold and manage assets entrusted to them in line with directions set by government. To this end, they undertake investments that include investing in foreign financial assets.

As Baran (2012) points out, the objectives of commodity SWFs include mainly motives associated with the stabilization of general government revenue, maintaining the balance of payments, and accumulation of savings for future generations. The objectives on non-commodity SWFs are mainly to maximize returns on invested capital and stabilize inflation. In 2015, commodity SWFs related to income derived from crude oil and natural gas accounted for approximately 56% of all SWFs in the world (SWFI, 2018b).

The history of both commodity wealth funds and wealth funds in general dates back to the middle of the last century (Chopra, 2013). The first fund to be set up at that time was SAMA Foreign Holdings (1952), followed by SWF set up by the Kuwait Investment Authority (1953), which was fed with surplus revenues from oil exports. Chopra (2013) distinguishes three eras in the development of commodity SWFs (Table 3.12). The first one is the period before the 1973 oil crisis, which saw the establishment of three funds. The second covers the period between 1973 and the beginning of the new millennium (2000), when another ten funds were set up. The third generation of SWFs consists of funds created after 2000.

Chopra (2013) emphasizes that SWFs are formed mainly during periods of rising oil prices in world markets. This is partly confirmed by the statistics of funds

Table 3.12 Sovereign wealth funds (SWF) according to their time of establishment

Period	*Number of SWFs established*
Before 1973	3
1973–2000	10
After 2000	8 (till 2013)

Source: Compiled by the author based on Chopra (2013).

established before 2015. It follows that, taking into account the period 1970–2015, in the years 2000–2009 – about 45% of the SWFs operating today were created, in the period 2010–2015 – about 21%, and before 1970 – 7.6% (SWFI, 2018b).

Among the ten largest SWFs in the world, in terms of assets held are two European funds and eight Middle Eastern funds (Table 3.13). This is a consequence of the distribution of global oil resources, as well as the share of individual countries in global exports of this commodity. The largest SWF is the Norwegian Global Fund (Norwegian *Oljefondet*). Although it was established relatively recently (1990), its assets significantly exceed those held by other institutions of this type (about USD 1 tr). It is also one of the leading funds in terms of investment and management transparency. Investment transparency is measured by the Sovereign Wealth Fund Institute, using the Linaburg-Maduell Transparency Index developed in 2008. The index ranges from 0 to 10. The higher its value, the greater the

Table 3.13 World's biggest sovereign wealth funds (SWF)

No.	*Country*	*SWF name*	*Asset value (USD bn)*	*Year created*	*Natural resource*	*Transparency index value*
1	Norway	Government Pension Fund-Global	1,032.69	1990	Crude oil	10
2	United Arab Emirates	Abu-Dhabi Investment Authority (ADIA)	828	1976	Crude oil	6
3	Kuwait	Kuwait Investment Authority	524	1953	Crude oil	6
4	Saudi Arabia	SAMA Foreign Holdings	494	1952	Crude oil	4
5	Qatar	Qatar Investment Authority	320	2005	Crude oil and natural gas	5
6	Saudi Arabia	Public Investment Fund	223.9	2008	Crude oil	4
7	United Arab Emirates	Mubadala Investment Company	125	2002	Crude oil	10
8	United Arab Emirates	Abu-Dhabi Investment Council	110	2007	Crude oil	Data unavailable
9	Iran	National Development Fund of Iran	91	2011	Crude oil and natural gas	5
10	Russia	National Welfare Fund	72.2	2008	Crude oil	5

Source: Compiled by the author based on SWFI (2018b).

transparency of the activities of the SWF concerned. The index includes ten categories. These are each time the openness/transparency of the SWF in terms of, for example, its formation/history, annual audit reports, ownership structure, returns on investment, objectives/strategies, contact details/website management, hiring external managers. The least transparent (Linaburg-Maduell index value = 1) commodity funds based on income from energy exports are SWF, respectively, from Mauritania, Venezuela, Algeria, Brunei, and Libya (SWFI, 2018a).

Oljefondet is based, like most commodity SWFs, on revenues from oil exports. Among the largest SWFs of this type, there are also funds that are additionally fed with funds from the export of natural gas. These include SWFs from Iran and Qatar. Revenues from the export of this fuel form the basis of funds from Algeria, East Timor, Mauritania, Mexico, Oman, Papua New Guinea, Turkmenistan, and the United States (New Mexico, North Dakota, Alabama, Louisiana, West Virginia, Texas).

SWFs contribute to the energy security of mainly energy-exporting countries. They make exporters independent of fluctuations in the prices of resources in international markets (an extreme case of which is the phenomenon of immiserizing growth described before), and prevent the emergence of the Dutch disease. SWFs consider fighting a Dutch disease as one of their major tasks (Wills, Senbet, and Simbanegavi, 2016). This argument is supported by Garg and Shukla (2021), who summarize the influence of the SWFs on the Dutch disease mitigation. According to authors such impact encompasses three dimensions. Firstly, SWFs protect economies from commodity price shocks. In times of high commodity prices, SWFs absorb excess liquidity in times of low prices support government expenditure and budgets. This argument is also supported by Aizenman et al. (2019); Coutinho et al. (2022); Dagher, Gottschalk, and Portillo (2012); Kinda, Mlachila, and Ouedraogo (2018); Mohaddes and Raissi (2017); or Van der Ploeg (2014). Secondly, SWFs reduce the volatility of real exchange rate misalignments by dampening the transmission of energy prices as presented by Aizenman and Riera-Crichton (2014); Raymond, Coulibaly, and Omgba (2017); Shehabi (2015); and Zeufack et al. (2016). Thirdly, by redistribution of tax revenues generated from the energy sector facilitate the economy's shift towards a sustainability as suggested by Heffron (2018). Apart from that, SWFs also address, among others, governance and institutional quality deterioration induced by resource abundance as proved by Tsani (2013). By insulating economies from energy price shocks and exchange rate volatility, SWFs provide energy demand security for exporting nations.

In sum, energy-related SWFs (or energy SWFs) play an important role in shaping the energy security of energy-exporting countries. They are a kind of complex financial instrument that to some extent eliminates the negative economic properties of energy commodities. This concerns in particular the low price elasticity of the supply of energy commodities, which results from a long investment cycle, high capital intensity of investments, and a high share of fixed costs in the total extraction costs. All this means that supply does not react flexibly to price changes (outside the opportunity margin of free generation capacity), which means that during periods of falling prices, the production of energy commodities remains at a slightly changed level. For the exporter, SWFs are not only a mechanism to stabilize income over time, but also to benefit from it, even in periods of downturn. If the exporter's energy security is treated as stability of revenues from the export of energy commodities, then energy SWFs are a tool for achieving this goal.

3.3 Energy demand security in natural gas market in the neoclassical trade framework – Empirical approach

The aim of this study is to investigate the influence of energy demand security on comparative advantage of developed, net gas-exporting economies. To do so, econometric modelling is used as a tool for testing the following research hypothesis: relative energy demand security has a positive and a statistically significant impact on relative comparative advantage of net gas-exporting countries.

This study fits into the following research gaps. First, highlighted by Nyga-Łukaszewska and Napiórkowski (2022) and Nyga-Łukaszewska and Chilimoniuk-Przeździecka (2017) calling for broader empirical investigation of energy demand security. Second, research *niché* indicated by Antoniadis (2017) and by Karatayev and Hall (2020) concerns extending, on the one hand, the discussion on the influence of oil rents on other than Black Sea energy-exporting economies, and, on the other, investigating energy security in resource-rich exporting nations other than Russia and the Caspian region. Thus, this study contributes to the existing scientific knowledge by looking at the energy demand security of high-income OECD net gas exporters. Choice of these countries, constituting coherent group without outlying observations, results from their high gas export levels combined with a comparable level of economic development.

This research departs from the existing literature in various ways. Firstly, study employs the concept of demand security, whereas most studies focus on supply security (Dike, 2013). Secondly, the analysis on demand security has so far been carried out for developing and emerging economies, like OPEC countries (Bollino and Galkin, 2021), Saudi Arabia (Ulatowski, 2016), Russia (Novikau, 2021). Rare perspective on demand security of industrialized nations delivers Nyga-Łukaszewska and Napiórkowski (2022). Thirdly, this study as suggested by Dike (2013) looks at the demand security through a set of indicators including simple measures as resources dependency – reflecting Karatayev and Hall (2020) approach, institutional quality – referring to Ramírez-Cendrero and Wirth (2016) perspective but also aggregate indices such as Energy Security Risk Index – resembling Ye et al. (2021) or Bollino and Galkin's (2021) logic. Fourthly, this study embeds the energy demand security comparative advantage analysis within a wider framework of international trade models (testing Ricardo and Heckscher-Ohlin trade approaches). In a methodological manner, it resembles to some extent approach of Nyga-Łukaszewska and Napiórkowski (2022). Differences to the above study include two aspects. Firstly, study includes a different set of variables on resources availability and their influence on economy and exports. Next to Energy Security Risk Index, there is also fuel exports measure showing commodities exports in relation to countries' merchandise exports, and institutional quality indice – describing quality of institutions.[40] Secondly, for the purpose of this book which focuses mainly on the natural gas market this category is narrowed down, wherever it was possible, from total natural resource rents to natural gas rents only.

In the methodological dimension this study investigates, similarly to Amoroso, Chiquiar, and Ramos-Francia (2011), if the pattern of comparative advantages of Norway *vis-à-vis* other developed, leading net gas exporters is related with productivity differentials or with differences in factor endowments. Using this conceptual framework results from the fact that there is a growing evidence (Leamer, 1995; Harrigan, 1997; Chor, 2010; Morrow, 2010) suggesting that both the Ricardian and the Heckscher-Ohlin trade determinants explain the countries' patterns of specialization regardless of the nations' incomes. Morrow finds this argument true for the analysis of developed and developing countries, while Leamer and Harrigan – for the OECD states. The below study recognizes the above suggestion along with arguments of Harrigan; Lai, and Zhu (2007), claiming that the Ricardian model has a greater explanatory power when analysing capital-rich economies, while Heckscher-Ohlin framework serves better when explaining performance of countries with different factor abundance. The same relevance of the factor endowment theory was also noticed by Debaere (2003).

Final model specification is a combined approach of Heckscher-Ohlin hypothesis and Ricardian approach. The former used in studies of Cuñat and Melitz (2012), Levchenko (2007), Nunn (2007), and Romalis (2004) suggests that export performance in a specific industry depends on country's relative human and physical capital endowment using a fixed effects model on a country and an industry level:

$$\ln X_{is} = \alpha_1 + \alpha_s + \beta_1 K_1 k_s + \beta_2 H_1 h_s + \varepsilon_{is} \tag{3}$$

where:

α_1 – country's fixed effect,
α_s – industry sector s fixed effect,
X_{is} – exports of country's sector s,
K_1 – country's relative physical capital endowment,
k_s – sector's s's physical capital intensity,
H_1 – country's relative human capital endowment,
h_s – sector's s's human capital intensity.

Ricardian approach relies on the assumption that country's export performance in a specific industry sector is linked to labour productivity resembling Golub and Hsieh (2000) and Costinot and Komunjer (2007) approaches. Model specification takes the following form:

$$\ln X_{is} = \alpha_1 + \alpha_s + \beta_1 LP_{is} + \varepsilon_{is} \tag{4}$$

where:

α_1 – country's fixed effect,
α_s – industry sector s fixed effect,
X_{is} – exports of country's sector s,
LP_{is} – labour productivity in a country's sector s.

Combining Heckscher-Ohlin and Ricardian approaches on a country not industry level similar to Nyga-Łukaszewska and Napiórkowski (2022) generates the following model specification:

$$\ln X_{it} = \alpha_1 + \beta_1 K_{it} k_{it} + \beta_2 H_{it} h_{it} + \beta_3 LP_{it} + \varepsilon_{it} \tag{5}$$

where:

K_{it} – country's *i* relative physical capital endowment at time *t*,
k_{it} – country's *i* physical capital intensity at time *t*,
H_{it} – country's *i* relative human capital endowment at time *t*,
h_{it} – country's *i* human capital intensity at time *t*,
LP_{it} – labour productivity in a country's *i* at time *t*.

Part of the model on: $\beta_1 K_{it} k_{it} + \beta_2 H_{it} h_{it}$ – accounts for the Heckscher-Ohlin specification, while $\beta_3 LP_{it}$ – refers to the Ricardian approach.

Including Amoroso, Chiquiar, and Ramos-Francia's (2011) concept of relativity of a country's *i* to a country's *j* performance and substituting export performance with revealed comparative advantage (RCA) index, one arrives at the following formula:

$$\begin{aligned}\ln(RCA_{it}) - \ln(RCA_{jt}) = \alpha_1 + \beta_1 (K_{it} - K_{jt}) k_{it} + \beta_2 (H_{it} - H_{jt}) h_{it} \\ + \beta_3 \left(LP_{it} - LP_{jt}\right) + \varepsilon_{it}\end{aligned} \tag{6}$$

where:

K_{jt} – country's *j* relative physical capital endowment at time *t*,
k_{jt} – country's *j* physical capital intensity at time *t*,
H_{jt} – country's *j* relative human capital endowment at time *t*,
h_{jt} – country's *j* human capital intensity at time *t*,
LP_{jt} – labour productivity in a country's *j* at time *t*.

Country sample included in this study encompasses industrialized leading world natural gas exporters. Developed nations were selected from the group of high-income OECD economies, while leading natural gas exporters were chosen on the basis of Statista data on leading gas exporters in 2020 (Statista, 2022) as a result group of selected nations includes (in alphabetical order): Australia, Canada, the Netherlands, Norway, and the USA. Apart from Norway, serving as a study's reference point, each of the other countries represents different continents: Australia – Oceania, Canada and the USA – America, the Netherlands – Europe. Asia remains underrepresented in this sample as majority of Asian economies are net natural gas importers. Qatar which is one of the world biggest LNG exporters and a high-income country is not included in the study as it is not an OECD member.[41] Alike Qatar, Russia, one of the biggest natural gas exporters in the world, is excluded from the analysis as it is not an OECD member and, additionally, according to the OECD database is categorized as the upper-middle income economy.[42]

Norway was chosen as a reference point in this study for similar reasons as highlighted by Nyga-Łukaszewska and Napiórkowski (2022). These include: Norway's "role model for the 21st century energy policy" (Kamprath, 2009) and efficient management of oil and gas revenues (IEA, 2017), which result in the highest positions of the Norwegian sovereign wealth fund in transparency rankings (as proved above). All of that makes Norway one of the most renowned energy exporters in the world, which, uniquely to other energy exporters, leads in the decarbonization efforts (KPMG, 2022). Including Norway as a reference point, a model specification assumes the following form:

$$\ln(RCA_{it}) - \ln(RCA_{Nt}) = \alpha_1 + \beta_1(K_{it} - K_{Nt})k_{it} + \beta_2\,(H_{it} - H_{Nt})h_{it} + \beta_3(LP_{it} - LP_{Nt}) + \varepsilon_{it} \quad (7)$$

where:

K_{Nt} – Norway's relative physical capital endowment at time t,
H_{Nt} – Norway's relative human capital endowment at time t,
LP_{Nt} – labour productivity in Norway at time t.

Summing up, the below study investigates the influence of the energy demand security on comparative advantage of developed energy exporting economies with Norway as a reference point. It employs an econometric modelling framework combining the Heckscher-Ohlin and Ricardian hypotheses. Heckscher-Ohlin approach is captured within the form of relative and human capital endowment while Ricardian assumption relies on the labour productivity.

3.3.1 *Variables description*

Dependent variable selection results from theoretical and methodological rationales. From the theoretical point of view, since Balassa (1965) comparative advantage has been countlessly measured by the RCA index. On the methodological side, this study uses Amoroso, Chiquiar, and Ramos-Francia's (2011) framework which as a regressant employs the RCA concept. Thus, dependent variable builds upon Amoroso, Chiquiar, and Ramos-Francia's (2011) study and includes the original Balassa's RCA concept.

The RCA indice, sometimes called Balassa index or B index, is a common tool in assessing a trade policy, but it has not escaped criticism. Stellian and Danna-Buitrago (2022) list just few of them. Among the most common ones there are sole reliance on exports data only, subjection to size bias, lack of additivity and asymmetry of results intervals. Including only exports data in the RCA indice, omits import data, which according to Stellian and Danna-Buitrago (2019) is crucial in creating comparative advantage. Size bias of the B indice, as explained by Leromain and Orefice (2014), correlates high values of the indice with strong comparative advantage, which might be achieved even if a country has small share in total exports. Lack of additivity of the RCA indice, demonstrated by Yu, Cai, and Leung (2009), does not allow for comparisons across commodities, countries, and time, thus makes it unuseful for studies on regional comparative advantage. Asymmetry of results intervals, suggested by Laursen (2015), results from the fact that comparative advantages are measured on the scale from 0 to ∞, while comparative disadvantages – 0 to 1. Acknowledging among others, the above-presented limitations of RCA indice, for the purpose of this study, author introduces its modified version, similar to Nyga-Łukaszewska and Napiórkowski (2022), where RCA is a ratio of studied country's (*i*) export (*X*) to its import (*M*) divided by alike ratio for the world (*w*) at time *t*.

$$RCA_{it} = \frac{X_{it}/M_{it}}{X_{wt}/M_{wt}} \tag{8}$$

where:

RCA_{it} – value of the RCA index of a country's *i* at time *t*,
X_{it} – country's *i* export value at time *t*,
M_{it} – country's *i* import value at time *t*,
X_{wt} – world's export value at time *t*,
M_{wt} – world's import value at time *t*.

Applying the relativity concept Amoroso, Chiquiar, and Ramos-Francia (2011) of framework to the RCA indice, the measure takes the following form:

$$\ln\left(\frac{X_{it}/M_{it}}{X_{wt}/M_{wt}}\right) - \ln\left(\frac{X_{Nt}/M_{Nt}}{X_{wt}/M_{wt}}\right) = \ln\left(RCA_{it}\right) - \ln\left(RCA_{Nt}\right) \tag{9}$$

where:

RCA_{Nt} – value of the RCA index of Norway at time *t*,
X_{Nt} – Norway's export value at time *t*,
M_{Nt} – Norway's import value at time *t*.

Data on exports and imports of goods and services captured as a share of GDP was obtained from the World Bank (2022) database.

In addition to the below study, in a manner similar to Levchenko (2007), Nunn (2007), and Romalis (2004), includes additional regressors in the form of energy demand security variables particular but also an energy supply security variable. They are treated, like institutions in Levchenko and Nunn studies, as the source of comparative advantage. Details for independent variables are presented in Table 3.14. Energy variables include, on the one hand, energy supply security variable in the form of the Energy Security Risk Index (ESRI), and on the other hand demand security proxies such as natural gas rents and fuel exports as a percentage of merchandise exports. Institutional quality is measured by the Worldwide Governance Indicator (Figure 3.12).

ESRI is an index of 37 metrics measuring broad aspects of energy security delivered by Global Energy Institute (2022). The index includes indicators describing geopolitical, economic, reliability, and environmental aspects. That includes metrics on fossil fuels' (hydrocarbons and fossil) production and reserves, hydrocarbons' imports and imports' expenditures (also with relation to GDP), energy

Table 3.14 Model-specific explanatory variables information

Variable type	*Symbol*	*Full name*	*Source*	*Relation with the literature*
Energy variables	ESRI	Energy Security Risk Index	Global Energy Institute	Boussena and Locatelli (2013) Romanova (2013)
	NGR	Natural gas rents (% of GDP)	World Bank	Dike (2013) Karatayev and Hall (2020)
	FE	Fuel exports (% of merchandise exports)		
Institutional quality variable	GOVER	Worldwide Governance Indicators	World Bank	Mehlum, Moene, and Torvik (2002) Robinson, Torvik, and Verdier (2006)

Source: Compiled by the author.

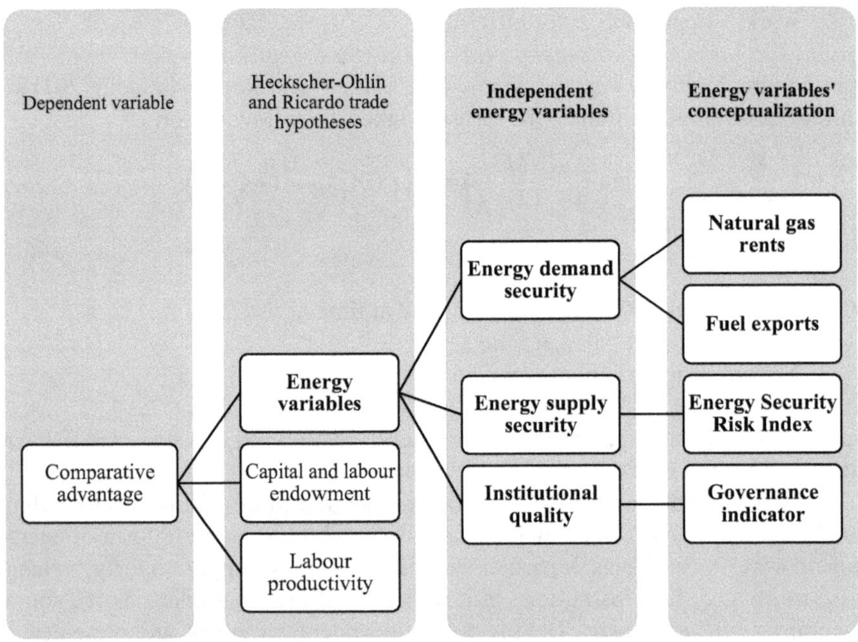

Figure 3.12 Model conceptualization with reference to the energy variables.

Source: Compiled by the author.

expenditures per household (per GDP) and its volatility, crude oil price and its volatility, petroleum stocks levels, energy efficiency (by different consumer types) and intensity, electricity capacity and transmission measures, transport sector metrics, energy-related CO_2 emissions (in different categories), and energy-related research and development expenditures (by different categories). Natural gas rents as a percentage of GDP are the difference between the value of natural gas production at regional prices and total costs of production related to GDP. Fuel exports comprise of the value of commodities in Standard International Trade Classification (SITC) section 3 (mineral fuels, lubricants, and related materials) related to the overall merchandise exports value. Worldwide Governance Indicators are aggregate indicators including six dimensions of governance: voice and accountability, political stability and absence of violence/terrorism, government effectiveness, regulatory quality, rule of law, and control of corruption. Relative average governance rank is an arithmetic average of individual ranks of the above six categories (Kaufmann, Kraay, and Mastruzzi, 2010; Worldwide Governance Indicators, 2021). Use of an arithmetic average gives equal weights to each of the six categories. Such a solution is dictated by a lack of uniformity on the importance hierarchy of these areas. It is also an elegant solution from the operational perspective.

Data has been collected the 1997–2019 period, which was the longest possible period given the objective to have a strongly balanced dataset. Data on trade variables (measured as percentage of GDP), GDP (constant 2015 USD), and labour force (count) has been obtained from World Bank's World Development Indicators database (World Bank, 2022). Data on remaining variables: physical capital (2017 USD), human capital (index), and share of labour compensation in GDP at current national prices (proportion) came from Penn World Table (version 10.0; Feenstra, Inklaar, and Timmer, 2015; University of Groningen, 2022). The two-year difference in base years between GDP and physical capital measures is noted, but – due to lack of large changes in price levels during that time – this isn't expected to have an impact on model's results.

Data for governance quality for the years 1997, 1999 and 2001 had to be supplemented and it was done with an average of neighbouring years. Data on ESRI ended in 2018. To maintain a strongly balanced panel, it was assumed that the value of growth between the years 2018 and 2019 was the same as for 2017 and 2018. Data on relative natural gas rents had to be supplemented for Canada and the USA for two periods: 2010–2013 and 2015–2017. This was done by assuming constant per period value changes between 2009–2014 and 2014–2018. These imputation methods were selected after a series of trend regression trials, which yielded either low values of R-squared or irrational forecasted values (e.g., large negative values).

The explanatory variables selection (Table 3.14) corresponds with the analysis of energy demand security on the grounds of international economics in particular. That is why natural gas rents refer to governments' revenues from the production of natural resources. Fuel exports variable shows the importance of energy resources' foreign sales in a country's international trade and resembles export dependence concept. Natural gas rents and fuel exports correspond with Dike's (2013) energy demand security concept, resembling, respectively, economic dependence and export dependence and resource dependency introduced by Karatayev and Hall (2020). Both of the explanatory variables can also be indirectly referred to an idea of energy export externalities introduced in Chapter 2 of this book and based on Bohi and Toman's (1996) concept of energy security externalities. Natural gas rents might be considered a proxy of income of exporters which builds export price externalities, while fuel exports can be regarded as a source of possible but indirect influence on the balance of payments and effective exchange rate constituting indirect export volume externalities. ESRI index is included in the research following the logic of Boussena and Locatelli (2013) and Romanova (2013) according to which demand and supply security are interconnected and emerges as the "new duel" in the 21st century. ESRI variable depicts supply security concerns in the group of net energy exporters. It is assumed that even in these countries, energy imports exist and, thus, may pose the supply security threat. Supply security variable is included only in the form of the aggregated index, not as a set of simple variables, as its relevance for considered study is limited since its main focus is energy demand security. Other explanatory variable – institutional quality – is included in the model specification following the logic of Robinson, Torvik, and Verdier (2006) as well as Mehlum, Moene, and Torvik (2002), suggesting that Heckscher-Ohlin-related phenomenon – the Dutch disease occurrence in resource-rich countries depends on the quality of institutions.

Explanatory variables representing relative resource endowment and productivity have been constructed according to the procedure presented by Amoroso, Chiquiar, and Ramos-Francia (2011). Each energy variable takes the following form:

$$\ln\left(X_{it}\right)-\ln\left(X_{Nt}\right) \tag{10}$$

where:

X_{it} – variable x for country i at time t,

X_{Nt} – variable x for Norway at time t.

Apart from independent variables specific for the design study, Amoroso, Chiquiar, and Ramos-Francia's (2011) framework also includes physical and human capital endowment along with differences in labour productivity. Relative physical capital is a per worker endowment by the fraction of physical capital to the GDP. The latter $\left(K_{it}/GDP_{it}\right)$ is a proxy for physical capital intensity reflected in Amoroso, Chiquiar, and Ramos-Francia (2011). Data on physical capital (in mn 2017 USD) was obtained from the Penn World Table, version 10.0 (University of Groningen, 2022). Data on labour force and GDP in constant prices (USD 2015) were collected from the World Bank (2022) database. Relative physical capital per worker variable can be written as:

$$\left[\ln\left(\frac{K_{it}}{L_{it}}\right)-\ln\left(\frac{K_{Nt}}{L_{Nt}}\right)\right]\times\frac{K_{it}}{GDP_{it}} \tag{11}$$

where:

K_{it} – country's i capital stock at time t,
L_{it} – country's i labour stock at time t,
K_{Nt} – Norway's capital stock at time t,
L_{Nt} – Norway's labour stock at time t,
GDP_{it} – country's i GDP at time t.

Relative human capital endowment is multiplied by a share of labour compensation in GDP at current national prices. The latter serves as a proxy of human capital intensity reflected in Amoroso, Chiquiar, and Ramos-Francia (2011). Data on human capital index (index based on years of schooling and returns to education) and share of labour compensation in GDP was obtained from the Penn World Table, version 10.0 (University of Groningen, 2022). Thus, relative human capital per worker variable can be written as:

$$\left[\ln\left(H_{it}\right)-\ln\left(H_{Nt}\right)\right]\times h_{it}/\hat{h} \tag{12}$$

where:
H_{it} – country's *i* human capital index at time *t*,
H_{Nt} – Norway's *i* human capital index at time *t*,
h_{it} – country's *i* share of labour compensation in GDP at time *t*,
$\hat{h}$ – average share of labour force in GDP for the whole panel.

Differences in productivity differentials refer to differences in the ratios of GDP and labour stock. Data on labour stock and GDP in constant prices (USD, 2015) were obtained from the World Bank (2022) database. The variable on differences in productivity differentiations can be written as:

$$\left[\ln\left(\frac{GDP_{it}}{L_{it}}\right)-\ln\left(\frac{GDP_{Nt}}{L_{Nt}}\right)\right] \tag{13}$$

where:

GDP_{Nt} – Norway's *i* GDP at time *t*.

Descriptive statistics for variables are presented (per cross section) as in Table 3.15 (excluding Norway as it serves as a reference point).

3.3.2 Modelling results

The model takes the form presented below:

$$\begin{aligned}\ln\left(RCA_{it}\right)-\ln\left(RCA_{Nt}\right)=\beta_0+\beta_1&\left\{\left[\ln\left(\frac{K_{it}}{L_{it}}\right)-\ln\left(\frac{K_{Nt}}{L_{Nt}}\right)\right]\frac{K_{it}}{GDP_{it}}\right\}\\&+\beta_2\left\{\left[\ln\left(H_{it}\right)-\ln\left(H_{Nt}\right)\right]\frac{h_{it}}{\bar{h}}\right\}+\beta_3\left[\ln\left(\frac{GDP_{it}}{L_{it}}\right)-\ln\left(\frac{GDP_{Nt}}{L_{Nt}}\right)\right]\\&+\beta_4\left[\ln\left(ESRI_{it}\right)-\ln\left(ESRI_{Nt}\right)\right]+\beta_5\left[\ln\left(NGR_{it}\right)-\ln\left(NGR_{Nt}\right)\right]\\&+\beta_6\left[\ln\left(FE_{it}\right)-\ln\left(FE_{Nt}\right)\right]+\beta_7\left[\begin{array}{l}\ln\left(GOVER_{it}\right)-\\\ln\left(GOVER_{Nt}\right)\end{array}\right]+\gamma_i+\delta_t+\varepsilon_{it}\end{aligned} \tag{14}$$

Table 3.15 Descriptive statistics for model's variables

	Relative comparative advantage	*Relative physical capital per worker*	*Relative human capital*	*Relative labour productivity*	*Relative average governance rank*	*Relative ESRI*	*Relative natural gas rents*	*Relative fuel exports*
Australia								
Min.	−0.6	0	−0.04	−0.37	−0.06	−0.13	−20.31	−10.14
Max.	0.07	0	0.06	−0.25	−0.01	0.21	−0.08	−0.63
Ave.	−0.34	0	0	−0.31	−0.04	0.12	−10.49	−0.95
Std. dev.	0.18	0	0.04	0.04	0.01	0.1	0.62	0.14
Canada								
Min.	−0.45	0	0.02	−0.71	−0.05	−0.12	−50.04	−10.77
Max.	0	0	0.05	−0.56	−0.01	0.2	10.75	−0.81
Ave.	−0.28	0	0.03	−0.63	−0.03	0.11	−10.64	−10.17
Std. dev.	0.12	0	0.01	0.05	0.01	0.09	20.18	0.3
Netherlands								
Min.	−0.35	0	−0.09	−0.55	−0.04	0.17	−20.27	−20.38
Max.	0.08	0	−0.06	−0.47	0.04	0.55	−0.56	−10.54
Ave.	−0.18	0	−0.08	−0.5	−0.01	0.33	−10.21	−10.93
Std. dev.	0.14	0	0.01	0.02	0.02	0.14	0.45	0.26
USA								
Min.	−0.91	0	0.02	−0.34	−0.19	−0.24	−50.74	−30.54
Max.	−0.21	0	0.07	−0.18	−0.04	0.27	0.28	−10.37
Ave.	−0.57	0	0.05	−0.27	−0.12	0.14	−20.74	−20.56
Std. dev.	0.22	0	0.02	0.05	0.03	0.14	10.92	0.75

Source: Compiled by the author.

Model's parameters were estimated using Ordinary Least Squares (OLS) with specific cross-section (γ_i) and period (δ_t) effects. The first step in the estimation procedure was to conduct the Hausman test, results of which (*p*-value = 0.000) indicated that fixed effects are the more efficient option. Since the results of the Breusch-Pagan LM test of independence (*p*-value = 0.000) indicated that residuals are correlated (see De Hoyos and Sarafidis, 2006), Generalized Least Squares (GLS) and – given the overoptimism of GLS in terms of standard errors – Panel-corrected Standard Error (PCSE) estimators substituted the original OLS estimator (Hoechle, 2007). The Wooldridge test for autocorrelation in panel data indicated no autocorrelation (*p*-value = 0.0567) and the results of the Modified Wald test for groupwise heteroskedasticity (*p*-value = 0.3314) show that variance of residuals is homogenous. Given the number of observations ($n = 92$),[43] lack of normal distribution of residuals (Jarque-Bera's *p*-value = 0.0062; Shapiro-Wilk's *p*-value = 0.000) is not an issue discounting the model. Results of the Levin-Lin-Chu (*p*-valuc = 0.000) and Harris-Tzavalis (p-value = 0.000) unit-root tests show that residuals are stationary; therefore, rejecting the notion that obtained model is a spurious regression. Lastly, results of Kao (Table 3.16) and Pedroni test for cointegration (Table 3.17) allow for a rejection of these tests' null hypothesis of no cointegration. Presented procedure is in line with Napiórkowski (2022).

Table 3.18 shows results for both estimators (GLS and PCSE) with Prob > chi^2 = 0.000 for both model and *R*-squared = 0.5725 for PCSE estimator. At a 5% level of statistical significance ($\alpha = 0.05$), decisions on whether individual coefficients are equal to zero are the same for both models. Coefficients of the average governance rank (GLS *p*-value = 0.746; PCSE *p*-value = 0.782), natural gas rents (GLS *p*-value = 0.158; PCSE *p*-value = 0.086), and fuel exports (GLS *p*-value = 0.227; PCSE *p*-value = 0.166) are not statistically different from zero. All other estimated coefficients are statistically significant and negative; hence, the higher is

Table 3.16 Results of the Kao test for cointegration

Test	*Statistic*	*p-Value*
Modified Dickey–Fuller *t*	−6.6248	0.0000
Dickey–Fuller *t*	−6.3515	0.0000
Augmented Dickey–Fuller *t*	−4.9972	0.0000
Unadjusted modified Dickey–Fuller *t*	−6.8912	0.0000
Unadjusted Dickey–Fuller *t*	−6.3773	0.0000

Source: Compiled by the author.

Table 3.17 Results of the Pedroni test for cointegration

	Statistic	*p-Value*
Modified Phillips–Perron *t*	2.5377	0.0056
Phillips–Perron *t*	−5.8709	0.0000
Augmented Dickey–Fuller *t*	−6.2459	0.0000

Source: Compiled by the author.

Table 3.18 GLS and PCSE results

Dependent variable = Relative comparative advantage		*GLS*		*PCSE*	
Variable	*Coefficient symbol*	*Coefficient value*	*p-Value*	*Coefficient value*	*p-Value*
Relative *K*	β_1	−65,002.340	0.353	−65,002.340	0.331
Relative *H*	β_2	−3.322	0.000	−3.322	0.000
Relative *LP*	β_3	−0.408	0.031	−0.408	0.015
Relative *ESRI*	β_4	−0.633	0.000	−0.633	0.001
Relative *NGR*	β_5	0.017	0.158	0.017	0.086
Relative *FE*	β_6	0.038	0.227	0.038	0.166
Relative *GOVER*	β_7	−0.213	0.746	−0.213	0.782
Constant	β_0	−0.399	0.000	−0.399	0.000

Source: Compiled by the author.

the advantage of cross-section *i* (Australia, Canada, the Netherlands, the USA) in the value of an explanatory variable over Norway, the lower is the advantage of that cross-section over Norway in terms of comparative advantage.

Figure 3.13 shows a summary of the econometric research results. Negative coefficients mean that whenever the variable's value for Norway increases relative to other analysed countries, the comparative advantage of Norway decreases. This line of reasoning applies to the ESRI, labour productivity, and human capital. Negative coefficients in ESRI mean that if the ESRI of Norway increases $(ESRI_{Nt})\uparrow$, relative to other analysed countries *i*, $\left[\ln(ESRI_{it})-\ln(ESRI_{Nt})\right]\downarrow$, the comparative advantage of Norway decreases $\left[\ln(RCA_{it})-\ln(RCA_{Nt})\right]\uparrow$. Negative coefficients in labour productivity mean that if productivity levels in Norway increase $(LP_{Nt})\uparrow$, relative to other analysed countries *i*, $\left[\ln(LP_{it})-\ln(LP_{Nt})\right]\downarrow$, the comparative advantage of Norway decreases $\left[\ln(RCA_{it})-\ln(RCA_{Nt})\right]\uparrow$. Negative coefficients in human capital mean that if human capital in Norway increases $(H_{Nt})\uparrow$, relative to other analysed countries *i*, $\left[\ln(H_{it})-\ln(H_{Nt})\right]\downarrow$, the comparative advantage of Norway decreases $\left[\ln(RCA_{it})-\ln(RCA_{Nt})\right]\uparrow$. One may conclude that the higher is the ESRI in Norway, the lower is the comparative advantage of Norwegian economy *vis-à-vis* other industrialized net natural gas exporters.

3.3.3 Discussion on modelling results

Obtained results suggest that the comparative advantage of Norway *vis-à-vis* other net gas-exporting high-income nations is related to both Ricardian productivity differentials and factor endowments. This argument is supported for OECD countries by Harrigan (1997, p. 26), who testing the neoclassical theory of international specialization found that "both factor supply and technology differences have

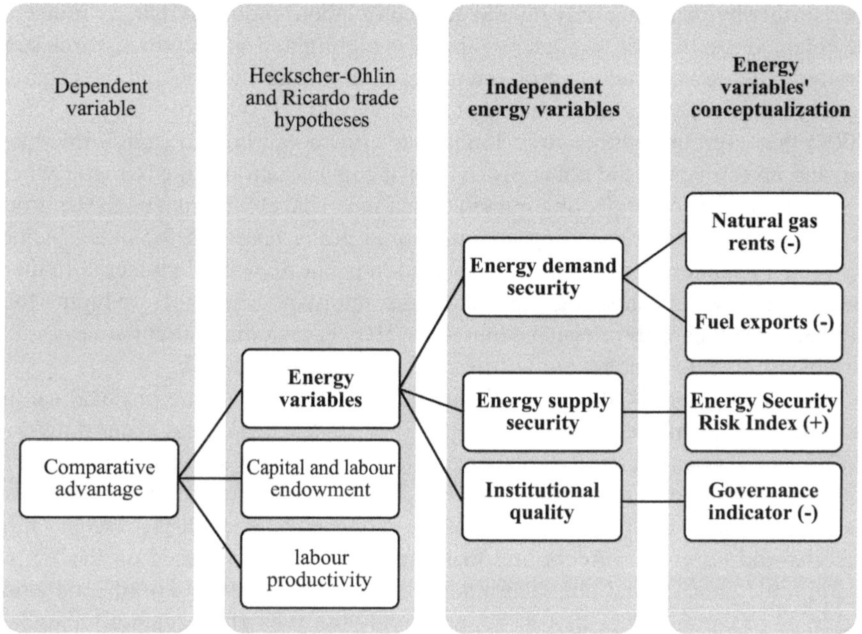

Figure 3.13 Model results' summary with reference to the energy variables.

+/− denotes statistical significance (+) of the variable or its lack (−)

Source: Compiled by the author.

important impacts on a country's pattern of specialization in the global economy, and that these factors must be considered jointly when formulating policies intended to effect the structure of production and trade." In part on the importance on factor endowments in the OECD economies, obtained results are also supported by the study of Fitzgerald and Hallak (2004), who confirmed that factor proportions explain two-thirds of observed differences in patterns of specialization between the group's poor and rich economies.

Yet, the negative Beta coefficients' values in labour productivity and human capital variables are interesting. One may expect that higher productivity differentials and greater human capital endowment should positively influence comparative advantage. Possible explanations behind the Beta coefficient signs may include arguments referring to the set of raw data, variables' construction, and specific situation of the benchmark country – Norway. Firstly, the set of raw data for labour productivity in the analysed group of economies proves that Norway is topping labour productivity OECD rankings, exhibiting significantly higher values than other countries. Secondly, aggregated data on Norwegian labour productivity do not distinguish between mainland and oil and gas sector. As IMF (2014) noticed that even though mainland labour productivity in case of Norway against other countries is relatively high, the same values for oil and gas sector are not that satisfying. That is why probably disaggregating labour productivity data or going even further by including only oil and gas sector labour productivity may influence the obtained results. Hence, such possibility is highlighted as a future research step. Similar variable construction problem might be an explanation behind the negative Beta coefficient's value in the human capital variable. It was proved by Gylfason (2001) that even though resource abundance crowds out human capital in education and investment, it did not apply to high-income countries, like Norway, where there are no signs of neglecting human education. That is why maybe in the group of high-income countries, using human capital proxy based on the index including years of schooling and returns to education is not relevant. In general, in these societies number of schooling years and, thus, returns to education are higher than in other emerging or developing economies. Hence, including other human capital variable might be an interesting future research recommendation.

Worth explaining is also lack of statistical significance of the physical capital variable. It was expected that, in line with Nyga-Łukaszewska and Napiórkowski's (2022) study, physical capital per worker would manifest statistical significance with high Beta coefficient's value. Additionally, it was assumed, in line with Romalis (2004) that in this group of countries capital-related quasi-Heckscher-Ohlin effect would be visible. According to Romalis's prediction, based on the US bilateral trade data, capital abundant countries capture a larger share of production and trade of commodities that more intensively use their (here: capital) abundant factors. For instance, capital-abundant countries capture larger shares of imports in the capital-intensive industries. Since the analysed group of countries is relatively capital abundant, it could have been expected that relative physical capital per worker would be not only relevant but also would be supported by high Beta coefficient's value.

There are two possible explanations behind the insignificance of the physical capital variable. First refers to the countries' sample composition used in this study and research of Nyga-Łukaszewska and Napiórkowski (2022). Above-described model includes apart from Canada, the Netherlands, Norway, and the USA, like in Nyga-Łukaszewska and Napiórkowski's, also Australia. Hence, there might be some unobserved effect connected with physical capital that is Australia-specific and thus influences the results. Second explanation refers to the importance of intangible, instead of tangible capital, for high-income economies. As it was proved by Piekkola (2011), tangible man-made goods are no longer major determinant of international competitiveness. Even though Piekkola's study was based on the EU economies, its conclusions might be applicable to other advanced nations. Piekkola claims that intangible capital is nowadays a main source of capital deepening in European countries. Thus, extending Amoroso, Chiquiar, and Ramos-Francia's (2011) framework by including intangible capital as a Heckscher-Ohlin factor proportion in the analysis of comparative advantages in the group of high-income countries, might be a future research recommendation. Any research efforts in this direction should recognize the argument of Che (2009) on possible data limitations while testing the hypothesis of intangible capital importance in advanced economies.

The most interesting modelling result is statistical significance of the ESRI. Relevance of that variable confirms the importance of energy supply security phenomenon in influence over comparative advantage in the analysed group of countries. It means that, even for net energy exporters, supply security concerns are valid source of comparative advantage. Probable explanation behind this result, in the analysed group of countries, might be the fact that, to some extent, majority of them imports crude oil, that according to argument of Podbregar et al. (2020), price (along with global coal reserves) is responsible for 90% of index variance. Additionally, high-price volatility of crude oil in the last 20 years combined with its relevance for ESRI index might also be a reason contributing to ESRI statistical significance.

On the other hand, the econometric modelling did not prove statistical significance of institutional governance, fuel exports, and natural gas rents variables, all of which constitute energy demand security framework. There are various possible explanations behind that.

In case of institutional governance, the first argument refers to Norway that was used as a benchmark country in this analysis. Even though Norway is said to have high-institutional capacity (Thurber, Hults, and Heller, 2011) and "good institutions and clever policies" that can serve as a role model for other countries (Cappelen and Mjøset, 2009), in a study, in which relative levels *vis-à-vis* other well institutionally equipped countries are included; general institutional quality loses statistical significance. It may also result from the fact that analysed group of countries is relatively homogeneous in terms of institutional quality and thus this factor does not affect the relative comparative advantage of these economies. Possibly greater differences in that respect might be visible in a sample consisting of developed and developing energy exporters. Thus, any research comparing the influence of institutional quality on comparative advantage of energy exporters might be an interesting next research step. To some extent, results of the econometric modelling confirm the argument of Meon and Sekkat's (2008), who argued that institutional quality does not affect total export levels. If RCA is, even in proposed formula, partially a proxy of export levels, the authors' argument holds true for this study. Thus, it can be concluded that institutional quality in high-income countries (net) exporting non-manufactured goods such as natural gas does not affect their RCA. Yet, this study due to the methodological approach does not statistically confirm the argument of Ramírez-Cendrero and Wirth (2016) that well-developed institutions in the form of oil and gas policy helped Norway escape the Dutch disease.

In like manner, this research does not find any statistical relevance of fuel exports. Possible explanation behind that refers to the relative weight of fuel sales in total foreign goods' exports in the analysed group of countries. Apart from Norway, in which the respective share ranged between minimum value of 43% in 1998 and maximum value of 70% in 2012, in other high-income economies average values between 1997 and 2019 amounted to 6% in the USA, 9% in the Netherlands, 20% in Canada, and 24% in Australia. Thus, fuel exports in other than Norway countries constitute only part of their merchandise exports. Thereby, fuel exports variable due to diversified exports and GDP structures does not influence relative comparative advantage of high-income net gas-exporting nations. Statistical insignificance of natural gas rents variable results on the one hand from strictly assumed *p*-value levels

(0.05) and, on the other, from relative importance of gas rents in the high-income economies. As long as the first explanation results from the modelling approach and does not need any further explanation, the second justification deserves more attention. Natural gas rents like fuel exports are captured in relation to other macro-economic variables. While in case of fuel exports – it is total merchandise exports, in case of natural gas rents – it is GDP. That is why probably effect of the relatively small rents in relatively high GDP (hereinafter: "size effect") is even stronger than in the case of fuel exports in total goods' exports. Apart from Norway, in which the respective share ranged between minimum value of 0.17% in 1998 and maximum value of 3.29% in 2012, in other high-income economies average share of natural gas rents in GDP, between 1997 and 2019, amounted to 0.41% in USA, 0.44% in the Netherlands, 0.95% in Australia, and 1.09% in Canada. Comparing these values for high-income economies with other natural gas exporters representing developing/emerging economies reveals significant differences. The same values for Algeria amounted to 2.9% and Russia 3.73%. Thus, any research effort aimed at comparing influence of natural gas rents on the comparative advantage between groups of developed and developing/emerging economies is highlighted as the next possible research direction.

This empirical study like any other research has limitations. They refer to methodological and conceptual approach, variables' construction, and countries' sample. Using Amoroso, Chiquiar, and Ramos-Francia's (2011) framework requires comparing selected countries against a benchmark nation. This approach, on the one hand, generates difficulties in results' interpretation and on the other – through a choice of a benchmark country – may significantly influence obtained results. In the conceptual dimension, selection of respective variables corresponding with energy demand security phenomenon is highly subjective. Even though this book's author made efforts to justify variables' choice on the theoretical grounds, one may always include other proxies for the analysed phenomenon. Additionally, in a methodological and conceptual manner, this study does not include any differences among the countries in their technological endowment.[44] The same refers to variables construction. Research data constraints, on the one hand, and the authors' willingness to maintain data and data source consistency across the panel, on the other, forced the use of specific variables. However, relaxing these assumptions may result in using different variables from a greater variety of sources. Lastly, selected countries' sample even though coherent in terms of their economic development and position in international gas market proved to be relatively heterogeneous in terms of "the country's size effect".

3.4 Energy demand security in natural gas market – summary

Depletable energy resources are still the most common sources of energy in the world maintaining a relatively strong position in global energy use. Uneven geographical distribution of proven resources deposits across the world and relatively limited resource substitution in the short- and medium-term forces energy-scarce countries to buy fuels abroad. Such trade relationship evokes challenges including physical supply disruption and price volatility. Both of these constitute prime concerns in the energy security research.

Trade in energy resources can be also explained by selected trade theories. Even though energy resources do not appear directly in the factor endowment theory, they are represented in neo-factor theories explaining Leontief's paradox, Rybczyński's theorem, and the Dutch disease (or the resource curse) idea. Energy resources either reduce or eliminate the alleged paradox or are the source of negative influence over the economies' relying too much on energy exports. These consequences include decrease in production, real wages, and employment in the manufacturing sector, but also a deterioration in the balance of the trade, an appreciation of the exchange rate (sometimes questioned), and a decrease in the country's international competitiveness. Interestingly, energy-related resource curse appearance might be connected to the quality of institutions in the exporting economy.

The above-presented scientific investigation takes the form of formalized research (Figure 3.14) with a hypothesis testing. It is opened with a theoretical insight into the energy security phenomenon. As literature on economics of energy security (in general) is "thin" (Metcalf, 2013), results obtained from even narrower demand security analysis are only "thinner". Thus, theoretical review in this book focuses on the detailed investigation of existing scientific achievements related to the demand security. Theoretical study is a type of the conceptual research category as it relates to the abstract idea and aims at re-examination of existing and development of new concepts which later are subjected to the empirical analysis (Figure 3.15).

The systematic review, employing critical analysis and synthesis, was based on the following inclusions criteria concerning the literature: (1) results were published between January 2000 and (late) November 2020; (2) materials appeared in one of the most popular scientific databases – Web of Science Core Collection or Scopus; and (3) research falls into the category of economics or management discipline of social sciences and exclusion criterion related to works published only in

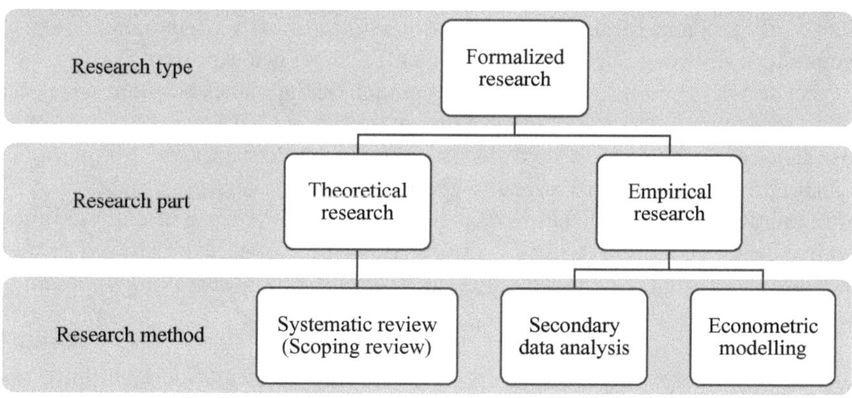

Figure 3.14 Research design summary.

Source: Compiled by the author.

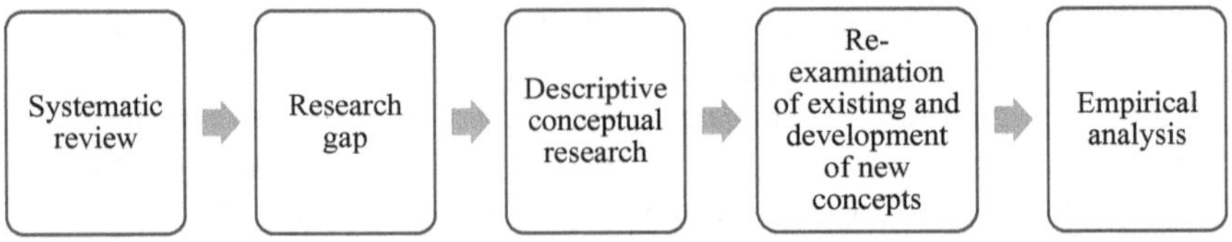

Figure 3.15 Research reasoning summary.

Source: Compiled by the author.

English. That allowed to identify a research gap. It relates to energy security from the perspective of the energy-exporting nations and within international economics' framework.

Theoretical analysis, provided in the descriptive manner, showed that demand security "entered scientific discourse uncritically" (cf.: Novikau, 2022). Additionally, it proved that it can be analysed similarly to the supply security phenomenon as its mirroring concept. At this stage of research, demand security strongly resembles supply security. The source of risks in both cases is international trade in energy commodities; for producing nations, it is export, while for consuming countries it is import. In this way, study confirms the argument of Boussena and Locatelli (2013) according to which energy supply and demand security emerge as the "new duel" in the 21st century and Romanova's (2013) assumption on phenomena's interconnection.

Embedding energy demand security in the supply security framework allows to present author's perspective on theoretical developments in demand security research. That includes provision of a "risk and tool" approach merging existing achievements of demand security studies and extension of the most common economic approach in security supply studies, externalities idea to the demand security analysis. Later, these concepts in combination with, offering great generalizability, the IEA's energy security idea are used to, on the one hand, investigate demand security determinants and, on the other, to test empirically its influence over the comparative advantage of the high-income OECD net gas exporters.

Proposed in the book "risk and tool" approach distinguishes between systematic and non-systematic risks following Nowrouzi et al.'s (2019) suggestion. Among those that cause the entire system to malfunction (systematic), the following can be distinguished: price fluctuations in energy markets, geopolitical stability of importing nations, global legislation changes undermining the use of exported fuels, negative macroeconomic dynamics observed on the global level, slowed demand for energy or sudden demand shifts induced by ground-breaking innovations changing the way the specific energy resources are used. Non-systematic risks as challenges referred only to the selected importing nations include changes in legislation in energy-importing markets (including taxes and competition), protectionism in the form of tariff and non-tariff trade barriers, sanctions including export embargoes, technological/financial or investment restrictions, increasing competition from emerging exporters entering the market, buyer-related breach of contract or buyer-default, contractual changes in existing export agreements, such as adjustment of the pricing formula forced by decisions of international arbitration communities, negative macroeconomic dynamics observed on the importing nation level, slowing demand for energy on the importing nation level, transit risk, and physical supply disruption.

The main economic tool behind demand security improvement is diversification, and it can be divided into three groups: transport-related, contract-related, and asset-related instruments. Transport-related tools include activities pertaining to the increased variety in export routes, means of transport, consuming countries, and transit countries. Contractual arrangements with the goal to ensure demand security refer mainly to the variety of contract durations in the exporter's portfolio, provision of specific contract conditions/clauses, and diversifying contract partners (companies). Asset-related instruments refer to ways in which exporters diversify their business (at the micro level) and economic activity (at the macro level). At the micro level, such diversification includes asset-swapping, investments in transport, storage and production, vertical integration in global value chains, and reducing core asset reliance, while at the macro level – it pertains to the economy's structural changes.

Applying externalities idea to the demand security analysis brings export volume and export price externalities. The former can be further divided into direct and indirect externalities. Export volume externalities can be observed in the long and medium terms, while export price externalities can be treated as short-term price shock adjustments. Direct externalities, in the case of exporters, may refer to the market power that the importer can exercise against an exporter. It refers to the ability to alter market prices of energy resources through changes in the quantities of purchased commodities. In the case of exporters, such a situation can be described as monopsony. In the group of the indirect energy demand externalities, emphasis is placed on merchandise trade balance and its effects on the exchange rate of the exporter's domestic currency. Export price externalities relate to the adjustment of exporter's economy to rapid fluctuations in prices. Their effects may be visible for exporting nations in two ways. First, through reduced national income, and second, as a result of lack of hedging strategies against price fluctuations. The first type of price externalities may be observed when decreased prices reduce export revenues and as a result contribute to decline in potential national income. Internalization of the above externalities may include financial mechanisms that guarantee long-term profits from energy exports, such as sovereign wealth funds (SWFs), hedging strategies against energy price fluctuations (inventories, excess in production capacity, energy-based financial instruments), and R&D spendings aimed at increasing the variety of applications of existing energy sources and diversifying export markets. SWFs and export market diversity address indirect and direct export volume externalities, while hedging strategies deal with export price volatility. R&D spending may be regarded as a type of an "umbrella" type of internalization strategy because they address export volume and price externalities.

Theoretical considerations on the nature of the demand security are followed by the analysis of methods used to assess the phenomenon. By distinguishing between simple, complex, aggregated, and portfolio theory measures, author concludes that assessment methods – just like definitions – rely on the ways of the supply security measurement. However, relatively quick progress of demand security research field resulted in a leap development omitting, on the one hand, use of most popular trade concentration and dispersion measures and, on the other hand, neglecting critical reflection and in-depth scientific discussion on the sense and applicability of the introduced measures.

Having researched demand security theory and empirics, this book's author made an attempt to analyse the phenomenon from the point of view of the neo-classical trade principles and its extensions. Thus, at the centre of the investigation, there are factor endowment theory and neo-factor proportion theories along with concepts based on them relating to natural resources and depletable energy resources in particular. These considerations include four key propositions, as suggested by Jones (1956), describing the properties of the standard H-O model with two goods and two production factors (such as: Heckscher-Ohlin theorem, Stolper-Samuelson, Factor-price equalization, and Rybczyński theorem), their extensions (e.g., reverse Rybczyński theorem) in particular related to depletable energy resources (e.g., Dutch disease) and these neo-factor explanations of the Leontief's paradox where natural resources play role. Apart from that, author also reaches for selected strategic trade policy models (e.g., Brander-Spencer with extensions), which intuitively might be used to describe demand security phenomenon, showing at the same time how they lose their relevancy with gas market specifics. Author concludes that factor endowment theory and its extensions can be applied to the analysis of the demand security phenomenon and holds to that argument in empirical study where next to Ricardian – Heckscher-Ohlin trade hypothesis is tested.

Empirical analysis of the demand security phenomenon in the 21st century follows energy security theoretical considerations provided in Chapter 2. Thus, this chapter describes the global gas market and its determinants with the use of the secondary data analysis and tests econometrically the hypothesis on the influence of demand security on comparative advantage of the high-income OECD gas exporters.

The analysis of energy security determinants for exporting nations is carried out in the IEA-definition spirit and includes factors influencing volume and price of exported energy as disruptions in the volume of the supplied product or its price volatility constitute the core of the energy security understanding of the IEA. Factors influencing volume of exported energy include resource and infrastructure base, non-price terms of contract and selected energy policy initiatives. An analysis of the group of net energy-exporting countries shows that it is dominated by countries with a significant share in the world's fuel resources and their production. The vast majority of these countries are developing nations or in-transition/emerging economies (e.g., Iraq, Iran, Nigeria, Russia). The exceptions in the group of net energy exporters are Australia and Canada. However, holding only vast resources does not decide about becoming a gas exporter. Only abundant resource base combined with efficient gas transport can be a necessary condition for energy exports. Even though gas transit, from the theoretical point of view, belongs to the supply security analysis, it can be a critical point in the gas export, determining not only its efficiency but also success. Transit risks resulting from rent-seeking, opportunistic behaviour are exacerbated, on the one hand, by the gas characteristics as a product transported via fixed infrastructure with capacity constraints and limited storage options and, on the other hand, by inherent features of energy investments such as high capital intensity and long-term period of return.

Non-price terms of contract refer, on the one hand, to the duration of the contracts between exporters and importers and, on the other, to the provisions such as take-or-pay clause or territorial restrictions. All of these terms are used to secure the interests of contract parties and exporters in particular. Long-term contracts for natural gas exports, even though, being shortened in the recent years reduce or eliminate possible opportunistic behaviours of an importer and guarantee demand and payoff of the capital-intensive infrastructural investment. Take-or-pay clauses, even though challenged lately by the international arbitration communities, ensure foreseeable and quantifiable cash flows. Territorial restrictions (export ban or destination clauses), even though unilaterally removed in selected contracts, insulate an exporter from the international competition.

Energy policies' impact on demand security has a cross-cutting character. Global, regional, or national legislation shifts impact energy exporters, importers, and transit countries as well. Due to the book's scope only selected policy initiatives are presented, but their choice results from their uniqueness. Thus, energy policy examples include by importers: regional attempt to build Energy Union in the EU and the Lithuanian national ban on gas imports from Russia and by exporters: the US regulatory process authorizing gas exports to strictly selected countries. EU's policy towards creation of the common energy market through increased infrastructural investments, first of all, increases the community's resilience to sudden energy disruptions. Its influence on an energy exporter includes the reduction of the supplier's market power in a respective importing economy (cf.: Bohi and Toman, 1996). Even stronger policy action against an exporter is the one presented in the Lithuanian example,[45] where as a result of geopolitical events, Russia was denied access to the domestic gas market other than transit to its Kaliningrad enclave. In contrast, the American case exhibits the exporter's perspective in which export allowance to a selected non-FTA destination is granted on the basis of two-stage scrutinized procedure. Only exports serving public interest can be authorized. In this way, regulatory process allows to adjust the quantities of the sold gas and to control exports' destinations. From the empirical point of view investigating the energy policy and demand security link might be carried out with a described novel agent-based approach.

Determinants influencing natural gas prices include price terms of contracts, energy subsidies, and SWFs. Gas pricing in the international contracts has experienced recently great amount of volatility. Firstly, changing market conditions enforced gas instead of oil indexation and secondly, shortening of the review periods in the price review clauses, rapidly adjusted prices, and increased contracts flexibility. From the point of view of the exporting nation decoupling of oil and gas prices in contracts, on the one hand, reduces the time energy corporations feed profits or losses from gas export and, on the other, diminishes gas exporters' susceptibility to oil market volatility by shifting the focus to spot gas-pricing mechanisms and the activity of regional gas-trading hubs. Such market changes are an important step towards the implementation of the market-based mechanisms which, at least, from the theoretical point of view should serve all market players.

Another price determinant in the natural gas market constitutes energy subsidies. Alike other subsidies' types, they can take various forms. These can be both the simplest direct subsidies, preferential tax policy, as well as business regulation or supporting the energy sector by providing services at a lower than market price or trade barriers (mainly non-tariff), administrative sales assurance, price controls, and restrictions on access to the energy market. Regardless of subsidies' type, their influence over energy market is similar. They reduce either production costs or prices for consumers. Energy subsidies for producers have become a domain of developed countries, and those intended for consumers are specific mainly to developing countries. In developing economies subsidies, usually targeted at consumers, are used to close the energy access gap and protect the poorest from the energy price shocks but they may also support country's industrialization. In contrast, in developed countries, subsidies are directed at producers and are supporting domestic fuel production for employment protection reasons. In energy-exporting countries, majority of subsidies cover hydrocarbons, among which there is natural gas. As the World Bank (2010) highlights, subsidies are an opportunity cost of lost export profits for energy-exporting countries, and for energy-importing countries – a budgetary burden. In the case of the former group of countries, subsidies have a particularly positive effect when domestic energy companies have a limited export potential. On the other hand, for the other group of countries, subsidies further improve the system of foreign exchange reserves (World Bank, 2010). Thus, their influence over energy demand (but also supply) security refers to the financial aspects and, by that, might impact the affordability dimension of energy security (according to APERC's definition).

SWFs are an instrument which contributes to the energy demand security of exporting nations in numerous ways. Firstly, as a kind of financial instrument, SWFs to some extent eliminate the negative economic properties of energy commodities. This concerns, in particular, their low-price elasticity of the supply, which results from a long investment cycle, high-capital intensity of investments, and a high share of fixed costs in the total extraction costs. In this way, SWFs activity guarantees incomes regardless of the export activity intensity. Secondly, SWFs reduce fluctuations in the prices of resources in international markets (an extreme case of which is the phenomenon of immiserizing growth described before), and prevent the emergence or even help fight the symptoms of the Dutch disease. Thirdly, SWFs reduce the volatility of real exchange rate misalignments by dampening the transmission of energy prices protecting energy-exporting nations from economic losses. Apart from the influence on the demand security, SWFs affect economies in other ways. Firstly, they support long-term economy decarbonization by redistribution of tax revenues generated from the energy sector. Secondly, SWFs also address the quality of institutions in energy-exporting economy protecting it from the energy-related governance deterioration.

The second part of the empirical study econometric-modelling study is designed with a goal to investigate the influence of energy demand security on the comparative advantage of developed, net gas-exporting economies. This econometric research departs from the existing literature in various ways. Firstly, study employs the concept of demand security; secondly, it delivers rare perspective on demand security of industrialized nations; thirdly, study depicts demand security through a set of simple measures on resources dependency, institutional quality and also aggregate indices such as the ESRI, and fourthly, this research embeds the energy demand security comparative advantage analysis within a wider framework of international trade models (testing Ricardo and Heckscher-Ohlin trade approaches). Country sample included in this study encompasses high-income OECD economies, which are at the same time leading world natural gas exporters: Australia, Canada, the Netherlands, Norway, and the USA. Research horizon stretches between 1997 and 2019. Time range results from the assumed research goal (to capture the phenomenon at the verge and beginning of the 21st century) and data availability issues.

In a methodological manner research builds upon Amoroso, Chiquiar, and Ramos-Francia (2011) where the pattern of comparative advantage of a benchmark country (Norway) is investigated *vis-à-vis* other developed, leading net gas exporters and is related to productivity differentials (Ricardian hypothesis) and to differences in factor endowments (Heckscher-Ohlin hypothesis). Dependent variable takes the form of the RCA index. Energy-specific independent variables include natural gas rents, fuel exports, the Energy Security Risk Index (ESRI), and governance indicator.

Natural gas rents and fuel exports correspond with Dike's (2013) energy demand security concept, resembling, respectively, economic dependence and export dependence and Karatayev and Hall's (2020) resource dependency idea. Both of the explanatory variables can also be indirectly referred to an idea of energy export externalities introduced in Chapter 2 of this book and based on Bohi and Toman's (1996) extended concept of energy security externalities. The ESRI index is included as a variable controlling for supply security concerns in the group of net energy exporters. Institutional quality is included in the model specification following the logic of Robinson, Torvik, and Verdier (2006) as well as Mehlum, Moene, and Torvik (2002), suggesting that the Heckscher-Ohlin-related phenomenon – the Dutch disease occurrence in resource-rich countries depends on the quality of institutions.

Obtained results suggest that the comparative advantage of Norway *vis-à-vis* other net gas-exporting high-income nations is related to both Ricardian productivity differentials and factor endowments. The econometric modelling did not prove statistical significance of natural gas rents, fuel exports, and institutional governance variables, all of which constitute energy demand security framework. The only statistically significant energy variable was the ESRI, proving that even for net energy exporters, supply security concerns are valid source of the comparative advantage. Thus, the hypothesis on the statistically significant impact of the relative energy demand security on the relative comparative advantage of net gas-exporting countries is rejected. Possible explanations behind variables' insignificance include methodological approach with Norway as a benchmark country, strict assumption on the *p*-value, sample's homogeneity, or relative insignificance of fuel sales in total foreign goods' exports in the analysed group of countries. Changed research perspective in the above areas is highlighted as a possible next research step. Obtained results may suggest that energy demand security for high-income net gas-exporting economies has different roots than resource dependence. Thus, Dike's (2013) economic/export dependence idea or resource dependence (Karatayev and Hall, 2020) in a proposed form cannot be treated as the demand security measure in the analysed group of countries. In sum, high-income net gas-exporting economies have other than the (depletable) resource-based demand security profile.

Looking for other than proposed demand security measures might include, based on the literature review, a set of measures relating to the possibilities of demand security internalization. As proposed in Chapter 2 (see Figure 2.15), these measures derive from the supply security "risk and tool" approach and energy security externalities idea. These measures might refer to short- and long-term tools. The former includes industry-specific spare capacity margins, which, in case of sudden changes in energy demand, allow the producer to regulate the production levels. That is why the higher the spare capacity margin of the gas-exporting industry, the better the demand security. The long-term diversification measures include transport-, contract-, and asset-related measures. Transport-specific measures in energy export might refer to number of export routes, variety of transport means (LNG vs. pipelines), or number and geopolitical stability of transited third country territories and gas-supplied countries. One may expect that producer using greater number of pipeline and LNG export routes to multiple consuming nations enjoys higher demand security. On the other hand, the greater the number of transited, politically instable countries or supplied regions, the lower the demand security. Contract-related diversification might be described through the average duration of the exporter's contract portfolio (in years), dummy variable on the existence of take-or-pay or territorial clauses or the number of contract partners. The longer are the contracts with the above clauses, the higher the exporter's demand security. On the other hand, the greater the number of contract partners (even from one country), the lower the exporter's demand security.

Asset-related diversification (e.g., in money terms) may pertain to investments in gas transport, storage and production, asset-swapping in importing countries strict about unbundling procedures, vertical integration of the international global value chains, and the reduction of the degree of the core asset's reliance. The higher are the above money values, the higher the demand security.

All of the above highlighted measures are general in their use. It means that they can be applied to developing and developed net gas exporters. On the contrary the last asset-related diversification tool might be called high-income countries' specific measure. It relates to the level of structural changes in the economy. The more diversified is the economy or the lesser is the importance (share of percentage) of the gas-exporting industry in the GDP structure, the higher the demand security of the exporter. Apart from the above-mentioned diversification tools that might serve as potential proxies for variables in demand security studies, one may also think about differences in technology endowment between different exporting countries. This measure might be regarded as high-income countries' specific measure only in a sense that wealthier economies are expected to be more technology endowed, on the one hand, and, on the other, the quality of technological endowment might be higher than in case of poorer economies. Thus, better technologically endowed countries would be expected to achieve higher demand security. These group of countries might be not only exporting energy resources but also energy technologies. Such technology-related variable may take the form of share of energy-related/"green technologies" exports of technologies in total merchandise exports or energy-related patents and trademarks per capita. Expectations about the nature of influence of respective variables' proxies on energy demand security cannot be easily translated into their influence over comparative advantage of high-income countries. However, more detailed selection of variables specific for advanced economies may at least influence factors' statistical significance. Nevertheless, the existence or the direction of the influence of demand security variables (specific only for industrialized countries) on comparative advantage is unknown. One may only assume that better performance in energy demand security might positively influence a country's comparative advantage.

All of these proposed alternative demand security measures can be discounted by various gas market risks either systematic or non-systematic. In the first group one may list long-term demand for natural gas, macroeconomic performance of the importing regions, and the price volatility levels. In the non-systematic risks set, there might be listed the quantifiable level of competition in the export markets (e.g., with HHI index) or dummy variables on the existence of unfavourable towards producers changes in legislation in gas-importing markets, adjustments of the pricing formulas forced by the international arbitration communities, or sanctions against competing suppliers. The last one proved to be especially important in the times of the Russian-Ukrainian conflict (as of 2022) when Russian suppliers have been denied European gas market access and as a result spot trading of American gas supplemented supply.

The Russian-Ukrainian conflict (as of 2022) might be called a "geopolitical twist" or even a "geopolitical game-changer" in the global natural gas trade. Even though territorially it is Europe-restricted, its influence spans across the continents and also in a merit sense through the economies. Firstly, non-transit Russian gas denial in Ukraine and Lithuania spurs across Europe and has been extended to oil as well. It means that European countries decide to cease not only gas but also oil imports from Russia. In this way, gas market dynamics impact hydrocarbon imports in general. Secondly, disrupted gas exports through Nord Stream pipeline, its maintenance checks and gas leakage posed again a question about supplier's reliability, which had already been challenged by gas conflicts in the beginning of the 21st century. Such doubts do not arise when the US gas exports are taken into consideration. Thus, thirdly, Russian invasion in Ukraine became an opportunity for other global gas players to intercept gas demand. In this way, at the beginning of 2022, the USA became the world's largest LNG exporter (EIA, 2022e) and top gas supplier in Europe (EIA, 2023). However, supplying gas to wealthy European states happened at the cost of poor Asian economies, as due to the conflict and soaring prices, gas supplies have been re-routed from poor Asian countries to Europe (and richer Asian states). Prime example of country affected by this change is Pakistan, where not only gas shipments did not arrive but also due to high coal prices country was forced to increase domestic lignite production. That brings another, fourth global consequence of the conflict for energy markets, which is influence over decarbonization schemes. In Europe, net-zero energy goal, already catalysed by the COVID-pandemic, has been additionally strengthened by the Russian-Ukrainian conflict and related geopolitical tensions. However, in Asia, the participance of which is crucial for the success of the global climate regime, due to increased fossil fuel consumption GHG emissions went up. Thus, decarbonization trend in the short term has been negatively affected. That is why Russian-Ukrainian conflict "twisted" existing trade relations prioritizing politically and economically Europe over Asia and changed the global gas and energy markets by influencing gas supply/demand and by challenging energy-related climate goals.

In sum, presented approach in this book is limited in its theoretical and methodological focus. Extending the above analysis outside the factor endowment approach into further international economic areas, energy economics or a wider economic framework might be an interesting direction for the future conceptual research. That includes, from the international economics field, among others: intra-industry trade, new "new" trade theory, strategic trade policy, imperfect competition, network economics, specific factors theory, differences in technology endowment, and linkages between exporting companies and governments etc., and from energy economics area, for instance, property rights or environmental externalities, while from the point of view a wider economic framework employing game theory findings. At the same time, using other than Amoroso, Chiquiar, and Ramos-Francia's (2011) methodology, such as network-based approaches allowing to measure the complexity of economies and economic agent behaviours might be a meaningful contribution to the demand security analysis.

Notes

1 According to the IEA, in the years 2000–2006, the extraction of shale gas in the USA ranged from 20 bcm to almost 40 bcm. Although the IEA data are not completely consistent with the data provided, for example, by the American Energy Information Administration, they are a source of internationally comparable data.
2 Initially, it was not treated as an energy source but only as a cause of dangerous explosions in coal mines.
3 The period of analysis determined by the availability of data.
4 By comparison, in the OPEC cartel established in 1960, there are two types of membership: founding members (the five countries that created the organization) and full members (all other cartel participants) (OPEC, 2022).
5 Under perfect competition, the marginal cost (MC) curve is the supply curve (Budnikowski, 2006).
6 The stability of the cartel may be jeopardized by the possibility of the prisoner dilemma (Prokop, 2009).

7 For a more extensive comparison of the GECF and the OPEC (Organization for Petroleum Exporting Countries) in the context of their market power, see Nyga-Łukaszewska (2009).

8 Whereas the dominant position of the OPEC in the crude oil market is determined by the monocultural use of crude oil in transport and the lack of generally available and affordable substitutes. The widespread use of electric cars is a sign of future changes in the oil market. However, currently, due to their relatively high cost, it is difficult to call them an affordable alternative. Rising oil prices in the 21st century are encouraging importing countries to use crude oil more efficiently and invest in finding alternative fuel sources for transport. As a consequence of high oil prices, its role in the long term may gradually decrease.

9 In the case of the OPEC, the producers outside the cartel include Russia, Norway, Mexico, and Kazakhstan. However, the potential of each of these countries separately in the production and export of crude oil is incomparably smaller than that of the OPEC countries.

10 Being aware that in economics a short term is considered to be the time during which the factors of production are unable to adapt to changes in the market, and in the long term they do adapt, it is assumed for the sake of simplicity of the analysis that a short term is a period of up to one year, a medium term is one to three years, and the long term is a period of more than three years. It is a typology that harmonizes with the specificity of the energy industry. Due to such a time horizon, natural gas storage facilities, which are part of short-term energy security, are not included in the scope of the analysis.

11 The level of economic development in the nomenclature used by both the World Bank and the United Nations.

12 For example, the best quality coal is anthracite. Poland, despite the fact that it has rich coal deposits, imports anthracite from abroad. This is due to the fact that this type of coal – according to information from the National Geological Institute – occurs only in trace amounts in the Lower Silesian Coal Basin (Malon and Tymiński, 2018).

13 The group consists of Afghanistan, Benin, Bolivia, Burkina Faso, Burundi, Cameroon, Central African Republic, Chad, Congo, Democratic Republic of the Congo, Comoros, Ivory Coast, Ethiopia, Gambia, Ghana, Guinea, Guinea-Bissau, Guyana, Haiti, Honduras, Liberia, Madagascar, Mali, Mauritania, Malawi, Mozambique, Nicaragua, Niger, Rwanda, São Tomé and Príncipe, Senegal, Sierra Leone, Togo, Uganda, and Zambia.

14 In the World Bank statistics, the countries of Central Europe are reported on together with the Baltic States and consequently form a group consisting of Bulgaria, Czechia, Croatia, Estonia, Hungary, Latvia, Lithuania, Poland, Romania, Slovakia, and Slovenia.

15 The group consists of Andorra, Antigua and Barbuda, Aruba, Australia, Austria, Bahamas, Bahrain, Barbados, Belgium, Bermuda, British Virgin Islands, Brunei, Canada, Cayman Islands, Channel Islands, Chile, Curaçao, Cyprus, Czechia, Denmark, Estonia, Faroe Islands, Finland, France, French Polynesia, Gibraltar, Greece, Greenland, Hong Kong, Hungary, Iceland, Ireland, Isle of Man, Israel, Italy, Japan, South Korea, Kuwait, Latvia, Liechtenstein, Lithuania, Luxembourg, Macao, Malta, Monaco, Netherlands, New Caledonia, New Zealand, Northern Mariana Islands, Norway, Oman, Palau, Poland, Portugal, Puerto Rico, Qatar, San Marino, Saudi Arabia, Seychelles, Singapore, St. Maarten (part of the Netherlands), Slovakia, Slovenia, Spain, Federation of St. Kitts and Nevis – St. Martin (French part), Sweden, Switzerland, Trinidad and Tobago, Turks and Caicos Islands, United Arab Emirates, United Kingdom, United States, Uruguay, and Virgin Islands (USA).

16 India uses natural gas to a much lesser extent than China. In 2016, it consumed about 50 bcm of this resource, of which about 22.5 bcm came from domestic production. Import is carried out exclusively via LNG vessels (BP, 2017).

17 Coal production in Ukraine decreased from 26 Mtoe in 2014 to 17 Mtoe in 2016 (BP, 2017).

18 Latest data available, at the time of book's preparation, from 21 February 2023.
19 At this point, due to the purpose of the study, the role of the so-called reverse points is omitted. Reverse points are points at the borders of the transmission systems of countries where there are facilities that enable the resource to be transmitted in the opposite direction to that originally assumed. Examples of such points are those at the Polish-German and Polish-Ukrainian borders, which enable the transmission of gas to the east. Reverse points may, admittedly, be an additional source of natural gas supply, but they are not directly related to the import of resources.
20 Apart from signatories there are also observer countries, including from the group of natural gas producers, for instance: Australia, Canada, and the USA. However, this group of countries, in comparison to the signatories, declared only political approval that has no further legally binding consequences. Energy Charter (2023b).
21 However, there is, for instance, a debate whether hydrogen can be transported via existing gas pipelines.
22 Compare with: UNESCAP (2023).
23 Another work in the context of the Ukrainian gas transit is Dieckhöner (2012). However, this chapter looks at the transit purely from the supply security perspective.
24 Other non-quantifiable elements of the price formula include periodic reviews of gas prices (review or re-opener). In turn, the quantifiable elements of the formula are the value of gas at the point of delivery and the value of competing fuels. As the quantifiable elements and the principles of periodic price reviews concern the value of natural gas, they will be discussed in the section on price conditions.
25 On the other hand, in view of the monetary nature of the penalty linked to non-compliance with this principle, it could also be included among price conditions.
26 The degree of integration of electricity markets within the EU in 2017 shows that while in the case of some countries there is a strong infrastructural integration with the EU market (Luxembourg), in others there is still much work to be done (Poland). It is worth noting that countries outside the continent are naturally characterized by a lower level of integration with the continent.
27 As noted by Pach-Gargul (2016), cooperation within the European Union is to include the following areas:

- energy security – in particular to increase the resilience of member states to discontinuity of energy supply, improve the diversification of routes, directions, and suppliers of energy commodities, encourage countries to engage in energy cooperation,
- internal energy market – more precisely, completing the process of integration of the EU energy market started in the 1990s,
- energy efficiency – in particular, reducing energy demand in construction and transport,
- retreat from coal used in economies (decarbonization of the economy) – related to the reduction of greenhouse gas emissions, acceleration of investments in low-carbon technologies and the EU's ambitious goal of taking on the role of global leader and research centre in the field of RES,
- research, innovation, and competitiveness – in particular, concerning clean transport, clean fossil fuels, and nuclear energy.

The European Union monitors the implementation of these priorities within the framework of periodic reviews. The main objectives in the field of energy security are those related to the construction of transmission infrastructure between member states. These include projects such as (European Commission, 2017b):

- BEMIP (Baltic Energy Market Integration Plan) for the integration of electricity markets of the Baltic States, to end their isolation from other EU markets; for this purpose, cross-border interconnections are to be established or expanded between

Lithuania and Sweden, Lithuania and Poland, Estonia and Finland (Balticconnector); in total, the EU had earmarked approximately EUR 1.1 bn for the purpose under various support programmes,
- connection of the Iberian Peninsula with the rest of Europe for the electricity and gas markets; in the former case, this involves an interconnection between France and Spain across the Biscay Bay, and in the latter, the construction of the Eastern Gas Axis connecting the Peninsula with France via the Eastern Pyreneans (Midcat project),
- integration of Central and South European gas markets by constructing the LNG terminal on the Croatian island of Krk, installation of gas interconnectors between Greece and Bulgaria and between Bulgaria and Serbia,
- development of the North Sea offshore grid for a more optimized deployment of renewable energy sources.

28 Green Deal strategy will be supported by other mechanisms. Example of such an initiative (having also consequences for the international trade flows) might be carbon border adjustment mechanism (CBAM). It is a type of carbon-related tariff that is to be levied on the carbon-intensive products entering the EU. By introducing CBAM, the EU intends to prevent the carbon leakage phenomenon.

29 According to the "Treaty of the Functioning of the European Union", energy falls into the category of shared competencies, like for instance: security of supply (article 122 TFEU), external energy policy (articles 216–218 TFEU), internal energy market (article 114 TFEU) and energy networks (articles 170–172 TFEU).

30 These are the USA – FTA countries. International Trade Administration (2023).

31 His approach also offers a possibility to investigate the same relationship for net energy consumers. Voudouris (2013).

32 This book's author is aware that the prices of commodities materials are recorded as spot prices and prices under long-term price formulas. The impact of spot prices on natural gas prices under long-term contracts will be discussed further in this chapter.

33 The "cost plus pricing" formula is historically the oldest pricing formula. It determines the gas price as a sum of the cost of production, transport, fixed costs, and profit margin.

34 No newer data available.

35 As Franza notes, since 2012, Russian natural gas prices in Europe have been significantly convergent with natural gas prices at the Dutch Title Transfer Facility (TTF) hub (Franza, 2014).

36 Subsidizing domestic production is aimed at eliminating or reducing imports of a particular good or at achieving other economic goals that are important from the point of view of the country (such as protecting employment, stimulating the development of a selected industry). In turn, the purpose of an export subsidy is to achieve an excess supply of a given commodity, so that it can be used for export or increase existing exports. The main difference between the identified types of subsidies is the moment when they are obtained. In the case of a subsidy to domestic production, it is the moment at which the entity undertakes to produce a particular commodity. On the other hand, with regard to a subsidy to export production, it is the moment when the company decides to export the commodity (Budnikowski, 2006).

37 Original writing.

38 The IMF also distinguishes pre-tax subsidies and post-tax subsidies.

39 Negative influence on trade balance does not hold true for export subsidies.

40 More on institutions and comparative advantage nexus can be found in: Nunn and Trefler (2014).

41 Qatar's presence in the OECD framework is limited to the participance in the OECD Development Assistance Committee. At this forum, Qatar is a provider of substantial concessional finance for development co-operation and humanitarian aid OECD (2023).

42 Moreover, in response to Russia's large-scale aggression against Ukraine (2022), the OECD Council has decided to suspend the participation of Russia in OECD bodies. OECD (2022).
43 Number of observations results on the one hand from multiple factors. Firstly, the research design; secondly, the desire to have as big number of observations as possible; thirdly, need to keep the data coherency (in terms of sources reliability); and fourthly, from the wish to maintain the panel balanced. Additionally, the sample size follows the argument presented by Gruszczyński, Kuszewski, and Podgórska (2009, p. 28).
44 Among the neoclassical models (H-O) allowing for influence of technological differences, one may highlight conceptual settings presented in Harrigan (1997) and Harrigan and Zakrajsek (Number of Harrigan and Zakrajsek, 2000).
45 But also on the EU level with the REPowerEU initiative.

References

Aizenman, J. and Riera-Crichton, D. (2014) *Liquidity and foreign asset management challenges for Latin American countries*. NBER Working Papers 20646. Cambridge: National Bureau of Economic Research.

Aizenman, J. et al. (2019) 'Fiscal space and government-spending and tax-rate cyclicality patterns: a cross-country comparison, 1960–2016', *Journal of Macroeconomics*, 60, pp. 229–252. doi:10.1016/j.jmacro.2019.02.006.

Al-Hassan, A. et al. (2018) *Commodity-based sovereign wealth funds: managing financial flows in the context of the sovereign balance sheet*. IMF Working Papers [Preprint], Washington, DC: International Monetary Fund.

Amoroso, N., Chiquiar, D., and Ramos-Francia, M. (2011) 'Technology and endowments as determinants of comparative advantage: evidence from Mexico', *The North American Journal of Economics and Finance*, 22(2), pp. 164–196. doi:10.1016/j.najef.2011.01.004.

Antoniadis, I. (2017) 'Exploring the linkage between oil and gas sector and competitiveness: a panel data analysis for the countries of the Black Sea region', *Scientific Bulletin – Economic Sciences*, 16, pp. 34–44. Available at: http://economic.upit.ro/repec/pdf/2017_1_4.pdf (Accessed: 21 December 2021).

Anway, S.P. and von Mehren, G.M. (2017) 'The evolution of natural gas price review arbitrations', in: *Global Arbitration Review,* Rowley, J.W., Bishop, D., Kaiser, G. (eds.), London: Law and Business Research, 2nd edition. Available at: https://www.bennettjones.com/-/media/Files/BennettJones/Shared/415Multi-Tier-Investment-Disputes.pdf (Accessed: 30 August May 2023).

APERC (2007) *A quest for energy security in the 21st century. Resources and constraints*. Tokyo: Institute of Energy Economics.

Balassa, B. (1965) 'Trade liberalization and revealed comparative advantage', *The Manchester School of Economic and Social Studies*, 33, pp. 99–123. doi:10.1111/j.1467-9957.1965.tb00050.x.

Baran, B. (2012) 'Znaczenie państwowych funduszy majątkowych na globalnym rynku kapitałowym', *Gospodarka Narodowa*, 9(253), pp. 39–59.

Bhattacharyya, S.C. (2011) *Energy economics. Concepts, issues, markets and governance*. London: Springer.

Boersma, T., Vandendriessche, M., and Leber, A. (2015) *Shale gas in Algeria. No quick fix*. Washington, DC: Brookings Institution. Available at: https://www.brookings.edu/wp-content/uploads/2016/07/no_quick_fix_final-2.pdf (Accessed: 2 May 2018).

Bohi, D.R. and Toman, M.A. (1996) *The economics of energy security*. 1st edn. Boston, MA: Kluwer Academic Publishers.

Bollino, C.A. and Galkin, P. (2021) 'Energy security and portfolio diversification: conventional and novel perspectives', *Energies*, 14(14), p. 4257. doi:10.3390/en14144257.
Boussena, S. and Locatelli, C. (2013) 'Energy institutional and organisational changes in EU and Russia: revisiting gas relations', *Energy Policy*, 55, pp. 180–189. doi:10.1016/j.enpol.2012.11.052.
BP (2017) *Statistical Review of World Energy 2017*. Available at: https://www.bp.com/en/global/corporate/energy-economics/statistical-review-of-world-energy.html (Accessed: 30 October 2017).
BP (2021) *BP Statistical Review of World Energy 2021*. Available at: https://www.bp.com/en/global/corporate/energy-economics/statistical-review-of-world-energy.html (Accessed: 2 March 2022).
Buckley, P.J. and Casson, M. (2021) 'Multinational enterprises and international cartels: the strategic implications of de-globalization', *Management and Organization Review*, 17(5), pp. 968–988. doi:10.1017/mor.2021.42.
Budnikowski, A. (2006) *Międzynarodowe stosunki gospodarcze*. 3rd edn. (revised). Warszawa: Polskie Wydawnictwo Ekonomiczne.
Cahil, B. and Palti-Guzman, L. (2023) *The role of gas in Ukraine's energy future*. CSIS Briefs, Washington, DC: CSIS. Available at: https://www.csis.org/analysis/role-gas-ukraines-energy-future (Accessed: 15 March 2023).
Cappelen, A. and Mjøset, L. (2009) Can Norway be a role model for natural resource abundant countries? in Augustin K. Fosu (ed.), *Development Success: Historical Accounts from More Advanced Countries*, WIDER Studies in Development Economics (Oxford, 2012; online edn, Oxford Academic, 24 Jan. 2013) [Preprint]. doi:10.1093/acprof:oso/9780199660704.003.0003, pp. 44–72
Che, N.X. (2009) *The great dissolution: organization capital and diverging volatility puzzle*. 13701. Munich: University Library of Munich, pp. 1–37. Available at: https://ideas.repec.org/p/pra/mprapa/13701.html (Accessed: 24 June 2022).
Chopra, A.S. (2013) 'Commodity and non commodity sovereign wealth funds – decision scorecard (DSC) analysis', *International Journal of Research and Development – A Management Review*, 2(1), pp. 46–51.
Chor, D. (2010) 'Unpacking sources of comparative advantage: a quantitative approach', *Journal of International Economics*, 82(2), pp. 152–167. doi:10.1016/j.jinteco.2010.07.004.
Chyong, C.-K. (2015) *Markets and long-term contracts: the case of Russian gas supplies to Europe*. Cambridge: University of Cambridge. Available at: https://www.eprg.group.cam.ac.uk/wp-content/uploads/2015/12/1524-Text.pdf (Accessed: 5 March 2018).
Chyong, C.-K. and Hobbs, B.F. (2014) 'Strategic Eurasian natural gas market model for energy security and policy analysis. Formulation and application to South Stream', *Energy Economics*, 44, pp. 198–211. doi:10.1016/j.eneco.2014.04.006.
Clements, B.J. et al. (2013) *Energy subsidy reform: lessons and implications*. Washington, DC: International Monetary Fund.
Costinot, A. and Komunjer, I. (2007) *What goods do countries trade? New ricardian predictions*. NBER Working Paper Series, No. w13691. Cambridge, MA: National Bureau of Economic Research. Available at: https://www.nber.org/papers/w13691 (Accessed: 30 May 2021).
Coutinho, L. et al. (2022) 'Limiting fiscal procyclicality: evidence from resource-dependent countries', *Economic Modelling*, 106(C), p. 105700. doi:10.1016/j.econmod.2021.105700.
Creti, A. and Villeneueve, B. (2004) 'Long-term contracts and take-or-pay clauses in natural gas markets', *Energy Studies Review*, 13(1), pp. 75–94.
Crocker, K.J. and Masten, S.E. (1991) 'Pretia ex Machina? Prices and process in long-term contracts', *The Journal of Law & Economics*, 34(1), pp. 69–99. doi:10.1086/467219.

Cuñat, A. and Melitz, M.J. (2012) 'Volatility, labour market flexibility, and the pattern of comparative advantage', *Journal of the European Economic Association*, 10(2), pp. 225–254. doi:10.1111/j.1542-4774.2011.01038.x.

Czerniewicz, K. (2015) *Sektor energetyczny Białorusi*. Warszawa: Ośrodek Studiów Wschodnich. Available at: https://oaspl.org/2015/07/15/sektor-energetyczny-bialorusi/ (Accessed: 20 May 2018).

D'Agostino, A.D. (2013) 'The social development dimension of energy security', in Sovacool, B. (ed.), *The Routledge handbook on energy security*. Abingdon: Routledge, pp. 205–217.

Dagher, J., Gottschalk, J., and Portillo, R. (2012) 'The short-run impact of oil windfalls in low-income countries: a DSGE approach', *Journal of African Economies*, 21(3), pp. 343–372. doi:10.1093/jae/ejr052.

Davis, M. et al. (2005) *Ukraine – the impact of higher natural gas and oil prices*. 38602. Washington, DC: World Bank. Available at: http://documents.worldbank.org/curated/en/838301468173971844/Ukraine-The-impact-of-higher-natural-gas-and-oil-prices (Accessed: 9 February 2018).

De Hoyos, R.E. and Sarafidis, V. (2006) 'Testing for cross-sectional dependence in panel-data models', *Stata Journal*, 6, pp. 482–496. doi:10.1177/1536867X0600600403.

Debaere, P. (2003) 'Relative factor abundance and trade', *Journal of Political Economy*, 111(3), pp. 589–610. doi:10.1086/374179.

Dieckhöner, C. (2012) 'Simulating security of supply effects of the Nabucco and South Stream projects for the European Natural Gas Market', *The Energy Journal*, 33(3), pp. 153–181. http://www.jstor.org/stable/23268097.

Dike, J.C. (2013) 'Measuring the security of energy exports demand in OPEC economies', *Energy Policy*, 60, pp. 594–600. doi:10.1016/j.enpol.2013.05.086.

EIA (2015) *Ukraine*. Available at: https://www.eia.gov/beta/international/analysis.cfm?iso=UKR (Accessed: 20 May 2018).

EIA (2016) *India*. Available at: https://www.eia.gov/beta/international/analysis.cfm?iso=IND (Accessed: 2 May 2018).

EIA (2017) *The United States Now Produces Nearly All of the Natural Gas that It Uses*. Available at: https://www.eia.gov/energyexplained/natural-gas/where-our-natural-gas-comes-from.php (Accessed: 20 May 2018).

EIA (2018) *United Kingdom*. Available at: https://www.eia.gov/international/analysis/country/GBR (Accessed: 2 May 2018).

EIA (2022a) *Iran*. Available at: https://www.eia.gov/international/analysis/country/irn (Accessed: 8 March 2022).

EIA (2022b) *Japan*. Available at: https://www.eia.gov/international/analysis/country/jpn (Accessed: 8 March 2022).

EIA (2022c) *Saudi Arabia*. Available at: https://www.eia.gov/international/analysis/country/SAU (Accessed: 2 March 2022).

EIA (2022d) *United Kingdom*. Available at: https://www.eia.gov/international/analysis/country/GBR (Accessed: 2 March 2022).

EIA (2022e) *The United States Became the World's Largest LNG Exporter in the First Half of 2022*. Available at: https://www.eia.gov/todayinenergy/detail.php?id=53159 (Accessed: 26 March 2023).

EIA (2023) *Europe Was the Main Destination for U.S. LNG Exports in 2022*. Available at: https://www.eia.gov/todayinenergy/detail.php?id=55920 (Accessed: 26 March 2023).

Enerdata (2018) *Global Energy Statistical Yearbook 2017*. Available at: https://yearbook.enerdata.net/total-energy/world-consumption-statistics.html (Accessed: 10 May 2018).

Energy Charter (2023a) *The Amendment to the Trade-Related Provisions of the Energy Charter Treaty*. Available at: https://www.energycharter.org/process/energy-charter-treaty-1994/trade-amendment/ (Accessed: 15 March 2023).

Energy Charter (2023b) *Members and Observers to the Energy Charter Conference*. Available at: https://www.energycharter.org/who-we-are/members-observers/ (Accessed: 15 March 2023).

European Commission (2004) *Commission Confirms that Territorial Restriction Clauses in the Gas Sector Restrict Competition*. Available at: http://europa.eu/rapid/press-release_IP-04-1310_en.htm (Accessed: 2 June 2018).

European Commission (2015) *Antitrust: Commission Sends Statement of Objections to Gazprom – Factsheet*. Available at: http://europa.eu/rapid/press-release_MEMO-15-4829_en.htm (Accessed: 2 June 2018).

European Commission (2017a) *Antitrust: Commission Invites Comments on Gazprom Commitments Concerning Central and Eastern European Gas Markets*. Available at: http://europa.eu/rapid/press-release_IP-17-555_en.htm (Accessed: 2 June 2018).

European Commission (2017b) *Communication from the Commission to the European Parliament, the Council, the European Economic and Social Committee and the Committee of the Regions. Communication on Strengthening Europe's Energy Networks'*. COM(2017) 718 Final. Available at: https://ec.europa.eu/energy/sites/ener/files/documents/communication_on_infrastructure_17.pdf (Accessed: 27 March 2018).

European Commission (2022) *REPowerEU: A Plan to Rapidly Reduce Dependence on Russian Fossil Fuels and Fast Forward the Green Transition*. Available at: https://ec.europa.eu/commission/presscorner/detail/en/ip_22_3131 (Accessed: 27 March 2023).

European Commission (2023) *A European Green Deal*. Available at: https://commission.europa.eu/strategy-and-policy/priorities-2019-2024/european-green-deal_en (Accessed: 27 March 2023).

European Council (2023) *Fit for 55*. Available at: https://www.consilium.europa.eu/en/policies/green-deal/fit-for-55-the-eu-plan-for-a-green-transition/ (Accessed: 27 March 2023).

Feenstra, R.C., Inklaar, R., and Timmer, R.M. (2015) 'The next generation of the penn world table', *American Economic Review*, 105, pp. 3150–3182. doi:10.1257/aer.20130954.

Fitzgerald, D. and Hallak, J.C. (2004) 'Specialization, factor accumulation and development', *Journal of International Economics*, 64(2), pp. 277–302. doi:10.1016/j.jinteco.2003.09.001.

Franza, L. (2014) *Long-term gas import contracts in Europe. The evolution of pricing mechanisms*. Hague: Clingendael International Energy Programme. Available at: http://www.clingendaelenergy.com/inc/upload/files/Ciep_paper_2014-08_web_1.pdf (Accessed: 2 April 2018).

Gabriel, S. et al. (2010) *Cartelization in gas markets. Studying the potential for a "Gas OPEC"*. 638. Statistics Norway, Research Department, Oslo: Statistics Norway. Available at: https://www.ssb.no/a/publikasjoner/pdf/DP/dp638.pdf (Accessed: 25 March 2018).

Gao, F. (2012) *Will there be a shale gas revolution in China by 2020?* Oxford: Oxford Institute for Energy Studies. Available at: https://www.oxfordenergy.org/wpcms/wp-content/uploads/2012/04/NG-61.pdf (Accessed: 3 May 2018).

Garg, R. and Shukla, A. (2021) 'The impact and implications of SWFs: a systematic review of literature', *Qualitative Research in Financial Markets*, 13(5), pp. 580–607. doi:10.1108/QRFM-08-2020-0171.

GECF (2021) *Annual Statistical Bulletin 2021*. Available at: https://www.gecf.org/_resources/files/flipbook/gecfasb2021/files/assets/common/downloads/publication.pdf (Accessed: 8 March 2022).

GECF Statue (2008) *Statute of the Gas Exporting Countries Forum*. Available at: https://www.gecf.org/_resources/files/gecf-meetings/gecf-statute.pdf (Accessed: 14 March 2023).

Global Energy Institute (2022) *Energy Security Risk Index*. Available at: https://www.globalenergyinstitute.org/energy-security-risk-index (Accessed: 2 February 2022).

Golub, S.S. and Hsieh, C.-T. (2000) 'Classical Ricardian theory of comparative advantage revisited', *Review of International Economics*, 8(2), pp. 221–234. doi:10.1111/1467-9396.00217.

Gruszczyński, M., Kuszewski, T., and Podgórska, M. (eds.) (2009) *Ekonometria i badania operacyjne*. 1st edn. Warszawa: Wydawnictwo Naukowe PWN.

Gylfason, T. (2001) 'Natural resources, education, and economic development', *European Economic Review*, 45(4), pp. 847–859. doi:10.1016/S0014-2921(01)00127-1.

Harrigan, J. (1997) *Technology, factor supplies and international specialization: testing the neoclassical model.* NBER Working Paper Series, No. w5722. Cambridge, MA: National Bureau of Economic Research. Available at: https://www.nber.org/papers/w5722 (Accessed: 30 May 2022).

Harrigan, J. and Zakrajsek, E. (2000) 'Factor supplies and specialization in the world economy', *Finance and Economics Discussion Series*, 2000, pp. 1–43. doi:10.17016/FEDS.2000.43.

Hartley, P. (2013) *The future of long-term contracts*. Crawley: The University of Western Australia. Available at: http://www.business.uwa.edu.au/__data/assets/pdf_file/0009/2356524/13-22-The-Future-of-Long-term-LNG-Contracts.pdf (Accessed: 2 June 2018).

Hartwick, J. (1977) 'Intergenerational equity and the investing of rents from exhaustible resources', *The American Economic Review*, 67(5), pp. 972–974.

Heffron, R.J. (2018) 'The application of distributive justice to energy taxation utilising sovereign wealth funds', *Energy Policy*, 122(C), pp. 649–654. doi:10.1016/j.enpol.2018.07.049.

Heidecke, L. et al. (2022) *The revision of the third energy package for gas*. Publication for the Committee on Industry, Research and Energy (ITRE), Policy Department for Economic, Scientific and Quality of Life Policies. Luxembourg: European Parliament. Available at: https://www.europarl.europa.eu/RegData/etudes/STUD/2022/734009/IPOL_STU(2022)734009_EN.pdf (Accessed: 19 March 2023).

Hoechle, D. (2007) 'Robust standard errors for panel regressions with cross-sectional dependence', *Stata Journal*, 7, pp. 281–312. doi:10.1177/1536867X0700700301.

Hotelling, H. (1931) 'The economics of exhaustible resources', *Journal of Political Economy*, 39(2), pp. 137–175. doi:10.1086/254195.

Hubbard, R.G. and Weiner, R.J. (1991) 'Efficient contracting and market power: evidence from the U.S. Natural Gas Industry', *The Journal of Law & Economics*, 34(1), pp. 25–67. doi:10.3386/w3502.

Hubert, F. and Ikonnikova, S. (2004) 'Hold-up, multilateral bargaining, and strategic investment: the Eurasian Supply Chain for Natural Gas'. Available at: https://www.academia.edu/16259704/Hold_Up_Multilateral_Bargaining_and_Strategic_Investment_The_Eurasian_Supply_Chain_for_Natural_Gas (Accessed: 19 March 2023).

Hubert, F. and Ikonnikova, S. (2011) 'Hold-up and strategic investment in international transport networks: gas pipelines in North Western Europe'. Available at: http://www.ms-hns.de/files/publications/holdup_-_strategic_investment_-_gas.pdf (Accessed: 22 January 2022).

Hubert, F. and Suleymanova, I. (2008) *Strategic investment in international gas-transport systems: a dynamic analysis of the hold-up problem*. DIW Discussion Papers, 846, Berlin: Deutsches Institut für Wirtschaftsforschung. doi:10.2139/ssrn.1429257.

IEA (2014) *World Energy Outlook 2014*. Available at: https://www.iea.org/publications/freepublications/publication/WEO2014.pdf (Accessed: 4 February 2018).

IEA (2017) *Energy Policies of IEA Countries. Norway 2017 Review*. Available at: https://iea.blob.core.windows.net/assets/7113f933-b252-434c-aa15-67c460475bc3/EnergyPoliciesofIEACountriesNorway2017.pdf (Accessed: 20 December 2021).

IMF (2014) 'Norway: selected issues', *IMF Staff Country Reports*, 2014(260), pp. 13–23. doi:10.5089/9781498374408.002.A002.

International Trade Administration (2023) *Free Trade Agreements*. Available at: https://www.trade.gov/free-trade-agreements (Accessed: 25 March 2023).

Jones, R.W. (1956) 'Factor proportions and the Heckscher-Ohlin theorem', *The Review of Economic Studies*, 24(1), pp. 1–10. doi:10.2307/2296232.

Joskow, P.J. (1988) 'Price adjustment in long-term contracts: the case of coal', *The Journal of Law & Economics*, 31(1), pp. 47–83. doi:10.1086/467149.

Kamprath, R. (2009) *Norway: a template for world energy policy*. Available at: https://ssrn.com/abstract=1577928. doi: 10.2139/ssrn.1577928 (Accessed: 20 December 2021).

Karatayev, M. and Hall, S. (2020) 'Establishing and comparing energy security trends in resource-rich exporting nations (Russia and the Caspian Sea region)', *Resources Policy*, 68, pp. 101746. doi:10.1016/j.resourpol.2020.101746.

Kaufmann, D., Kraay, A., and Mastruzzi, M. (2010) *The worldwide governance indicators: a summary of methodology. Data and analytical issues*. World Bank Policy Research Working Paper No. 5430, Washington, DC: World Bank. Available at: http://papers.ssrn.com/sol3/papers.cfm?abstract_id=1682130 (Accessed: 10 June 2022).

Kinda, T., Mlachila, M., and Ouedraogo, R. (2018) 'Do commodity price shocks weaken the financial sector?' *The World Economy*, 41(11), pp. 3001–3044. doi:10.1111/twec.12667.

Konoplyanik, A. (2010) *Evolution of gas pricing in continental Europe: modernization of indexation formulas versus gas to gas competition*. International Energy Law and Policy Research Paper Series. Dundee: University of Dundee.

Koplow, D. (2004) 'Subsidies to energy industries', in Cleveland, C. and Ayres, R.U. (eds.), *Encyclopedia of energy*. 1st edn. Amsterdam: Elsevier Academic Press, pp. 749–764.

KPMG (2022) *Norway Tops KPMG's First-Ever Net Zero Readiness Index*. Available at: https://home.kpmg/cn/en/home/news-media/press-releases/2021/10/norway-tops-kpmg-first-ever-net-zero-readiness-index.html (Accessed: 1 February 2022).

Lai, H. and Zhu, S.C. (2007) 'Technology, endowments, and the factor content of bilateral trade', *Journal of International Economics*, 71(2), pp. 389–409. doi:10.1016/j.jinteco.2006.07.002.

Laursen, K. (2015) 'Revealed comparative advantage and the alternatives as measures of international specialization', *Eurasian Business Review*, 5(1), pp. 99–115. doi:10.1007/s40821-015-0017-1.

Law of the Republic of Lithuania on Natural Gas No. VIII-1973. Law on Amendment of Articles 2, 45, 46, 57 and 62. Available at: https://www.e-tar.lt/portal/legalAct.html?documentId=f32ecd80828711ed8df094f359a60216 (Accessed 25 March 2023).

Le Coq, C. (2004) *Long-term supply contracts and collusion in the electricity market*. SSE/EFI Working Paper Series in Economics and Finance No. 552. Stockholm: Stockholm School of Economics.

Le Coq, C. and Paltseva, E. (2012) 'Assessing gas transit risks: Russia vs. the EU', *Energy Policy*, 42, pp. 642–650. doi:10.1016/j.enpol.2011.12.037.

Leamer, E.E. (1995) *A combined Ricardian and Heckscher-Ohlin model of comparative advantage*. Reihe Ökonomie/Economics Series 17. Vienna: Institute for Advanced Studies (IHS). Available at: http://hdl.handle.net/10419/68641 (Accessed: 30 May 2022).

Leonard, M. et al. (2021) *The geopolitics of the European Green Deal.* European Council on Foreign Relations. Available at: https://ecfr.eu/publication/the-geopolitics-of-the-european-green-deal/ (Accessed: 20 March 2023).

Leromain, E. and Orefice, G. (2014) 'New revealed comparative advantage index: dataset and empirical distribution', *International Economics*, 139, pp. 48–70. doi:10.1016/j.inteco.2014.03.003.

Levchenko, A.A. (2007) 'Institutional quality and international trade', *The Review of Economic Studies*, 74(3), pp. 791–819. doi:10.1111/j.1467-937X.2007.00435.x.

Łoskot-Strachota, A. (2020) *More EU, less Russia. Transforming gas transmission rules in Central and South-Eastern Europe.* OSW Commentary, Warszawa: Ośrodek Studiów Wschodnich. Available at: https://www.osw.waw.pl/en/publikacje/osw-commentary/2020-10-14/more-eu-less-russia-transforming-gas-transmission-rules (Accessed: 23 March 2023).

Makarov, I., Chen, H., and Paltsev, S. (2020) 'Impacts of climate change policies worldwide on the Russian economy', *Climate Policy*, 20(10), pp. 1242–1256. doi:10.1080/14693062.2020.1781047.

Malon, A. and Tymiński, M. (2018) *Węgiel kamienny.* Warszawa: Państwowy Instytut Geologiczny. Available at: http://geoportal.pgi.gov.pl/surowce/energetyczne/wegiel_kamienny (Accessed: 1 July 2018).

Masten, S.E. and Crocker, K.J. (1985) 'Efficient adaptation in long-term contracts: take-or-pay provisions for natural gas', *The American Economic Review*, 75(5), pp. 1083–1093.

Matuszak, S. and Kardaś, S. (2017) *Arbitraż w Sztokholmie: strategiczny sukces Ukrainy, doraźne korzyści Gazpromu.* Warszawa: Ośrodek Studiów Wschodnich. Available at: https://www.osw.waw.pl/pl/publikacje/analizy/2017-12-28/arbitraz-w-sztokholmie-strategiczny-sukces-ukrainy-dorazne-korzysci (Accessed: 2 June 2018).

Mehlum, H., Moene, K., and Torvik, R. (2002) *Institutions and the resource curse.* Oslo: Department of Economics, University of Oslo. Available at: https://www.econstor.eu/bitstream/10419/63059/1/354828169.pdf (Accessed: 2 October 2021).

Meon, P.-G. and Sekkat, K. (2008) 'Institutional quality and trade: which institutions? Which trade?', *Economic Inquiry*, 46(2), pp. 227–240. doi:10.1111/j.1465-7295.2007.00064.x.

Metcalf, G.E. (2013) *The economics of energy security.* NBER Working Papers 19729. NBER. Cambridge: National Bureau of Economic Research.

Michałek, J.J. (2004) 'Subsidies in the context of the World Trade Organization', *Reflets et perspectives de la vie économique*, xliii(1), pp. 25–38. doi:10.3917/rpve.431.0025.

MIT (2011) *The future of natural gas. An interdisciplinary MIT study.* Cambridge, CA: MIT Press.

Mohaddes, K. and Raissi, M. (2017) 'Do sovereign wealth funds dampen the negative effects of commodity price volatility?' *Journal of Commodity Markets*, 8, pp. 18–27. doi:10.1016/j.jcomm.2017.08.004.

Morrow, P.M. (2010) 'Ricardian–Heckscher–Ohlin comparative advantage: theory and evidence', *Journal of International Economics*, 82(2), pp. 137–151. doi:10.1016/j.jinteco.2010.08.006.

Mullerhin, J.H. (1986) 'Complexity in long-term contracts: An analysis of natural gas contractual provisions', *Journal of Law, Economics & Organization*, 2(1), pp. 105–117.

Murshed, M. (2017) 'Is energy subsidy helping to achieve energy security?' *The Independent*, 13 January. Available at: http://www.theindependentbd.com/printversion/details/76311 (Accessed: 6 February 2018).

Napiórkowski, T.M. (2022) *Praktyczna analiza danych za pomocą metod ilościowych.* Warszawa: Oficyna Wydawnicza SGH.

National Environmental Policy Act (1969) Available at: https://www.energy.gov/nepa/articles/national-environmental-policy-act-1969 (Accessed: 25 March 2023).

Natural Gas Act (1938) Available at: https://www.energy.gov/sites/prod/files/2013/04/f0/2011usc15.pdf (Accessed: 25 March 2023).

Neumann, A. and Hirschhausen, C. (2004) 'Less gas to Europe? An empirical assessment of long-term contracts for European energy supply', *Zeitschrift fuer Energiewirtschaft*, 28(3), pp. 175–182.

Nojszewska, E. (1995) *Podstawy ekonomii*. Warszawa: Wydawnictwa Szkolne i Pedagogiczne.

Novikau, A. (2021) 'What does energy security mean for energy-exporting countries? A closer look at the Russian energy security strategy', *Journal of Energy & Natural Resources Law*, 39(1), pp. 105–123. doi:10.1080/02646811.2020.1794108.

Novikau, A. (2022) 'Rethinking demand security: between national interests and energy exports', *Energy Research & Social Science*, 87, p. 102494. doi:10.1016/j.erss.2022.102494.

Nowrouzi, A. et al. (2019) 'Optimizing Iran's natural gas export portfolio by presenting a conceptual framework for non-systematic risk based on portfolio theory', *Energy Strategy Reviews*, 26, p. 100403. doi:10.1016/j.esr.2019.100403.

Nunn, N. (2007) 'Relationship-specificity, incomplete contracts, and the pattern of trade', *The Quarterly Journal of Economics*, 122(2), pp. 569–600. doi:10.1162/qjec.122.2.569.

Nunn, N. and Trefler, D. (2014) 'Chapter 5 – Domestic institutions as a source of comparative advantage', in Gopinath, G., Helpman, E., and Rogoff, K. (eds.), *Handbook of international economics*. Oxford: Elsevier, pp. 263–315. doi:10.1016/B978-0-444-54314-1.00005-7.

Nyga-Łukaszewska, H. (2009) 'Czy porozumienie głównych producentów gazu ma szanse stać się nowym OPEC w światowym handlu gazem ziemnym?' *International Journal of Management and Economics*, 26, pp. 127–148.

Nyga-Łukaszewska, H. (2017) 'Wydobycie węglowodorów niekonwencjonalnych w USA a bezpieczeństwo energetyczne kraju', *Polityka Energetyczna – Energy Policy Journal*, 20(3), pp. 105–116.

Nyga-Łukaszewska, H. and Chilimoniuk-Przeździecka, E. (2017) 'Modelling energy security and international competitiveness: the export perspective', *Entrepreneurial Business and Economics Review*, 5(2), pp. 71–84. doi:10.15678/EBER.2017.050204.

Nyga-Łukaszewska, H. and Napiórkowski, T.M. (2022) 'Does energy demand security affect international competitiveness? Case of selected energy-exporting OECD countries', *Energies*, 15(6), p. 1991. doi:10.3390/en15061991.

OECD (2013) *Analysing energy subsidies in the countries of Eastern Europe, Caucasus and Central Asia*. Paris: Organisation for Economic Cooperation and Development.

OECD (2022) *Statement from OECD Secretary-General on Further Measures in Response to Russia's Large-Scale Aggression against Ukraine*. Available at: https://www.oecd.org/newsroom/statement-from-the-oecd-council-on-further-measures-in-response-to-russia-s-large-scale-aggression-against-ukraine.htm (Accessed: 26 March 2023).

OECD (2023) *Qatar Becomes Participant in the OECD Development Assistance Committee (DAC)*. Available at: https://www.oecd.org/countries/qatar/qatar-participant-dac.htm (Accessed: 26 March 2023).

OPEC (2022) *OPEC Member Countries*. Available at: https://www.opec.org/opec_web/en/about_us/25.htm (Accessed: 8 March 2022).

Pach-Gargul, A. (2016) 'Unia Energetyczna – nowy etap polityki energetycznej Unii Europejskiej?' *Finanse, Rynki Finansowe, Ubezpieczenia*, 3(81), pp. 213–224. doi:10.18276/frfu.2016.81-19.

Parry, I., Black, S., and Vernon, N. (2021) *Still not getting energy prices right: a global and country update of fossil fuel subsidies*. IMF Working Papers. WP/21/236. International Monetary Fund, Washington, DC: International Monetary Fund.

Parsons, J. (1989) 'Estimating the strategic value of long-term forward purchase contracts using auction models', *Journal of Finance*, XLIV(4), pp. 981–1010.

Piekkola, H. (2011) 'Intangible capital: the key to growth in Europe', *Intereconomics*, 46(4), pp. 222–228. doi:10.1007/s10272-011-0387-2.

Pietkova, M. (2022) 'Weekly data: Lithuania becomes the first European country to ditch Russian gas', *Financial Times*, 11 April. Available at: https://www.energymonitor.ai/tech/networks-grids/lithuania-ditches-russian-gas/ (Accessed: 25 March 2023).

Piotrowski, J. (2015) 'Subsydiowanie produktów energetycznych', *Unia Europejska*, 6(235), pp. 34–45.

Pirani, S. and Yafimava, K. (2016) *Russian Gas Transit Across Ukraine Post-2019: pipelines scenarios, gas flow consequences, and regulatory constraints*. OIES Paper NG 105. Oxford: Oxford Institute for Energy Studies. doi:10.26889/9781784670542.

Podbregar, I. et al. (2020) 'The international energy security risk index in sustainable energy and economy transition decision making—a reliability analysis', *Energies*, 13(14), p. 3691. doi:10.3390/en13143691.

Poprawa, P. (2018) *Co się kryje pod terminem niekonwencjonalne złoża gazu ziemnego*? Warszawa: Państwowy Instytut Geologiczny.

Prokop, J. (2009) 'Problem kartelizacji gałęzi o strukturze oligopolistycznej', in Kopycińska, D. (ed.), *Wybory konsumentów i przedsiębiorstw w teorii i praktyce*. Szczecin: Uniwersytet Szczeciński, pp. 146–155.

Ramírez-Cendrero, J.M. and Wirth, E. (2016) 'Is the Norwegian model exportable to combat Dutch disease?' *Resources Policy*, 48, pp. 85–96. doi:10.1016/j.resourpol.2016.02.010.

Raymond, H., Coulibaly, D., and Omgba, L.D. (2017) 'Exchange rate misalignments in energy-exporting countries: do sovereign wealth funds matter?' *International Economics*, 152, pp. 124–144. doi:10.1016/j.inteco.2017.05.005.

Rentschler, J. and Bazilian, M. (2017) 'Reforming fossil fuel subsidies: drivers, barriers and the state of progress', *Climate Policy*, 17(7), pp. 891–914. doi:10.1080/14693062.2016.1169393.

Reuters (2012) *RWE Transgas Says Wins Contracts Dispute with Gazprom*. Available at: https://www.reuters.com/article/us-gazprom-rwe-dispute/rwe-transgas-says-wins-contracts-dispute-with-gazprom-idUSBRE89N0Z620121024 (Accessed: 2 May 2018).

Robinson, J.A., Torvik, R., and Verdier, T. (2006) 'Political foundations of the resource curse', *Special Issue in Honor of Pranab Bardhan*, 79(2), pp. 447–468. doi:10.1016/j.jdeveco.2006.01.008.

Romalis, J. (2004) 'Factor proportions and the structure of commodity trade', *The American Economic Review*, 94(1), pp. 67–97.

Romanova, T. (2013) 'Energy demand: security for suppliers?' in Dyer, H. and Trombetta, J. (eds.), *International handbook of energy security*. Cheltenham: Edward Elgar, pp. 239–249.

Salvatore, D. (2011) *International economics trade and finance*. 10th edn. New York, NY: Wiley & Sons.

Schulte, S. and Weiser, F. (2019) 'Natural gas transits and market power: the case of Turkey', *Energy Journal*, 40(2), pp. 77–100. doi:10.5547/01956574.40.2.ssch.

SCM Agreement (1995) Available at: https://www.wto.org/english/docs_e/legal_e/24-scm.pdf (Accessed: 25 March 2023).

Shehabi, M.R. (2015) *An extraordinary recovery: Kuwait following the Gulf War*. Economics Discussion/Working Papers. The University of Western Australia, Department of Economics, Perth: The University of Western Australia, pp. 15–20.

Siddi, M. (2021) *What does Euroepean Green Deal mean for EU-Russia relations?* Available at: https://www.europeanleadershipnetwork.org/commentary/what-does-the-european-green-deal-mean-for-eu-russia-relations/, London: European Leadership Network. (Accessed: 15 March 2023).

Statista (2022) *Leading Gas Exporting Countries in 2020, by Export Type (in Billion Cubic Meters)*. Available at: https://www.statista.com/statistics/217856/leading-gas-exporters-worldwide/ (Accessed: 1 June 2022).

Statista (2023) *Gas Inflow for Transit from Russia to Europe in Ukraine from February 1, 2022 to February 28, 2023, by Entry Point (in Million Cubic Meters)*. Available at: https://www.statista.com/statistics/1308480/ukraine-russian-gas-transit-volume-by-route/ (Accessed: 15 March 2023).

Stellian, R. and Danna-Buitrago, J. (2019) 'Revealed comparative advantages and regional specialization: evidence from Colombia in the Pacific Alliance', *Journal of Applied Economics*, 22(1), pp. 349–379. doi:10.1080/15140326.2019.1627722.

Stellian, R. and Danna-Buitrago, J.P. (2022) 'Revealed comparative advantage and contribution-to-the-trade-balance indexes', *International Economics*, 170, pp. 129–155. doi:10.1016/j.inteco.2022.02.007.

Stern, J. (2005) *The future of Russian gas and Gazprom*. Oxford: Oxford University Press.

SWFI (2018a) *Linaburg-Maduell-Transparency-Index*. Available at: https://www.swfinstitute.org/statistics-research/linaburg-maduell-transparency-index/ (Accessed: 20 February 2018).

SWFI (2018b) *SWF Rankings*. Available at: https://www.swfinstitute.org/sovereign-wealth-fund-rankings/ (Accessed: 20 February 2018).

Thurber, M.C., Hults, D.R., and Heller, P.R.P. (2011) 'Exporting the "Norwegian Model": the effect of administrative design on oil sector performance', *Energy Policy*, 39(9), pp. 5366–5378. doi:10.1016/j.enpol.2011.05.027.

Treaty of the Functioning of the European Union (2012) *Official Journal of the European Union*. C 326/47, 26.10.2012. Available at: https://eur-lex.europa.eu/LexUriServ/LexUriServ.do?uri=CELEX:12012E/TXT:en:PDF (Accessed: 23 March 2023).

Tsani, S. (2013) 'Natural resources, governance and institutional quality: the role of resource funds', *Resources Policy*, 38(2), pp. 181–195. doi:10.1016/j.resourpol.2012.11.001.

Ulatowski, R. (2016) *Analiza porównawcza polityki energetycznej importerów i eksporterów surowców energetycznych na przykładzie Niemiec i Arabii Saudyjskiej perspektywa geoekonomiczna*. Warszawa: Wydawnictwo Naukowe Scholar.

UNEP (2004) *Energy subsidies: lessons learned in assessing their impact and designing policy reforms*. Geneve: United Nations Environment Programme.

UNESCAP (2023) *Energy Transit*. Available at: https://www.unescap.org/sites/default/files/Presentation%20-%20Energy%20Transit.pdf (Accessed: 15 March 2032).

University of Groningen (2022) *Penn World Table Version 10.0*. Available at: https://www.rug.nl/ggdc/productivity/pwt/?lang=en (Accessed: 10 June 2022).

US Government (2016) *United States Self-Review of Fossil Fuel Subsidies Submitted December 2015 to the G-20 Peer Reviewers*. Available at: http://www.g20chn.org/English/Documents/Current/201609/P020160919419901132079.pdf (Accessed: 5 February 2018).

Van der Ploeg, R. (2014) 'Guidelines for exploiting natural resource wealth', *Oxford Review of Economic Policy*, 30(1), pp. 145–169.

Vavilov, A. (2015) *Gazprom. An energy giant and its challenges in Europe*. London: Palgrave Macmillian.

von Hirschhausen, C., Meinhart, B. and Pavel, F. (2005) 'Transporting Russian gas to Western Europe — A simulation analysis', *The Energy Journal*, 26(2), pp. 49–68.

von Moltke, A., McKee, C. and Morgan (eds) (2017) *Energy subsidies: lessons learned in assessing their impact and designing policy reforms*. New York: Routledge Taylor&Francis Group.

Voudouris, V. (2010) 'Towards a unifying formalisation of geographic representation: the object–field model with uncertainty and semantics', *International Journal of Geographical Information Science*, 24(12), pp. 1811–1828. doi:10.1080/13658816.2010.488237.

Voudouris, V. (2011) 'Towards a conceptual synthesis of dynamic and geospatial models: fusing the agent-based and object – field models', *Environment and Planning B: Planning and Design*, 38(1), pp. 95–114. doi:10.1068/b3600.

Voudouris, V. (2013) 'Energy policy and security through the lenses of stochastic portfolio theory and the ACEGES model', in *Global Energy Policy and Security*. London: Springer, pp. 1–10. doi:10.1007/978-1-4471-5286-6_1.

Voudouris, V. et al. (2014) 'Exploring the production of natural gas through the lenses of the ACEGES model', *Energy Policy*, 64, pp. 124–133. doi:10.1016/j.enpol.2013.08.053.

Wagbara, O.N. (2007) 'How would the gas exporting countries forum influence gas trade?' *Energy Policy*, 35(2), pp. 1224–1237. doi:10.1016/j.enpol.2006.03.017.

Waloszyk, M. (2014) *Law and policy of the European gas market*. Cheltenham: Edward Elgar.

Williamson, O. (1983) 'Credible commitments: using hostages to support exchange', *American Economic Review*, 73(4), pp. 519–540.

Wills, S.E., Senbet, W.L., and Simbanegavi, W. (2016) 'Sovereign wealth funds and natural resource management in Africa,' *Journal of African Economies, Centre for the Study of African Economies (CSAE)*, 25(2), pp. 3–19. doi:10.1093/jae/ejw018.

World Bank (2010) *Subsidies in the Energy Sector: An Overview*. Available at: http://siteresources.worldbank.org/EXTESC/Resources/Subsidy_background_paper.pdf (Accessed: 5 February 2018).

World Bank (2014) *Data Bank. World Development Indicators*. Available at: http://databank.worldbank.org/data/reports.aspx?source=2&series=EG.IMP.CONS.ZS&country=# (Accessed: 22 March 2022).

World Bank (2018) *Access to Electricity (% of Population)*. Available at: https://data.worldbank.org/indicator/EG.ELC.ACCS.ZS?locations=AO-CG (Accessed: 2 May 2018).

World Bank (2022) *World Development Indicators*. Available at: https://databank.worldbank.org/source/world-development-indicators# (Accessed: 10 June 2022).

World Energy Council (2016) *Unconventional gas: a global phenomenon*. London: World Energy Council. Available at: https://www.worldenergy.org/wp-content/uploads/2016/02/Unconventional-gas-a-global-phenomenon-World-Energy-Resources_-Full-report-.pdf (Accessed: 2 May 2018).

World Governance Indicators (2021). Available at: www.govindicators.org (Accessed: 10 June 2022).

WTO (2006) *World Trade Report 2006: exploring the links between subsidies, trade and WTO*. Geneve: WTO.

WTO (2023) *Agreement on Subsidies and Countervailing Measures ("SCM Agreement")*. Available at: https://www.wto.org/english/tratop_e/scm_e/subs_e.htm (Accessed: 25 March 2023).

Ye, R. et al. (2021) 'Natural gas security evaluation from a supply vs. demand perspective: a quantitative application of four As', *Energy Policy*, 156, p. 112425. doi:10.1016/j.enpol.2021.112425.

Yegorov, Y. and Wirl, F. (2009) 'Ukrainian gas transit game', *Zeitschrift für Energiewirtschaft*, 33(2), pp. 147–155. doi:10.1007/s12398-009-0017-x.

Yegorov, Y. and Wirl, F. (2010) *Gas transit, geopolitics and emergence of games with application to CIS countries*. USAEE Working Paper, 10-044. Available at: 10.2139/ssrn.1560563.

Yu, R., Cai, J., and Leung, P. (2009) 'The normalized revealed comparative advantage index', *The Annals of Regional Science*, 43(1), pp. 267–282. doi:10.1007/s00168-008-0213-3.

Zajdler, R., Hara, T., and Staniłko, J. (2012) *Formuły cenowe w kontraktach długoterminowych na dostawę gazu do Unii Europejskiej*. Warszawa: Instytut Sobieskiego. Available at: http://sobieski.org.pl/wp-content/uploads/Formuly_cenowe_w_GKDT_IS20120420180045.pdf (Accessed: 15 March 2018).

Zeufack, A. et al. (2016) *Optimal allocation of natural resource surpluses in a dynamic macroeconomic framework: a DSGE analysis with evidence from Uganda*. The World Bank, Washinton, DC: World Bank. doi:10.1596/1813-9450-7910.

Conclusions

Analysis provided in this book focused on answering a research question, attaining research goals and investigating assumed research hypothesis. Such design of a study allowed to come up with several conclusions.

Within the theoretical goal, the literature review proves that energy security studies, and energy demand security, in particular, is on the rise in scientific research in the 21st century. Even though the absolute numbers of scientific investigations in energy demand security are still moderate, their growth dynamics are significant. This research also shows dominant position of either Asian or North American institutions in the above research efforts. European universities are relatively less vocal about energy security. Their position improves with narrowing down the analysis to energy supply and, to lesser extent, energy demand security in particular. Worth mentioning is also the fact, that the research perspective delivered by the Central European institutions, specialized in economic studies, is rather rare. Additionally, majority of published works on energy demand security constitute articles or conference proceedings making even book chapters rather missing perspective. Thus, the above book not only fills in the research gap in the merit sentence – by delivering energy demand security perspective from the international economics point of view but also in a functional dimension – by providing additional voice in the discussion on the phenomenon recorded outside the ongoing mainstream articles' discussion.

This research depicts energy demand security within a broader energy supply security framework looking for common features and areas of differences. In this way, study systematizes different literature strings and shows phenomenon origins along with its determinants. However, this research goes beyond that in an effort to organize energy demand security studies. Firstly, it extends one of the most popular – in economics – energy supply security definition – into energy demand security framework. This way, the research offers new perspective in the energy demand security analysis encompassing externalities and possible ways of their internalization. Secondly, this study in a theoretical dimension sets energy demand security into neoclassical trade theories, highlighting that these concepts might be applicable for the analysed phenomenon. By systemizing and organizing energy demand security research, the author achieves the assumed theoretical goal.

Achieved theoretical goals correspond with assumed empirical aims. Extended theoretical energy demand security framework serves as a basis for description of energy security determinants, while neoclassical trade theories build foundations for econometric modelling process. Factors influencing energy demand security in the natural gas market are presented in the global perspective to capture the complexity of the analysed phenomenon in the 21st century. But wherever that is possible, due to data aggregation and availability constraints, the analysis presents the breakdown into OECD and non-OECD (developing) countries. The research delivers a snapshot view of the natural gas market outlining the most recent (at the time of final book preparations) changes referring to, e.g., price- or non-price contractual terms but also GECF's potential in influencing market competition. Such description precedes the econometric analysis, which employs neoclassical trade frameworks and extends them with energy demand security variables. In this way, energy demand security is included as a determinant of a comparative advantage of high-income net natural gas exporters. At the same time, this study offers, on the one hand, another perspective on factors shaping comparative advantage – by including elusive phenomena such as energy demand security and, on the other hand, empirically embeds energy demand security of high-income countries in the Heckscher-Ohlin/Ricardo modelling frameworks. This way, the research delivers modified methods of assessing comparative advantage and energy demand security constituting a new research stream and bringing additional voice in the scientific discussion on empirical assessment of both phenomena.

Achieving theoretical and empirical goals is subjected, on the one hand, to the research question and, on the other hand, it corresponds with testing the research hypothesis.

As long as part of the hypothesis on increased relevance of energy demand security phenomenon in the 21st century can be confirmed by the theoretical conclusions, its relevance for a comparative advantage of high-income OECD nations is questioned. Theoretical considerations support claim that since the beginning of the 2000s, there is a growing number of research in energy demand security studies. Empirical model, within its specification, confirms rather the importance of supply, not demand security, for high-income OECD net natural gas exporters. This claim has three implications for future research. Firstly, from the theoretical point of view, this conclusion may speak in favour of analysing energy supply and demand security as mirroring concepts, building together energy security idea. Secondly, from the empirical point of view, the above argument suggests that even when looking at the net energy exporters, it might be essential to include the energy imports' perspective. One may expect that the smaller is the surplus of energy exports over imports, or the more price-volatile are energy imports over exports, the greater might be possible influence of supply security concerns over a country's comparative advantage. Thirdly, the research shows that energy security (in analysed group supply security) can be treated as a part of comparative advantage of nations. Fourthly, study proves, what has been already acknowledged for supply security research, that demand security is highly contextual phenomenon. It means that energy demand security might be different for various regions or groups of/ countries depending on their individual economic and energy situation.

Achieving the ultimate goal connected with analysing energy demand security with its determinants in the natural gas market in 21st century delivered a set of conclusions of theoretical, empirical, and practical nature. Since first two sets of conclusions have already been described above, at this point the author focuses only on the implications for policy practice. Firstly, this study proves that discussion on energy demand security exists and additionally that the perspective of exporters is noticed. Secondly, the research shows that this optic also refers to developed nations, which so far have rather been neglected in the analysis. Dominance of developing or emerging economies in energy demand security studies, to some extent, biased the discussion towards development and economic growth issues. Including in the analysis developed countries with relatively high GDP growth levels shifts the debate to comparative advantage, and also, possibly in the future, to innovation capacity, technological stewardship, and sustainability issues. Thus, policy shaping in this group of countries should include these aspects while designing effective energy demand security framework. Drafting such strategies is, however, not possible without relying on a description of possible risks and tools used to contain them. Thus, third practical policy-oriented conclusion refers, on the one hand, to the set of threats that are associated with security of gas exports and also, on the other hand, the instruments mitigating the above dangers. Risk abatement strategies should include policy responses to systematic risks that are independent from exporters, but foremostly ought to focus on non-systematic risks that are specific to exporters' trade relations. While the former threats (e.g., decarbonization requirements) can be addressed with long-term, preventive measures, the latter (e.g., physical import disruption) might be accommodated only by a well-designed and tested network of effective short-term responses protecting from an *ad hoc* budget instability. Such a time-sensitive "risk-tool box" may serve not only developed but also developing exporters in each case requiring adaptation to individual country's circumstances. In this way, framework is of a common use and application. Fourthly, the econometric research results indicate possible directions of energy policy in high-income net natural gas exporting countries. Depending on the energy exports and imports levels, policy design in these countries should include both supply and demand security concerns. In case of the latter, policy-makers should not focus solely on volume of exported resources or resource rents, but rather ought to take into consideration a wider perspective including geopolitical, economic, and environmental aspects. This argument resembles energy policy needs pyramid of which higher order needs resonate strongly in the group of developed countries. Fifthly, this study in a number of places refers to Norway as a benchmark for standards in managing the resource wealth and an example of escaping from the Dutch disease symptoms. Thus, Norwegian experience, policy framework, and institutional solutions can serve as a "golden standard" in energy demand security policy, especially for newcomers in natural gas exports (net), like the USA.

This research, as any other, has its limitations. They result from conceptual approach, sample choice, methodological constraints, and data limitations.

Firstly, this research investigates energy demand security only from the economic perspective, and international economics in particular. However, including geopolitical aspects may enrich the analysis. It has been recently proven by the Russian-Ukrainian conflict (as of 2022) that political unrest can have significant consequences also for gas exporters, especially high-income ones. These effects are the most visible in Europe, where Russia is a dominant pipeline gas supplier. With the rising Russian demands on settling the payments in Russian rouble only, selected EU countries decided to withdraw from already-existing contracts while the others accepted offered conditions. The former ones, having the access to interconnecting facilities or LNG terminals, shifted their import contracts towards other suppliers, for instance, the USA or Norway. The length of the Russian-Ukrainian conflict and its further developments will show whether this trend will continue in the future. Exporters, regardless of their economic position (developed versus developing/emerging) are more interested in longer-term commitments allowing for foreseeable investment processes rather than short-term solutions, which admittedly generate windfall profits, but at the same time increase transactional costs. That is why from the business perspective, in countries with low state participation in energy-exporting companies, there might be little motivation to contain political commitments related to energy exports. One may expect that in the periods of rising global energy or natural gas demand in particular, exporters can be even less willing to organize *ad hoc* LNG shipments. But without doubt, Russian-Ukrainian conflict imprinted on the natural gas market dynamics and dispute effects will be visible in the long-term horizon, as some of the European countries, on the margins of COVID-pandemic, have already urged towards withdrawal from the use of fossil fuels. It seems that the Eastern conflict may only deepen this trend. One of the examples of such approach is Lithuania's declaration, according to which, it decided not only on the fossil exit but also on giving up on imports of Russian hydrocarbons as a result of the geopolitical situation. However, such a perspective is not included in this study and, thus, the author highlights it as a possible next research step.

Secondly, this book focuses, wherever possible, on the group of developed countries, to some extent neglecting the perspective of emerging and developing net gas exporters. The rationale behind such an approach stems from the literature review which showed relatively well-investigated energy demand security of developing countries next to a research gap indicated for developed nations. Thus, any effort aimed at comparing energy demand security approach between developed and developing nations might be an interesting future research step. Moreover, the perspective presented in this book delivers mostly optics of the European countries, neglecting Asian/Oceanian gas market developments. Hence, any effort complementing this geographical perspective in demand security analysis is highlighted as a future research step.

Thirdly, this study in a methodological sense has its limitations. Firstly, it focuses only on a selected group of international economic theories. Even though the author tried to motivate and explain the above choice, still one may argue that there might be additional aspects relevant for energy demand security analysis, which have not been included in this research. Some of such possible areas of investigation include highlighted previously concepts from international economics or energy economics field or ideas in a category of a wider economic framework. Secondly, by design of a scoping review, this research focuses only on scientific databases (selected). Thus, it neglects information recorded outside the scientific and business discourse, often included in the form of experts' comments, discussions, etc. Taking into consideration these perspectives on energy demand security may be subjected to the so-called grey literature review, which might broaden the phenomenon's description. Both of the above-depicted methodological aspects are beyond the scope of this study, but the check of their relevance for energy demand security is worth further investigation in the future.

Fourthly, as this research relies on secondary data, it cannot escape the data limitations problem highlighted in the empirical and theoretical parts. In empirical dimension, this issue is connected with both data availability and data aggregation level. Data availability constraints affected the choice of selected variables, which described energy demand security in the modelling approach. Even though the research uses internationally renowned databases, this problem could not have been resolved. Data aggregation standards influence the construction of variables included in empirical modelling. For instance, willingness to capture resource rents with a reference to budget incomes or, even more precisely, energy export revenues met an obstacle in the form of World Bank data aggregation levels. The institution provides resource rents' data with reference to GDP only. At the same time, desire to keep sources' coherence did not allow for other variables' construction. Thus, capturing energy demand security within different than proposed variables is a recommended next research step. In the theoretical dimension, data limitation problem refers mainly to the choice of databases included in the scoping review. Even though Web of Science and Scopus are the biggest and the most representative databases for social sciences, extending in the future considerations other scientific databases might be another research direction.

Summing up, energy demand security constitutes an interesting research topic both from theoretical and empirical point of view. Widening the research to other group of countries or deepening the analysis towards more precise measures under relaxed conceptual and methodological approach might be a future research direction. Nevertheless, the analysed phenomenon is worth understanding not only from the scientific point of view but also from the practical perspective. Hence, enriching scientific dialogue with reliable journalistic debate may contribute positively to scaling up the unbiased discussion on energy demand security.

Appendix

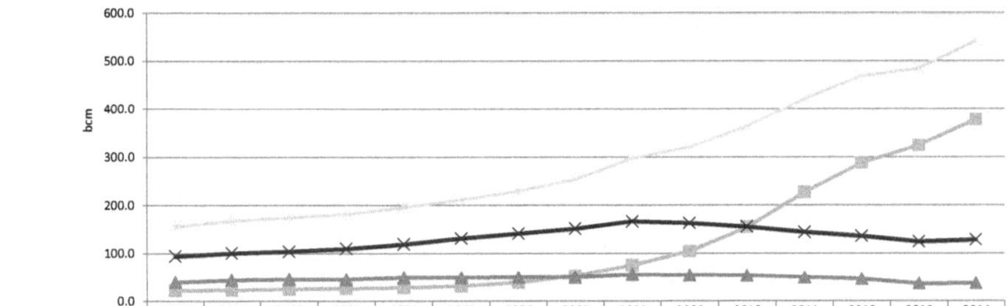

	2000	2001	2002	2003	2004	2005	2006	2007	2008	2009	2010	2011	2012	2013	2014
Shale gas	23.1	23.5	25.3	26.9	28.5	32.1	39.4	53.6	76.1	104.7	155.0	227.6	287.9	324.4	378.8
Coal bed methane	39.0	44.2	45.7	45.3	48.7	49.0	49.8	49.6	55.7	54.2	53.4	49.9	46.4	36.5	37.1
Tight gas	94.2	100.3	103.9	109.5	119.1	130.6	140.8	151.4	166.2	162.5	155.1	144.0	135.4	124.0	127.7
Unconventiona gas total	156.4	168.1	174.8	181.7	196.3	211.7	230.0	254.6	298.0	321.4	363.5	421.5	469.7	484.9	543.6

Shale gas — Coal bed methane — Tight gas — Unconventiona gas total

Figure A.1 Unconventional gas resources in the USA between 2000 and 2014 (bcm).
Source: Compiled by the author based on IEA (2020).

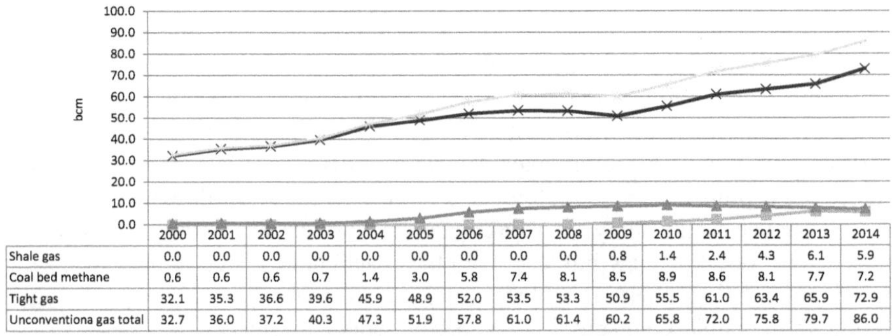

	2000	2001	2002	2003	2004	2005	2006	2007	2008	2009	2010	2011	2012	2013	2014
Shale gas	0.0	0.0	0.0	0.0	0.0	0.0	0.0	0.0	0.0	0.8	1.4	2.4	4.3	6.1	5.9
Coal bed methane	0.6	0.6	0.6	0.7	1.4	3.0	5.8	7.4	8.1	8.5	8.9	8.6	8.1	7.7	7.2
Tight gas	32.1	35.3	36.6	39.6	45.9	48.9	52.0	53.5	53.3	50.9	55.5	61.0	63.4	65.9	72.9
Unconventiona gas total	32.7	36.0	37.2	40.3	47.3	51.9	57.8	61.0	61.4	60.2	65.8	72.0	75.8	79.7	86.0

Shale gas — Coal bed methane — Tight gas — Unconventiona gas total

Figure A.2 Unconventional gas resources in Canada between 2000 and 2014 (bcm).
Source: Compiled by the author based on IEA (2020).

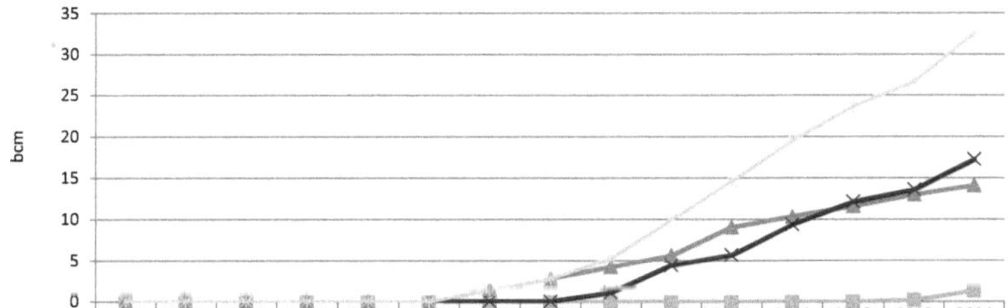

	2000	2001	2002	2003	2004	2005	2006	2007	2008	2009	2010	2011	2012	2013	2014
Shale gas	0	0	0	0	0	0	0.0	0.0	0.0	0.0	0.0	0.0	0.0	0.2	1.3
Coal bed methane	0	0	0	0	0	0	1.4	2.8	4.2	5.6	9.0	10.3	11.6	13.0	14.1
Tight gas	0	0	0	0	0	0	0.0	0.0	1.1	4.4	5.6	9.3	12.1	13.6	17.2
Unconventiona gas total	0	0	0	0	0	0	1.4	2.8	5.3	10.0	14.6	19.6	23.7	26.8	32.6

Shale gas — Coal bed methane — Tight gas — Unconventiona gas total

Figure A.3 Unconventional gas resources in China between 2000 and 2014 (bcm).
Source: Compiled by the author based on IEA (2020).

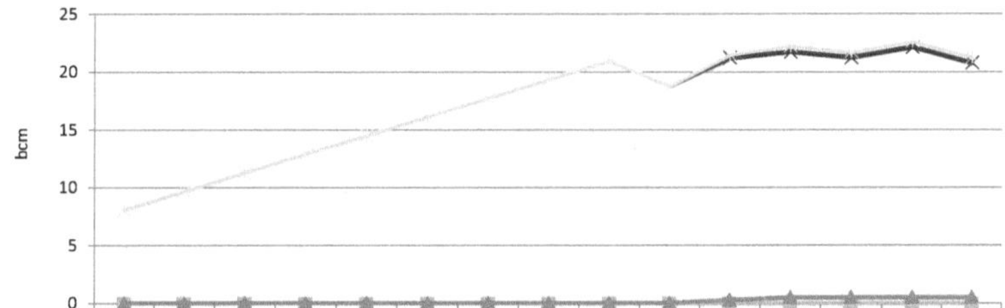

	2000	2001	2002	2003	2004	2005	2006	2007	2008	2009	2010	2011	2012	2013	2014
Shale gas	0	0	0	0	0	0	0	0	0	0	0	0	0	0	0
Coal bed methane	0.0	0.0	0.0	0.0	0.0	0.0	0.0	0.0	0.0	0.0	0.3	0.5	0.5	0.5	0.5
Tight gas	8.1	9.7	11.3	12.9	14.5	16.2	17.8	19.4	21.0	18.8	21.2	21.7	21.2	22.1	20.8
Unconventiona gas total	8.1	9.7	11.3	12.9	14.5	16.2	17.8	19.4	21.0	18.8	21.5	22.2	21.7	22.6	21.3

Shale gas — Coal bed methane — Tight gas — Unconventiona gas total

Figure A.4 Unconventional gas resources in Russia between 2000 and 2014 (bcm).
Source: Compiled by the author based on IEA (2020).

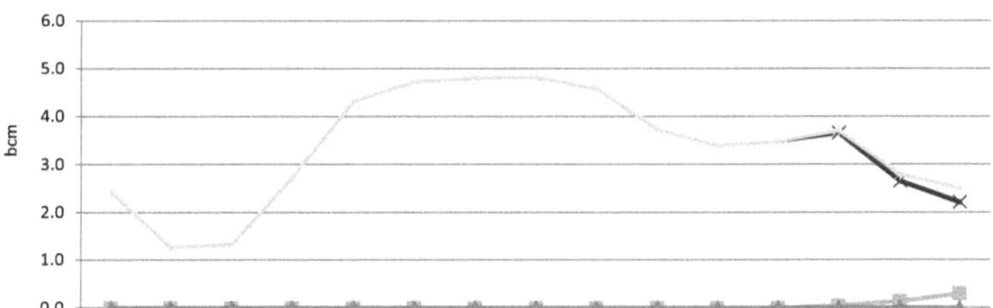

	2000	2001	2002	2003	2004	2005	2006	2007	2008	2009	2010	2011	2012	2013	2014
Shale gas	0.0	0.0	0.0	0.0	0.0	0.0	0.0	0.0	0.0	0.0	0.0	0.0	0.1	0.1	0.3
Coal bed methane	0.0	0.0	0.0	0.0	0.0	0.0	0.0	0.0	0.0	0.0	0.0	0.0	0.0	0.0	0.0
Tight gas	2.4	1.3	1.3	2.7	4.3	4.7	4.8	4.8	4.6	3.7	3.4	3.5	3.7	2.7	2.2
Unconventiona gas total	2.4	1.3	1.3	2.7	4.3	4.7	4.8	4.8	4.6	3.7	3.4	3.5	3.7	2.8	2.5

Shale gas — Coal bed methane — Tight gas — Unconventiona gas total

Figure A.5 Unconventional gas resources in Argentina between 2000 and 2014 (bcm).
Source: Compiled by the author based on IEA (2020).

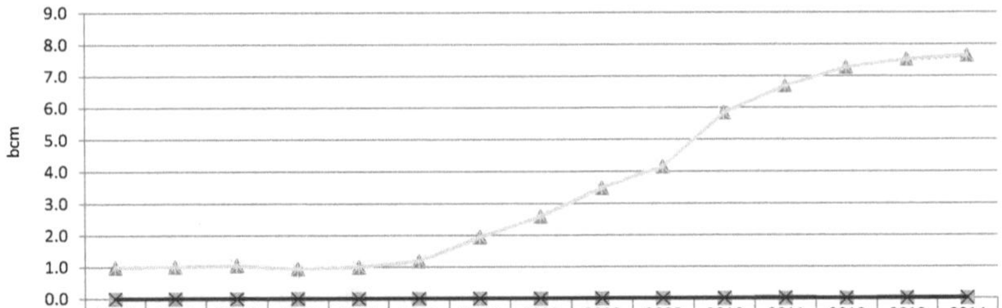

	2000	2001	2002	2003	2004	2005	2006	2007	2008	2009	2010	2011	2012	2013	2014
Shale gas	0.0	0.0	0.0	0.0	0.0	0.0	0.0	0.0	0.0	0.0	0.0	0.0	0.0	0.0	0.0
Coal bed methane	1.0	1.0	1.0	0.9	1.0	1.2	1.9	2.6	3.5	4.2	5.8	6.7	7.3	7.5	7.6
Tight gas	0.0	0.0	0.0	0.0	0.0	0.0	0.0	0.0	0.0	0.0	0.0	0.0	0.0	0.0	0.0
Unconventiona gas total	1.0	1.0	1.0	0.9	1.0	1.2	1.9	2.6	3.5	4.2	5.8	6.7	7.3	7.5	7.7

Shale gas — Coal bed methane — Tight gas — Unconventiona gas total

Figure A.6 Unconventional gas resources in Australia between 2000 and 2014 (bcm).
Source: Compiled by the author based on IEA (2020).

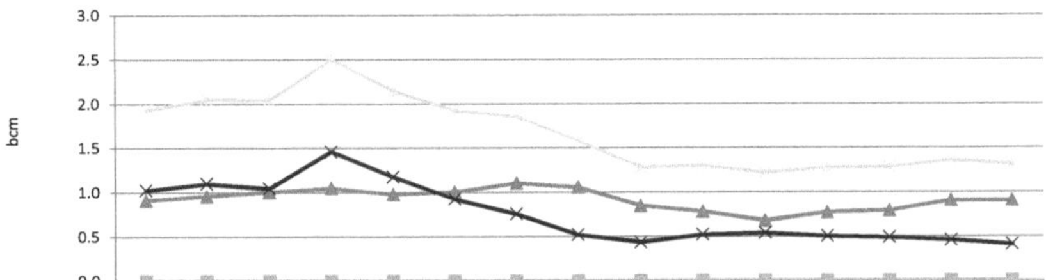

	2000	2001	2002	2003	2004	2005	2006	2007	2008	2009	2010	2011	2012	2013	2014
Shale gas	0.0	0.0	0.0	0.0	0.0	0.0	0.0	0.0	0.0	0.0	0.0	0.0	0.0	0.0	0.0
Coal bed methane	0.9	1.0	1.0	1.0	1.0	1.0	1.1	1.1	0.8	0.8	0.7	0.8	0.8	0.9	0.9
Tight gas	1.0	1.1	1.0	1.5	1.2	0.9	0.8	0.5	0.4	0.5	0.5	0.5	0.5	0.5	0.4
Unconventiona gas total	1.9	2.1	2.0	2.5	2.1	1.9	1.9	1.6	1.3	1.3	1.2	1.3	1.3	1.4	1.3

Shale gas — Coal bed methane — Tight gas — Unconventiona gas total

Figure A.7 Unconventional gas resources in Germany between 2000 and 2014 (bcm).
Source: Compiled by the author based on IEA (2020).

Reference

IEA (2020) *Gas*. Available at: https://www.iea.org/ugforum/ugd/ (Accessed: 20 June 2021).

Index

Note: **Bold** page numbers refer to tables; *italic* page numbers refer to figures and page numbers followed by "n" denote endnotes.

Kolibri 360 GmbH
Ferdinand-Jühlke-Straße 7
99095 Erfurt, Deutschland
produktsicherheit@kolibri360.de